CENTERS FOR THE URBAN ENVIRONMENT

CENTERS FOR THE URBAN ENVIRONMENT

Survival of the Cities

VICTOR GRUEN

VNR VAN NOSTRAND REINHOLD COMPANY
NEW YORK   CINCINNATI   TORONTO   LONDON   MELBOURNE

Published for

THE VICTOR GRUEN FOUNDATION
FOR ENVIRONMENTAL PLANNING
Los Angeles, California

Van Nostrand Reinhold Company Regional Offices:
New York Cincinnati Chicago Millbrae Dallas

Van Nostrand Reinhold Company International Offices:
London Toronto Melbourne

Manufactured in the United States of America

Published by Van Nostrand Reinhold Company
450 West 33rd Street, New York, N.Y. 10001

Published simultaneously in Canada by Van Nostrand Reinhold Ltd.

15 14 13 12 11 10 9 8 7 6 5 4 3 2 1

Library of Congress Cataloging in Publication Data

Gruen, Victor, 1903-
     Centers for the urban environment.

     1. Cities and towns—Planning—1945-   2. Shopping
centers. I. Title.
HT166.G76   309.2'62   73-1161
ISBN 0-442-22877-5

Foreword by the Foundation

This book represents an expression of the efforts of the Foundation to bring about a greater public understanding of the decisive role which "Environmental Planning" should and must play if the ecological and biological balance of our planet, which is essential for the continuous existence of the human species, is to be assured.

The Foundation devotes itself to this task by undertaking research, education directed toward the appreciation of environmental values, and by maintaining, operating and making available an environmental library.

Victor Gruen, as founder and president of the Foundation, undertook the task of writing this book, making use of research, information and illustrative material which we were able to put at his disposal.

To Victor Gruen, and to all friends of the Foundation who have helped in the shaping of this book, we extend our sincere thanks.

The Foundation worked to the greatest degree on this book under the directorship of Dr. Claudia Moholy-Nagy, who died tragically on September 21, 1971, at the age of 35. Her idealism, dynamism, devotion and wide knowledge remain an inspiration to us all.

The Victor Gruen Foundation
for Environmental Planning
Tracy Susman
Director

Introduction

Victor Gruen is one of the world's preeminent architects. To my mind, he deserves designation as the foremost "environmental architect" of our time.

In a very real sense Gruen's career traces the evolution of architecture and urban planning over the last half-century. Born and educated in Vienna (a city which has beneficently "imprinted" so many of its inhabitants with convictions about the supreme importance of life-centered urban amenities), Victor, like many of his contemporaries, was influenced in the early stages of his career by the ideas of Le Corbusier.

In 1938 Victor came to the United States, driven from Austria by Adolf Hitler. Had it not been for his resilience and versatility, he might have been overwhelmed by the prospect of starting over in a strange country. However, Victor mastered the American idiom, and by the early 1950s he was ready to build the first of his large-scale urban development projects—Northland Shopping Center in suburban Detroit. After pioneering the regional shopping center concept and many subsequent variations, Gruen and his associates (an interdisciplinary team of engineers, economists, planners and architects) turned their creative energies toward revitalizing the decaying downtown areas of such cities as Ft. Worth, Rochester and Fresno—work that culminated in Victor's last book," The Heart of Our Cities."

The next phase of Victor's remarkable career encompasses the ideas and concepts of this book. Having enlarged his angle of vision, Gruen is now a total environment planner who believes that cities must be unifying, "multifunctional" centers if their living values are to be conserved.

Gruen's two earlier books were largely about urban America. This one has a global overlay, for his work is now international in its scope and importance.

From the beginning, Gruen has been willing to tackle large-scale projects requiring bold concepts that could only be nurtured by planning teams. Victor is not an individualistic "hero architect": his name is not associated with skyscrapers or singular buildings. His skill is the skill of a creative team

captain. He knows that technology, economics and environment can only be meshed together into a buildable project if the right generalist-specialist minds are brought to bear on the problem at hand.

I believe the two personal qualities which have done most to lend distinction to Gruen's work are his capacity for intellectual growth—and his instinct for holistic planning. As this book attests, Victor is still groping for new truths and a better understanding of the lessons of design history. He has a refreshing way of not letting his ego get between himself and his work, a trait that allows him to acknowledge graciously that his own creation—the "unifunctional" shopping center—has contributed to urban sprawl and added to the errors of an auto-centered society. Victor is emphatically not a man of dogmas: he is eminently educable, and he goes out of his way to praise the outstanding work of others.

Gruen's instinct for holistic planning enables him to evaluate large-scale plans and the interrelated vectors and forces that determine the livability of a city or a region. Along with Lewis Mumford, twenty years ago Gruen saw that automania could cause us to suffocate our cities, and he perceived that architecture conceived apart from its related transportation systems would, in the long run, be misconceived.

As an environmental architect, Gruen understands the crucial—and often ignored—interreacting factors which either impair or enhance the community itself once a particular project is completed. And even as his work has become more expansive, he has never forgotten the importance of small-grained things that delight the eye and add life-giving qualities to a community. He realizes, for example, that it is more important to put the bicycle back into the city than to build an SST, and he has steadfastly maintained that all urban planning which ignores the human-scale and humane values will inevitably erode "the urbanity" of our cities.

Gruen understands the ecology of urban environments. It is central to his thinking that the ultimate test of any plan or project is whether it not only adds a humanizing dimension to the lives of individuals, but improves what the Greeks called the public happiness by making the common estate and the common experience richer and more meaningful for all.

One of the best things about this book is that it abounds in "for instances." Gruen likes to bring his theories down to earth—and he helps his readers take them apart by presenting a series of projects and planning case studies to evaluate. These studies are invaluable: by inviting analysis of specific mistakes and specific successes, they help bridge the gap between abstract planning and the immediate decisions faced by the designers of ongoing projects.

As a surgeon for sick cities, Gruen is ever alert for evidences of entropy. He contends that most of the world's large cities are now mere "human agglomerations" plagued by ill-planned changes that are anti-city in character. He argues that much of the "modern" trend toward "unifunctional centers" (industrial centers, civic centers, shopping centers, old-age centers, financial centers, educational centers, cultural centers, etc.) is contributing to the sickness of our cities and the downfall of true urbanity.

This kind of honest analysis (some of it the result of a self-skeptical attitude) has led Victor Gruen to the major conclusions of this book. I will not attempt to describe them in this introduction, except to warn the reader that his experience has caused him to favor "radical" solutions.

The brilliant young architect-critic, Paul Spreiregen, has summarized our urban predicament in these words:

"The real problem, the real frontier for the architectural profession, and the city planning profession and for our whole society, is the question of how we are going to live . . . We lack great visions of what we could be aiming for."

Some of this needed vision is contained in Victor Gruen's book—and some of it is incorporated in the best projects executed by him and his colleagues.

For my part, I am encouraged by the scope and temper of this volume. It is a vital contribution to the urgent dialogue about the future of human settlements that is certain to dominate our lives in the remaining years of this century.

STEWART L. UDALL
Washington, D.C.

Foreword by the Author

There now exists a growing awareness that the shaping of the urban environment is one of the tasks on which the future of mankind, of civilization and culture, will depend. This awareness causes concern to the "thinkers" and is expressed in action by the "doers."

Our hope to achieve decisive improvements of the existing deplorable conditions is somewhat hampered by the fact that most of the "thinkers" are not willing to actively participate in those measures which they themselves have intellectually determined as necessary, whereas most of the "doers" are so busily engaged in action, that no time is left to get acquainted with "theories."

I have been led into the position of being a "thinker" and a "doer" at the same time. This is not a comfortable position. It is like standing on a bridge, with a view toward reality on one side and idealism on the other, hoping that the bridge might act as a connecting link between "thinkers" and "doers."

As a "thinker" I have devoted my life to observing, learning, contemplating, writing, lecturing, and teaching. As a "doer," I have immersed myself in working with teams of friends and associates, in the planning and designing, and with some luck, implementation of structures and their composite into environmental units.

A bridge opens up fascinating views in all directions but it is also an unsheltered place, exposed to the stormy weather which characteristically prevails where a "high" of lofty thinking adjoins a "low" of materialistic aims.

It is an uncomfortable position and this is going to be an uncomfortable book, at least for the author. He is exposing himself to the criticism of the highbrows, who, with some right, will find that the book is insufficiently academic and pure. It will be looked at with suspicion by the "practical" man because it calls for his engagement in matters which go far beyond short-range, materialistic, egocentric aims. The book is not written for any of the countless specialized professional or business groups; it therefore avoids, to the highest degree possible, the usage of technical, academic, or business lingo which, though understandable to a specific group of readers, represents for others, a secret code. Because of my conviction that the shaping of the urban environment does not fall into the preserved activity range of any special group, but must be a matter of serious concern for the scientist, the professional, the politician, the entrepreneur, the student, and in fact for every urbanite, I have striven in writing this book, to relate those thoughts and experiences which should be of interest to all.

My publishers approached me in 1969 with the proposal of writing a sequel to the book *Shopping Towns USA,* which was written in the years 1958 and 1959 and which appeared in print in 1960. I worked on it together with the economist Laurence Patten Smith, who died in 1967. With his death I lost a close personal friend and collaborator and the world lost a man who not only had outstanding experience in his own field of economics, but also a creative approach to his profession which enabled him to dare to analyze new concepts and new ideas and to respond to them positively.

When Larry and I worked on *Shopping Towns USA,* we found ourselves in an exceptional position. Not only had a new environmental planning concept been born, but, by happy coincidence, effected by persons who were willing to take unusual risks. At the time the book was written, there were in existence only a small number of representative examples of the new planning concept. Larry and I, together with our respective organizations had been actively engaged in many of them. Even at that time, it was clear to us that the importance of the concept, the "regional shopping center," reached far beyond its application to retail trade in suburban areas. This was the reason why we chose as title *Shopping Towns USA.* With this title, we wanted to indicate that the role of the new planning concept could expand beyond the goal of creating merely machines for selling, and could satisfy the demand for urban crystallization points and thus offer to the suburban population significant life experiences.

The success both of the book and the new building type was considerable. The concept of the regional shopping center, once limited to a handful of examples in the United States spread all over the world, and shopping center development and construction became a large industry. The book is still regarded in all developed countries as a kind of handbook or "bible" for the planning, economics, architectural treatment, and operation of regional shopping centers. However, the assignment of writing a sequel to the former book did not, at least for me, indicate that I should rest on my laurels and point with pride to the effects which pioneering work had triggered in this field. Though I do not wish to deny that the regional shopping center as one of the first breakthroughs in large-scale environmental planning has been significant, I can only regard it, as I pointed out even when writing the former book, as an experimental proving ground for different, larger, and, for the future of our urban pattern, more decisive ventures.

To circumscribe the basic conditions and thus directions which thought and action concerning the urban environment will have to take, I start this book with an exposure of "Horizons and Restraints."

Acknowledging the role of the regional shopping center as a springboard for further development, I deal in the second chapter with "The Regional Shopping Center: Its Contribution to Environmental Planning," and I trace in the third chapter, "Twenty Years: Shopping Towns International," the quantitative and qualitative development of this building type, connecting this with observations based on my personal experience and pointing out those misunderstandings which tend to dilute the high quality of the original concept. Chapter 4, "The Unifunctional Center: Its Rise and the Downfall of Urbanism," reflects the gnawing doubts as to whether the shopping center or any other unifunctional center can make a real contribution to urbanism.

In Chapters 5 and 6, "The Multifunctional Center" and "Urban Cores," I attempt to establish a more suitable, alternate solution to the unifunctional center.

Chapter 7 is, finally, an attempt to summarize the experiences gained in unifunctional and multifunctional centers and to bring them into context with the overall question of "The Emerging New Urban Pattern."

There exists a danger that those of my readers who are involved in the planning, designing, and developing of shopping centers might concentrate their attention on Chapters 2 and 3 and that those whose interests are directed toward the future might skip those parts of the book which deal with practical application and turn to the more future-oriented Chapters 4 to 7. If this should be the case, I would feel that I have failed in my task. One of the aims of this book is to bridge the gap between thinkers and doers and to stress that the ability to create the large overall mosaic of the urban environment depends on mastering the countless little pieces which form the whole.

We live in an age of specialization, where labels are attached to anybody involved in creative work. I have found myself at various stages of my activity in the embarrassing situation of having such labels pinned to me. I was characterized as the "Father of the Shopping Center" and later as the "Father of the Downtown Mall," and for a long time revitalization projects for city cores were referred to by journalists as "Gruenizing" the city center. I have always refused energetically the responsibility for these "Fatherships" because I have never aspired to be an expert in any specific field of architecture or planning. However, there have been two cases of public recognition which I have really appreciated. These were when *Fortune* Magazine bestowed on me the title of "Architect of the Environment" and when Rice University presented me with a beautiful plaque nominating me "Architect of the People."

There is now raging all over the world an intensive discussion concerning the future of human settlement. "The City for the Year 2000" has become the catch phrase to which symposia, conventions, books, and articles are hitched. Ideas for this fabulous city for the year 2000 range all the way from gigantic man-made mountains of the vertical city, to the idea that the city will completely disappear and mankind will live spread out over the whole world and perhaps over the moon as well.

In this book, I am not asking for the moon. I am convinced that what we will be confronted with at the turn of the century will be based to a large degree on what has been created by our forefathers and to an even larger degree on what is being planned today.

A sequel to *Shopping Towns USA* (which dealt with the beginnings of the development of *one* planned environmental unit) should, I feel, deal with new, future-oriented environmental planning elements, as they now begin to become apparent in the form of multifunctional centers, as building stones for a superior urban pattern.

VICTOR GRUEN

Contents

7 THE EMERGING NEW URBAN PATTERN

CENTERS FOR THE URBAN ENVIRONMENT

1

Figures 1-1—1-2 Conservation of nature—or pollution through misuse of technology?

HORIZONS AND RESTRAINTS

In order to be meaningful, concern regarding any specific part of the human environment must be related to the wider horizons of settlements for human beings. It must be based on the awareness that environmental planning is the key to human survival on this planet. Though our "horizons" must be wide, in order to discuss with validity a specific urban planning element, we must apply self-discipline, setting into focus a specific theme, so as not to expose ourselves to the danger of saying something about everything and therefore little about something. We must self-impose certain restraints.

The specific theme on which I want to concentrate, "Centers for the Urban Environment," has been selected because I feel that it has significance in the framework of the broad outlines of the horizons. I believe that quality, shape, and structuring of the urban settlements have decisive influence on ecological problems. I submit further that centers as the accents and high points of the urban scene are generators of form and content for urban agglomerations. The entire concept of this book is of course based on a number of suppositions:

First, that human life on this planet will continue for some time, destroyed neither by natural events, nor by those forces which man himself has unleashed.

Second, that the human animal's herd instinct which makes him gather in groups, tribes, and nations, and which made him settle in hamlets, villages, towns, and cities, will endure.

I respect everybody's right to reject these suppositions, but obviously, without accepting them, this book could not be written and should not be read.

I have optimistically assumed that mankind will not destroy itself through tools of ecological destruction. The existence of just such a danger has long been pronounced by scientists. In recent times it has been annunciated as a serious threat by government leaders all over the world and has been forcefully brought to the attention of a sensation-hungry audience through the efficiency of modern mass media. But even though the spreading of the message of the threatened extinction of the human race is sometimes motivated by the wishes of government to distract people from other unpleasant events, the disquieting fact remains that something is happening, something which we might term "the unintentional suicide of mankind."

Since *Homo sapiens* emerged from the Ice Age, he has always been engaged in fighting or taming nature. As a means of self-preservation he has destroyed forests, slaughtered animals, dug up the earth's surface, and mined her seas and mountains. But even though man was able to inflict serious wounds on the skin of this planet, the regenerative powers of nature were generally able to heal the damaged tissues.

It is the unique accomplishment of our era that, for the first time, we are able to destroy faster than nature can replenish. This triumph is partially due to our growing numerical strength and partly to the unparalleled ability of producing more and more effective tools for conquering nature. We are producing and consuming more goods than ever before, and in the whirl of that activity, amassing such amounts of waste products that we are puzzled as to how to dispose of them. *Homo sapiens* is winning the millenium-old war against nature. The "enemy" can no longer regroup his forces, heal his wounds, with sufficient speed. If man does not call a halt to this war of attrition—he will win. The balance of forces will be upset with finality. Nature will die, and man, realizing too late that he is himself part of nature, will suffocate in the stench of the corpse. We men are starting to experience the gathering of the first fruits of victory. We have proven that we can poison water, air, and land faster than ever before and faster than nature can purify them. We can kill animals faster than they can breed, destroy plant life faster than it can renew itself. We can pollute rivers and even oceans

Figure 1-3 The first men.

Figure 1-4 The last tree.

with such efficiency that all the mountain springs and glaciers of the globe cannot keep up with us. We can even, if we set our minds to it, use up oxygen faster than all the trees which have been spared and all the waters of this globe can replenish it. If all this should not suffice, we can unleash the powers of the split atom and kill all living matter, including ourselves, once and for all.

We *can* do all of these things. We have the capability and we even seem to have a certain compulsion to use it. A few more victories behind the banners of overproduction of people and goods will spell finis for all organic life on this our planet earth. But we are not really forced nor obliged to make use of this capability. We may awaken from our drunkenness caused by that powerful drug called "technological progress"; we may yet in time recognize that man is an integral part of nature and that by protecting and saving this planet's environment we can save ourselves.

Science is academically divided into "humanities" (human sciences) and other types which, by implication, are "inhuman." In our emphasis on short-term, materialistic gains, we have allocated to human sciences only a secondary role to "applied" sciences or to technology. Technology—and technological progress—have become the expressions of mankind's highest ambitions. Through mass hypnosis man has been cowed into a condition of slavish servility to the monstrous tools he himself has created. He stoically accepts mass murder by movement machines, the undermining of his physical and mental health, the destruction of his living environment—in the same manner as our forefathers accepted destruction by such natural events as earthquakes, volcanic eruptions, lightning and storms, as by divine forces. In our blind admiration for the achievements of technology we are even willing to overlook that "progress" is directed one-sidedly to quantitative standards, whereas quality has received only scant attention. We are being swamped with

Figure 1-5 Mass murder of fish through pollution of water.

Figure 1-6 Pollution of water through trash.

Figure 1-7 Pollution by the automobile.

Figure 1-8 Smog—the effect of pollution of air.

shoddy merchandise and incompetent services which could not pass the lowest quality standards set up in many civilized countries for the products of agriculture and livestock raising.

This condition becomes obvious when under the pressure of public opinion certain manufacturers of certain products are called upon to show greater responsibility and when, in specific cases, governmental regulations are enforced. For example, when the American tobacco industry was attacked on a broad front for selling a product which causes cancer, it pointed out, with a certain legitimacy, that its contribution to the poisonings of mankind was modest in comparison with the achievements of industry generally and of the automobile manufacturers specifically. In order to defend their own position they played the role of "environmentalists," attacking vehemently all the other bigger polluters of the air we breathe. When they were forced by law to print on the packages of their product the warning that its use may cause cancer, they asked, with some justification, that similar labels should be attached to every automobile in the salesrooms.

One generally assumes that the producing of

shoddy and dangerous merchandise is simply motivated by the desire to make private profits. However, the situation is not very different where basic industries are nationalized, as is for example the

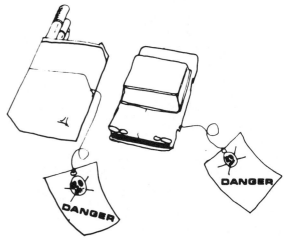

Figure 1-9 Why danger-labels only on cigarettes? Why not on cars?

case in Austria. Under the pressure of an intense public campaign for environmental protection, the various industries were forced to respond. The nationalized oil industry pointed out that though they were scientifically in a position to remove life-endangering chemicals from their products, it was not practical to do so for the following reasons:

First, it would cost a lot of money which would have to come out of the taxpayer's pocket. It was calculated that measures which would hold existing pollution of air and water at its present level would cost four percent of the gross national product. Any measure to improve the existing situation even modestly would cost eleven percent of the gross national product.

Second, the products of the automobile industry (which in Austria are nearly all imported) are so faulty that they would not be able to operate with improved gasoline.

Thus the oil industry shifted the responsibility for their dangerous products to the inefficiency of the automobile industry, and finally, the representatives of the oil industry declared that the trouble was really the fault of governmental planning, especially as far as road building was concerned. They pointed out that fast-moving traffic creates "nearly no" problems of poisonous gases, whereas slow-moving traffic, caused by many holdups at crossings and by traffic congestion, increases the problem a thousand-fold. The conclusion of the oil industry, then, was that if only the Ministry of Planning would create more and better constructed roads, which would permit automobiles to move faster and without stopping, a great part of the problem laid at the doorstep of the oil industry would be solved. The oil industry even went so far as to recommend that in densely built-up areas, where obviously fast-moving traffic could not be achieved, large pedestrian zones should be created.

On a much broader front, ambitious competition has started in order to decide who should be given the "Oscar" for pollution. The large industries insist that the first prize should be given to individual households for the trouble they cause by heating dwellings with coal, coke, or oil. The oil and automobile producers would like to present the award to industry generally or to the households. All of them consider agriculture with its use of chemicals for fertilizing and plant protection, a deserving candidate. Inasmuch as in Austria large segments of industry and agriculture are either nationalized or subsidized by the government, the fight is carried into the governmental arena. The various ministries responsible for planning, agriculture, finance and social welfare feel that they themselves

Figure 1-10 Who should get the Oscar? Individual heating? Industry? Oil refineries? Dumping? The automobile?

are innocent and that the other ministries should take care of the matter.

The example of little Austria illustrates that the battle for human survival is just as problematic in countries with authoritarian or communist or socialistic systems as in capitalistic ones. Thus it would appear that the real trouble with our much-praised advanced technology is that it is actually "underdeveloped." Its products, though quantitatively impressive, are qualitatively faulty and shoddy, and actually each of them should bear the warning "use of this product is dangerous to human life and health." What we need is some real progress in our so-called "technological progress." We can change direction on the dead-end road of "unintentional suicide" if we go into reverse gear. It is the human scientist whom we need at the wheel—at whose disposal we should put the use of our awe-inspiring technological tools, and under whose direction we should improve their quality.

If we change direction from striving for short-term, avarice-motivated, self-defeating aims to the long-term goal of protecting and enriching organic life, we can yet reestablish the biological balance and save ourselves.

Within the overall global environmental crisis, we are confronted with extremely critical conditions in our urbanized areas. In these concentrations of population, every human expression, positive or negative, is most acutely present and experienced. Cities are not only the birth and gestation places of ideas, spiritual life, artistic creation, economic achievements, and so on, but also of unrest, revolts, and continuous ferment. They are not only "melting pots" of racial, ethnic, and economic groupings, but also the breeding grounds for the eruption of hostilities. In the city, because it represents concentrations of large numbers of humans, we find the strongest manifestations of human achievements and of human failures. The urbanized areas are also the places in which the deadly conflicts between humanity and its technological apparatus burst most vehemently into the open. The shortsighted or naïve are therefore inclined to oversimplify and to blame the city for the lion's share of our environmental problems. They want to solve the ecological crisis by dissolving the city, or by escaping "back to nature." They overlook the fact that if everybody were to move out into the countryside, there would soon be no nature left. Those who call today for the abandoning of the cities, may find themselves tomorrow in the position of asking for the abandoning of counties, of states, of nations, and finally for the abandoning of our planet. Escape from unpleasantness is an understandable but foolish proposition. It is as futile as trying to run away from oneself.

On the American continent for a long time there existed the opportunity to escape. In the United States, mass emigrations evolved in the escape from the East Coast to the Middle West, from the South to the North, from the Middle West to the West, from the city to the suburbs, from the suburbs to the metropolitan regions. The escapees acted like sloppy picnickers who, disgusted with the trash they had thrown away, moved on to a new picnic ground, only to spoil it in the same manner. Wherever they went, the troubles they had run away from soon stared them in the face again. By now, however, all the picnic places have been spoiled; by now there is on the American continent, hardly any place left to escape to.

"Back to rural life," "back to small town life" are escapist slogans. If they were followed, we would only succeed in wiping out the last vestiges of nature, landscape and agricultural land. We would on the one hand definitely lose the creative values of an urban society; on the other hand, we would not regain the idyllic aspects of country life. We would succeed only in spreading out and rendering unmanageable, the symptoms of the urban crisis.

If escape is not a valid response, then we can obviously act in only one way: we must improve our urban scene by environmental planning. The task is a formidable one. We are confronted not only with the cleaning up of the mess now existing in urbanized areas all over the globe but also with the task of taking care of additional urban population which grows at an unprecedented pace.

The worldwide trend of growth of urban population proves that the human "herd instinct" is still fully operative. The general worldwide population explosion seeks an outlet, not in rural areas nor in villages or small towns, but mostly in and around cities, especially the large ones. Part of the reason is that because of technological progress less work-

Figure 1-11 Industrialized man behaves like a sloppy picnicker.

ers are needed for the growing of food, the raising of livestock, the mining of minerals, and more are needed by industry, public and private administration, by trade and professions, and education, all of which are best located in the city. Thus the entire brunt of the population explosion, and in addition, the migration from rural areas, has to be absorbed by urbanized areas.

In a relatively short time the demographic pattern of nearly all nations has changed from one in which the majority consisted of farmers or inhabitants of villages and small towns into one in which the overwhelming majority has become urbanized.

City	Population of Metropolitan Area in 1960	Population of Metropolitan Area in 1968
New York	10,695,000	11,551,000
San Francisco	2,783,000	2,999,000
Boston	2,589,000	3,239,000
Paris	6,094,000	8,197,000

Figure 1-12 Growth of metropolitan areas.

City	Population of Incorporated City	Population of Metropolitan Area
New York	7,964,000	11,551,000
San Francisco	697,000	2,999,000
Boston	697,000	3,239,000
Paris	2,591,000	8,197,000

Figure 1-13 Population in incorporated cities and metropolitan areas in 1968.

Source: Demographic Year Book of United Nations issued 1969

How can one explain the phenomenon of the ever-growing attractive power of cities, especially large conurbations, in light of the undeniable fact that our cities are steadily deteriorating with respect to the quality of human life and living conditions? The city attracts and will continue to attract people because it has one inherent quality: it offers choice, and choice is an ingredient of individual freedom. Only in the city, and especially in the large one, is there a wide choice of working places, of educational opportunities, of goods, a choice of cultural, spiritual, and entertainment experiences. The city offers choices as far as the people one wants to talk with, live with, work with, and fall in love with. It offers a choice between sociability or anonymity and privacy. It allows choice in one's personal style of living as "conformist" or "nonconformist" because the unusual is more easily accepted in the city than in the village. It is the city which offers exposure to different people, different impressions, different experiences. The chances for human personality to unfold and develop are greatest in the cities.

Many of the qualities of the city which we can summarize under the term "urbanity," however, are now being diluted and eroded. Though our urbanized areas are growing quantitatively and spatially as never before, their quality of "urbanity" is diminishing dangerously. This saddening phenomenon is created by the fact that mankind is winning the same Pyrrhic victories in the areas of the urban environment as in the battle with the natural environment.

Cities should be viewed as organic structures of a living organism. A city consists primarily of people and exists for people. Its structures, its communication systems, its utility lines, all are means only to serve the needs and aspirations of people. Whenever the mechanical servants of the urbanite start to interfere with human interests—when they threaten and endanger "organic" (that is, human) life—then the urban environment is in jeopardy.

Our task of shaping and reshaping the urban environment needs clearly defined, new directions. The goals of our efforts must be stated. They must not be the winning of hollow victories against organic life, human health, and life fulfillment, because in that case, the victors would be the vanquished. We cannot afford to fool ourselves any longer by measuring success or failure of an urban organism by applying purely materialistic measuring sticks. Neither the statistics dealing with the percentage growth rate of a city, nor those which enumerate the mileage of urban freeways, the number of automobiles, of television sets, or of washing machines, are meaningful indicators for the quality of urban life. We will have to change our judgment criteria. A new approach can be found if we put man into the central position of all our planning and actions.

The urban environment for which we must strive then becomes simply one in which are achieved optimal environmental conditions for the urbanite—for his physical and psychological health and safety—through a framework and structuring which is able to create and safeguard those qualities which we summarize under the term "urbanity." This goal implies on the one hand, greatest concern for organic life, and on the other hand, the need for concentrating population and urban functions on limited and strictly defined land areas.

Without imposing such restraints on size, shape, and form of cities, we are bound to experience failure with regard to a number of goals:

1. Without such restraints we cannot create or re-create the values of urbanity.
2. Without them we cannot succeed in reestablishing the balance with natural forces.
3. Without them we destroy the chances for the urbanite to communicate with nature and landscape and thus to regenerate his physical and psychological health.
4. Without them we render futile all efforts to serve the urbanite with those amenities, facilities, opportunities, and experiences which are the prerequisite for urban life.
5. Without them we reduce the availability of a multitude of choices which form an essential part of human freedom.

Figure 1-14 The Rockefeller Center—an example of positive urbanity.

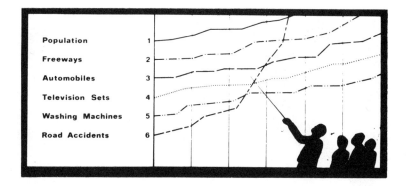

Figure 1-15 Chart of urban growth rates: We point with pride!

To combine the goals of optimal environmental conditions and highest achievable compactness is an extremely complex and difficult task. *But it is not superhuman.* The dangerous conditions which now prevail, as expressed in the global ecological crisis and in the urban crisis, were not brought about by superhuman forces, but by human actions. I therefore submit that failure brought about by people can be erased and converted into contributions to human progress, also by people. The vast arsenal of scientific and technological tools can be mobilized equally well for the advancement of organic and human life as for their destruction. We just have to decide whether we want to continue to utilize our ingenuity to set up technology as tyrant or as a servant to humanity.

To create cities as defined, compact, organically structured organisms with strong interaction of all urban functions in a small-grained composition of sociological and functional diversity safe from pollution of biologically essential matter, we will have to make fullest use of the sum total of our knowledge and our skills. Urban planning based on the principle of the priority of human and environmental values must aim at and can succeed in removing the many-faceted urban crisis. It can resolve the "transportation crisis" by shortening the distances between related urban functions, between residences, working places, and places for cultural, educational, social, artistic, political, entertainment, sports, and health preserving and curing facilities. To make the close relationship, the small-grained intermingling of functions possible, we do not have to deny technology. Quite to the contrary, we have to improve some of its poorly developed, life and health endangering tools, and we have to invent nontoxic new ones.

We can resolve the pollution crisis by correcting faulty, misconceived technical equipment which we now use to produce goods, heating, cooling, power, and transportation. By putting a stop to wastage and pollution of land, we can reduce the involuntary wastage of time, nervous energy, and effort.

By interweaving all expressions of human life within the urban tissue, we can restore the lost sense of commitment and belonging; we can counteract the phenomena of disorientation, isolation, and lonesomeness and awaken a sense of identification and participation.

By sacrificing certain short-term, egocentric, materialistically motivated and antisocial desires, we can achieve the potentially greatest possible individual freedom of life expressions.

Singly directed efforts, not related to an overall context, are often destined to impotence. Though each one of them might be in itself important and praiseworthy, well-meant efforts toward "beautification," "environmental hygiene," "nature protection," or "slum clearance," together with efforts to create better public housing and more inspired architecture, renewal and revitalization of historic city cores, protection of our architectural past, can only be effective if seen and understood in the context of the entire problem. The same holds true of course for the special theme of this book, because the planning and designing of centers for the urban environment can be successfully approached only in relation to urban problems generally.

The environmentally planned city, will be, like every organic entity, a cellular organism. In such an organism each cell consists of a nucleus and a protoplasm. Groupings of cells combine into more developed sub-organisms. Within an urban organism, such groupings might be neighborhoods, boroughs, townships. Each of these groupings will have as its nucleus, a "center" serving a total range of urban functions, graduated however, in size and character, in a direct ratio to the size of the grouping. This "polycentric" organization has always been typical for the organically grown city; it has however, been perverted in our technologically dominated epoch.

To trace the conditions and characteristics of centers within the existing urban agglomerations and to outline the emerging pattern of new types of centers or revitalized old ones aiming for a better urban environment is the task I have set myself in this book.

2

Figure 2-34 Southdale: Partial view of the Garden Court with bird-cage and light-sculptures (see page 33).

THE REGIONAL SHOPPING CENTER

Its Contribution to Environmental Planning

What is the explanation for the phenomenon that significant contributions toward environmental planning have been made just in the field related to trade and commerce? One would assume that commerce—a rather materialistically motivated activity—should have shown, in this respect, less ambition than, let us say, building activity in public buildings, churches, and the quantitatively largest expression of it, housing. Maybe an explanation lies in the fact that commerce as represented by retail stores plays the role of a meeting point between men and products. The store offers the opportunity of a face-to-face encounter between our mass-production society and the individual. It is the place in which agricultural products and goods manufactured in factories all over the world are exchanged against the money earned in the producing process. Thus, the merchant represents the middle man between anonymous industry and the desires, tastes and even moods of the individual. The merchant has learned through centuries that he can play this role of "broker" successfully only if he presents the merchandise, whether produced through agriculture or industry, in a most effective manner. Whenever scarcity of products exists and competition is small, his efforts in this respect can be minimal. But when there is an abundance of products and strong competition within the distribution system, then the individual store can be successful only if it also offers, besides economic advantages to the buyer, a certain amount of attractivity.

As long as the public environment, that is, the streets with their sidewalks, public places, and squares, are safe and agreeable, the efforts of the individual merchant in the area of showmanship can be concentrated on the appearance of the exterior of his store, on the show windows and their display, and on the achievement of a pleasant shopping atmosphere and an effective display of the merchandise inside and outside the store. Whenever the public environment becomes hostile, then merchants are forced to band together and to create, separated from the hostile public environment, a more pleasant and sympathetic environment for trade. As examples serve the open markets of antiquity, the agora of Athens, the Roman forums, the bazaars in the cities of the Orient, and in the

Figure 2-1 A historical etching showing a medieval merchant offering his wares to a customer.

nineteenth century the great arcades and galleries, all witnesses of the necessity of overcoming the disturbing characteristics of an unattractive, "hostile public environment."

As long as the public environment is basically attractive, the ambitious merchant can generally concentrate his attention on the creation of the intimate environment of his own enterprise. Great merchants have employed for this purpose, especially in the nineteenth and twentieth centuries, the services of architects, designers, graphic artists, and even painters and sculptors. Examples are

Figure 2-2 The oriental bazaar.

Figure 2-3 The Carson Pirie Scott store in Chicago.

Sullivan's Carson Pirie Scott Store in Chicago and the V. C. Morris Store, designed by Frank Lloyd Wright, in San Francisco.

But when the public environment becomes, for one reason or another, plagued by conflicts and disturbances and therefore hostile, then the merchant is forced to call on the help of planners, urbanists, and architects to create environmental conditions which, separated from the hostile overall public environment, will give him a chance to survive. And because the merchant is the immediate contact man with the individual, he has to develop an acute understanding for those needs and requirements which the ordinary citizen consciously or subconsciously demands from a good environment.

These were the reasons why, in the nineteenth century, the "covered arcade" building type made its appearance in central city areas. The conditions of the streets were rendered so disagreeable and unsafe that walking on narrow or nonexistent sidewalks became an unpleasant experience. Thus merchants, banding together, in cooperation with many outstanding architects, created new, exclusively pedestrian, weather-protected areas in the middle of building blocks, connecting one major street with another. The excellent book *Passagen, Ein Bautyp des 19. Jahrhunderts* by Johann Friedrich Geist (published by Prestel in 1969) traces in an encyclopedic manner, the development of the nineteenth-century arcade. In this definitive and richly illustrated book, however, the author predicts the death of this building type. This pessimistic pre-

Figure 2-4 The V. C. Morris store in Maiden Lane, San Francisco, designed by Frank Lloyd Wright.

Figure 2-5 A 19th century arcade, in Naples, Italy.

Figure 2-6 A 19th century arcade, in Leeds, England.

diction has not quite come true. In many active city core areas, for example in Brussels and also in Paris, new arcades following closely the nineteenth-century concept are being constructed. It is also interesting to note that in those city cores such as Bologna and Bolzano in Italy and Bern in Switzerland, where special pedestrian amenities were provided by means of colonnades, the nineteenth-century arcades were never introduced. It is also worthwhile to remember that in the cities of the United States, until the years after the end of World War II, the activity of constructing new stores or remodeling old ones was concentrated in the downtown areas. From my own experience, I can say that, after my arrival in New York in 1938 until about 1944, nearly all my projects were located in either Manhattan or the downtown areas of Los Angeles, Seattle, Portland, and many other cities.

Figure 2-8 The colonnaded streets of Bern.

Figure 2-7 A contemporary arcade in Osaka, Japan.

However, the situation of a highly hostile urban environment arose in the spreading suburban areas of the cities of the United States rather earlier and more forcefully than in the cities of Europe, Japan, and other industrialized nations. It is in the context of this situation that the development of a new building type, "the regional suburban shopping center" has to be understood. Even during the war it was already apparent that a revolutionary change in the distribution pattern would be in the offing. When, in 1943, the publication *Architectural Forum* devoted an issue to "Architecture 194X," inviting a number of architects to prophesy what would happen after the war ended, I contributed an article on the "Shopping Center," illustrating it with sketches and drawings reflecting the concepts of separation of pedestrian and automobile traffic, of the creation of pedestrian areas, and of the "one stop" shopping environments.

Figure 2-9 Sketch of a shopping center by the author. From the "Architectural Forum," 1943 issue entitled "Architecture 194X." Original text read:
"How can shopping be made more inviting?

"Shops could be grouped in one building surrounding a landscaped area, as in this scheme. With the exception of the main entrance the outside is modest in character. No advertising disturbs the appearance of the residential streets. Each end of the block has parking space and loading and unloading are carried on behind screen walls. For the shoppers there is a covered walk connecting all the stores, a restful atmosphere and protection from automobile traffic.

"All necessities of day-to-day living can be found in the shopping center: post office, circulating library, doctors' and dentists' offices, and rooms for club activities, in addition to the usual shopping facilities. Shopping thus becomes a pleasure, recreation instead of a chore.

"Larger centers could be built on the same principle, covering several blocks. Automobile traffic could be diverted around such centers or if necessary, under them."

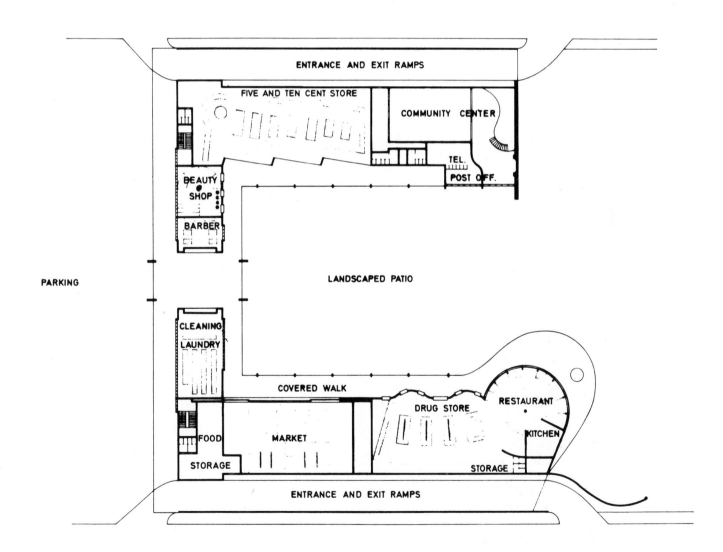

U.S. PREDECESSORS TO THE REGIONAL SHOPPING CENTERS

In order to appreciate the contribution the regional shopping center has made to environmental planning, it might be helpful to review the history of its predecessors.

Some suburban concentrations of shopping facilities had been constructed in the United States in the 1930s and 1940s prior to the involvement of the United States in World War II. Some of these were products of careful planning. I am referring especially to the Country Club Plaza in Kansas City, Missouri, Westwood Village in Los Angeles, and some of their imitators. In certain ways they are forerunners not only of the regional shopping center but also of the "satellite town." They were conceived and constructed within integrated patterns of new communities and functioned as cores for the new developments. They also represented multifunctionality to a higher degree than the building type "regional shopping center." They included places of entertainment and offices. However, hav-

ing been constructed in the years "B.C." (Before Combustion engine), no attention had been paid to separation of vehicles and people because the insatiable appetite of the individual car was still not evident. Garages and other parking facilities had therefore to be added to them later in similar fashion as became necessary in central city areas.

Another significant difference between these "shopping villages" and the "regional shopping center" was that department stores or other large stores were not generally represented in them, but smaller merchandising units which served the new community satisfactorily found a place there.

Architecturally, these developments tried to achieve a European, and specifically a Mediterranean, character. Italian and Spanish forms were not only adopted, but various Latinate building elements, ornaments, and sculptures were imported. Inasmuch as the demand for elements such as churches, chateaus, and the like, was at that time minimal, typical Mediterranean towers and turrets crowned banks, movie houses and supermarkets. Even if one might smile about the naivety of this eclecticism, it must be conceded that these shopping villages achieved an architectural unity rarely found in today's representatives of regional centers.

Figure 2-10 Country Club Plaza.

POSTWAR DEVELOPMENT

When the "war to end all wars" was, for the United States and its allies, victoriously ended, pent-up desires and postponed developments burst into the open and caused, as one effect, "the exploding metropolis." Government action promoted suburbia by assisting war veterans in the fulfillment of their dreams for a free-standing house with a garden. Private construction activity which had been at a standstill during the war years, caught up with the backlog, concentrating on those areas where land was easy to get and the cheapest available—in the regions around large cities. Motor cars and gasoline, which had been scarce during the war years, suddenly became available in abundance and the automobile population grew at a staggering rate. As far as trade was concerned, great opportunities arose. The shortages of the war years were over and, though nobody in the United States had starved because of the war, the "nice things of life," as symbolized by nylon stockings, had been scarce and were suddenly in abundant supply and demand. Yet though there was certainly a high demand for shopping goods, the stores, and especially the department stores, had lost physical contact with their customers, who had escaped to suburban and regional developments many miles distant. At first hesitatingly, and then in droves, the merchants

Figure 2-11 A typical "miracle mile" development.

followed their customers to the suburbs. They settled along arterial roads in endless rows in order to catch the eye and the pocketbook of their potential customers as they drove by on the way between their homes and work. Huge neon signs competed with each other for the attention of the customer. But soon it became obvious that the arterial roads were overworked. They could not fulfill two completely diverse and conflicting functions: that of serving the movement of thousands of automobiles and the function of stopping people in order to induce them to buy. Roads became hopelessly congested by those who parked cars along the curbs, by those who walked from stores situated on one side of the street to those located on the opposite side, and by trucks delivering and collecting goods. Finally the stores had to make some kind of arrangement to permit their customers to park their cars more easily, by arranging parking lots behind their buildings. This created a strange phenomenon. Most of the customers no longer paid any attention to the show windows and prestige entrances directed toward the main street, but entered the store from the rear parking lot, through a little back door which usually served also as entrance for employees and the place where merchandise was carried in and garbage carried out. This is the pattern which arose in those famous strip developments often touted as "miracle miles" which sprang up

in all major metropolitan areas. The "miracle" was achieved by concentrating some important and representative stores continuously on both sides of a main thoroughfare with parking spaces behind the stores. However, the greater the "miracle" of merchandising success became, the more intense became the "misery" for those who wanted to drive on the road in order to reach their destinations and for those who wished to engage in shopping. Thus the same situation referred to earlier as a "hostile public environment," which triggered off the development of the nineteenth-century arcade, repeated itself. The time was ripe for a new idea, for a new concept, for a new type of common effort by merchants to assure their continued existence by establishing a superior environment for their shoppers. The new concept, though urgently needed, was not born overnight. in the years between 1945 and 1950, there raged dissent and ambivalence. The large department stores especially, with their huge investments in downtown areas, were by no means unanimous as to whether or not they should join the flight to suburbia. Many realized at that time that an engagement in suburban areas might not only interfere with their own business success in city centers but might in fact contribute to downtown deterioration. How well founded these apprehensions were is discussed in Chapter 6 of this book.

The degree of indecisiveness which prevailed is

highlighted by a special issue of the *Architectural Forum* of August 1950, dealing with what was then called "suburban retail districts." I quote from this article:

The isolated branch department store in the suburbs is headed for trouble. A major new building pattern is appearing out in the great automobile trading areas which surround all the big U.S. cities. This is the integrated suburban retail district, planned and built under a single ownership. Perhaps the best place to study it is in the case history of the J. L. Hudson Company of Detroit, which stands next to Macy's New York as the biggest single department store in the country. The Hudson Company is planning to build a $15 million retail district on a 103 acre site out in Detroit's suburbs. This district will be almost wholly dependent upon automobile traffic. As the focal point of this development, J. L. Hudson is planning a branch department store big enough to gross $20 million a year. No department stores of this size have ever before been built in suburbia although Allied Stores have already under construction a suburban district six miles north of downtown Seattle.

Both "Hudson" and "Allied" are counting on integrated shopping districts including directly competitive stores to bolster their huge suburban investments. The shrewd merchants who own J. L. Hudson's believe that "competition is good for us downtown, and it will be equally good for us in the suburbs."

Census findings show an even sharper suburban movement than business had expected. Suburban populations were up 70% in some districts, compared to gains as low as 2% inside some big U.S. cities. Even more important than this great population shift is the fact that middle and upper income families are the ones who have moved to the suburbs. Census findings on retail sales show what is happening: 1948 suburban retail sales were up 226% over 1939 as compared to a rise of only 177% for stores inside the 32 biggest U.S. cities.

About half of all existing retail stores probably should not be in business at all: they are non-profitable, constantly failing enterprises. Another 25% are marginal undertakings; only a strong 25% enjoy steady prosperity.

Today's backers of the suburban retail district believe that "you could pull business up a mountain—if you have the right stores in the right relationship to each other." But most of them spend hundreds of thousands of dollars to find out what are the right stores and the right relationships and where these integrated developments should be located. The golden hunches of the real estate genius have given way to market analyses.

The quoted article also contains certain theories which had been set up for the new building type by "experts" in the field. Some of them are excellent examples of the "clouded crystal ball." There are statements that shopping centers should under no circumstances be larger than 20 to 50 acres, and others that claim that more than 525,000 square feet of stores could not be placed on a piece of land without repeating the evils of downtown congestion. In relation to these theories, the *Architectural Forum* stated:

When the J. L. Hudson Company announced a plan for 1,250,000 square feet of rental area, it was generally felt that this was utopian. Department stores were until recently, divided roughly into two groups: those who founded branch stores and those who did not. Those who did, tended to try to get a jump on their competitors by seeking out so-called "hot spots." Frequently these were in highway strip developments where parking shoppers and road crossing shoppers mixed to make a first rate traffic hazard. Wherever they went, the department stores could not seem to persuade themselves to get off the sidewalk—although the majority of shoppers entered from the rear of the store from the parking lot.

The *Architectural Forum* then editorializes on the architect's place in the suburban retail district and states:

Perhaps the most important thing that can be said about the architect is that he is in a position of leadership almost unparalleled in his practice. The suburban retail district promises him both a design freedom and a planning responsibility of staggering proportions. The architect is no longer the last man to climb aboard—at the mercy of zoning ordinance, of the real estate broker etcetera. He has a chance, as he has never had before—to control outside as well as inside space. For his new job he needs to combine skills ranging from those of the traffic engineer and city planner to those of the chain store and leasing specialists—not because he would dream of undertaking these jobs but because he will need to coordinate the work of dozens of experts in a dozen fields. The J. L. Hudson Company for example, called in Victor Gruen before the officers had even decided to build a branch department store or an integrated center.

This editorial is then followed by some plans for "suburban retail districts" including the one I originally developed for what was later to become, in a completely different form, Eastland Center in Detroit.

In those years, four large regional shopping centers were created almost simultaneously. In each one, architects borrowed heavily, intentionally or unintentionally, from the urbanistic forms of the past, without however, imitating past architectural expressions, as had been the case in the shopping villages of the prewar days. It is interesting to note that there existed a relation between background, education, and urban heritage of the architects and their creations.

North Gate Center near Seattle (architects, John Graham and Associates) with its location in the "New West" of the United States, leaned on the pattern of the traditional downtown main street, creating a long, stretched development on both sides of a street, from which, however, automobiles were excluded.

Shoppers World near Framingham in the Boston area (architects, Ketchum, Gina and Sharp) adopted the New England commons as a point of departure.

The Northland Center in Detroit and Southdale Center near Minneapolis (architects, Victor Gruen

Figure 2-12 North Gate Center, near Seattle.

Associates) were, in their planning approach, clearly influenced by the European heritage of three of the partners, myself included.

All four centers, which can be regarded as the pioneering deeds of the new building type, the "regional shopping center," contributed new ideas and concepts.

NEW OPPORTUNITIES AND PROBLEMS

In these prototypes are expressed the new opportunities and new problems which the regional suburban shopping center as a building type of the second half of the twentieth century opened up. This building type is of historic significance because its planning, design, and execution on virgin land offered opportunities and raised questions which had not previously been experienced in private projects.

The task of creating not a single building for one merchant, but one which would harmoniously combine as many as a hundred, was a unique proposition. It was further complicated by the task of in-

Figure 2-13 Shopper's World, Framingham.

cluding in the composition, non-retail functions, the necessity of grouping all functions around public spaces which in themselves should be of environmental interest, the aim of successfully separating the "human functions" from traffic functions and parking areas, the necessity of composing all elements which were often of considerable size (1,000,-000 square feet of built up area and more), estimating the economic strength of such a large composition of structures in advance, and of preplanning the transportation needs in detail. Those who participated in the designing, planning, and operational structuring of the first large regional shopping centers had to break new ground whether or not they were consciously aware of being innovators of a new building type.

None of these participants was quite prepared for this task. Architects had for a long time been trained only in the design of the individual structure. The opportunity to design groupings of structures around preplanned open spaces had been rare. Merchants had great experience in the layout of individual stores, in the methods of merchandising floor by floor, but they were certainly not prepared for the role which the regional shopping center forced them to play: namely the one involving new urban development working methods, the practice of teamwork, new rules and regulations. New attitudes toward such practices as protection of shoppers from rain and sun had to be developed, as did a new outlook on landscaping, street furniture, selection of works of art, general design control, concern for individual smaller stores, handling of deliveries, and, most important of all, the creation of a desirable environmental scene and a harmonious integration with surrounding residential areas.

"MACHINES FOR SELLING" OR "SHOPPING TOWNS"

Within the general goal of providing better environment for trade, there were two distinct philosophic approaches, which expressed themselves in various shopping centers and which are still in competition with each other. There are those who feel that the most direct approach is the only economically responsible one, that shopping centers should be scientifically designed "machines for selling," and that everything which distracts the shopper from "doing his duty" in making the cash register ring as often as possible should be discouraged. The narrow path system, which permits the shopper to look into windows on both sides at the same time, the elimination of any function which is not directly connected with the activity of selling and buying, and emphasis on the purely mechanical aspects of

parking, on moving from the parked car directly into the stores are the governing ideas. In sharp contrast to this is the approach which I personally have always favored and which expresses itself in the title of the book *Shopping Towns USA:* that the merchant has always been and will always be most successful where his activity is integrated with the widest possible palette of human experiences and urban expressions. This conviction expresses itself in the inclusion of as many non-retail urban functions within the complex of the center as feasible, in creating opportunities for cultural, artistic, and social events and in striving for an environmental climate and atmosphere which in itself becomes an attraction for the inhabitants of a region. A decision as to whether one or the other approach has proven more successful can only be made if one disregards certain special conditions. Shopping centers with mediocre environmental conditions are extremely successful when located in a densely populated and economically potent income area, and, on the other hand, some centers providing excellent environmental conditions have only modest success because their influence area is not strong enough. It is, after all, quite obvious that the missing prerequisites of a sufficiently large and economically strong population as well as of good accessibility cannot be overcome by any skill of planning, design, or environmental excellency. But in all those cases where prerequisites of equal quality are present, it can be stated by now, without any doubt, that those centers which provide superior environmental conditions and the greatest mixture of urban functions prove to be the most successful. To demonstrate that in this respect we are only at the beginning of utilizing all potentials and meeting all challenges is one of the purposes of this book.

The new conditions, new challenges, new problems which arose in those pioneering days, I believe I can most clearly relate to the reader by describing my personal experiences concerning two centers. Even now, after my involvement with dozens of centers containing about 40 million square feet of rentable area and taking into consideration my acquaintance with hundreds of other centers in all parts of the world, these two regional shopping centers represent for me best, the basic features and qualities of the new building type.

The Northland Story

In 1948, during an unplanned stop in Detroit (airplanes were grounded due to bad weather), I visited that city and its surroundings, including, because of my great interest in stores, the largest, or second largest (the placement depending on whether or not you included Macy's liquor department), department store in the United States, the J. L. Hudson Company. Aside from the question of whether this store was first or second in the United States, its importance with regard to one specific city is certainly unmatched. Hudson's is for Detroit what the Eiffel Tower is for Paris.

Having made various unsuccessful attempts during previous years at having one of my shopping center dreams implemented, I tried a selling job on the most unlikely customer. The J. L. Hudson Company, a family enterprise, was run with an iron hand by one of the merchant princes of America, Mr. Oscar Webber, who was also one of the greatest men I have had the privilege of meeting. To him and the entire Webber family, the store was not just a merchandising unit but the expression of pride and prestige of a family which passed the "empire" along from one generation to another as in a constitutional monarchy. I also knew that Mr. Webber detested the vulgarity and cheapness of suburban commercial development and that he fervently believed in the slogan that it is better to have "all one's eggs in one basket." However, on my two days' crisscross tour of Detroit, I had noticed not only that this world capital of the automobile was spreading and sprawling in all directions, but also that commercial development of tremendous impact was taking place on the periphery, including a large number of department stores. During a discussion with the store architect, Mr. Fred Wilkins, I learned:

1. That it was unimaginable that anybody could approach the President of the company, Mr. Oscar Webber.
2. That there was a group of younger executives, headed by Mr. James B. Webber, Jr. (who was then General Manager), which had been for some time restless about the general merchandising situation in Detroit and who had tried, in vain however, to persuade the President to participate in some of the mushrooming suburban developments.

A few days after my talk with Mr. Wilkins, I wrote a long exposé to Mr. James B. Webber, Jr., giving him my views on the future position of the J. L. Hudson Company, in the hope that I might get some reaction. It was only a few days later that I received a response which indicated that if I should again be in Detroit, the younger Webber would be interested in discussing the situation with me further. I happened to be in Detroit two days later. At that time I had the pleasure of hearing from Mr. Webber that he completely agreed with my analysis, that he had come to the same conclusions, but that all his efforts to persuade the President had failed because the

latter staunchly refused to join any suburban development due to his conviction that they were poorly planned, of apalling quality, and that the image of the J. L. Hudson Company would be sacrificed through any such participation. I then explained that I did not have the slightest intention of advising Hudson's to participate in any second-rate development; I would rather encourage them to build their own centers, established and designed in the great image of the parent company. This appeared to him as a new avenue which he might be willing to explore. It was only a few weeks later that I was invited back to Detroit, this time for an audience with the great man himself. This day, which I will never forget, started not only the Northland story, but a story which continued into Eastland, Westland, Southland, a number of further outlying centers, and a most enjoyable cooperation which is still continuing.

I have related this personal experience for the record and in order to scotch all the wild rumors which crept up when I, head of a comparatively small organization, was suddenly entrusted with designing the largest regional shopping center then contemplated. It was at that time rumored that I had been in school with Mr. Webber, or was related legitimately or illegitimately to him, or had some other "pull." The fact is that my success was due to a chain of coincidences and perhaps some initiative.

In chapter 3 of this book, I talk about the motivational quality of the developer. Rarely have I found conditions regarding motivation more favorable than in the case of the J. L. Hudson Company and specifically Oscar Webber. Once he agreed to the proposition of planning and constructing a suburban shopping center through the efforts and in accordance to the standards of his company, he stated that this was not a sufficiently long-term goal. He insisted on a study for a 15-year period which would establish a general strategy for at least four major centers and would enable him to take all preparatory steps to bring such a plan to stagewise implementation in the interest of the present generation of Webbers and for future Webbers or Hudsons. He urged me to enlist the help of as many specialists as needed and to organize a team.

The first result of the teamwork was the establishment of a general set of goals:

1. Four centers were to be established within 15 years starting from the opening date of the first one. (This schedule was in fact exactly adhered to.)
2. Each of the centers had to be large and powerful and in each one a J. L. Hudson store of between 300,000 square feet and 450,000 square feet in size had to be established. (Mr.

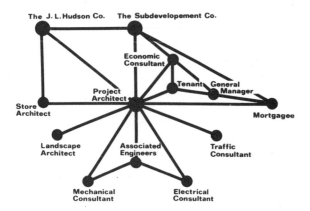

Figure 2-14 Organizational chart of the team which was set up in 1949 for the development of suburban regional shopping centers for the J. L. Hudson Company. (From Architectural Forum of August 1950).

Webber insisted that a department store, in order to serve its purpose, had to be large and that a little Hudson store was as unthinkable as a small giant.)

3. Inasmuch as it was realized that the suburban area of Detroit was almost completely dependent on private automobile traffic, ample parking space was to be provided and thus land areas of at least 100 acres for each center would be acquired.

4. The quality of each center should match in every respect the quality of a Hudson store and every means should be used in order to encourage the tenants, if necessary by subsidies, to attain this high quality standard for their show windows and interiors.

Figure 2-15 The Detroit Region with indication of the predetermined locations of Northland, Eastland, Westland, and Southland.

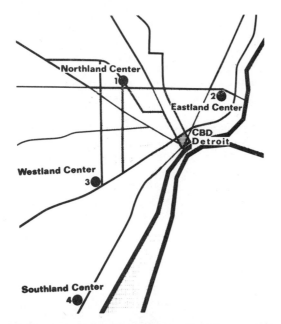

The first part of the work period was devoted to searching for appropriate sites which would fulfill the prerequisites of supporting population, of accessibility, and of physical qualifications of the land. Inasmuch as Mr. Webber insisted on strictest secrecy, one of my partners, Karl O. Van Leuven, Jr., and I were locked for weeks in the firm's conference room, permitted to leave only under strictest controls in the case of physical needs. We then proceeded to develop ideas for the planning of the Eastland Center, destined to be constructed first because the land was immediately available. After many experimentations, we developed a plan which was published in the *Architectural Forum* of August 1950 and which I now regretfully consider "the biggest egg" I ever laid. It was egg-shaped. A number of stores were ranged around an oval parking area in ring shape form, not less than 3,300 feet long.

Luckily, this egg was never hatched. The outbreak of the Korean War and the subsequent building restrictions gave us a chance to think again. The generosity of the client gave us the opportunity of developing alternative after alternative and, when the building restrictions were lifted, the land for Northland Center (which we had always recommended as the first one to be used) had become available and a new plan had been completed. The new plan was described in the *Architectural Forum* of June 1954 in a major article, as follows:

This is a classic in shopping center planning, in the sense that Rockefeller Center is a classic in urban skyscraper group planning, or Radburn, N.J., in suburban residential planning.

Northland is a planning classic because it is the first modern pedestrian commercial center to use an urban "market town" plan, a compact form physically and psychologically suited to pedestrian shopping.

Up to now, pedestrian shopping centers have been based either on a vehicular tradition (the strip street) or on an unsuitably diffuse rural village tradition (the common).

Northland's plan will repay study by city planners too: its flexible market-town use of open spaces looks like a natural for coping with rehabilitation of blight-spotted decaying shopping districts. And although in the aggregate this is an enormous project, it is full of ideas for individual store owners and architects who have had great freedom here.

Other points about Northland will become yardsticks. For instance, its high standards in public signs; its uninhibited, generous and lighthearted use of art. Best guarantee that the force of Northland's example will be heeded: it is proving enormously successful for both its department store and other tenants, sales already exceed estimates for five years hence.

The development of this plan and of every one of the concepts which at that time had to be newly invented was achieved in the framework of the closest teamwork which I have ever experienced.

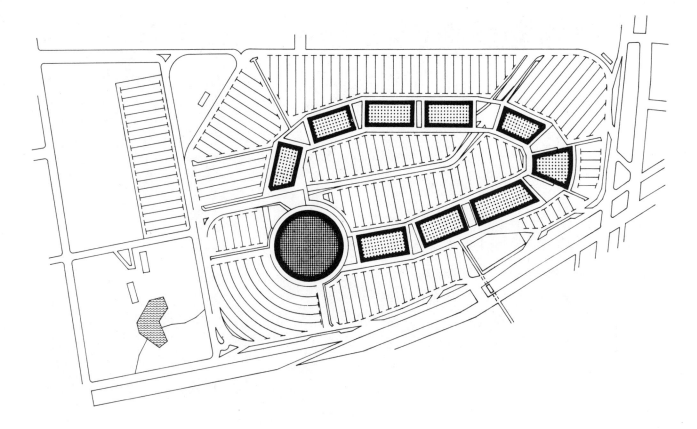

Figure 2-16 First design approach for Eastland. (From the "Architectural Forum" of August 1950).

Daily meetings were held with Oscar Webber at 9 A.M. (two minutes' delay caused a minor explosion); an office which we set up around the corner from the J. L. Hudson store employed over a hundred

Figure 2-17 Northland Center: Basic layout with department store in the center and tenant buildings grouped around malls and garden courts surrounding the major magnet.

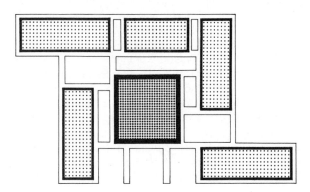

people. We worked with consultants like Larry Smith and Company for economics, Lloyd B. Reid for transportation, H. E. Beyster Corporation as associate engineers, and many others.

Oscar Webber was not only the best client an architect could expect, but also a man of very definite convictions. It was always possible to convince him but it was certainly a task which made hard thinking and a battle of the wits necessary. As an example, take the question of introducing art in the form of sculptures and mosaics into the pedestrian areas, a proposition which at first Mr. Webber refused even to listen to, but after half a year of arguing, agreed to, with his usual insistence that, if something was done, it had to be done properly and that no costs should be spared. We also had some minor troubles about color schemes, concerning which Mr. Webber assured me that I would have complete liberty to choose any color I wanted, "as long as it is brown." I bowed to his wishes and invented more shades of brown than one would think possible.

Figure 2-18 Public spaces at Northland: Sculpture by L. Saarinen.

Shortly before starting working drawings, two economic consultants judged the future income possibilities of the project in widely differing manners. Homer Hoyt proceeded along intuitive lines and furnished a highly optimistic picture, whereas Larry Smith had, on the basis of experiences of other suburban developments, calculated with greatest accuracy, and had come to the conclusion that the center as planned was:

1. Much too large.
2. Much too costly.
3. That its possible yearly income potential after five years would be around $50 million and that the project as it now existed could never attain financing.

Smith proved to be absolutely right with regard to the last statement. In spite of the formidable credit rating of the Hudson Company, no insurance firm was willing to finance the project as it was conceived. At this point, what may sound today like a fairy tale, happened. Oscar Webber said he personally, on the basis of his knowledge of the attractive power of the Hudson's, and the quality of the project and its location, was convinced that the project would be successful. If no outside financing was available, he

would proceed anyhow, with the company's capital. His decision proved to be the right one. As soon as the center was under construction and the first leases signed, he was stormed by offers for financing by various institutions. The business volume of the center in the first year was $100 million. When Webber teasingly asked Larry Smith how it was possible that he could underestimate the gross income of a center in a manner in which the first year's business was double the one which he had forecast for the fifth year, Smith was able to give him a very convincing explanation: "Sir," he said, "I am only an economist; I can only judge on the basis of past experience; I was not aware of the potentials of the new type development you were creating. However, if you ask me the next time, I will be able to give you the correct answer."

The planning of the long-term suburban development for the J. L. Hudson Company, interwoven with the planning for Northland and Eastland, was an exhilarating but also demanding activity. Six years went by between the decision to build the four regional centers and the opening of the first one, Northland Center, in 1954. This is not actually an excessive period if one considers that we were faced with terra incognita and that practically everything had to be newly invented, considered, and fought for. I still remember the zoning battles when the Hudsons and we met in mass meetings, the outraged groups of suburbanites who were alarmed about the possibility that the attracted automobile traffic would disturb their quiet residential streets, and that they would have from their houses a view of the ugly backyards of the usual commercial enterprises with their litter and truck traffic. It took half a year of persuasion, with the help of models, slide-presentations and other illustrations of the projected superior environment before the conviction slowly grew that the center might constitute an asset to the community and not a disturbance. (When, a few years later, similar meetings took place with regard to Eastland Center, we hardly had to do any talking; at that time it was the vast majority of the community who demanded a project like Northland.)

THE INDIVIDUAL VERSUS THE CORPORATE CLIENT

Looking back, I now realize how fortunate it was that in the cases of the first large centers which we designed, we were dealing with private clients or family enterprises such as those of the Hudsons and Daytons, the Strawbridges, the Magnins, and many others. Later we worked successfully with both private and corporate clients, but there is no doubt in my mind that the private client was inclined to be more daring, more willing to embark on innovations, and able to make faster decisions. Whenever working with large corporations, we were somehow faced with the "technocratic bureaucracy" which is nearly as ponderous as the governmental type. Just to illustrate the difference by one example: our contract with the J. L. Hudson Company was written on two pages and was decided within one hour between Mr. Webber and myself. A contract which we once closed with the R. H. Macy Company was about 40 pages long and was actually only signed half a year after the project was completed.

THE ARCHITECT'S ROLE

The role which we as architects played is partly described by the article in the *Architectural Forum* which I cited, but the role went even further. In Northland, we also planned the interiors and merchandising layout of the department store and of a large number of tenants' stores, and designed the landscaping, selecting every tree in cooperation with a landscape architect. We also worked with the sculptors in their studios. In other words, we enjoyed the position of team leaders with respect to the whole as well as to every detail.

Summarizing, I feel justified in stating that in the work for Northland, all problems of the "open regional shopping center" were present and most of them were resolved in a manner which still has full validity:

1. *Site Selection and Land Acquisition:* Achieved on the basis of study of the influence area, as far as economic and accessibility aspects were concerned, it proved to be accurate.
2. *Environmental Planning.* The introduction of a green belt between the public road network and the transportation area of the center made a great contribution to safeguarding the environmental character of the surrounding areas.

   The separation of transportation areas from human activity areas was achieved partly in the horizontal sense (as far as private automobile traffic was concerned) and partly in the vertical sense (as far as goods moving traffic was concerned).
3. *Accessibility.* The preexisting (and later improved) public road network was connected efficiently with an inner transportation loop establishing easy access and egress in all directions.

   Parking areas were provided in a most generous manner (about 10 parking spaces per 1,000 square feet of rentable area). Separated parking lots further distant from the center core were arranged for employees. For public transportation (buses and taxis), a special separated roadway was constructed which brought passengers to two covered stations located immediately adjoining the core area, and to taxi stands.
4. *Functional Concept.* A central heating and climatization plant was constructed on the periphery of the center area, directly adjoining a public road. In this location also are the central maintenance shops and a fire and police station. For the supermarket, a pickup station (climatized) was constructed on the fringe of the parking area and connected to the basement of the supermarket by an underground conveyor system.
5. *Planning of the Center Core.* The center core amounted to a tight group of buildings clustered around open public spaces. Inasmuch as Northland Center was planned for only one department store, this four-story building is located at the central point of the core and all other buildings, consisting of basement and one floor and containing tenants' stores, are grouped around the central feature. Thus the department store is actually furthest removed from the parking areas. It therefore performs

Figure 2-19 Aerial view of Northland center taken 1956. Note the green belt between public road network and parking area; inner transportation loop connecting with public road network; central heating plant in left hand corner of the site and employees parking lot in the foreground.

the role of magnet, ensuring that the visitors of the center pass other stores before they reach the department store.

6. *Basement.* The basement area extended under all buildings and under some of the open spaces. The demand for basement space, especially for furniture and home furnishing stores, was so great that plans were modified during actual construction to increase basement availability.

7. *Urban Design.* The open spaces between buildings were shaped in accordance with the pattern found in European cities. Narrow walks and lanes lead the customers from the transportation area into a series of generously dimensioned squares and plazas, each one of different size and character. Thus the shopper finds in Northland, an ever changing scene. Overly long, straight-lined malls were avoided.

The intent of the design was to create urban

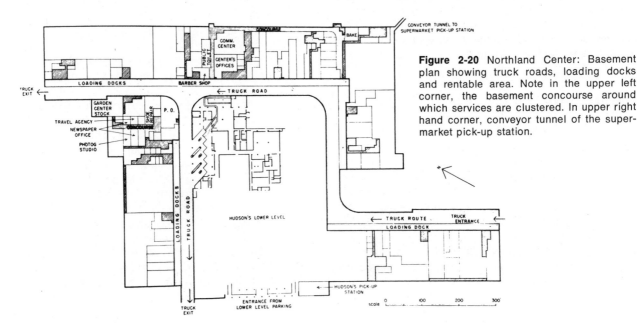

Figure 2-20 Northland Center: Basement plan showing truck roads, loading docks and rentable area. Note in the upper left corner, the basement concourse around which services are clustered. In upper right hand corner, conveyor tunnel of the supermarket pick-up station.

Figure 2-21 Northland Center: One of the spacious pedestrian courts. Note the covered walkways along tenant stores to the right, and along the department store to the left.

open spaces in which large paved surfaces were enriched by small-scale tree groups, flower beds, ponds, and fountains. Thus an opportunity for large meetings and other public events was created and that opportunity has been, from the opening day on, continuously made use of.

All buildings are surrounded by colonnades, protecting walkers from inclement weather or hot sunrays. Connecting covered walkways afford the possibility of crossing from one structure to the other without being exposed to the weather.

At the time Northland was designed, it was not possible to overcome the insistence of the individual merchants that their customers should be given the choice of entering their stores either directly from the parking lots or from the pedestrian areas. After a year of operation they realized that the attractiveness of the pedestrian areas persuaded most shoppers to enter into the center core before deciding which individual store they wanted to visit. I would therefore conclude today that it was a mistake to furnish show windows and entrance doors for all tenants stores on two sides, and it is interesting to note that this fault was rectified when the third shopping center for the Hudson Company, Westland, was constructed.

Figure 2-22 Northland Center: In the large courts, trees and bushes have grown up to give a park-like appearance. (Photograph taken in 1967).

8. *Provisions for Future Enlargement.* The final size of Northland was predetermined. It was not fully implemented in the beginning, however, although all preparations of structural character were made for the purpose. All tenant buildings were prepared for a second floor and the department store was also prepared for an additional story. In two places, basements and foundations were provided for additional buildings. To a large degree this pre-preparation for growth poten-

tial has been utilized in the years since the opening of the center.

9. *Pre-merchandising.* The idea of determining ahead of time the locations and sizes of various types of tenant stores was new at that time. It met with considerable resistance. Enterprises which wanted to rent supermarkets were disappointed when they found out that only one supermarket would be included in the center. The representatives of large, powerful chain stores refused initially to accept restrictions as to the number and size of units they were permitted to rent. It was to a large degree due to the insistence and perseverence of Mr. Horace Carpenter, who was in charge of leasing, that the pre-merchandising pattern was adhered to.

10. *Architecture.* The goal of the architectural design was to achieve impressiveness and unity by simplicity and straightforward design. Standardization was used for the tenants' buildings, and the department store's exterior reflected a spirit of restraint. Great attention was paid, on the other hand, to the proportions of the buildings and to the quality of all utilized materials. The usual outgrow of technical equipment above the "official roof line" was completely suppressed. Even television antennae were not permitted and all stores were connected to a central antenna.

11. *Graphics.* A graphic artist of outstanding reputation and ability, Mr. Alvin Lustig, was retained. Compared with other developments

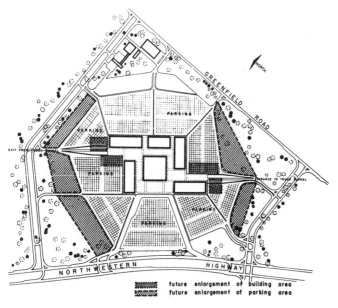

Figure 2-23 Northland Center: Original plan for future enlargement provided by the architects. A large amount of the planned expansion has in the meantime been carried out. The additional floor for the department store, also planned from the beginning, has been constructed.

Figure 2-24 Northland Center: Plan of the main level indicating the original pre-merchandising plan.

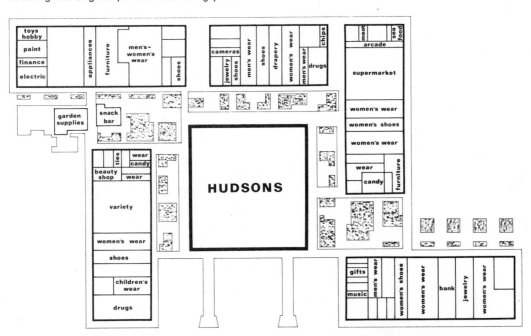

Figure 2-25—Northland Center: The department store, and adjoining low building, housing tenant stores. This photograph was taken in 1970 after the additional floor had been added to the department store and a sign affixed. Note in the foreground, the bus road and in front of the department store, two bus stations.

there is a small quantity of graphic expression, but it is of the highest quality. The name of the center itself is announced only through symbols and lettering on signboards of sculptural quality at those points where the public road network enters into the internal road system. The high water tower is used as an impressive symbol of Northland Center.

Figure 2-26 Northland Center: The water tower used as a symbol for the center.

The most amazing fact is possibly that there was no sign on the department store. Mr. Webber felt, quite correctly, that no one in his right mind could imagine that a building of such size and height could be anything else than a J. L. Hudson store. (Later, when the department store was enlarged, a sign was added.)

Signs for the individual stores were subject to sign control by architects and the graphic artist, but this control did not try to interfere with individual expressions. Tenants faced with sign control, which determined the size of letters and the provision that exposed neon tubing could not be used, were at first aghast; however, when they found out that these restrictions were imposed on everybody, they concluded that they could save a lot of money in being freed from the obligation of trying to outdo each other.

12. *Cooperation with the Community.* The clients believed that good relations with the community would be a key to success. Therefore Northland provides a large public auditorium, a theater, and a post office. The use of the outdoor areas by civic groups, such as garden clubs (which compete in taking care of the various flower beds), theatrical groups, amateur orchestras and so forth, is encouraged. Northland established its own police force, smartly uniformed, which performs a public service by finding lost children, locating automobiles when a shopper cannot remember where he has parked one, and preventing wild bicycle riding and similar disturbances.

Figure 2-27 Public events in Northland Center.

13. *Tenants' Role.* A tenants' association was formed which arranged for public events, and special decorations for holiday seasons, and which was in charge of enforcing the various controls concerning for example, opening hours, the hours at which show windows had to be kept illuminated, as well as the general appearance of stores and especially the prevention of paper signs pasted on show windows. The rental pattern was based on guaranteed minimum rents and percentage rents above a certain sales level. In contrast to later-constructed shopping centers, the developer himself paid for all shop fronts and also for certain parts of the interior features of stores. This raised the overall cost of the shopping center but also improved the quality of appearance of the stores, and with that, generally, the sales figures and the subsequent percentage income for the developer.

14. *Amenities.* All of those elements which could heighten human experiences were provided in the public areas with the greatest generosity. This is expressed in the arrangement for drinking fountains, telephone automats, letter boxes (which, through a chute arrangement, drop each letter into the underground delivery road for collection by the post office), ample provision of rest benches and litter baskets, and last but not least, in the richness of planting, fountains, ponds, sculptures, and mosaics.

The sum total of these conceptual measures established Northland from the beginning as the most successful regional shopping center in the United States, visited daily by between 50,000 and 100,000 persons.

Northland is, even after 17 years, still one of the most successful shopping centers in the world. It is being constantly enlarged within the framework of the original expansion plans and it enjoys a growing popularity.

The Southdale Story

There is a tie between the Northland story and the Southdale story—a family tie. Mr. Oscar Webber, referred to by the Daytons as "Uncle Oscar," had taken on a paternalistic role after Mr. Dayton senior died and left six Dayton sons in control of the family store.

It was Webber who persuaded the "Dayton boys" to put the fate of the expansion of their store into the hands of my organization. Each of the Dayton brothers actually had their own strong professional interests but, as so often happens in a "merchant prince" family, they had promised their father to stick to the store if anything should ever happen to him—and what a great team these six young men formed. Each one assigned to himself a special sphere of responsibility. The man with whom we worked most closely was Mr. Bruce Dayton, an intellectual with a lively interest in modern art.

The first project which we did for the Daytons was actually not a suburban one, but involved a medium-sized department store in the downtown area of Rochester, Minnesota.

I had the opportunity of visiting with the Daytons in connection with the Rochester store and with the suburban expansion project at various seasons. Whenever I got there it was either freezingly cold with snow masses covering the streets and countryside, or it was unbearably hot. From these personal experiences, under which I suffered greatly, I came to the conclusion that a shopping center patterned after Northland would never do. I concluded that open public pedestrian areas in a climate of extremes, which is typical for the Minnesota area, could not be a total success. So I carefully prepared the Daytons for the shocking idea of establishing completely weather protected, covered and climatized public areas, referring to such examples as the Galleria Vittorio Emanuele in Milan and many of the nineteenth-century arcades. The Daytons reacted with enthusiasm, but it was obvious to all of us that new concepts would have to be arrived at in order to achieve an economically possible solution.

A second condition occurred which made a complete rethinking of the Northland concept essential. In contrast to Detroit, where the J. L. Hudson Company was undisputed king, there existed in Minneapolis a second powerful store operated by Allied Stores Incorporated. They had officially declared their intention of constructing their own regional shopping center, not very far from the location which the Daytons had selected, and they had actually purchased the land. The situation was difficult. On the one hand, both parties realized that their competitive developments would damage each other. On the other hand, the two companies were not on speaking terms. Thus one part of the Southdale story is concerned with the role I had then to play for the first time, as matchmaker, a role often repeated in later years. A "marriage" was finally arranged, and so Southdale had to be designed for two magnets (quite in contrast to Northland). The marriage contract was not exactly ideal. Though Allied did agree to become a participator in the center, they would not agree to participate in the central heating and air conditioning plant or to have the same architects or even the same construction firm. This demonstration of independence did not exactly ease the planning task.

Figure 2-28 The Galleria Vittorio Emanuele in Milan, Italy.

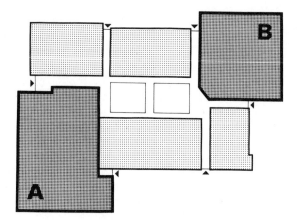

Figure 2-29 Southdale: Upper activity level indicating the location of the two department stores and the arrangement of the tenant stores around the large Garden Court and a number of lanes. The lanes indicated on this level lead to upper parking lots.

Though the clients were from the beginning receptive to the idea of an enclosed center, they had a hard time withstanding the dire warnings of numerous self-appointed shopping center "experts." They were generally warned that such a scheme could not succeed:

1. Because it had never been done before.
2. Because it would create staggering expenses as far as capital and operating costs were concerned.
3. Because a center with two activity levels, as we envisaged, would destroy the balance of shoppers' traffic.

If we had not been fortunate enough to have clients who dared to think independently and who were willing to take certain risks, Southdale could never have been built, and maybe all its later imitators would also never have come into being.

Though we profited tremendously in the planning of Southdale from the experiences gained from the planning of Northland, it became obvious that some entirely new concepts had to be developed for a center which was to be enclosed and climatized and which was to have two department stores within its limits. It was obvious that a roofing over and climatizing of a center like Northland with its vast public areas would not be economically feasible. The concept of a climatized public area could only be achieved if we could compress the center core, and this in turn was only possible by utilizing the third dimension. Thus Southdale has actually two and a half public activity levels. The half is in the basement where, around a basement concourse, service shops, repair shops, a children's play area and zoo,

Figure 2-30 Aerial view of Southdale and its surrounding area. This photograph was taken in December 1970. In the foreground is the building site of the enlargement which was then under construction.

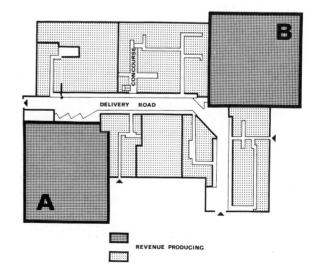

Figure 2-31 Southdale: Schematic plan of basement level. About half of the surface is used for revenue producing purposes. Note the basement concourse directly accessible by a stairway from the Garden Court of the lower sales level.

eating facilities, and the center's offices are located. The other activity levels (lower and upper) were made equally accessible from the transportation area through the arrangement of inclined parking lots, half of which ramp down to the lower level and the other half upwards to the upper level. The extrovert arrangement of Northland, whereby entrances and exits to all stores were provided from the parking lots as well as from the pedestrian areas, became for Southdale, illogical and physically impossible. For such an arrangement, it would have been necessary to introduce for every single store, expensive double doors with temperature buffer zones between them. Thus the Southdale Story also includes the event of the birth of the first "introvert" center. Customers enter only through arcades or side streets and, after passing along these narrow and low arcades, reach the impressively sized, three-story-high Central Garden Court. Through this concept, we were able to prove that additional expenses for roofs and climatizing for the public areas could be offset by a number of savings:

1. The need for duplicating store fronts and entrances disappeared.
2. The possibility of introducing "open store fronts" for all tenants who adjoin the climatized pedestrian areas created the possibility of savings.
3. The concentration of the building mass on about half the land area otherwise needed, made possible by the introduction of two major shopping levels, created savings for foundations and roof areas.

However, after solving the economic equation, we were still faced with the question of how we could create the type of pleasant outdoorish shopping atmosphere which we had planned for Northland. The design and treatment of the covered pedestrian areas and shaping of the garden court took on decisive significance. By introducing skylights and a large, continuous, glazed vertical opening in the garden court, we succeeded in establishing a psychological connection with nature and also the possibility of growing trees, plants, and flowers. The particular character of this garden court at Southdale was created through a carefully designed psychological type of illumination, through an abundance of plants, tree groups, and ponds, through easy-on-the-foot type of pavement, through the sidewalk café, which, with its umbrellas, gives the impression of being in the open, and through a much more daring use of works of art than ever before undertaken—a possibility which was open to us because of the intense interest and knowledge of Bruce Dayton. One of the outstanding American sculptors, Mr. Harry Bertoya, supplied the enchanting "golden trees" which reach from the floor to the high ceiling of the garden court.

A new technical solution which was introduced in Southdale was a "heat pump system," completely automatically operated to provide heat and refrigeration.

The arrangement for cooperation and teamwork was similar to the one established in Detroit. We set up a local office in Minneapolis headed by Mr. Herman Guttman, who, after he brilliantly supervised this complex project, became a partner of Victor

Figure 2-32 Southdale: Exterior view. Southdale is an introverted center, no stores being accessible from the parking lots, of which a part slope downwards to the lower level and a part slope upwards to the upper level.

Figure 2-33 Southdale: General view of the Garden Court. In the foreground right, one of the golden tree sculptures by Harry Bertoya, and the sidewalk cafè.

Gruen Associates. Here again, we not only planned the center as a whole, but designed interiors for the Dayton store and many other individual stores. When Southdale opened in 1956, it could be proved that the skepticism expressed by so many during the planning process was unwarranted. The capital expense per square foot was actually lower than that of Northland, and the operating costs were kept within very reasonable boundaries and gladly accepted as charges by the tenants. The fear that two shopping levels would destroy the balance of shoppers' traffic proved groundless. Through the happy coincidence that a candy store chain had rented one space on the lower level and one on the upper level, it was possible to compare the sales volumes in the two locations. They proved year after year to be the same. The garden court proved itself as an urban space, of city-wide interest. Inasmuch as it is the largest weather-protected space in the entire area, it became not only a meeting ground but also, in evening hours, the place for the most important urban events, as for example the yearly ball of the Minneapolis Symphony. However, even after Southdale had had its successful opening, the shopping center industry still hesitated to build anything similar and it was not until a number of years later that anything comparable was tried.

Today, however, those concepts which were first realized in Southdale Center have become the basis for the vast majority of regional shopping centers all over the world.

How has this prototype of the enclosed shopping center fared in the 15 years since its opening? Up until 1970, Southdale had been expanded, growing from 640,000 square feet to 800,000 square feet of rentable area. In 1971, it was again enlarged—to 1,180,000 square feet.

The sales volume (before the latest enlargement)

Figure 2-35 Southdale: Partial view of the Garden Court. In the foreground, pond. (Stairways, well designed, are popular with customers).

Figure 2-36 Southdale: Photograph taken on the occasion of a Minneapolis Symphony Ball held in the Garden Court of Southdale Center.

Figure 2-37 Southdale: One of the side lanes. This photograph shows the typical "open storefront" treatment.

had increased 175 percent. The developers state:

It has been profitable, and today it is a valuable property. Southdale has stimulated development within a radius of a mile from the center. That covers an area of several thousand acres.

CONCLUSIONS

The Northland story and the Southdale story should contribute to an understanding of the problems which were faced and resolved through "pioneering centers" in the United States. They also make it clear that a number of problems which could not at that time be quite foreseen have not been successfully resolved; for example:

1. The ugliness and discomfort of the land-wasting seas of parking which surround the centers and which render impossible any close integration with the surroundings.
2. Partly connected with the first problem, the inability to absorb other urban functions which are drawn to the immediate vicinity of centers

into the physical context of the center itself.

By virtue of its achievements and also by accentuating certain shortcomings, the regional shopping center has been a decisive factor in environmental planning. It erased the artificial barriers between architects and planner and created a model for the teamwork necessary for large-scale environmental developments. One of the major contributions made by this building type is that it has proved that a separation of mechanical functions and human functions is not only possible but that it creates significant human and economic values. In the pursuit of designing regional shopping centers we have relearned the long-lost art of shaping enjoyable animated urban spaces, whether open or covered, and in doing so we have gained experiences of great significance in the designing of multifunctional centers and new town centers and the revitalization of existing urban cores. Thus it appears that once more trade, in following its own economic interests, has made, as so often throughout history, a meaningful contribution to the shaping of the urban environment.

3

Figure 3-49 Eastridge Center: Main court. (See case study II on page 76)

TWENTY YEARS: SHOPPING TOWNS INTERNATIONAL

This chapter attempts to trace the development of regional shopping centers within the last 20 years. It takes as a point of departure, the book *Shopping Towns USA*. The chapter title indicates recognition of the fact that an environmental building type created and first developed in the United States has now attained significance throughout the world.

QUANTITATIVE GROWTH

As one of those who pioneered the new planning concept, I do take some satisfaction from the fact that this concept has in the last 20 years experienced a dynamic quantitative growth, not only in its birthplace, the United States, but over all continents in all developed and developing countries, completely independent of political and economic systems. Planning and construction of shopping centers are vigorously carried forward in Europe (especially Germany, France, Italy, Sweden, Denmark, the Netherlands, Belgium, but also (at least in project form) in Czechoslovakia, Hungary, Russia and Rumania), in South Africa, Japan, Canada, and in Central and South

American countries, in Australia, the Philippines and other parts of the world.

According to data released by the International Council of Shopping Centers at their convention in 1970, shopping centers accounted for 37 percent of the total retail trade in the United States and Canada in 1966. On the basis of trend projections, it is estimated that by 1976 there will be 16,000 shopping centers within the United States and Canada, which would then account for more than 50 percent of the retail trade. Another prediction states that by 1980, shopping centers alone will account for the annual employment of 18 million persons in the Western Hemisphere.

These figures sound impressive, but they obviously reflect a very loose determination of what constitutes a "shopping center," including under this term, any grouping of stores, even if such groupings should only consist of one or more supermarkets, or possibly a supermarket with a variety store.

Within the framework of this book, I am interested in those regional shopping centers which, by virtue of their size, the existence of at least one major department store branch, and the existence of a large number and variety of other retail stores and customers' services, establish important crystallization points within suburban or regional areas.

In order to obtain realistic data concerning the quantitative development of the "regional shopping center," I turned to my old friend, Samuel O. Kaylin, with whom I had the pleasure of cooperating for 20 years and who, because of his continuous involvement in this field, I regard as a reliable and objective expert. (Mr. Samuel O. Kaylin was editor of *Chain Store Age* from 1939 to 1968 and editor of *Shopping Center Age* from 1961 to 1963; he was Director of Publications of the International Council of Shopping Centers from 1968 to 1970 and is now working as a consultant on a series of studies concerning shopping centers for Harvard University.)

I have tried to arrive, together with Kaylin, at a determination of minimum size for a regional shopping center in the United States. I proposed that as a rather arbitrary cutoff point we should establish that a regional shopping center in the United States and Canada should be regarded as one with a minimum size of 400,000 square feet of gross rentable area. Kaylin felt that this was a reasonable assumption on the following basis: "A regional center ought to have at least one full-line department store (requiring at least 150,000 square feet) and a reasonably wide selection of tenant stores and, in addition, one junior department store." Considering the sizes of American merchandising enterprises it would be difficult to place these enterprises in much less than 400,000 square feet. He concludes, "400,000 square feet is as good a cutoff point as any."

I wish to add to this statement that this cutoff point would not be applicable to other continents, quite especially to Europe. Europe reflects in every respect a much smaller-grained pattern and therefore sizes of department stores and of all other stores are considerably smaller. A regional center with the necessary variety of enterprises could, in Europe, easily be established with 200,000 square feet of gross rentable area.

If one assumes that, for the United States, a center with 400,000 square feet can be regarded as a regional center, the following facts evolve: the last year for which exact research data exist is 1965. At that time Kaylin found a total of 389 regional centers, which together had 267,110,000 square feet of gross rentable area. They provided a total of 1,658,810 parking spaces. Kaylin attempted to extend the 1965 figure to 1971 and concludes that by the end of 1971 there will probably be 750 regional centers in the United States.

As far as Canada is concerned, he estimates that 28 regional centers will exist by the end of 1971. In the case of Canada, however, he warns that there, centers upward of 250,000 square feet could be regarded as regional types, because they serve people in an extended region with a wide range of goods and services. (On this basis, the number quoted (28) would have to be increased.)

I inquired from Kaylin what he thought of the newspaper reports which stated that 10,000—12,000 new centers would have to be added in the next 15 years. He felt that this all depended on the size of the new centers. If they were all to be small—let us say 50,000 square feet—one would probably need more than 10,000. If they were all to be large—let us say 1,000,000 square feet each—then only very few would be needed. He states,

I think therefore that a look into the future should really be based on population and income projections as related to sales per square foot. To refine such a projection, one would have to break calculations down state by state, allocating future space needs in proportion to population growth in various states or geographic regions or territories. As for dividing up future space between shopping centers and other types of locations, like freestanding stores, stores in the city cores, and locations on suburban arterial roads, some very high fraction, possibly 80 percent, would have to be assigned to shopping centers of all sizes.

QUALITATIVE DEVELOPMENT

In contrast to the quantitatively impressive growth, it must be observed that qualitative development has lagged behind. One is forced to the conclusion that the inventiveness which expressed itself so clearly in the first pioneering centers has given way to repetition and routine. Within the framework of the unifunctional shopping center (that is, the one which to the highest degree serves only the function of selling and buying merchandise), no decisive new ideas, concepts, or improvements have appeared. The first tidal wave has receded and we are left in brackish water. This statement may be regarded as subjective and, in order to be sure that it had a sound foundation, I checked it with Samuel Kaylin, who wrote, "As to innovations in regional centers, it is obvious that the blueprint was drawn up 20 years ago. Even the enclosed shopping center was designed in principle, when Southdale Center was opened." Meaningful progress had been made in the field of general planning, by applying certain planning principles developed during the pioneering days of the regional shopping centers to the multifunctional centers within the existing urban tissue and in the planning and construction of new towns. These promising developments, however, will be discussed in later chapters and discussion presently will be restricted to the 20 years of historic development of the "unifunctional shopping center."

It is believed that a critical analysis of this development is useful and necessary because, quite evidently, whether we like or dislike, approve or disapprove of the past, present, and, unfortunately, continuing trend of suburbanization, we must realize that the effect of this development will be felt for a considerable time to come. As long as this condition exists, unifunctional suburban shopping centers will continue to proliferate. However, I am convinced that, even within the framework of the unifunctional shopping center, important improvements can be achieved if certain misunderstandings created by thoughtless, mechanical application of rules and regulations could be clarified and eliminated.

HISTORIC REVIEW

Let us first take a brief look, through the eyes of the historian, at the evolution which has taken place in the last 20 years, especially with respect to the large regional shopping centers. Even within such a short time span, one can discern certain historic periods.

The period of the so-called "open center" has been replaced by the period of the enclosed climatized center. Whereas in 1956 the first such "enclosed center"—Southdale near Minneapolis—could be constructed only because of the daring and vision of the clients, it has recently been publicly noted that at the present time about 90 percent of all regional shopping centers in the United States are constructed as enclosed types. A similar prevalence exists throughout the world.

A side effect of the switching from the open center to the enclosed is that the pattern has changed from utilizing only one building level for sales functions to constructing two and sometimes three activity levels. As far as merchandising methods are concerned, the original pattern of the center with only one major magnet (represented by a department store branch), which was paralleled by the insistence of major tenants to be the only representative of their special trading field, has undergone a radical change. In contrast to the former insistence on "exclusivity clauses" in leases, we now find that all stores, including the large department stores, insist on the condition that competitive enterprises are included because of the growing conviction that competition makes a large shopping center attractive to the customer. The pattern has thus changed to a high degree, and this healthy competition has brought with it an upgrading of customer conditions and services. New large centers have two to three major magnets (in the form of department store branches) and quite a number of secondary magnets (in the form of junior department stores, large speciality stores, etc.). Samuel Kaylin confirms that this is one aspect in which important changes have

taken place. New centers with as many as four to five department stores are referred to in shopping center lingo as "blockbusters." The motivation for the creation of these "blockbuster centers" is to stave off all possible competition and to assure decisive dominance. These "blockbuster centers" could be viewed in a similar way as the fusion of industrial enterprises into large trusts. Kaylin points out that a trade area that can support four department stores may not necessarily be able to support an additional 150 smaller tenants. If instead of one mammoth center with four department stores, two of them, each containing two department stores, were to be built, space would then be leased to about 150 other merchants. However, with the four large department stores tied together into one center, space would probably be leased to only about 80 tenants— a number that is likely to be more in keeping with the needs of the trade area than 150. There is also a certain, but not yet very strongly expressed, trend to integrate other functions into the shopping and selling environment. This trend is exemplified by the inclusion of some office buildings, some cinemas, even small theaters, certain other entertainment facilities, and, in rare cases, indoor sport facilities. However, this promising trend is expressed only weakly, in the face of strongly developed specialization which is so typical of our era. The specialists in the shopping center field—developers, financers, or architects—insist on sticking to their specialty and are extremely hesitant about extending their field of action.

This attempt to furnish a historic analysis and to pinpoint certain historic periods suffers from the shortcoming that it does not quite reflect reality. The fact is that all shopping center types, even the ones which one would have to historically characterize as "prehistoric," continue to be planned and constructed in some parts of the world. Let us review some of the major prototypes:

Figure 3-1 shows a shopping center which relies for accessibility on existing public roads but which provides parking spaces behind the stores. The delivery of goods also takes place there. This ar-

Figure 3-1

rangement—left over from the old strip development—creates a split personality for the center. The representative storefronts face the public road, but the customer enters at a rear door, very often the same one through which merchandise is carried in and garbage carried out.

Figures 3-2 and 3-3 show centers which also rely for accessibility on the public roads but where parking is arranged in front of the stores. In this manner, it is possible to bring about a separation between the customer's traffic and delivery and service traffic (which takes place at the rear of the stores). Storefronts and signs can then be logically arranged facing the parking area, where the customer can see them from the public road as well as from the parking lot.

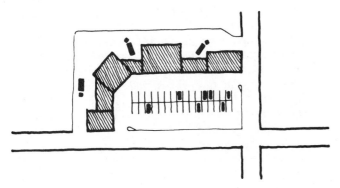

Figure 3-2

Figure 3-3

Figure 3-4 still relies on the public roads for accessibility but surrounds a block of stores on three sides with parking facilities and reserves the rear for goods delivery and services. This type of arrangement exists in many cases in Europe where the rentable area is then usually utilized by a supermarket in combination with a variety store and a few smaller stores or services.

Figure 3-4

Figure 3-5 is the first one which introduces a separate area for pedestrians in the form of a pedestrian mall. This prototype can either exist by attaching itself to a public road or by introducing its own circulatory road system which is then connected to the public road network.

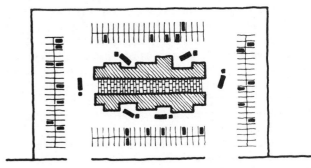

Figure 3-5

Figure 3-6 is just a variation of the theme. Both arrangements have the disadvantage that the delivery traffic is not separated from customer traffic and that the customer is given the choice of entering the store either from the parking area or through the pedestrian mall. We refer to this type

Figure 3-6

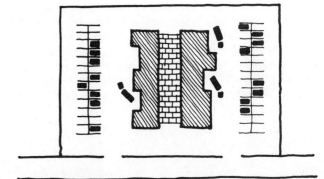

as "extroverted centers" and they are often plagued by the fact that the pedestrian mall lacks "animation."

Figure 3-7 represents a regional center with two major magnets. Access to parking is accomplished by its own circulatory road which is then connected at two or three points to major public roads. The prototype suffers from the fact that there is no separation between the delivery traffic and the customers' traffic. Centers of this type are executed either as "extroverted centers" (with show windows, signs, and entrances to the stores directed to both the parking area and the pedestrian mall) or as "introverted centers." In the latter case, all show windows, entrances, and signs are directed toward the mall, which can be reached only through arcades from the parking area. Thus, pedestrian movement is concentrated in the mall, which then becomes truly animated. The duplication of expenditures for show windows, doors, and signs is avoided. A superior pedestrian environment is created.

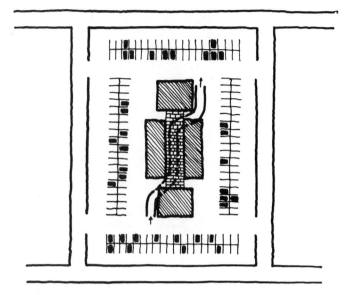

Figure 3-8

Figure 3-9 shows a similar arrangement for a shopping center when only one major department store is available. Here also, a basement with delivery roads should exist in order to avoid the conflicts and the wastage of land which always occurs when deliveries are made on the surface.

Types shown in Figures 3-5 to 3-9 can be executed as "open centers" or as "enclosed climatized centers."

The number of basic prototypes is enlarged when it comes to the introduction of more than one magnet (department store).

Figure 3-9

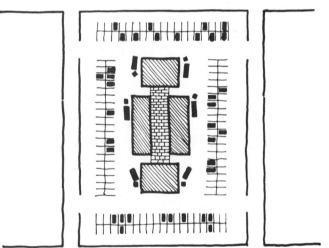

Figure 3-7

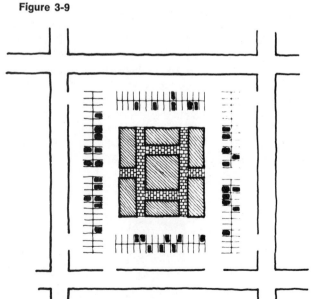

Figure 3-8 shows the same arrangement as 3-7 but enhanced by the introduction of a basement into which an underground delivery road (represented by the broken line) is incorporated. This prototype effects a separation between customers' traffic and delivery and service traffic.

Figure 3-10 indicates the main pedestrian flow pattern in the case of one department store (this illustrates schematically the arrangement exemplified by Northland Center near Detroit).

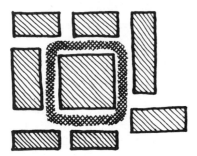

Figure 3-10

Figure 3-11 is a variation of the theme as exemplified by the Old Orchard Center near Chicago.

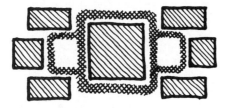

Figure 3-11

Figures 3-12 to 3-15 illustrate typical arrangements when three department stores are introduced. In each case, the intensity of pedestrian movement would tend to flow from one of the main magnets to the others, as indicated. We find that in prototypes 12 and 13 a balance of intensity of the pedestrian flow can be achieved, which benefits the tenants' stores because it is equally distributed between the magnets. In those two cases, the distances which the pedestrian has to walk from a central point are kept reasonably short. (Figure 3-13 shows schematically the approach exemplified by Randhurst Center near Chicago.)

Figure 3-12

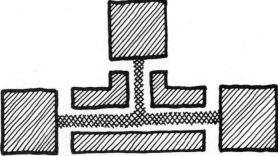

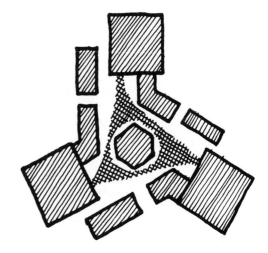

Figure 3-13

The prototype shown in Figure 3-14, which places one of the department stores in the middle of a very long mall, tends to bring about a concentration of pedestrian traffic in the center of the mall and therefore establishes an imbalance, giving the centrally located department store and the adjoining stores a greater exposure to pedestrian traffic than the two department stores on the extreme ends. The danger that the mall becomes too long and that, because of being arranged in one straight line, it does not provide any variety and surprise for the customer, is also a disadvantage.

Figure 3-14

The prototype in Figure 3-15, representing an L-shaped mall, also creates an uneven distribution of the pedestrian flow and therefore unequal opportunities for the three department stores and the adjoining tenant stores. If the three department stores are of approximately equal size and quality, the exposure to pedestrian traffic will tend to be the strongest at the location in the corner of the "L."

Preferable is a T-shaped arrangement (Figure 3-12), which could easily be adopted for four magnets by enlarging the T-shaped mall to a cross mall.

Figure 3-15

Finally, *Figures 3-16 and 3-17* show two approaches to the center with two magnets. Figure 3-16 represents the simplest and most often used solution. Figure 3-17 is a variation as it was utilized, for example, in Southdale, near Minneapolis, where the mall is considerably widened to a court and the large stores are arranged in diagonal positions. Thus space for additional tenant stores is gained on both ends of the pedestrian area through the considerable width of the court, and opportunities for the placement of kiosks and for the holding of public events are created.

Figure 3-16

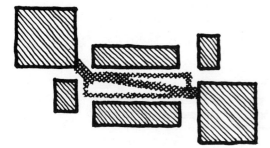

Figure 3-17

NEED FOR IMPROVEMENT

This small number of prototypes, which I have schematically illustrated, encompasses, to the best of my knowledge, all the solutions which are being applied, and it is significant to note that all of them already existed 20 years ago. Since then, the great incentive of inventing something basically new has disappeared. What a small group of architects, planners, developers, merchants, and a few consultants created in the pioneering days has since then been followed by an army of shopping center "specialists" leaning heavily on pseudoscientific literature and masses of statistics and superficial rules. There is no doubt that certain improvements have been made in building techniques, in climatization, and in building economics, but in contrast to the pioneering years of the shopping centers, one now only rarely finds centers which deserve to be called to public attention in professional magazines and one has to sadly agree that, as usual, imitation falls short of the original.

This is a situation which, in my opinion, is avoidable and warrants change. If a change of attitude cannot be brought about, then we are faced with a steady deterioration of those qualities which have made the prototype "planned regional shopping center" such a success. If we cannot at least match, and if possible, surpass those planning and design standards which are the underlying reasons for the worldwide success of the idea, it may in the long run bring the entire concept into discredit with shoppers and merchants and thus promote the downfall of the entire shopping center concept.

THE ECONOMIC EQUATION

All shopping centers, whether excellent, mediocre, or downright poor, are created in order to provide economic gains. This is equally true whether they are constructed in the framework of a free-market society, or created in the framework of a mixed society (by mixed economic groupings where government has a controlling influence), or even in countries with a socialist economic system. In one form or another, the wish to create a revenue-producing operation is the dominant motivation. If we accept this fact as an established reality, it is then obvious that in those cases where shopping centers have fallen short with regard to quality, especially in the last 20 years, a misunderstanding concerning economics must be at the root.

I have repeatedly observed that when a new shopping center comes into existence, two steps are taken simultaneously, the "setting of the corner stone," and the "cutting of corners." The average developer not only believes that saving on capital costs is the key to economic success, he is also often misguided concerning the ways and means by which capital costs can be reduced. At the danger of being platitudinous, it must be restated, that economy is an equation of a number of inter-related factors. The equation reads $I - (A + O) = RR$

I = Yearly income
A = Yearly amortization of investment capital
O = Yearly operating and maintenance costs
RR = Yearly available revenue and risk-reserve

The essence of economy is not understood if the four factors of the equation are not considered simultaneously, with equal emphasis. If a qualitatively good center requires, for yearly capital amortization (A) − 70, for yearly operating and maintenance (O) − 10, and achieves, as yearly income (I) − 100 − then it is obviously preferable to a "cut-price" model in which $A = 60$, $O = 15$, and $I = 80$. It is, of course, perfectly legitimate and logical to save on capital costs as long as this saving can be achieved without increasing operating and maintenance costs and without cutting, as a long-term consideration, the income potential. It is indeed a fact that the construction costs per square unit of regional shopping centers have, in spite of inflation, risen only slightly, and that this has been achieved to a large degree by perfectly legitimate cost savings as growing experience has brought about improved techniques. However, in the majority of cases, shopping center standards have suffered seriously because capital investments have been cut by methods which interfere seriously with long-range income potentials.

Architecture, according to Vitruvius, is the art of providing "firmness, commodity and delight." Firmness and also security have to be provided, even by the most cost-conscious developers, because in all civilized countries they are pretty well assured by building legislation. As far as commodity is concerned, it has also to be provided to the largest degree in order to establish rentable space and the necessary assisting service facilities. Thus cost-cutting is expressed first in one small portion of the overall consideration for "commodity," that which concerns the so-called public areas, for example pedestrian walks and parking areas.

Hardest hit by cost-cutting is usually the third component of Vitruvius' formula—"delight." Inasmuch as the attraction of a shopping center and therefore its financial success depend on its acceptance by the shopping public, it is obvious that providing "commodity" and "delight," especially in the public areas, are key factors.

But it is not only the lack of understanding concerning the interaction of the three main factors of economy by the developer and the professionals whom he retains which has a deteriorating effect on shopping center planning; there exists besides, a large number of preconceived ideas on how cost savings can be achieved. Because they are based on lack of knowledge or on superficial ideas, they fail to achieve any real cost saving and very often succeed in creating additional capital expenses. At the same time, they may interfere with the functioning and therefore the financial success of the center.

MISUNDERSTANDINGS

I would like to attempt to trace and categorize some of the prevailing misunderstandings. I am fully aware that it is difficult to do so in any kind of meaningful order because hundreds of factors are interconnected and must be observed simultaneously. If the fashionable term "system engineering" is anywhere fully applicable, then it is in the field of planning and designing a regional shopping center which not only has clearly defined economic aims, but which, because it constitutes a meeting ground between goods and human beings, has to take into consideration human needs, requirements, and aspirations, and is therefore influenced also by sociological and psychological motivations. In this attempt I will follow the organizational pattern of *Shopping Towns USA.* I will not, however, repeat those thoughts which were expressed rather thoroughly at that time, assuming that my readers are familiar with the book. What I will discuss here reflects in part the changing conditions which have occurred during the last 20 years and also those new experiences to which I have been exposed.

In *Shopping Towns USA,* I started with a discussion of the "prerequisites," and I will repeat this pattern here. The prerequisites are conditions which precede the activity of development, of planning and design, and determine to a large degree whether or not a center should be planned at all.

PREREQUISITES

The Motivational Quality of the Entrepreneur

Accepting as a fact that the impetus for development action is the profit motive (and it is not of great significance whether such profit accrues to a private party, a corporate structure, a cooperative, a city government, or to the state), it has to be concluded that the profit motive can express itself in a wide range of variations and aberrations. Some of them form a suitable prerequisite for the development quality; others are unsuitable. When unsuitable prerequisites exist, then all efforts expended through planning and development actions will prove to be impotent. Superior development quality can be achieved only if the satisfaction of specific interests can be brought into harmony with the requirements of the public interest, such as the interests of society as a whole, the quality of the environment and human needs.

The English language offers two expressions with regard to the entrepreneur which at least facilitate a superficial distinction between undesirable motivations and the more desirable ones. In English one uses the terms *promoter* and *developer*. In the French language only the term *promoteur* is available. In German it would be possible to distinguish between *Bauunternehmer* or *Bautraeger* and *Entwicklungsgesellschaft*.

The term *promoter* indicates an individual or a group which aims for a short-term, speculative gain. The promoter employs the following methods: he produces with a minimum of capital investment a product which, with the help of persuasion through public relations efforts, he sells as quickly as possible to users of the product or to a third party. He does so with the aim of making a capital gains profit, sometimes referred to as "making a fast buck." Depending on the quality of the other prerequisites, which will be discussed later, and on the degree of judgment and sophistication of potential buyers, the promoter can either cash in heavily (he can and does get away with murder) or he can only make a reasonable profit. Inasmuch as he plays poker, the possibility that he may go bankrupt is not excluded. The promoter is like any other seller of shoddy merchandise, inclined to emphasize superficialities like promotion and "packaging." He will pay little or no attention to matters which influence long-range success: cost of upkeep, maintenance, and operation, functioning of the center, and harmonizing private with public interests. An admirably frank American promoter, who has extended his activities to France, told me, when I pointed out to him that a center he had planned would not function: "I am selling even before construction starts. There is a sufficiently great number of inexperienced buyers around to enable me to do so. Après moi le déluge!" Short of a miracle (which would be the exception rather than the rule), the motivations of the short-term speculative promoter do not constitute a suitable prerequisite for a successful center.

The long-term developer on the other hand, might provide positive responses to the prerequisite of motivational quality. He might be motivated to plan and construct a superior center for manifold reasons:

1. He might himself be one of the principal participants of the center, e.g., one of the department stores, or he might represent a group of participating enterprises.
2. He might wish to enhance the desirability and therefore the value of other large real estate holdings which he controls and which he plans to exploit for large subdivisions, for new towns, tourist facilities, employment facilities, etc.
3. He might, as a banking or insurance institution, be interested in long-term revenue as it accrues from percentage rents (which reflect successful operation of a center).
4. He might intend to stay in business as a developer of centers within one country for a long time and he therefore would be desirous of building up a reputation for excellency of performance.

Thus I can state summarily, that the decisive prerequisite of motivational quality is present only if the entrepreneur is motivated by long-term "enlightened" self-interest.

Supporting Population

The population which is to support the economic success of a center might be:

1. Presently existing.
2. Partly existing and partly predictable through urban growth.
3. Partly existing and partly achievable through the deed of constructing the center and intensive utilization of surrounding land.
4. Created possibly in connection with development of new urban units such as new cities, new towns, or large-scale urban developments.

The possibility of constructing a center and the determination of its size and character depend in all four above-mentioned cases on the basic economic rule of supply and demand. Demand for a center depends on the size of the supporting population, on the quantity of requirements of this population, and on their economic ability to fulfill these requirements. The population to which I am making reference is the one which can be regarded as residing or working in the "influence area" of the projected center. Thus, the prerequisite of a "supporting population" will be nonexistent or insufficient if the size of the population is too small or if the desire and ability of it to acquire goods is insufficient.

The demand for a center will also be influenced by the supply of shopping goods already distributed by existing facilities. However, this supply of shopping facilities (existing competition) must be evaluated not only quantitatively but also qualitatively. Generally speaking, in the case of an existing suburbanized area, there should be no unfulfilled demand, as one will usually observe that nobody goes around naked and nobody starves. If, in mechanically computed economic reports concerning existing competition, it is demonstrated that after deducting all existing competition there is still a great demand left over, then the reason for this can only be that not all existing competition was accounted for. However, in spite of sufficient supply of shopping facilities, the planning of superior facilities in the form of a new center will still frequently create a new demand, at the cost of existing "poorer" competition. As a guide for planning, therefore, the quality of existing supply will have to be analyzed and the new supply represented by the projected center will have to offer sufficiently superior standards of size, quality, and amenities in order to create that needed demand.

I have related the term "supporting population" to the term "influence area" before. "Influence area" again is not an absolute term. It depends partly on the quality of accessibility, but it also depends on size, quality, and comfort of the projected center. In relation to these factors, the radius of the influence area of a center may not only be radically different in various directions, but it might vary generally from anything between half a mile and thirty miles. Thus it can be readily seen that there exists a strong interdependence between so-called prerequisites and a number of deliberate actions through planning, which, by improving the quality of supply, also influence the second factor of the equation, namely demand. Yet this influence by planning is limited. If for one reason or another a demand either does not exist or cannot be created, if the prerequisite of "supporting population" is completely absent, then even the noblest efforts to create a well-planned center are doomed to failure. On the other hand, it must be acknowledged that if a large, unfulfilled demand exists and if, through scarcity of available land, the owner of a land parcel finds himself in a monopoly position, then even a qualitatively poor center will succeed economically.

Paradoxically, I have found that "monopoly positions" for centers, as they are often created by public or large-scale private planning, have a negative influence on quality. Because in the case of new cities or new towns such a planning procedure determines in advance the logical locations and sizes for centers of various character (neighborhood centers, town centers, city centers), the spur of competition is removed from the developer, and with this removal of fear from competition, the urge for superior performance is also unfortunately re-

duced. (I refer to the regional plan for Paris, the new towns in England, Scandinavia, the United States, and other parts of the world for example.)

In such cases it is obviously necessary to ensure high quality of planning, construction, and performance of a center by establishing defining parameters for performance. It appears obvious that those who have provided the opportunity of "monopoly locations" are entitled and obliged to establish binding parameters.

Because of the interdependence which exists between the "givens" of the supporting population and those which can be deliberately shaped by planning, it is obviously futile to have the size, character, merchandising pattern, and leasing pattern predetermined through an economic expertise. An initial effort on the part of the economic consultant is needed only in the direction of a fact-finding report in order to establish the existence and size of demand. In this initial effort, the economists should be able to develop a series of hypotheses based on varying sizes of influence areas and of the influence of existing shopping facilities under various assumptions concerning the size and quality of the projected new center. A responsible economist will refuse to go beyond this study before he receives basic answers to pertinent questions from the "center team." Such questions may be related to:

- The size.
- The availability of major tenants and participants.
- The accessibility.
- The attractiveness.
- The quality.
- The comfort and amenities.
- The implantation of related urban functions.

It is therefore obvious that the "center team" must be formed by the developer at the time of the formulation of the intent to act in a specific region or area. The team would include the developer, the planner and architect, the economic adviser, and the construction engineer. If the developer is desirous of getting a meaningful and valid answer to the question of whether he should proceed with the center development at all and if so, what the size and quality of the projected center should be, the work of all team members must start simultaneously with a feasibility study.

The Site

The land necessary for the development of a center must obviously be available and must fulfill certain minimum requirements.

1. It must be legally available. That means its use for the purpose of constructing a center should not be prevented by zoning regulations, density regulations, or other restrictions.
2. It must be sufficiently large. However, size is not an absolute factor. I will prove later on that even the traditional unifunctional regional shopping center of, let us say, 1 million square feet of rentable area can, depending on deliberate planning action, be constructed on a land area varying from 100 to 20 acres.
3. There should be no insurmountable problems concerning the shape of the land or physical characteristics. We have described desirable and undesirable characteristics of the site at great length in *Shopping Towns USA*. Experience in the last 20 years however, has shown that many obstacles concerning difficult site problems can be overcome by planning and construction techniques. As an example, I would like to mention the project for a center in the city of Lausanne in Switzerland (see figures 3-18, 3-19, 3-20). There it was possible to prove that a successful center can be constructed in spite of the fact that the available land was not only very limited in size and shape, but further complicated by the fact that the site, through the existence of the valley of a former river, is located many levels below the ground level.

In the book *Shopping Towns USA*, we referred to two further prerequisites, namely "the tenants" and "financing." Though it is true that a regional shopping center depends on the active interest of major stores and other participants, it is also true that the interest of such necessary tenants can mostly be solicited if the major prerequisites are provably existent and if planning is of superior character. Often, of course, temporary difficulties exist, occurring when the general economic climate is poor or when all available major tenants are engaged in other projects to such an extent that they have to postpone expansion plans. Such situations usually influence only the timetable and not the basic decision. Similar conditions exist concerning financing. Difficulties in this respect occur on a worldwide or national basis in case of money shortage, but in a free-market society, they are usually resolved within a certain time period. Generally, it will be found that if the major prerequisites are provably existent and if planning is of superior quality, financing will be available and difficulties in this respect may have an influence on the timetable but not on the final realization of the enterprise.

Accessibility

I would, however, want to add to the original listing another prerequisite, and that is the one of accessibility. It is obvious that a selected location, even if the prerequisite of supporting population is fulfilled, would be unsuitable if this population could not reach the center within acceptable standards of time consumption and comfort.

A center in order to function must be accessible to people and to goods, with the stipulation that such accessibility must not only be possible but must also conform to qualitative standards, such as travel time and comfort. It is obvious that here again planning plays a major role. In planning for accessibility, it is often overlooked that there are a number of alternatives available. Accessibility for customers can be created by the medium of usage of private automobiles, by public transportation, and by pedestrian movement. Too often only one possibility, that of accessibility by private automobile is considered and the other two alternatives are completely neglected. Accessibility of goods can be created through the media of the truck, railroad, and conveyor belts.

In all highly developed countries it is now realized that there exists an upper limit for the growth of private automobile traffic within urbanized areas. This realization is partly based on the dangerous environmental effects of the usage of combustion engines for individual mass transportation and partly on the realization that the appetite for space of the

Figure 3-18 Center in Lausanne, Switzerland: Location of the center. To the right, the old city center. The dotted lines with arrows indicate pedestrian access roads which all lie on different levels. The dark shaded area is the major department store.

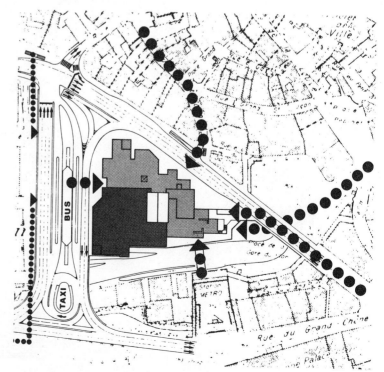

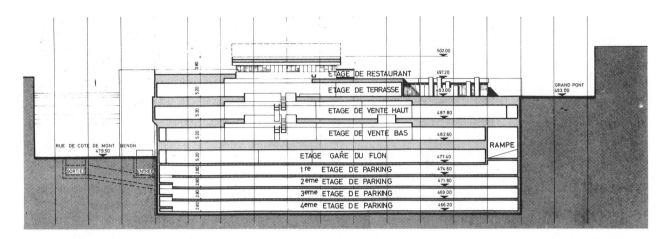

Figure 3-19 Lausanne: Section revealing that the street level is identical, on the right side with the terrace and on the left side, with the lower activity level.

Figure 3-20 Lausanne: Perspective view of the projected center. The land area of this project is about 118,000 square feet. Revenue producing area: 417,300 sq. ft. Income producing area (parking) 534,000 sq. ft. Nonproductive surface 205,700 sq. ft. Air raid shelter, 13,700 sq. ft. Total built up area: Approx. 1,162,500 sq. ft.

individual car is insatiable and can practically never be fulfilled. There is therefore little doubt that within the next 20 years governmental agencies will be forced to discourage the use of automobiles for routine trips in urbanized areas and to provide alternatives in the form of public transportation.

Since a large shopping center, and to a still greater degree a multifunctional one is an undertaking requiring a long amortization period, it is wise to examine all possible avenues in order to provide for a mixed pattern of accessibility. It is interesting to note that even the first pioneering centers, like Northland near Detroit, Southdale near Minneapolis, and many others, provide special facilities for public transportation (buses) and semipublic transportation (taxicabs). Though in the beginning there was great skepticism as to whether this would have any influence on the magnitude of customers' traffic, it has been proven that over the years, the percentage of those who take advantage of public and semipublic transportation grows steadily. In the centers located within densely populated areas, public transportation plays a larger role than individual transportation. The project Tête Défense in Paris anticipates that 60 percent of the customers will use public transportation. The center Midtown Plaza in Rochester, New York, depends on pedestrians and public transportation to a higher degree than on visitors who arrive by private car.

There is a general belief prevailing that provision of a large number of parking spaces (on the ground or in structures) in itself guarantees an economic success for merchants. In the prehistoric days of the shopping center this superstitious belief was so strong that for a time the term "parking centers" was utilized in order to impress on the public the superior service offered to them. A shopping center in France proudly carries the name Cap 3,000 (the number 3,000 indicating the number of parking spaces).

I am calling this belief superstitious because it omits consideration of the prerequisite accessibility. The investment for many thousands of parking spaces and of the land which has to be utilized for this purpose can prove to be completely lost if the surrounding and supporting road network does not possess the needed open traffic capacity to take care of the movement needs of the stored vehicles during peak hours. Such peak hours occur in shopping centers typically at closing time when it has been found that the drivers of about 60 percent of all parked cars wish to leave practically simultaneously. If they find out that this involves a waiting time of more than half an hour, they may judge that the accessibility comfort of the center is insufficient and may never return. The effect of this consumer's attitude is then that a major capital invest-

ment is lost. Thus, the prerequisite of accessibility may very well have a determining effect on the possibility of a center project or it may at least have an influence on the projected size. On the other hand, it is essential to investigate carefully whether accessibility cannot be markedly improved by taking advantage of existing public transportation media or by creating and encouraging use of public transportation and pedestrianism.

Ideally, the best safeguard to achieve long-range good accessibility is to ensure that choices are offered; that is to say, that access for people and for goods is made possible by various media. In such a case it will, however, be necessary to provide a functional separation of the various media from each other; that is:

- Separation of goods-moving traffic from customers' traffic.
- Separation of public transportation roads from automobile roads.
- Separation of pedestrian ways from all vehicular traffic (this involves also the provision of safe pedestrian ways for those who walk toward the center buildings after having parked their cars).

If one considers the great variety and diversity in accessibility patterns, then it becomes obvious that the blind belief in certain statistical data concerning the needed "parking ratio" is absurd. American experts, for example, have announced that on the basis of "scientific research," a shopping center needs 5.5 cars per 1,000 square feet. This formula has extended powerful influence. It has found reflection in planning and building legislation and in leasing agreements all over the world. Yet, like any other mechanically arrived at formula, it is absolutely worthless. The parking space demand of a shopping center depends on numerous factors. The most important ones are:

1. The size of a center and the goods and services which it offers. Generally it can be stated that the customer will remain longer in a very large center where he can satisfy a wide range of requirements and desires. The parking needs per 1,000 square feet of rentable area will therefore generally be lower in large centers than in small centers which contain only facilities serving everyday needs.
2. The availability of other means of access, namely public transportation and pedestrian access. In extreme cases, such as with large department stores in the centers of big cities, only 2 to 10 percent of the customers will arrive by private car. In a widely spread suburban area, where no public transportation is avail-

able and where nobody in his right mind would walk from surrounding areas through the vast parking deserts to the center, 90 to 95 percent of all customers arrive by car.

Under certain conditions, when the center is of superior size and quality and when accessibility for private automobiles is excellent, business activity will be of such intensity that a much larger ratio than the usually quoted one of 5.5 cars per 1,000 square feet will be necessary. Northland Center offers 10 parking spaces per 1,000 square feet.

Because it is served by public transportation and pedestrian traffic, another successful center, Midtown Plaza in Rochester, New York, manages to operate successfully with a parking ratio of about 3 spaces per 1,000 square feet. Thus it seems that with regard to accessibility and provision of parking space, there is, as in all other questions of center planning, no other solution than to analyze and plan every individual center in accordance with its specific needs and conditions.

The blind acceptance by legislators and tenants of mechanically computed parking ratio formulas has led to curious phenomena. The promoter-type developer, particularly, demonstrates that he provides the standard parking ratio by indicating the necessary number of spaces on the plans which form the basis for approval by authorities and acceptance by the tenants. This "paper parking" has, very often, not the slightest resemblance to reality.

Because a shopping center in order to be successful, must rely on the rotative use of one parking space by many customers during its opening time, "rotation" becomes an important consideration. Efficient rotation however, can only be achieved if the maneuvering of cars in and out of parking spaces is made as simple as possible. If individual parking spaces are too narrow, the loading of merchandise into the cars becomes a problem, and in the usage of a narrow and short parking space, the inexperienced or careless driver will often, by bad placement of his car, occupy two parking spaces instead of one. Thus it can often be proven that the number of parking spaces shown on paper is reduced in practice by 30 to 50 percent. It has been generally found that if one considers irregularities of the land, reservation of some space for pedestrian ways in the parking area, and a good system of "internal distributing roads," the necessary minimum requirements for the individual parking space in the United States and Canada is about 500 square feet, and in Europe and other parts of the world where smaller cars are used, 300 square feet.

In the case of constructed parking facilities (garages, deck parking), the space demand per parking space might be somewhat higher because

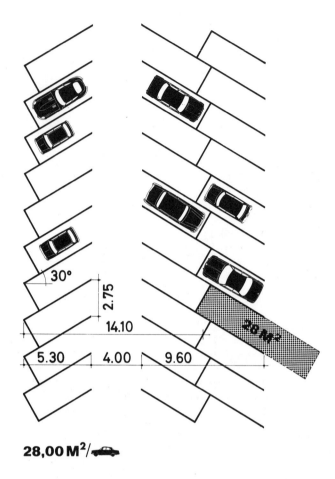

28,00 M²/

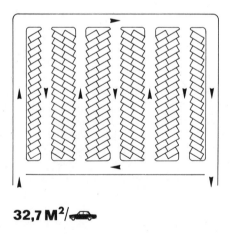

32,7 M²/

Figure 3-21 Parking study for European car sizes reveals that the net need per car parking space is 300 sq. ft. If the necessary internal driving lanes are added, the required area per parking space is 350 sq. ft. For American cars, 25% would have to be added to these figures.

of supporting columns, as well as the space occupied by ramps, elevators, stairways, escalators, etc. Those who plan a garage for a shopping center in accordance with the standards used for office buildings, make a serious mistake. They overlook the fact that in office building garages, one parking space is used by the same car during the entire day and that drivers who are using the space regularly acquire greater skill through familiarity of the parking arrangement—all conditions which do not exist as regards the customers of a shopping center. Thus garage facilities for shopping centers must be considerably more generous than for office structures.

The "Center Team"

It could, of course, be questioned whether the forming of a "center team" is a prerequisite for the development of a successful center. Yet it is certainly an important requisite. Years of experience have shown that it can be a decisive factor. The center team is composed of a large number of professionals and experts. The larger and the more complex a project grows, the greater might the number be.

The most important member of the team is, of course, the developer and his organization. The organization of the developer himself might be already composed of many departments guided by department heads. There might be a leasing department, a legal department, a financing department, a public relations department, a real estate department, etc.

Other members of the center team will be the planner and designer, to whom we might also refer as the architect, a transportation consultant, an economics consultant, representatives of the various engineering fields, a landscaping architect, cost estimators, etc.

In order to function properly, this team will obviously need one personality who will coordinate and guide all the efforts. This one personality will have to possess certain qualities without which an economically strong project of superior environmental qualities cannot be created. I am referring to the qualities of creativity, imagination, inventiveness, and leadership. When qualities are missing, then obviously only mediocre imitations of what has already been done by others can result. The leader of the team should have a combination of qualities and qualifications which are not easily found. In

Figure 3-22 If garage parking is used, space demands increase to about 470 sq. ft. for European cars. Again, for American cars, 25% would have to be added to this figure. Note: this layout is for a specific garage structure, i.e. that of the projected center Glatt in Zurich, Switzerland. More regular shaped garages would diminish the space demand per car.

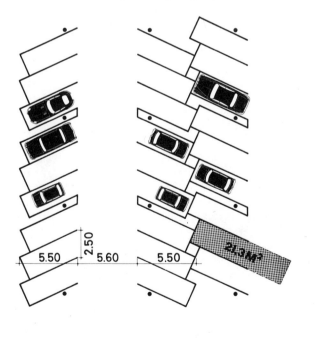

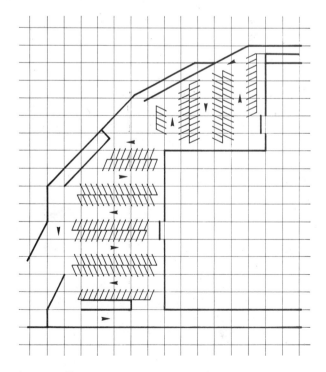

21,33 M²/🚗   **43,65 M²/🚗**

order to be successful in the leading and coordinating position, he must be a strong personality. Though he must be willing to stand up for his convictions, he must be just as willing to consider and accept advice of all other members of the center team and he must, through his knowledge and experience, gain their respect. Though he must be extremely knowledgeable in the fields of planning, design, and architecture, he must also be a "generalist" in the sense that he should be sufficiently informed concerning the fields of economics, transportation, and engineering to be able to comprehend and appreciate the advice of the other team members and the wishes and aims of the developer. In the case of a shopping center, he must be familiar with the problems and usages of merchandising and he must know something about the legalities involved in leasing.

It is obvious that it is difficult to find a personality who combines all these qualifications or possesses them in equally strong measure. In all likelihood, the leader of the center team will be an architect—an architect not in relation to a professional title or license, but in accordance with the original meaning of the Greek word *architekton;* a guiding spirit, the coordinator of a vast army of craftsmen. I know of cases where the *architekton* had been trained as an engineer, landscape architect, economist, but in all these cases, he had acquired through self-teaching and experience, those additional skills and knowledges which made him in fact the architect.

It must also be granted that there are many who have gone through a complete academic training as architects and who might not fulfill, to any appreciable measure, the conditions which I have enumerated above. Though experience in planning and designing environmental units, that is to say, groupings of buildings and open spaces, is certainly a requirement for the team leader, I do not believe a developer should insist that his architect qualify as a "shopping center specialist." A specialist who devotes himself exclusively to one narrow field of architecture is exposed to the danger of repeating "pet recipes" endlessly, losing the ability to see beyond the boundaries of his specialized field, and thus any chance of employing creativity, imagination, and inventiveness.

Similar considerations concern the selection of other members of the team. The transportation consultant should not be a highway specialist who lives under the impression that the world consists exclusively of freeways and a few disturbing inhabited areas in between. He should be a man who considers all types of movement as equally important and who will even concede that the old, nearly forgotten habit of setting one foot in front of the other might still be practical. The economist should

not just be a specialist for shopping center market analysis but should have a much broader outlook if all potentials of a location are to be utilized.

Now that I have—in restating certain facts about the prerequisites—hopefully succeeded in clarifying some of the misunderstandings which have developed over the last 20 years, I will turn to the actual planning process, following again basically, the organization of the book *Shopping Towns USA.* I will neither repeat nor enlarge upon what has been stated in the former book, but try to pinpoint those conditions and planning approaches where I believe clarification is necessary.

THE PLANNING SCHEDULE

The division of the entire planning process into various phases as it was outlined in the earlier book has found general worldwide acceptance:

1. Exploratory phase.
2. Preliminary phase.
3. Final planning phase.
4. Construction phase.
5. Opening phase.

However, I have found that the purpose and the execution of the exploratory phase are not fully understood.

The real purpose of the exploratory phase is to establish the feasibility of a projected center. In order to be of value, this feasibility study should be undertaken by the entire center team with greatest objectivity. Both the entrepreneur and the members of the team should be fully prepared mentally for the eventuality that the outcome of a feasibility study might be negative and that the specific project might therefore have to be abandoned.

In all contractual relationships between the entrepreneur and the other members of the center team, provision should be made for this possibility by giving the entrepreneur the right to terminate his relationship with all members of the center team if the result should be negative. A conscientious team of high standing will, if their combined studies show that a project is for one reason or another not realizable, state this bluntly. This of course means the sacrifice of an assignment and it is therefore recommended that the honoraria for the feasibility study be generous or that a special provision be made for separate payment in case the project has to be abandoned. The feasibility study, however, will never yield any conclusive results to the entrepreneur if he uses the services of the members of the center team haphazardly at various times or if he himself formulates an advance program which might be too ambitious or too restrictive. I have repeatedly experienced that the architect is retained only after the work of the economic consultant and the transportation consultant has been concluded and when a site has been definitely selected and bought. Whenever this happens, the architect is not in a position to formulate a program which may overcome or take advantage of the conditions inherent in the quality of the prerequisites pertaining, for example, to the influence area or to accessibility. In that case, the exploratory period becomes nothing more than an architectural exercise garnished with artistic sketches and possibly a pretty model. The entrepreneur loses every chance of finding out how economically viable the project actually is or what the possible parameters for economic success are.

On the other hand, I have experienced cases in which the entrepreneur has accorded the center team the necessary amount of freedom. In such cases he had only generally established the intention of constructing a center in a certain area. He held options on various pieces of land which could then be studied as alternative possibilities. He had not formulated a definitive program as to size, or major tenants and other participants. He expected from the center team, an investigation into various possibilities and subsequent advice concerning the degree of feasibility of various sites and a number of alternative planning concepts.

I have described a successful application of such an approach in Chapter 2 when relating the Northland story.

During all phases of the project, the work of the various center team members must be synchronized. It is, for example, impractical for the economist first to finish his work and for the other team members to follow. The same holds true for the transportation consultant. Because of the interdependence of all factors, a close step-by-step cooperation by all team members is essential.

The preliminary phase should start only when the decision to move forward with the project is made and when the basic program has been defined. The purpose of the preliminary phase is to clarify all planning and programming factors to such a degree that a reliable economic projection can be made concerning capital cost, operating and maintenance cost and revenues. A further aim is to obtain at least approval in principle for the project from all authorities. At the end of the preliminary phase it should also be possible to enter into negotiations concerning leasing of major elements of the center. For this purpose, it will be necessary at the end of the preliminary phase to design and publish a descriptive brochure.

The purpose of the final planning stage is to refine all findings of the preliminary phase, make those changes which might—because of special wishes and requirements of major tenants—become necessary, and to finalize the entire project in a manner which completely defines the entire construction program. Ideally, it should be feasible at the end of the final planning phase to obtain competitive bids from construction enterprises. It should also be possible at the end of this phase to arrive at an exact economic projection which reflects the expected capital and operating and maintenance costs as well as revenues. If this procedure is followed, then the differences between estimated capital investment cost and actual cost after completion of the construction should be minimal. Such differences between estimated and actual costs might arise in connection with excavation and foundation or in relation to minor changes which are made during the construction period upon the request of the entrepreneur. The above-described procedure is often followed in the United States, but only rarely in most European countries where construction contracts are often awarded at the end of the preliminary phase and various construction firms are charged with furnishing working drawings. The effect of this procedure is usually that actual final construction costs exceed estimates considerably.

The "construction phase" should be divided into two phases: the first concerns all the work which the entrepreneur has to perform; the second one relates to the finishing work of the individual tenants and participants. For each of these two partial phases, sufficient time should be permitted. Experience has shown that the predetermined opening dates could often not be met because the tenants were not able to perform their work—provide the fixturing for the stores, stock their stores with merchandise, and train their personnel in the short time available after the construction work of the entrepreneur was completed. The amount of work which the tenants undertake varies from case to case and country to country. In most European countries it is agreed that the entrepreneur should only provide the shell of the buildings, whereas the tenants at their own cost provide for the entire interior work including distribution of electrical, plumbing, heating and air conditioning lines, partitions, etc. It is a wise measure for an agreement to be made with the construction enterprise working for the entrepreneur, to the effect that he will not undertake any work for tenants and participants and to state so in a parallel agreement with the tenants. In this manner it is possible to employ a much larger range of construction firms of all types and avoid the overburdening of the main construction enterprise during the most critical time period when the center nears completion.

PLANNING THE CENTER

One of the earliest decisions which has to be made—especially in the case of the large regional center—is whether one wishes, due to a misunderstood spirit of building economy, to utilize only two dimensions, namely, the length and the width of a site, or whether one considers that the usage of the third dimension, namely, that of height, may bring advantages. I personally believe that only the second avenue can lead to superior results, not only with regard to building economies but also with regard to a better functioning center. When stating this, I have experienced surprising resistance which I firmly believe is based entirely on misunderstandings.

Misunderstanding 1: A one-story building is cheaper than a two-or three story-one. If the ground conditions are not completely abnormal, this statement is easily proven to be wrong. The wider a building spreads on one level, the more foundations are necessary and the larger the roof becomes. Also all the distribution lines for water, gas, electricity, and climatizing become elongated.

Misunderstanding 2: The construction of a basement is uneconomic because it is expensive and because it can be rented only at a lower price. Actually, on the basis of one measuring unit, a basement is cheaper than any other floor. Its building height can be lower than those of selling floors and it does not need any facade treatment. The basement provides space for essential functions of the center which otherwise absorb valuable, potentially productive space. For example, all delivery and storage areas and most of the technical equipment can be placed most advantageously underground. The other uses which can most advantageously be placed in underground levels, will be discussed later.

Misunderstanding 3: Whenever the idea of a basement deliveries system is mentioned, one hears the protest of the entrepreneur: "I don't want a truck tunnel! Truck tunnels are too expensive." The term "truck tunnel," which still spooks around, is applied completely erroneously. To my knowledge, arrangements which could properly be termed "truck tunnels" have been constructed for regional shopping centers only twice, and that was in the late forties or early fifties. As far as I remember, there exists one truck tunnel on Crenshaw Boulevard in Los Angeles, and one in the Lakewood Center near Long Beach. Both were created following the mentality of the suburban "subdivision technique." The subdividing developer started with the construction of a truck tunnel by actual tunneling operations and then proceeded with subleasing land parcels

either on one side (as in the example on Crenshaw Boulevard) or on both sides (as in Lakewood Center) of the tunnel, to individual developers, giving them the right to connect the basements of their own buildings to the preconstructed truck tunnel. (See Figure 3-23 for truck tunnel arrangements.) The advantage which the subdivider offered was that the delivery problem was solved in advance and that the space above the truck tunnel could be used for parking, for roads, or as pedestrian areas. Inasmuch as the tunneling of an underground truck road did not resolve any other problems of a well-planned shopping center, it was, as far as I know, never repeated. The trucking service and delivery facilities that are introduced in a basement level which covers the same ground area as the entire shopping center represent a completely different concept. The delivery road moves between an established "column grid" of the entire building and is different from the rest of the basement area only in the fact that it is usually depressed by three feet in order to create loading docks on both sides and add the amount of height necessary for truck movement. The only cost which the introduction of a truck, delivery, and service road in a basement involves concerns the ramps which connect this road with the surrounding terrain.

Earlier I stated that the development of a center on more than one level does not increase capital expenditure and, in addition, brings about functional advantages. The major advantages are:

1. Economy in the use of land.
2. Shorter walking distances for the customer and therefore a greater exposure of all stores to the pedestrian stream.

Figure 3-23 Schematic drawing of a truck tunnel. The basements of the stores adjoin the truck tunnel and are connected by stairs to the store area (2). Beyond the stores lies the parking area (3). This illustration represents the arrangement on Crenshaw Boulevard in Los Angeles. In the case of Lakewood Center, the truck tunnel is located beneath the pedestrian mall.

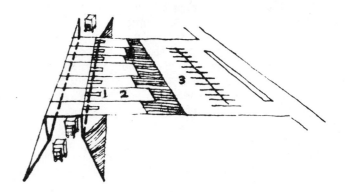

Figures 3-24 through 3-29 schematically show the changing conditions concerning these functional requirements on the basis of differing arrangements for floor levels. For all cases I have assumed a highly simplified plan for a center with 1,000,000 square feet of rentable area, of which 500,000 square feet is occupied by two department stores and the remaining 500,000 square feet by tenant stores. For purposes of simplification, I have assumed that the space needed for non-rentable areas (mainly pedestrian areas) is on the average, 30 percent of the total built-up area.

Figure 3-25 shows a center in which the department stores are two stories high, but all other stores and the pedestrian mall are only one story high.

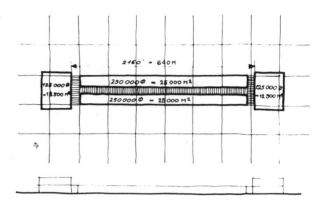

Figure 3-25 A center in which the department stores are two stories high, but all other stores and the pedestrian mall are only one story high. The land requirements are 250,000 sq. ft. for the department stores and 500,000 sq. ft. for the tenant stores. The nonrentable area however, will be just as large as in the case of 3-24, i.e. 300,000 sq. ft. so that the total land area required is 1,050,000 sq. ft. The length of the pedestrian mall is the same as in 3-24.

Figure 3-24 shows a center in which all buildings are only one story high.

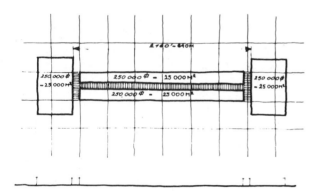

Figure 3-24 A center in which all buildings are only one story high. The land required by the buildings is therefore 1 million sq. ft. plus 300,000 sq. ft. for nonrentable area, together 1,300,000 sq. ft. The length of the main pedestrian mall is about 2,160 feet.

Figure 3-26 shows a center built with two sales levels for the department stores as well as for the tenant stores.

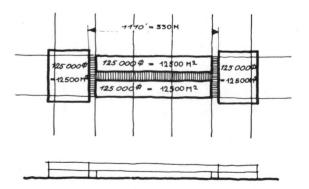

Figure 3-26 A center built with two sales levels for the department stores and for the tenant stores. The land requirements are 250,000 sq. ft. for the department stores and 250,000 for the tenant stores, plus 30% for nonrentable area (150,000 sq. ft.) in all, 650,000 sq. ft., exactly one half of the land requirement of illustration 3-24. The length of the pedestrian mall is about 1,110 feet which is near the upper limit of the walking distance which the average customer is prepared to accept.

Figure 3-27 shows a plan which introduces a basement level. The department stores have two additional levels above the basement, the tenant stores only one.

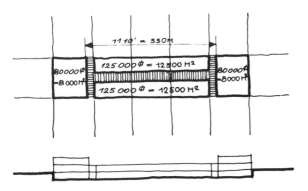

Figure 3-27 A plan which introduces a basement level. The department stores have two additional levels above the basement, the tenant stores only one. The land area required is 160,000 sq. ft. for the department stores, 250,000 sq. ft. for the tenant stores, together 410,000 sq. ft. However, for the nonrentable areas (because the length of the mall remains the same) the same area is needed as in Figure 3-26 (150,000 sq. ft.) totalling 560,000 sq. ft.

Figure 3-28 shows a plan for a center with a basement and two levels for the department stores and the tenant stores.

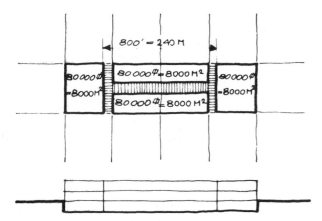

Figure 3-28 A plan for a center with a basement and two levels for the department stores and for the other tenants. Land requirements are 160,000 sq. ft. for the department stores, 160,000 for the tenant stores, together 320,000 sq. ft. plus 30% (96,000 sq. ft.) for nonrentable space, totalling 416,000 sq. ft. The length of the mall shrinks to about 800 feet.

Figure 3-29 finally shows a plan similar to the one of Figure 3-27 but with four levels for the department stores.

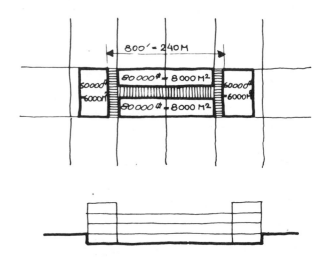

Figure 3-29 A plan similar to the one of 3-27 but with four levels for the department stores. The land requirement is 120,000 sq. ft. for the department stores, 160,000 for the tenant stores, together 280,000 sq. ft. The nonrentable area is equal to the one of 3-28 (96,000 sq. ft.) making a total of 376,000 sq. ft. The length of the mall is the same as that in Figure 3-28 (800 feet) which represents an acceptable walking distance between two magnets.

Figures 3-30 to 3-33 clarify the various possibilities through a number of sections.

As long as ground parking is employed, it is not easy to achieve more than two major sales levels which can be equally supplied with pedestrian traffic. This situation changes when constructed parking in the form of parking decks is introduced. In this case, it is possible to relate two parking levels to each major shopping level.

Let me now try to summarize the effect which these various plans have on land usage.

1. The most land-wasting and at the same time the poorest functioning center would obviously be the one shown in Figure 3-24 employing only one building level. Here, as we have seen, the land needed for the center buildings alone is 1,300,000 square feet, or about 30 acres. If we assume that for such a center, ground parking with a ratio of six cars per 1,000 square feet would be provided, parking would use a land area of about 70 acres, so that the total space demand for a center of 1 million square feet of rentable area would be 100 acres.

Figure 3-30 Section 1: A design without a basement, with the tenant stores one story high and the department stores two stories high.

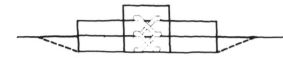

Figure 3-31 Section 2: Section through a center with a basement, tenant stores one story high and the department stores, two stories high. The dotted line indicates the ramps to the delivery road.

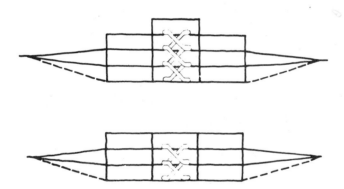

Figures 3-32—3-33 Section 3 and section 4: Sections through centers with basements and two selling levels (or one additional selling level for the department stores). In these cases, in order to achieve an equal amount of pedestrian traffic on both sales levels, the parking levels are arranged in such a fashion that they slope half a level upwards to the upper level, or half a level downwards to the lower level.

2. Better results would be achieved if three building levels were to be created in Figure 3-28. If parking is arranged on the ground level, such a center would utilize about 80 acres (considerably less than the 100 acres which would be needed for a one-level center). If parking were to be arranged on five constructed parking levels as shown in Figure 3-34, then the total land used would be reduced to about 24 acres. Thus it becomes apparent that in the case of a 1-million-square-foot regional shopping center which is basically unifunctional, land requirements can vary radically, dependent on the type of arrangement, ranging from 24 acres to 100 acres.

	U.S.	EUROPE
RENTABLE AREA	1,000,000 sq. ft.	100,000 m²
LAND AREA REQUIRED FOR RENTABLE AREA	8 acres	3.4 hectares
NUMBER OF PARKING STALLS (6 per 1,000 sq. ft./ per 100 m2 of rentable area)	6,000	6,000
SPACE DEMAND PER PARKING STALL	500 sq. ft.	30 m²
TOTAL AREA REQUIRED FOR PARKING	3,000,000 sq. ft.	180,000 m²
LAND REQUIRED FOR PARKING IF ON GROUND	69.8 acres	18 hectares
LAND REQUIRED FOR PARKING IF ON 5 LEVELS	14 acres	3.6 hectares

THEREFORE:		
TOTAL LAND REQUIRED FOR 3-LEVEL SHOPPING CENTER IF:		
a) Ground parking is used:	77.8 acres	21.4 hectares
b) 5-level constructed parking is used	22 acres	7 hectares

Figure 3-35 This tabulation gives information concerning the land requirements for a shopping center and its parking, if one assumes a sensible plan in which the center consists of a basement and two additional levels. The Tabulation was prepared for United States and European conditions in order to reflect the differing parking requirements.

Figure 3-34 Application of this principle to a regional shopping center consisting of basement, two levels for the tenant stores, and three levels for the department stores. The method of relating parking levels to shopping levels, however, makes it feasible to enlarge the number of sales levels and of related parking levels. The drawing indicates that the lowest parking level would be used for center employees, the next two levels would be related by short and easy ramps to the first sales level and the two upper parking levels would be related by similar ramps to the upper sales level.

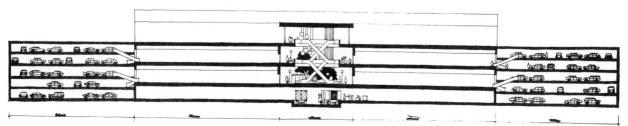

CASE STUDY I

Example of a multilevel shopping center employing deck parking:

Project Name: Forum Steglitz

Location: West Berlin, Germany

Architect: Georg Heinrichs

Consultants: Prof. S. Poloyi/R. Von Kamar

Developer: Forum Steglitz KG

Special Features: A shopping center with five activity levels four of which are used mainly for sales, the top (fifth) level being utilized for sports and entertainment facilities and to a small extent for offices. Of special interest is the mechanical equipment used for the movement of people and goods. For people, moving ramps, escalators, and elevators are provided: for goods, eight delivery towers, which are clearly expressed on the exterior of the structure.

Description: Land area 96,870 square feet. Rentable area, 304,630 square feet. Parking is supplied on seven levels and offers approximately 720 parking spaces plus 20 parking spaces for trucks.

Figure 3-36 Forum Steglitz: Exterior view.

Figure 3-37 Forum Steglitz: One typical activity level with parking related to it in a horizontal sense.

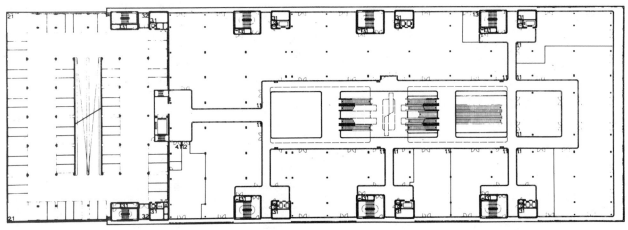

Figure 3-38 Forum Steglitz: Interior view. Note the plastic skin ceiling.

I have noted the function of land use as an important one. Generally, very little attention is paid to this function in the United States, Canada, and the New World generally; whereas in Europe one is forced to pay greater attention to it because land is considerably more expensive and very large parcels in desirable locations are not usually available. The reason why the function of land use is not sufficiently appreciated in the United States is that, at least for the time being, land is in most cases still in ample supply and can be bought at a low price. Yet I believe that this negligent attitude is a mistaken one for the following reasons:

1. From the point of view of center economics, one should not consider the price which is paid for fallow or agricultural land before a center is constructed, but rather the value which this land will have when the center is completed. Now, after 20 years of shopping center existence, we know that the land value around and near major centers experiences dynamic rises and is sought after for the construction of various buildings serving other urban functions,

such as apartment developments, hotel developments, laboratories, office buildings, etc.

2. The vast parking areas arranged on the ground create on the one hand an unattractive desert of tin roofs separating the entire center horizontally from all other urban functions and therefore from potential walking customers, and on the other hand, make necessary walking distances from a parked car to the center buildings often in excess of 600 feet which causes discomfort for the package-laden customer, especially in bad weather. From observing the illustrations, it becomes obvious that the greatest saving in land economy can be achieved through deck parking.

I am, of course, completely aware of the fact that constructed parking is considerably more expensive than ground parking as far as capital investment is concerned. Most economists therefore declare that constructed parking can only be recommended if the price per space unit of land is as high or higher than the construction cost for one space unit of garage structure. This statement, I believe, needs some modification.

1. One should not regard the purchase price of the land, but the *future* land value as the key factor.
2. Maintenance and upkeep costs within a garage are lower than they are for open parking, where the surface has to be regularly renewed and where, in cold-weather areas, business disturbances can occur and considerable expenditure for snow removal can be necessitated.
3. Deck parking creates additional customer comfort and therefore increases the attractive power of the center. It shortens the walking distances to about one-fifth. It provides weather protection for the cars and the walking customers. It therefore should be evaluated as a potential business increasing factor in the same manner as economists now evaluate the provision of a weather-protected, climatized pedestrian area.
4. The feasibility of collecting parking charges is considerably enhanced if protected parking spaces are provided.

If all these modifications are taken into consideration, it may very well be provable that, even in those cases where initial land costs are low, the construction of parking facilities can provide economic advantages. This should be especially true if low-cost prefabricated garage structures are utilized.

Yet I am aware of the fact that deck parking or garage parking of any form is, in the case of the unifunctional center where the parking spaces are used only during the limited business hours of the stores, much harder to justify than in the case of the multifunctional center where the hours of usage can be increased due to the different peak hours of the various functions integrated in the center. I will discuss this benefit, as one of many, when dealing with multifunctional centers.

When I stated my case for the construction of basements in regional shopping centers, I mentioned that there were other uses which could be advantageously assigned to a basement. In a regional shopping center, just as in an organically grown city, there is a need for lower-priced rentable space. There are also certain types of merchandise which need comparatively large areas for their display and sale but which do not attract large numbers of customers. I am referring for example to stores for furniture, major appliances, wallpaper and floor covering, and similar enterprises. Stores of this type have been arranged successfully in the following manner: on the lower sales level, they rent a comparatively small space, sufficient for stairways or escalators leading downward and for an entrance and display space directly in contact with the customer pedestrian flow. They rent a much larger

space in the basement for the display and sale of their merchandise. This type of arrangement has the additional advantage that valuable show window frontages along the pedestrian ways are not utilized for the less interesting displays of this type of merchandise.

A second group of enterprises which benefit from a basement location are service facilities: repair shops of all types, travel agencies, barber shops, beauty parlors, saunas, real estate offices, auto-driving schools, etc. In many cases they have been successfully arranged around a basement concourse which is made accessible by means of a stairway from the lower activity level. Such a basement concourse exists, for example in Southdale Center, where one finds not only the above-mentioned facilities but also the offices of the center management and a large children's play area with a miniature zoo.

SURROUNDING AREAS

In the book *Shopping Towns USA*, Larry Smith and I dealt with the planning of surrounding areas and the planning for growth under "Part II, Planning." At that time, we recommended that attention should be given to surrounding areas in order to prevent the establishment of so-called "pirating" enterprises which would constitute unfair competition by relying on the center's attractive pull. Such enterprises would also profit from the parking facilities and other amenities which the center provides and thus save on capital and operating costs. At the same time, they would not be subject to any of the controls and standards which the center sets up and would succeed economically because their considerably lower investments and operating costs would enable them to underbid the merchants of the center.

This reasoning of 20 years ago still holds true. However, we went beyond this protectionist recommendation and pointed out that a reciprocal relationship exists between a center and its surrounding area. We said at that time:

A well planned center can exert a highly favorable and invigorating influence on the area surrounding it, and a well planned surrounding area can add, in large measure, to the prosperity of the center. Conversely, a poorly planned or unplanned commercial grouping of stores can have a deteriorating effect on its surrounding area, while the success of even the best planned center can be endangered by a poorly planned or blighted surrounding area.

We finally made the recommendation that center developers should acquire considerably more land than necessary for the center and its parking facilities, and we showed examples as to how the future use of this land could be master planned. A number of developers followed our recommendation and profited materially in the years following the opening of the center by the sale of such surrounding land parcels. However, as will be discussed in the following chapters, I now feel that because land surrounding regional centers gains appreciably in desirability and value, the utilization of center land and its surrounding territory has to be regarded much more seriously and from new points of view, which make an intimate integration of a large number of urban activities possible.

As far as planning for growth is concerned, here also I have not markedly changed the opinions expressed in *Shopping Towns USA.* However, my conviction that a meaningful urban organism must be designed from the beginning for its optimal final size has been fortified. Growth must in all cases be preplanned, and such planning for future growth is only justified when it can be established with reasonable certainty that growth of the supporting population will occur within the foreseeable future, that is to say, within a time span of 10 to 15 years. The expectation of this growth must be well founded because planning for growth involves initial capital investments which can only be amortized in the future. Such investments concern the cost of land and the capital cost for the entire "infrastructure" (roads, heating and climatization plants, pipelines, etc.). Funds have also to be expended in order to make the center within each enlargement phase workable and attractive. Another factor which has to be considered is that construction activities around the center, which is a necessary operation for enlargement purposes, can have an unfavorable influence on operation and business. Thus it has been found in many cases that if supporting population growth can be expected within a time span of five to six years following the center's opening, it is economically advantageous to construct the center from the beginning to the size which will finally be required, accepting the disadvantage that certain areas may not be rented advantageously from the beginning. I have experienced cases where developers decided to build a center in stages, even though the supporting population was provably available at opening time. Reasons given for such a procedure are shortage of funds or the desire to establish experimentally whether the findings of the center team were correct. These seem to me invalid motivations for a development in phases, and ones which will almost certainly have negative effects on the entire economic success of the center.

PLANNING FOR MERCHANDISING

A well-planned center constitutes a major capital investment and considerable yearly costs for maintenance, upkeep, and operation. All of these costs have to be carried by those who participate as tenants in center activities. This participation is expressed through payments.

It is now generally accepted procedure that a center receives its income from three sources:

1. A minimum rent which is fixed and expressed as a rent per square foot or square meter.
2. A percentage rent which the tenants pay only after they have achieved a certain gross income per square foot or square meter of the rented area and for which only the percentage factor is determined in the lease.
3. Various charges for heating, climatizing, cleaning of public areas, and certain other services which the shopping center management offers.

The fixed minimum rentals are usually calculated in such manner as to enable the shopping center developer to fulfill his financial obligations with regard to repayment of building loans and for general upkeep, maintenance, and management costs. The profit of the developer accrues mostly from the percentage rental. Thus it is in the interest of the developer within a few years of opening to achieve a situation by which the majority of all tenants succeed in their business activities to such a degree that percentage rentals are being paid. It is therefore obvious that the developer has a vital interest in the prosperity of all tenants. This interest should cause him to create a center with balanced success opportunities.

The center team has a number of tools at its disposal to bring about this condition of balanced success opportunities. Since each one of the merchants is dependent on shoppers' traffic, it is obvious that such traffic must be distributed along the frontages and entrance doors of all stores in an equitable manner. It is therefore essential to guide shoppers' traffic from arrival points (whether they are ground parking facilities, structured parking, pedestrian ways, or stations of public transportation) into the pedestrian areas of the center in such manner as to provide for an equal "irrigation." If a center has more than one main sales level, then it becomes essential to make arrangements resulting in an equal share of shoppers' traffic for each of the levels.

I have dealt with this question in the discussion of the prerequisite accessibility in a general manner, and would like to add here only remarks about some specific cases. Though it is generally true that parking areas of about equal size should surround the center on all sides, especially in the case where a center relies heavily on private automobile traffic, this rule cannot apply when a center site is so located that entrances and exits can only be provided on one, two, or three sides. In that case, those parking areas which are not directly accessible from the surrounding road network would remain empty, with the exception of peak hour times, and those tenants who depend on traffic generated from such parking areas would be at a disadvantage. In such a case, it is wiser to move the buildings of the center away from the middle of the site and as closely as possible to those boundaries where access is not available.

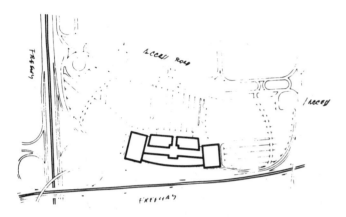

Figure 3-39 Shopping center in the Paris region for which I developed a master plan, moving the center as close as possible to the edge of the site where no access possibilities exist. (In the actually executed plan, the center core was moved into a central position on the site).

I have referred earlier to two basic concepts, those of the "introverted" and "extroverted" centers. The extroverted center provides for show windows and entrances which are directed toward the parking facilities, and for additional ones which are directed toward the public pedestrian areas. I have come to the definite conclusion that this arrangement is detrimental to the guiding of shoppers' traffic. The reasons are the following:

1. Shoppers' traffic is split. Some of the shoppers who enter from the parking area might never be exposed to the public pedestrian areas and thus to the other stores.
2. The provision of two store fronts, two entrance doors, two sets of show windows is wasteful, not only as far as capital investment is concerned but also as far as utilization of the rentable area and the operation of each individual store is concerned.

The introverted center, in contrast, provides for show windows and entrances to the individual stores exclusively from the public pedestrian areas (malls, courts, arcades, etc.). In the case of the introverted center the shopper is guided from arrival points through a limited number of short arcades into the main pedestrian area. He then experiences all the amenities of the public areas and is given the chance to establish contact with all stores in the course of his shopping trip. The concept of the introverted center offers a number of advantages:

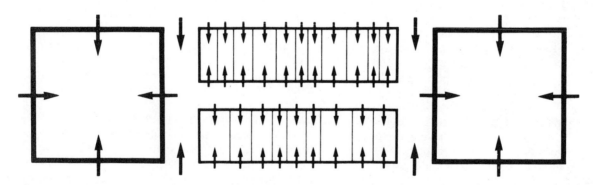

Figure 3-40 Schematic sketch of an extroverted center.

Figure 3-41 Schematic sketch of an introverted center.

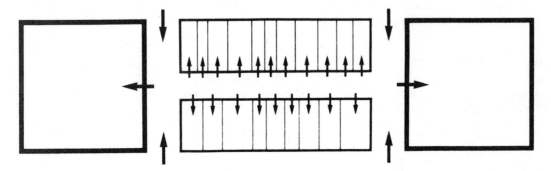

1. Savings of capital and operating costs for the entrepreneur as well as for each of the individual tenants, because only one set of store fronts and entrance doors are necessary.
2. The possibility of an attractive treatment of the exterior of the center core which is freed from individual signs and advertising.
3. The possibility of employing fully all those measures which bring about a balanced shoppers' traffic stream within the center complex.

Ideally, in the case of an introverted center, there should be no entrance to any individual store from the arrival areas. Regrettably, it has rarely been possible to convince the operators of department and other large stores to accept this simple disciplinary rule, and they often insist that in their case an exception should made and direct entrances from arrival areas be provided. It is highly doubtful that this insistence brings marked advantages to the large stores. They will often find that the entrances which lead from arrival areas into their stores are used by customers who do not have any intention of making a purchase in their specific store, but simply use it as a shortcut into the public pedestrian area. This type of shopper then creates the same disadvantage for the large store as automobile through-traffic creates for a city core.

It is significant that in those cases where department stores are connected with the ownership and therefore with the well-being of the entire center, they will take a much more reasonable attitude toward this detail of planning. In Northland Center, for example, the large Hudson store is the one which has the least amount of direct access from arrival areas.

Also with regard to the interior arrangements, essential for an aimful guidance of pedestrian streams, the basic attitude of the major department store or stores is of great significance. These stores are referred to in shopping center language as the "magnets" or "poles" of attraction. They achieve the quality inherent in these terms due to their size, their public image, their advertising, and the quality of their services. From the viewpoint of creating equal well-being for all tenants of the shopping center, it is desirable to place the magnets in such manner that the shoppers' traffic which they engender will flow past the doors and show windows of smaller tenant stores. It is therefore desirable that they be located on the extreme ends of public pedestrian areas if there are two or more such magnets, or in the very center of the public pedestrian routes if there is only one such magnet.

As far as their relation to entranceways or arcades from arrival areas is concerned, they should be rather distant from such points in order to encour-age the shopper to walk by other stores before he reaches the powerful magnet. Where department store operators take a narrow viewpoint of shortsighted self-interest, they usually protest against such an arrangement and, because they are in a strong negotiation position, they will only too often win the argument. I am characterizing this attitude as "shortsighted" because it has been proven without any doubt that the success of the magnet stores is closely related to the success of the entire center.

The customer who seeks a wide variety of shopping experiences will prefer a center in which both large stores and many smaller ones exist. The continuous existence of such small stores, however, can only be safeguarded if, through an equal distribution of shoppers' traffic, their economic life is assured. In view of this it is therefore also necessary to bring about an area balance between large (magnet) stores and individual smaller business enterprises. Where exactly the optimal rate of mixture lies is hard to determine, but it can generally be stated that department stores and other mass merchandising establishments should not occupy more than 50 percent of the entire rentable space.

The task of the center planner is to shape the pedestrian ways in such manner that they offer comfort and delight. Comfort will depend to a large degree on the walking distances necessary for a shopping trip. The shorter the length to which a pedestrian walk system can be held, the greater are the chances that a shopping trip covering a good part of the entire center will be undertaken. If pedestrian ways are overly long, then the individual customer will undertake only one part of the shopping trip; if by some unfortunate circumstance, a certain part of the long pedestrian way should prove less attractive than another (this could happen if one magnet were weaker than the others), then the danger exists that one part of the entire center will "dry off."

In this connection it is interesting to note that if two or more main shopping levels are established (which shortens the walking distance on each of the levels), the shopper will willingly move from one level to the other because technological tools enable us to assist the walker in successfully overcoming vertical distances (by means of escalators, moving ramps etc.). However, when utilizing two or more shopping levels (an arrangement which has been made possible through the covered climatized mall), a strong visual connection between the two levels is essential.

Physical Requirements

In Figure 3-42 we have indicated certain dimensions which are necessary in order to bring about such a

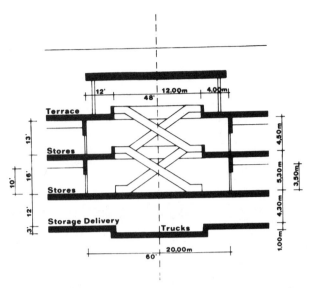

Figure 3-42 Section through the main mall area of a three level center giving average dimensions for floor surfaces, widths of balconies on upper levels and widths of opening between levels and to skylight.

visual connection. They are based on the fact that the upper sales levels will have to provide balconies along all sides of the public space which, at certain distances, are connected with each other by bridges. These balconies, which become the only route for shoppers' traffic, must be generously dimensioned. If the space between these balconies is not sufficiently wide, then the possibility of achieving for the shopper, the visual experience of being in one spatial unit that just happens to have more than one level, is lost. This visual experience, however, is essential, for otherwise those shoppers who arrive on the lower sales level might never be aware of the existence of the upper one and vice versa. Since access to natural light for the public pedestrian areas appears to be psychologically desirable, this need should be satisfied for the shoppers on the lower level by ensuring that the openings to upper levels are generously dimensioned.

Balance

A balanced diversification for a large shopping center can only be achieved if size and location of all shopping units (tenant stores) are carefully predetermined. A true balance can only be achieved when shoppers' traffic with regard to quantitative and qualitative characteristics is equally distributed throughout all public areas. (These public areas or pedestrian ways may be located on one or a number of levels.)

I have discussed earlier the relationship which should exist between the so-called "magnets" and all other tenant units. But beyond that, it is vital for the economic success of a center that the size and placement of each individual enterprise is predetermined. This need is very often completely disregarded, especially by the promoter-type entrepreneur who proceeds by selling space on a "first come-first served" basis and tries to sell as much space as possible to each interested party. The result of such a policy is not an integrated center, but an agglomeration of a number of stores lacking any functional relationship. The task of planning size and location of each shopping unit, often referred to as "pre-merchandising," is an extremely complex one. It entails the problem of arriving, by a predetermined intellectual effort, at results approaching those which in cities of organic growth have been achieved over a time span of centuries.

The listing of shopping units, service facilities, eating establishments, institutions, etc., which are usually represented in a large regional center, reads like a classified telephone directory containing anywhere from 50 to 200 different categories. One has to deal with some very large units, a smaller number of medium-sized ones, and a large number of small ones. To this list are added some "miniature" participants which are often placed in kiosks within the pedestrian areas; these may be newspaper stands, flower stands, refreshment booths, key and lock smiths, etc. One has to further distinguish between mass-merchandising enterprises and specialty stores. Within both categories there are some who depend on a high intensity of shoppers' traffic because their unit sales are comparatively small, and there are others who need a much lower intensity of such traffic because their unit sales are comparatively high.

There are some enterprises which depend strongly on visual contact with the shopper, which is achieved by their signs, show window displays, and entrance doors; there are others less dependent on direct visual contact because they cater to established needs and the shopper will therefore seek them out. (Into this category fall large food markets, various service facilities and repair shops, larger restaurants, etc.) Space requirements for various types of merchandise are radically different. It is evident that $10,000 worth of gold watches can be sold in a much smaller area than the same value of wallpaper. The need for show window frontage varies of course greatly with the type of merchandise sold.

WHAT IS SHOPPING?

Before we can intelligently discuss an approach to pre-merchandising, it is necessary to clarify the meaning of the term "shopping" and to investigate the question, "Who are the shoppers?" "Shopping" is an entirely different type of activity than "buying." Buying is the result of a predetermined and exactly defined aim. A decision to buy a specific article leads the buyer to one specific store or even to one specific counter where he brings his predetermined "project" to realization. The activity of shopping is approached with a certain degree of aimlessness and usually with a generous supply of free time and a flexible amount of funds. The aim of a shopping trip is not necessarily only that of buying certain goods which are urgently needed. Shopping has become a kind of professional vocation. It involves the comparing of price, style, and quality, but it is also influenced by the desire of spending some time for sociability and a wish for exposure to human experiences and entertainment.

The typical "shopper" may have a shopping list prepared but is perfectly willing and, in fact, hopeful that in the pursuit of the "shopping activity," inspirations for the purchase of goods of all types which are not on the list might be gained. These inspirations may occur in the form of reminders concerning articles which one really needs but had not previously thought of, or emotional involvement with an article which will subsequently be purchased although not really needed. Shopping is typical of an affluent society and of a life pattern in which people have leisure time on their hands.

The activity of shopping has some positive effects on the shopper, who is exposed to thousands of various articles. The experience widens the horizons, sharpens judgment, elevates taste. Through the sharpening of the sophistication of the shopper, the merchants, in order to remain competitive, are forced to increase their own demands on suppliers and steadily raise the quality, novelty, and value of their goods.

Shopping, when it is taken seriously, is a time-consuming and rather tiring activity. The center which wants to attract and hold the professional shopper will therefore provide opportunities for rest and relaxation. Rest benches and attractively landscaped seating areas, eating facilities (all the way from refreshment stands and snack bars to small cafés and restaurants), movie theaters, lecture rooms, etc. serve this purpose. If the center can enable the shopper to combine his shopping activity with other important tasks, such as a visit to the doctor or to a bank or post office, it will gain appreciation and goodwill from the shoppers.

WHO THEN, ARE THESE SHOPPERS?

In a typical regional shopping center, the largest part of the shopping army is represented by the suburban housewife. She is usually a woman with some time on her hands, because the number of working hours which in earlier times had to be spent on cooking, cleaning, washing, child-rearing, and sewing or knitting, has been vastly reduced through technological gadgets, through pre-prepared foods, and by the fact that children are taken care of from an early age by the school system. Thus, our typical shopper is really a "shopperess." In a typical suburban community she is starved with respect to certain experiences which only life within a truly central urban environment can offer. The activity of shopping becomes for her a substitute for these cultural, social, and spiritual experiences. But she also takes shopping very seriously as one of the virtues of a good homemaker. She acquires skills and an experience in her shopping profession which are highly superior to those of a non-shopper, represented by those who are regularly employed and who are to a large degree represented by the male sex. Thus, even most of the shopping for masculine needs is done by women, with the exception of those things which have to be tried on and fitted such as suits or shoes.

To the shopperess a shopping trip is simultaneously work and an enjoyable utilization of free time. If she has to take preschool-age children with her,

Figure 3-43

then she is somewhat hampered in her efficiency as shopperess. For this reason, shopping centers often provide nurseries and children's playgrounds where youngsters can be "checked in" in order to free the hands and mind of the shopperess for the pursuit of her profession. The shopperess has a certain sporting instinct; she is a devoted bargain huntress, willing to battle at certain counters, partly in order to save money and partly to prove to herself her superior shopping ability. This dedication to bargain hunting is equally strongly expressed in those who have to count their pennies and in those who have ample pecuniary means.

In spite of the fact that a man is rarely a professional shopper, he still plays an important role in the success of the center, though it might be sometimes only a symbolic one. He still has, or believes he has, some power of decision when it comes to major investments for home furnishings or other exceptional purchases. In such cases the shopperess usually makes the preselection in order to save the shopping layman time and trouble. The final decision is then made by both either during evening openings or on Saturdays, or even at times when the stores are closed, through the activity of window shopping, which does assume great importance. It is therefore recommended that the public areas of centers remain open into the late night hours and on Sundays and holidays and that all shop windows are illuminated during those times.

From a shortsighted point of view, the nonprofessional shopper (the man and the working woman), may seem preferable to the individual merchant because they make their purchases quickly and are not as price conscious as the professional shopper. Yet, in facing reality, one has to concede that it is the great mass of professional shoppers on which the economic success of the center depends. If centers find themselves in locations where their potential customers are to a large degree employed, then the economic success will depend to a very high degree on opening hours. If such opening hours are not distinctly different from the working hours of plants and offices, it might prove impossible to attract a sufficiently large number of professional or nonprofessional shoppers.

As far as the economic status of the shoppers of a suburban regional shopping center is concerned, it usually excludes the extremes on the low and on the high side of the economic scale. The very rich are usually not numerous enough and they often have unorthodox ways of satisfying their desires. They are catered to by certain exclusive stores; they often make purchases on trips to other cities or countries; they are willing to order merchandise at a higher price from stores who will deliver; and so on. The very poor, because of their limited funds, can buy only necessities and therefore cannot act as shoppers. Also, in our compartmentalized and segregated suburban areas, the poorer residents are usually far distant from the influence area of a regional shopping center. The shopper of the typical regional shopping center is middle class. He may be lower, middle, or upper middle class. On the basis of this realization, all the attempts which have been made to segregate a center through pre-merchandising planning into various economically oriented subunits seem to me extremely unwise. Such segregation destroys the balance and diversity of the center and disregards some of the basic behavior patterns of the shopperess. The shopperess with a limited pocketbook will also, from time to time and on certain occasions, be interested in luxury items, and even the one with an unlimited budget has a professional pride in being a successful bargain-huntress. If one considers the essence of the term "shopping," one will also arrive at the conclusion that a rigid division of the entire center into certain subdivisions which cater to men's needs or to women's needs is not desirable. On the other hand, certain groupings of stores selling related shopping goods may be justifiable.

THE "PARTICIPANTS" OF A CENTER

Let us examine in greater detail the main participants in a typical regional shopping center:

1. One or more large department stores. Because of their superior size (anywhere between 60,000 and 400,000 square feet) and because of the breadth and depth of the assortment they offer, they actually represent shopping centers in themselves. A full-scale department store is in fact a collection of stores satisfying all possible human needs under one roof. (In the United States, with the exception of special gourmet shops, the sale of food is usually excluded, whereas in Europe, it is often represented in a department store.)

2. Shopping units of secondary size are either junior department stores or branches of large chain stores. They usually do not represent a full range of all departments and normally their merchandise is more standardized and available at a lower price than in the full-scale department store.

3. The third important shopping unit is the supermarket. Large representatives of this species represent again a complete shopping center with regard to all types of food and household needs. The role of the supermarket in the regional shopping center is, however, different

from the isolated supermarket located in much closer relationship to a residential area. The so-called "neighborhood market" is in a superior position to serve the standard needs of the residential population and it is therefore unreasonable to assume that a shopper would visit a regional center just for the purpose of shopping for food. However, the existence of at least one supermarket in a regional shopping center is justified for the following reasons: it has to cater to the needs of that population which lives in the immediate influence area of the regional center, and it has to afford to the shopperess of the center the possibility of satisfying her wishes with regard to the acquisition of food or household goods at the same time as she does the rest of her shopping.

These facts have to a large degree been recognized. Whereas in early shopping centers we found a large number of huge competing supermarkets, this merchandising type is represented in the newer centers usually only by one unit.

One could assume that a regional shopping center could function satisfactorily when the three "giants" (the department stores, junior department stores, and supermarket) are represented. These giants after all have the possibility through mass buying techniques to offer a large selection of merchandise at competitive prices. The advantages derived from mass buying techniques and large organization, however, are accompanied by certain disadvantages. The large organization cannot respond with the same sensitivity and speed to individual ever-changing wishes and tastes and to the demand for certain specialized articles as can the small entrepreneur. In an organically grown city we therefore find large stores surrounded by dozens and sometimes hundreds of shops and boutiques, which partly cash in on the buying streams which the large stores attract, but which also render a special service to the shopper and the buyer because they can cater to certain needs a larger organization must disregard. It is therefore not surprising that around a large supermarket in a suburban area we will find dozens of small shops offering special pastries, delicatessen, imported foods, quality cuts of meat, vintage wines, etc.

The same condition exists in shopping centers in relation to department stores and junior department stores on the one hand and dozens of specialized enterprises on the other. The coexistence of the giant enterprises and the more human-sized small ones is essential for the success of the center. Though it appears evident that the small merchants are dependent on the attractive pull of the giants, it is often overlooked that we are here faced with a pattern of interdependence and that the giants are just as dependent on the existence and success of the small units. By now this interdependence has been at least generally recognized by the large stores. They realize that they have a vital interest in the selection and placement of other tenants and in the achieving of quantitative and qualitative balance. In many cases they reserve the right to approve the selection and placement of tenant stores. I have repeatedly been asked to assist department stores in the task of determining whether existing plans for a shopping center fulfill the requirements of quantitative and qualitative balance. This question becomes especially significant when two or more department stores are to be located in one center and when the question therefore arises whether each of them has—with respect to sound balance—an equal chance to succeed.

Evaluation System

I have therefore developed an evaluation system which tries to shape a basis for judgment. I am, of course, aware of the fact that the application of the system can only give approximate results because important factors, dependent on the skill of the individual merchandising entrepreneurs, cannot be established in advance. Yet if the character and size of each proposed tenant store is known and if possible the names of the proposed tenants are established, the evaluation system can at least permit an approximate forecast concerning quantitative and qualitative characteristics of each participant and therefore the balance of the entire center.

The evaluation system employs two scales: one relates to quantitative characteristics, namely, the amount of shoppers' traffic created by each participant in relation to one measuring unit (1 square foot or 1 square meter of its rental space). The second scale relates to the qualitative characteristics of the participants—that is to say, the ability to attract shoppers who are interested in merchandise of higher quality, greater styling, and therefore of higher price.

A certain number of points are allocated to each type of enterprise on the basis of quantitative and qualitative rating. One then multiplies the number of quantitative points by the areas which each of the participants occupies, and afterward proceeds in the same manner concerning the qualitative points. By adding the two figures and by dividing the result by two, one arrives at an average evaluation per size unit, and by multiplying this figure with a number of square units, at a total evaluation.

The ratings which I have used for the quantitative system are:

For major poles of attraction (magnets)
such as department stores 100

For secondary poles of attraction such as
supermarkets, junior department stores,
and major chain stores 80

For smaller participants which attract a
considerable number of shoppers because
they have comparatively low unit sales
(such as fashion stores, shoe stores, etc.) ... 70

For stores which attract a smaller number
of customers because they have a high unit
sale per customer and therefore need only
a small number of customers in order to
achieve their business volume 30

For the qualitative rating system the points are
as follows:

For stores which sell high-quality and
therefore high-priced merchandise 100

For stores which cater to all income levels
(food stores, department stores, snack
bars, etc.) 80

For stores selling low-cost merchandise 30

In order to illustrate one application of this evaluation system, I will use the case of a projected shopping center in France. In this case, the management of one of the department stores asked for our advice because of its intuitive feeling that the location which the plan of the center indicated for its store was disadvantageous as far as balance was concerned. The two illustrations schematically show the lower and upper sales level of the projected center. Two department stores are located as magnets. They are of about equal size and employ similar merchandising methods. They have therefore been completely omitted from the evaluation procedure. The dotted line indicates the division of the influence area of each one of the two magnets. The division line is created by the fact that a central court, to which two main pedestrian entrances from arrival areas lead, marks a clear division. This court also contains the means of vertical communication (escalators) from one level to the other. All rental units are indicated on the plans by size and shape, the number of points relating to the quantitative and qualitative rating systems, and underneath, the average between the two. The intensity of the gray shading indicates roughly the average rating value. An analysis of the plans and tabulations revealed the following:

The total rentable area
in the influence zone of
department store one is ..... 219,800 square feet

The total rentable area
in the influence zone of
department store two is ..... 302,500 square feet

This in itself already points to an absence of balance as far as floor areas are concerned. As far as the quantitative rating is concerned, it shows:

In the influence zone of department
store one,
on the lower sales level .... 53.4 points
and on the upper sales level .... 61.21 ″

The comparative value for department
store two,
on the lower level .... 68.26 ″
on the upper level .... 71.32 ″

As far as the qualitative rating is concerned, it points to:

For the influence area of department
store one,
on the lower level .... 53.78 points
on the upper level .... 54.42 ″

The related figures for department
store two,
on the lower level .... 82.51 ″
on the upper level .... 88.51 ″

If one now averages quantitative and qualitative points, one arrives at:

For department store one,
on the lower level .... 53.65 points
on the upper level .... 57.72 ″
Average 55.68

For department store two,
on the lower level .... 75.44 ″
on the upper level .... 80.38 ″
Average 77.91

If one multiplies these average evaluation points by the available total rentable area (with the exception of the department stores) one arrives at:

For department store one, on both
levels 12,238.464
For department store two, on both
levels 23,567.775

If one assumes the total rentable area (with the exception of the department stores) to be equal to 100, it shows that a serious imbalance exists. The evaluation gives 34.2 percent to the influence zone of department store one and 65.8 percent to the influence zone of department store two.

In this specific case, the apparent imbalance was so great that it could have been eliminated only by a radical change of plans. However, work on the plans had progressed so far that, for reasons of time pressure, the developer could not agree to a major change of the project though he readily agreed that it would have been in his own best

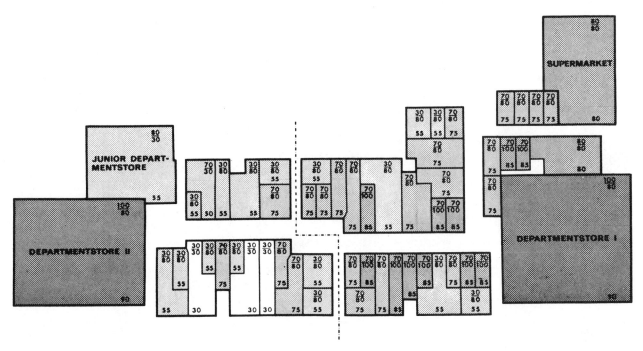

Figure 3-44 Merchandising plan of lower level of regional shopping center in France, illustrating evaluation system.

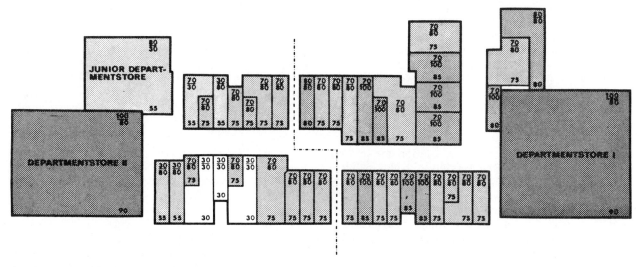

Figure 3-45 Merchandising plan of upper level.

long-term economic interest to do so. He did, however, agree to readjust the pre-merchandising plan by relocating certain tenant units in order to at least approach a more balanced arrangement.

SHOPPING ATMOSPHERE

We turn now to the third component of Vitruvius' formulation of the term "architecture" (firmness, commodity, delight). Whereas rules for firmness can be established by exact data supplied by engineering and the qualities which make up for commodity can be established empirically, we find ourselves in a much more complex situation when it comes to the task of discussing the measures which may bring about the quality of delight or enjoyment.

Here we find ourselves in the realm of dealing with conscious and subconscious desires, with psychological needs and aspirations. We are faced with the problem of considering emotional reactions and we can approach this question only through sensitivity and intuition based on a deep interest and knowledge of human behavior patterns. Yet provision of a superior "shopping atmosphere" is one of the decisive contributions to the economic success of a center. In making this statement I may be accused of possessing qualities which in our materialistic age are regarded with suspicion and mistrust. One may suspect me of being a "dreamer" and an "idealist"—both of which terms are often used as an expression of insult. I am perfectly willing to declare myself guilty on both counts. I believe that dreams, ideas, creativity and imagination are essential ingredients for any worthwhile creation in the field of planning and architecture. I also suspect that the explanation for the fact that the wave crest of development of regional shopping centers was reached during the pioneering days, and that the development since then has ebbed into brackish water, is to a large degree due to the fact that one has given up dreaming and instead relies on statistics, rules, and the computer.

I will, however, agree that in architecture and planning, dreaming alone will not bring about realization and that the architect and planner who wants to see his dream implemented has to combine the qualities of a dreamer with the ones of a realist. In order to assuage the suspicion that I might be too much of a wild dreamer, I would like to state now that providing "human experiences" or "delight" has, from the economic viewpoint of the "cost-benefit ratio" decisive implications. A raising of the entire capital budget by 2 or 3 percent can create those qualities which I have tried to subsume as "delight," "shopping atmosphere," or "human experience." This insignificant raising of the entire building budget, however, can express itself on the income side of the ledger in an impressive manner, possibly raising revenue by 20 to 30 percent, thus often becoming the deciding factor between success and failure.

The merchant as contact person between agricultural and industrial products on the one hand and human beings on the other has always been "environment conscious" when it comes to the shaping of the exterior and interior of his own store. In the framework of the planned shopping center, however, the need and the opportunity to create superior environmental conditions has attained new dimensions. The regional shopping center as a new building type has made its greatest contribution where and when it fully recognized the need of providing a superior environment as a basis for its success. In the foreground of these considerations, of course,

are those features which will provide physical comfort. The shopping center has reacted to the need for safety from traffic dangers, to protection from poisonous fumes and disturbing noises, by separating areas for pedestrians from those for disturbing mechanized traffic. It has generally reacted to the desire for protection from wind, snow, rain, direct sun rays, etc., by providing devices such as colonnades, arcades, canopies, etc., along the store fronts. In order to camouflage any remaining disturbing noises, it has introduced piped music. With the construction of enclosed, climatized centers, a further step has been made in providing ideal climatic conditions and complete weather protection.

In providing a year-round climate of "eternal spring" through the skill of architects and engineers, the shopping center consciously pampers the shopper, who reacts gratefully by arriving from longer distances, visiting the center more frequently, staying longer, and in consequence contributing to higher sales figures. Once it was found that the pampering paid off, new amenities were created. A superior shopping center with enclosed climatized pedestrian areas provides lockers where overcoats, galoshes, umbrellas, and packages can be stored. Comfortable means for vertical transportation—ramps, escalators—luxurious public washrooms to give the shopperess a chance to freshen up, drinking fountains (including miniature ones for the children), public telephone booths (so that the shopperess may explain to her husband that she will be late to cook the dinner because she still has to do some shopping), groups of sitting arrangements to encourage social chat, and dozens of other similar comfort-giving arrangements. But beyond comfort, the shopperess also expects consideration of her senses: seeing, hearing, smelling and touching. The eye of the shopper reacts negatively to disorder, litter, dirt, and visual confusion created through a profusion of signs, advertising, and other expressions of visual pollution. The eye reacts positively to a skillful combination of quietude and pleasant stimulation. The sense of calmness can be created by architectural unity, by introduction of expressions of nature—trees, bushes, flowers—and by employing those colors which, by association, are connected with the greenery of forests, the cool blueness of water, and the beige of sand and dunes. Stimulation on the other hand, is achieved by sparing use of the colors which we associate with fire and light, such as yellow, orange, and red.

Similar protection is necessary as far as the sense of smell is concerned. All those smells which are created by cooking and baking facilities must be isolated and eliminated by special ventilation ar-

Figure 3-46 Colonnades in an "open" shopping center. (Note roof in background for protected cross walk).

rangements. The sense of touch has to be considered specifically with regard to pavements. Here exists also a connection with the sense of hearing. Very hard pavements are unpleasant to walk on and create the noise of clicking heels. Any type of pavement suitable for rubber tires is not conducive to the satisfaction of the sense of touch within the walking areas of a center.

CASE STUDY II

Eastridge Center, in San Jose, California

Owner/Developer: Bayshore Properties Inc. and Homart Development Company

Architect: Avnar Naggar, A.I.A.

Structural Engineer: Butzbach, Bar-Din and Dagan

Mechanical and Electrical Engineer Yoshpe Engineers

Civil Engineer: George S. Nolte & Associates

Project Electrical Engineer: Edward S. Shinn & Associates

Landscape Architects: Lawrence, Halprin & Associates

Traffic: Barton-Aschman Associates

Mall Lighting: Evans and Hillman, Inc.

General Contractor: The Taubman Company

Special Features: An unusual spatial arrangement and an extremely inspiring atmosphere for the public spaces has been achieved. This has been accomplished by ignoring the usual vertical and horizontal division of interior space and employing an extremely imaginative use of irregular angles. Also, the floor surfaces, varied by means of plat-

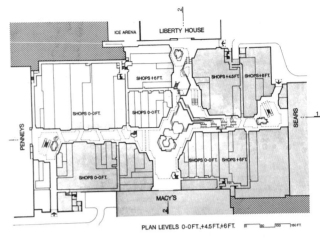

Figure 3-48 Eastridge Center: Floor plan of lower activity level.

forms and terraces, add to the pleasant sensation of spaciousness. This shopping center, offering 1,400,000 square feet of revenue-producing area, exemplifies an excellent mastering of architectural forms and lighting and the use of works of art.

Figure 3-47 Eastridge Center: Exterior view. A good example of the type of treatment possible with an introverted scheme.

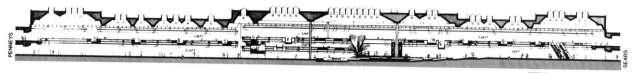

Figure 3-50 Eastridge Center: Typical section.

LONGITUDINAL SECTION 1-1

Figure 3-51 Eastridge Center: Change of levels inside the mall.

CASE STUDY III

Ghirardelli Square: In downtown San Francisco, California

Renewal Architects: Wurster, Bernardi and Emmons

Developer: William M. Roth

Landscaping: Lawrence, Halprin and Associates

Special Features: Within a block of old factory buildings (previously the Ghirardelli Chocolate and Coffee Plant), a new multi-level center containing a large number of highly specialized stores, restaurants, and also a theater, art galleries, and small offices has been created. The existing architectural features have been to the highest degree conserved, only one new building being added, which was designed to fully respect the architecture of the existing buildings. The largest undertaking in this project was the construction of a three-level underground parking garage. This was made possible by the fact that the project is located on a natural hill which could be utilized for the placing of the parking facilities.

Ghirardelli Square cannot properly be categorized as a regional shopping center, but neither can it be classified as "core revitalization." Representing an unusual constellation of functions and utilization of space, this project succeeds in satisfying the desire for a pleasantly atmosphered center where people can socialize as well as satisfy necessary shopping needs.

Figure 3-52 Ghirardelli Square: One of the original buildings.

Figure 3-53 Ghirardelli Square: A view over the square.

AUTHORITARIAN OR LIBERAL?

To which degree should the architect control the overall design of the center in all of its aspects? A regional shopping center represents a preplanned and predesigned architectural unit. It will achieve the expression of unity only if sufficiently strong and forceful overall design vocabulary can be employed. Yet, on the other hand, a regional shopping center also constitutes a federation of individual enterprises which are characterized by diverging needs and requirements.

The architect is obviously faced with a dilemma. In observing hundreds of centers I have noted that this dilemma was often approached from two viewpoints which are radically different from each other. The first one we may call the "authoritarian" attitude the second one we may call the "extremely liberal" attitude. Those who believe in the former try to enforce an overall discipline which extends to the treatment of each individual store front, to all of their graphic expressions, their color treatment, etc. The result of such an approach can be aesthetically very pleasing, but it disregards the "human factor" not only in relation to the individual merchants who find themselves unable to fulfill their individual needs and requirements, but also toward the individual shopper who is expecting stimulation through variety. The extremely liberal viewpoint, which tends to bow indiscriminately to every whim of the center's tenants, necessarily loses sight of the need for unity and order. Those who act according to this viewpoint will end up creating chaos.

The only feasible solution is one which recognizes through architectural treatment the fact that in a center there exists a relationship similar to that in a federated state. All of those matters which concern the entire federation must be taken care of by the central government, and those matters which are of more local concern can be taken care of by the individual states. In our case, the central government is represented by the developer and the center team. Their task concerns the planning and construction period, but also the operation period. They must attain and preserve a strong and suitable framework within which the greatest opportunities for the individual expressions of each member of the federation (all the participants or tenants) can be achieved. In order to create the strong framework, it is necessary that there exist a clear outline and delineation of public and private activity areas. Also, there must be a definition of architectural surfaces and spaces which are subject solely to the decision of the developer and the center team and a related clear delineation of surfaces and spaces which are subject to the decisions of the individual tenants. The freedom for individual expression within the "private sphere" should be as great as possible, with the condition however, that certain behavior rules must be set up which prevent various forms of individual expression clashing with others or with the overall interest of the entire federation. For this reason, it is necessary to set up certain rules and regulations concerning minimum standards for the quality of store fronts, treatment of store interiors, size and character of signs, standards of display techniques and also for store opening hours, hours at which show windows should be lit, prevention of disturbing noises, or smells etc.

STIMULATION AND CALMNESS

The senses of the shopper will be pleased and stimulated if there exists a sensitive balance between calmness and harmony on the one hand and of stimuli on the other. The fact that a shopping center consists of public areas, in the form of pedestrian walks of different sizes, shapes, and heights, and of private areas like store fronts, displays and store interiors, supplies the designer with a basic direction. Inasmuch as it is the inherent purpose of the center to stimulate the shopper into the activity of buying, it is evident that strong stimuli will be created by the individual participants by the effectiveness of their store fronts, signs, displays, and the interiors of their private areas. Thus, by contrast, it appears necessary that, in order to make these stimuli effective, the public areas should provide for a completely different atmosphere, one of restfulness, and harmony. A successful interplay between public and private areas will be achieved only if a distinctive separation and differentiation between the two is created. In open shopping centers this decisive difference exists to a large degree automatically. In this case, the public areas have a different climate from the store interiors. They are intimately connected with nature, with the sky and its ever-changing coloring. Building materials for pavements and wall surfaces must be of different character because on the outside they have to fulfill certain physical characteristics to withstand weather conditions. The introduction of landscaping —by trees, shrubbery, and flowers—will be easily achieved. Artificial lighting for evening and night hours will for outdoor spaces have, of necessity, a completely different character from that which is employed for the interior of the private spaces.

In those centers where enclosed climatized public areas are provided, many of the natural restraints are removed. The designer is no longer forced to utilize exterior type materials for walls, ceilings, floor coverings, lighting, etc. Because the restraints are lifted, he may then neglect to utilize all means available to stress the desirable differentiation in character between public and private areas. If, as I have often observed, identical materials and construction methods are used for public and private spaces, if there are no distinct differences in heights, shapes, and spaciousness, if the lighting techniques used for public areas are the same as for store interiors, and if open storefronts reach from floor to ceiling—then all differentiations are wiped out. The overflowing of private environment into public creates confusion, sterility and uniformity and complicates orientation.

VIVE LA DIFFERENCE

For the shaping of a successful and attractive shopping environment, the designer should keep in mind the French saying "vive la différence!" The operators of large department stores recognized the truth of this statement long ago, and have developed a mastery of the art. They introduce within the overall selling space, mostly along its borders, individualistically treated departments referred to as "boutiques" or "shops." They not only separate these from the overall selling area by strong visual means, but they give them a distinctive character through different ceiling heights, different decor, different floor treatment, and different lighting. Inasmuch as the designer appeals to the psychological and emotional reactions of the shopper, he uses means and methods which by association evoke in the shopper certain emotional reactions. He even, though climatic conditions no longer force him to do so, employs for the treatment of public areas in an enclosed center, materials and building methods of an "outdoorish" character. To reach this aim, he must have at his disposal certain sur-

faces which permit him to express the separation effectively. Besides floor areas, ceilings, and columns, he creates around each individual private space (i.e., between and above the storefronts) so-called "neutral strips" of sufficient size to achieve continuity and cohesion of the shape and character of the public space. He does so also with the aim of separating the strong individual expressions and stimuli of the distinct private spaces from each other.

ARCHITECTURE OF PUBLIC SPACES

For the architectural treatment of public spaces a very simple rule emerges: anything which would be typically employed for the treatment of a private space should be avoided for treatment of the public space. This concerns floor coverings, wall treatments, ceiling treatments, colors, textures, and illumination. As far as illumination is concerned, the customer expects within the individual store a certain amount of overall brightness in order to select the merchandise. For various types of merchandise certain overall lighting levels, expressed in footcandles, have been scientifically established, and also the coloring of lighting as it best suits different types of merchandise has been given great attention. These rules do not apply to public areas. In principle, the brightness level of public areas should be lower than that of private, because otherwise the private participant can never succeed in making visual stimuli effective. This general rule holds true also for the natural light which is permitted to filter through skylights or similar arrangements into public areas of an enclosed climatized center. It is also unnecessary to create equal overall brightness. Artificial lighting should be of "out-

Figure 3-54 Partial elevation of lower and upper levels for Center Glatt with an indication of horizontal and vertical neutral strips, separating various tenant stores from each other and establishing a continuity of the architectural areas of the public space.

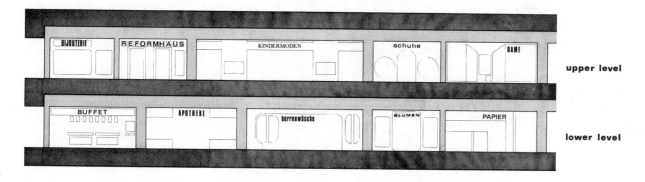

upper level

lower level

doorish'' character. A solution will not be found by approaching lighting design with mechanical, scientific methods. Psychological facts become much more important than physical ones. Though, for safety reasons, a certain minimum brightness level should be created, major attention should be given to lighting which has festive character: low wattage, visible light sources create by association the sense of festivity which we experience in the case of candlelight, the crystal chandelier, or lights on a Christmas tree.

ACCESS OF NATURAL LIGHT

In discussing the required dimension for the public areas of centers with covered pedestrian walks, I have stated that access of natural light to such covered malls is a psychological necessity. Natural light, however, should not just infiltrate through horizontal skylights. There should be offered to the shopper the possibility of looking through vertical or slightly inclined glass areas toward the sky to strengthen the "outdoorish character" of public areas. Thus the shopper does not lose contact with changing light conditions between morning and night and with changing weather and moving clouds. Such glass areas should be transparent. In order not to interfere with the effectiveness of the climatiz-

ation system they should be directed preferably toward the north or east, and they should be protected against direct sunrays by overhangs, louvers, or similar devices.

AMBLING AND STROLLING

The public spaces of a center are utilized by the shopper for activities similar to those which one could once experience in organically grown town or city centers before they were invaded by motorized traffic. Old habits which many thought were extinct experience a revival. The activities of walking, promenading, ambling, strolling, which imply leisurely propulsion, interrupted by stopping to view shop windows, to strike up acquaintances or renew old ones, having a social chat, sitting down for a few minutes or in a sidewalk café for a longer time in order to watch others walking by are characteristics of this newly rediscovered mode of living.

The designer who wants to create a successful shopping atmosphere will have to react to these phenomena. He should offer to the stroller a continuity of interesting experiences. He fails to do so if he permits large uninteresting areas like empty walls, uninteresting windows of banks or saving institutions, and frontages of mass merchandising to interfere with the continuity of experience.

Figure 3-55 Ambling and strolling.

URBAN DESIGN

The designer will do well to study the anatomy of the organically or sensitively planned old urban pattern which consists of a rich vocabulary of clearly defined urban spaces. Through narrow and intimate lanes one reaches in surprising fashion spacious ones of different sizes and shapes. There are no endless, straight, and uniform avenues; there is always something new and unexpected around the corner. So, obviously, the straight-lined, long-stretched mall which one experiences in its totality when entering at one end and through which one could shoot a cannon ball, does not appear to be a valid response to the psychological needs of the stroller. Even the major public areas should be broken up and, at certain strategic points, should widen into generous plazas. These "town squares" can establish not only strategic positions for vertical transportation between various levels, but also create natural meeting places and give an opportunity for the arrangement of public events, such as concerts, folk dancing, exhibits, fashion shows, etc. The entranceways from arrival areas to the main shopping streets can, through their dimensioning and their treatment, assume the role of sideways and byways, of intimate lanes and mews. The abilities of the sensitive urban designer can find full expression in the shaping of the public environment of a center and can at the same time meet the divergent needs of the different types of center participants.

Figure 3-56 Rich flora in a climatized shopping center. (Cherry Hill near Philadelphia, Pennsylvania, USA—architects Victor Gruen Associates.)

OUTDOOR ATMOSPHERE

There are many other means which the urban designer, together with the landscape architect, can employ to create the specific outdoorish character of public areas. The introduction of natural light will prove to be not only a purely psychologically founded necessity, but it will facilitate the introduction of trees, plants, and flowers. In climatized shopping centers it has been found that the eternal springlike controlled climate is especially favorable to the growing of subtropical flora.

The addition of ponds, fountains, sculptures, aviaries, and ice skating rinks will contribute to the enlivenment and enjoyment of the public area.

TWENTY YEARS' SHOPPING TOWNS INTERNATIONAL

It will be noted by the reader that in this chapter, which deals with the development of shopping centers within the last 20 years, I have only sparingly introduced illustrations of centers constructed in this long time period, in spite of the fact that thousands of them have been built.

My motivation for abstaining from this possibility lies in the fact that any selection which would fit into the physical size of this book would necessarily have to be unfair. Though I fully recognize that some of the centers constructed in the last two decades are superior to others, it seems to me that few of them have created something radically different or new in relation to the pioneering centers.

4

Figure 4-9 Del Amo area in Los Angeles, California: A number of unifunctional centers, each surrounded by its own parking area. In the upper half of the picture, the Del Amo financial center in construction. In the lower half, various competing shopping centers. (See Case Study II, page 92)

THE UNIFUNCTIONAL CENTER

Its Rise and the Downfall of Urbanism

Though nearly all urban agglomerations throughout the world are growing dynamically in size and number of inhabitants, their quality of "urbanity" is diminishing simultaneously and at the same speed.

URBANITY

In referring to "urbanity," I relate this term to three interdependent conditions which I believe form its essence:

1. The opportunity for direct human communications.
2. The opportunity for the free exchange of ideas and goods.
3. The enjoyment of human freedom as expressed by a nearly inexhaustible access to a multiplicity of choices.

The "urbane" city has attracted people throughout centuries because it offered those three conditions. Freedom of choice especially is a persuasive attractor. It not only implies the availability of choice with regard to many types and places of employment, education, enrichment of spirit and mind by expressions of art, and possibilities of amusement; it also permits, at different times and for different moods and temperaments, the choice between privacy and sociability, a choice between singleness, twosomeness, or of experiencing life expression within groups or with masses of people. Urbanity leads to a rubbing of shoulders among various economic, sociologic, and ethnic groups. It therefore promotes integration and tolerance. Contact with others can sharpen the wits, improve skills, and develop the intellect.

THE "ANTI-CITY"

If the term "city" is understood to be synonymous with the term "urbanity," then I feel moved to submit that most of the large cities today, or at least those parts of them which are populated by the majority of their inhabitants, no longer qualify under this term. Lacking a better term, we would have to refer to them as "human agglomerations" which spread and disperse over ever-increasing stretches of land which were once covered by forests, meadows, or fields.

Within the limited and delineated space of an "urbane" city, there exists a small-grained pattern in which certain functions may be grouped, and where vital and intimate relationships between all these groupings exist, comparable to the pattern of a tightly woven fabric. The indiscriminate endless stretching of the fabric enlarges the small functional groupings (as if the fabric were seen through a magnifying glass) into huge unifunctional ghettos. Time-and energy-consuming traveling distances then bring about a fragmentation which is expressed in segregation along economic, sociologic, and ethnic, as well as functional lines. Thus, the "anti-city" implies a negation of the three conditions of urbanity.

The growth of the "anti-city" has been made feasible through the availability of certain tools of technology: the automobile, telephone, radio and television. Its growth has been aided and abetted by government policies, by planning legislation such as zoning regulations and land usage restrictions. The "anti-city" proliferates inescapably through the working of a vicious circle. As sprawling and compartmentalization grow, so too does the dependency on the private automobile vehicle as the only feasible method of moving people and goods in a thinly "underdeveloped" area. Simultaneously the use of public transportation of any type becomes decreasingly applicable and practical. The more we are forced to use autos and trucks, the greater becomes the need to tear the urban tissue apart with streets, expressways, and freeways, parking lots and garages. The greater the nuisance and dangers created by automotive traffic become, the greater becomes the necessity to separate those functions which depend on very large quantities of vehicular traffic from others which depend on a somewhat smaller quantity. This then means that certain urban functions, like working functions of all types, shopping functions, major places of assembly, etc., have to be separated from residential

functions. The more unbearable the effects of automotive traffic (congestion, danger, noise, pollution) become the greater becomes the desire to escape the holocaust, and the agglomeration spreads wider and faster. With further spreading, the problems of distance and compartmentalization become even more apparent, and so it goes on ad infinitum.

The title of this chapter pinpoints a relationship between the rise of the unifunctional centers and the downfall of urbanism. By citing these two phenomena in conjunction with each other, I do not wish to imply that the downfall of urbanism should be regarded as a direct result of the rise of the unifunctional center. It is by no means the root of all evil, but rather a symptom; and as it appears to me, a significant one. Only the "anti-city" constitutes a fertile breeding ground for the phenomenon of the "rise of the unifunctional center." This rise on the other hand, is highlighting and aggravating the absurdity of fragmentation. If the foolishness and the absurdity can be recognized as the inescapable result of our sins of commission and omission, there may exist some hope that we can stitch the pieces and fragments together again.

THE RISE OF THE UNIFUNCTIONAL CENTER

The regional shopping center exemplifies one important type of unifunctional center. Though certain other unifunctional centers existed before the regional center's triumphant ascendancy throughout the world, there is no doubt that its phenomenal success has encouraged imitation with regard to segregating other urban functions into huge unifunctional groupings. For example:

Industrial Centers. (Or, as they are sometimes called, "industrial parks," because they do not contain a single tree.) These appear to be justified when they group industrial enterprises with irremovable disturbing characteristics or those which depend on certain transportation media, such as a railroad or shipping, into ensembles located in such a manner that, with relation to prevailing winds and distances, their disturbing qualities might be counteracted. But only too often such industrial centers are wrongly located and include employment facilities which, thanks to progressing technology, no longer create any disturbances. Employment-providing facilities like laboratories, research facilities, or smaller, electrically operated plants are potentially good neighbors to all urban functions including residences.

Civic Centers. These are huge conglomerations of governmental office structures in which bureaucrats

Figure 4-1 The vicious circle.

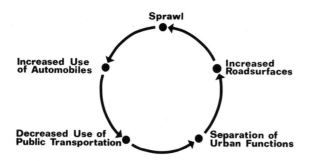

meet only bureaucrats and are estranged from those whom they are supposed to serve. Like all unifunctional centers, they create traffic peaks at opening and closing times. They are active during working hours, but they become deserted and sometimes unsafe in the evening and during holidays.

Financial Centers. These are agglomerations of banks, stockbrokers, and stockmarkets, where the ticker tape talks to the computer and vice versa.

Cultural Centers. These are concentrations of museums, galleries, exhibit halls, located in splendid isolation from those who might want to participate in culture.

Centers for the Performing Arts. These represent the ingenious idea of concentrating a number of theaters, an opera house, and concert halls on one isolated land area. Since it is unreasonable to expect that their visitors will profit from the close relationship of the various showplaces by partaking during one shopping trip in a concert, a drama, and an opera, the only effects are that they flatter the ego of their sponsors and create chaotic traffic congestions during the short time spans when all the showplaces begin or end their performances simultaneously.

Educational Centers. Whether high-school or university campuses, these constitute ghettos for the young; inasmuch as they assume considerable size they prove an effective means of institutionalizing the "ivory tower," of estranging the younger generation from the older one, and the studying population from the working one. They promote the remoteness of youth from the sociological and political life of their country and substitute college politics in its place. They certainly contribute to the idea that everything which is outside of the "youth ghetto" has to be regarded as the hostile "establishment."

Old Age Centers. Since we segregate the young, it seems logical that we must also segregate those politely called the "senior citizens." For them we build ghettos which often assume the size of towns, and in which the inhabitants are carefully isolated from everyone under the age of sixty-five and where, through this isolation, the elderly age even faster, concentrating on discussing with one another, various dysfunctions and diseases, whether real or imagined.

Office Centers. Here offices of private corporations are concentrated in heaps of skyscrapers, traffic-logged at office opening and closing times and deserted during the evenings, nights, Sundays and holidays.

Church Centers. Some promoters had the idea that worshipers of all denominations could not be ex-

pected to have religious or spiritual experiences within the profane atmosphere of parts of the urban agglomerations in which they might live, work, or shop. If such church centers provide for a complete coverage of all denominations, they might show signs of life on Friday evenings, Saturdays and Sundays; but they constitute wastelands at other times.

This listing can by no means make a claim as to completeness. We have amusement centers, restaurant centers, radio and TV centers, automotive centers, and, of course, huge centers for the dead in the form of cemeteries. In Germany there even exist "Eros Centers," implying presumably that eroticism is to be concentrated into certain ghettos and therefore to be excluded from the general urban scene. All of these unifunctional centers have a number of qualities, characteristics, and effects in common.

Enforced Mobility

All such centers cause "enforced mobility." Mobility is generally hailed as one of the great accomplishments of our age. One overlooks, however, the essential distinction between "voluntary mobility," which might indeed be an asset enabling an individual to widen his horizons by traveling to other parts of the country and the world, and "involuntary mobility," which is forced upon the individual when he has to change his place of residence in order to find employment, when his income decreases and he is thus forced to look for a cheaper shelter, or when his income increases and, as is often the case, our caste system forces him to move to the appropriate higher income residential ghetto. Involuntary mobility is also caused by the existence of unifunctional centers.

With Figure 4-2 I have tried to illustrate graphically, in a simplified schematic way how this en-

Figure 4-2   The suburban labyrinth.

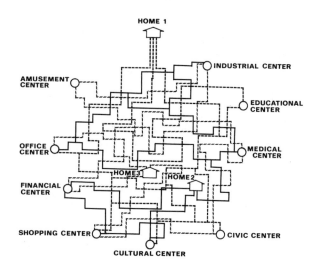

forced mobility acts in relation to three typical family units. The three symbols indicate: one family unit of the upper middle class, one of the middle middle class, and one of the lower middle class. Each one consists of the following members: husband, wife, a grown-up daughter, and a grown-up son.

Within a regional agglomeration each one of these families will live in a specific residential ghetto, the location of which reflects its environmental desirability. Thus, the upper middle class family will live as far as possible removed from the disturbances of our technological civilization. The lower income family has no choice but to live in the midst of the turmoil. The middle income family will be situated in a residential development somewhere in between.

Within regional agglomerations there are a number of unifunctional centers. In order to simplify matters, I have indicated only some of the significant ones, which are:

- An industrial center
- An office center
- A civic center
- An educational center
- A cultural center
- An amusement center
- A financial center
- A medical center
- A shopping center

I am now making the following assumptions:

1. The lower middle class family: the father is a blue-collar worker; the mother makes a living as an employee of the medical center; the son is a salesman in the shopping center; the daughter is a secretary in the office center.
2. The middle middle class family: the father is a bank clerk in the financial center; the mother is a housewife; the son is a student; the daughter has a job in the cultural center.
3. The upper middle class family: the father is a banker; the mother is a lady of leisure; the son is a student; the daughter is an assistant to a physician.

If each of the twelve individuals who make up the three typical families would have no other requirements than to move from home to the one unifunctional center which provides for employment or education then each of them would suffer only by the fact that the distances to be overcome are considerable and much time and nervous energy have to be expended for the trip. The matter is, however, complicated by the fact that each of the twelve individuals has certain additional needs and requirements, desires and aspirations which necessitate trips to other unifunctional centers. For example, the young woman who works as a secretary in the office center may also have the need to do some shopping, go to a beauty parlor, visit a doctor,

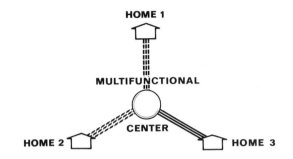

Figure 4-3 The introduction of one multifunctional center would dissolve the labyrinth.

or might even desire to attend an evening class, see a theater performance, etc. What has been said about the secretary holds true for every one of the other individuals. We are faced with the fact that a multiplicity of individual requirements and desires is contrasted by the limited unifunctional characteristics of specialized centers. Thus during the time unit of a day, a week, or a month, each one of the twelve individuals will be subjected to "enforced mobility" in order to satisfy requirements and desires in practically every one of the unifunctional centers. The result is a dizzy crisscross pattern of long and complex movements. To make this movement possible, an extensive system of roads has to be provided, as well as sufficient space for the storage of automobiles within each of the unifunctional centers. To translate this schematic drawing into one reflecting reality, one would have to assume that, in order to relate to the economic basis for the existence of the number of unifunctional centers which I have indicated, a regional agglomeration would not just be populated by three families or twelve persons but by 300,000 families. It is left to the imagination of the reader to visualize the total aggregate of "enforced mobility" which results through sterility and conformity.

Sterility and Conformity

If a specific urban function is located in one particular concentration, then it follows that that particular function is necessarily absent from all other areas. If everything connected with culture is herded into one "cultural center," this implies that expressions of culture must be absent from the remainder of the regional agglomeration. This of course holds true with respect to every other specific urban function. Thus each of the residential areas, carefully compartmentalized in accordance with shadings of sociological characteristics, creates a climate of conformity and intolerance and also, because each one lacks the admixture of any other urban functions, of sterility and boredom. Beyond that, each one of the unifunctional "concentration camps" is—because of the one-sidedness of its purpose—also plagued by uniformity and sterility. Unifunctional centers in combination with unifunctional residential developments create economic, sociologic, and ethnic segregation, intolerance and, as a consequence, civic unrest.

The Financial Burden

The pattern created by unifunctionalism results in economic waste as far as public and private expenditures are concerned. To fully appreciate the weight of this burden, one has to consider time as a factor. I do not subscribe to the saying "Time is money." Time which is spent voluntarily for any kind of individual pursuit cannot be measured by merely applying materialistic considerations. However, time which is spent involuntarily as a result of enforced mobility results in measurable sacrifices for the individual and in public economic waste.

I have noted earlier the vicious circle which evolves in human agglomerations. Involuntary movements derive from thousands of "points of origin" and are directed to a large number of unifunctional "points of destination." The pattern is so diluted and

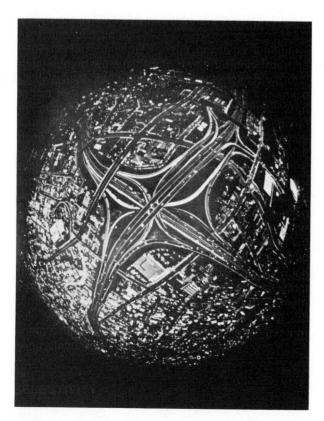

Figure 4-4 Freeways conquer the world!

so unpredictable that any attempt to satisfy movement needs through public transportation is doomed to failure. Therefore, a huge public investment is necessary to construct a road network which, in order to fulfill its tasks, must include complex facilities like freeways, overpasses, bridges, ramps, cloverleafs, etc. The vast area of the regional agglomeration must be furnished with many types of utilities, all of which must be maintained, repaired, and operated. There must also be established and operated a network of public facilities, police stations, fire stations, and a system of kindergartens, and primary and high schools. The listing of public expenditures which arise directly from the pattern of sprawl, low population density, and unifunctionalism could be endlessly continued.

As far as private expenditures are concerned, I have already referred to the waste inherent in the expenditure of "involuntary time." But the unifunctional "anti-city" pattern causes additional expenses which the inhabitant of a truly urban environment avoids. "Enforced mobility" implies that all those who do not own or cannot operate an individual motor vehicle are disfranchised as far as their participation in income-producing activities, social, educational or any other human activities are concerned. Thus our typical four-member family will be forced to own and operate four motor vehicles. In their place of residence, they will have to provide space and shelter for these vehicles and they will have to pay for the acquisition, and the operation.

The owners and developers of each one of the unifunctional centers will in turn have to provide storage space in the form of parking lots or garages for each of their regular or casual visitors. Inasmuch as this storage space always has to be provided for the possible maximum of users, which might (depending on the character and type of the unifunctional center) need it only for short time spans once or twice a day or for somewhat longer periods when the unifunctional center affords employment (30 to 40 hours a week), a considerable and to the largest degree wasted investment is involved.

On the basis of experience one arrives at the conclusion that for each car, one parking space has to be provided at the place of residence and three to four in context with the unifunctional centers. If one considers that the storage of one automobile requires 500 square feet of space, one finds that for one of our three typical families one must provide between 16 and 20 parking spaces, requiring a land space of between 8,000 and 10,000 square feet. If one considers that for the 300,000 families of a regional agglomeration, 4,800,000 to 6,000,000 parking spaces must be provided, one realizes that the sacrifices of land, capital investments, and maintenance costs are astronomically high.

THE DISPERSED CENTER

The need for multifunctionality is so overpoweringly evident and economic pressures to bring it about so great that even within the pattern of sprawling population agglomerations it has forced recognition. But inasmuch as this multifunctionality is the result of happenstances, neither planned, nor intended, the results are perversions of the concept of a multifunctional center. What we are usually faced with is a spatial accumulation of a number of unifunctional centers, with the result that new problems are created without any of the old ones being resolved.

CASE STUDY I

Case Study I: The Area Around Northland Center Near Detroit When the developers of this large unifunctional shopping center decided, upon my advice, to purchase considerably more land than needed for the shopping center, this was done with a number of motivations:

1. Land at that time was exceedingly cheap. The purchase did not involve great financial sacrifices and it

was reasonable to expect that land prices generally would rise.
2. They wished to protect the center from "pirating" competition.
3. A green buffer zone was to be created to protect existing and future residential developments from any disturbances caused by the traffic volume of the center.
4. There existed the vague notion that in accordance with the old saying "Where pigeons are—pigeons fly," there could rise at some unforeseeable time in the future a demand for land for other urban functions.

The fact that this vague notion became reality just a few years after the opening of the center was a surprise both to the developers and to me. It would be unfair to judge, with the help of hindsight, that a sin of omission was committed when in fact the center was from the beginning not planned to function as an efficient multifunctional center. It would be, on the other hand, irresponsible not to face the facts which have been demonstrated in this case and in many others, or not to draw conclusions relating to them for the future.

Let us take an objective look at the conditions as they exist today in the land areas around the center. It opened for operations in 1954. Giving in to the pressures for the purchase of land at steadily rising prices, the surplus land

Figure 4-5 Air view of Northland, near Detroit, in 1956.

owned by the center developer was sold to various groups and entrepreneurs. The land outside the property boundaries also appreciated in value and was therefore utilized for structures at an increasing pace. What was once cheap agricultural land—in fact a cow pasture—has now become high-priced real estate. Around Northland Shopping Center today there exist thousands of dwellings, hotels and restaurants, laboratories and small plants, office buildings, civic and cultural amenities, and facilities serving a dozen other urban functions. Though they are all within a limited distance of the "mother center" as the crow flies, they are in practice (for reasons I will presently discuss) hermetically isolated from one another.

Practically every one of the functions which I have enumerated before is shaped and organized as a "sub-unifunctional center." There are a residential center, a hotel and restaurant center, an office center, an industrial center, a cultural and amusement center, and others. The core area of each of these centers, which consists of the buildings needed for each specialized function, is surrounded by the required storage areas for automobiles. Each of the car storage areas, of course, has to be served by a distributing road network, and so we find, besides the loop road around the parking area of the mother center, a whole series of loop roads around each individual parking area of every specific "daughter center." Thus, if any one should venture to move on foot from any of the daughter centers to another, or from the daughter centers to the mother center or vice versa, he would expose himself to the rather unenjoyable experience of walking through a sea of stored automobiles and then of crossing one or more of the highly frequented access or loop roads. Should a person manage the crossing alive, he would still be confronted with the necessity of traversing another huge parking area. In actuality, such venturesome people do not exist. Thus the comparatively short distances are, in fact, overcome by using one's automobile over a complex road system involving considerable mileage.

The result is that this agglomeration of many unifunctional centers, though in their sum total representing multifunctionality, has led to transportation problems which even major investments for new roads and signalization cannot satisfactorily solve.

In spite of the fact that the mother center, because of its formidable success has been repeatedly enlarged, the combined building volume of the daughter centers is today considerably greater than that of Northland Shopping Center.

Based on this case study, one is forced to the conclusion that the "dispersed center" does not resolve the problems typical of the unifunctional centers such as enforced mobility, sterility and conformity, or economic waste, but that, on the other hand, it creates additional problems.

Figure 4-6 Air view of Northland in 1970. Note: Divided highways have been converted into freeways. Unifunctional subcenters have sprung up around the mother center.

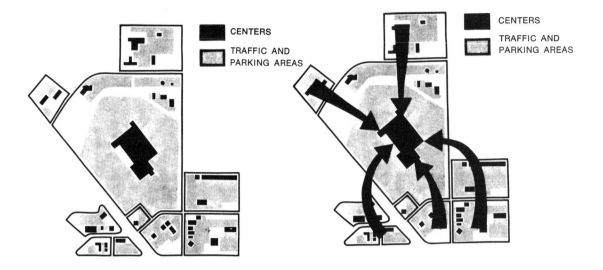

Figures 4-7—4-8 The dispersed center (Northland), existing conditions—integration would have resolved the problem.

CASE STUDY II

Case Study II: The Del Amo Area in Los Angeles In this area within the last twenty years private entrepreneurs have developed a number of unifunctional centers all serving specific functions, some of which are in direct competition with each other. There are a number of shopping centers here, and there is the Del Amo Financial Center, which consists of headquarter offices for various banks and rental areas for individual tenants with businesses related to financial activities. Every one of the unifunctional centers is forced to provide the facilities needed for accessibility of people and goods and the related storage areas for vehicles according to maximum needs for peak hours. Thus each one is surrounded by a "deadly zone" devoted to parking and traffic and thus is hermetically closed off from intercourse with the visitors and users of the other centers. This hermetic enclosure can only be broken by piercing it with the private automobile. In this area, various attempts have been made to bring about cooperation of individual unifunctional centers through bridging some of the gaps. Up to now, these efforts have been without success.

Figure 4-10 A view of the Del Amo financial center. Architects: Victor Gruen Associates.

CASE STUDY III

Case Study III: Parly 2 near Versailles in the Region of Paris, France In this development we are faced with three unifunctional centers. There is a large regional shopping center, a large residential center and a laboratory and research center. The same problem which I have discussed with regard to the other case studies, namely that of seclusion of each of the unifunctional centers, exists here also. It is, however, interesting to note that in contrast to other cases of dispersed centers, where joint action was difficult because of the varying ownership patterns and specialized interest of each developer, we are faced here with a situation in which one promoter developed the three unifunctional centers almost simultaneously. This phenomenon can probably only be explained by assuming that within the organization of the promoter there were three specialized departments staffed by experts for a certain type of unifunctional center who were not conscious of the advantages to be gained by pooling their skills.

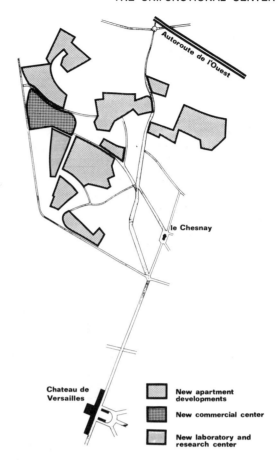

Figure 4-11 Land uses at Parly 2 near Versailles in the region of Paris, France.

CASE STUDY IV

Case Study IV: A "Chancery Center"
A very special project for a unifunctional center was seriously contemplated for Washington, D.C., which is already rich in unifunctional centers such as the huge ghetto for bureaucrats established in the Federal Triangle, and the John F. Kennedy Center for the Performing Arts. The new center seriously projected for Washington was a Chancery Center. President Johnson asked Congress in February 1967 to support a plan by the State Department to carve out an enclave north of Washington Circle to be used exclusively for foreign chanceries. In spite of governmental pressure, the plan was never executed. The most pointed and poignant criticism came from the international diplomats themselves who stated that "they did not want to be ghettoized." Some of the representatives of the new African nations expressed their fear that the proposal was nothing else but an attempt to bring about apartheid. Thus, in testimony, James W. Symington, the State Department Chief of Protocol stated: "I have received strenuous expressions of non-interest."

A QUESTIONABLE CONCEPT

In spite of having been involved personally in the creation of at least one type of unifunctional center, namely the regional shopping center, I have long realized that the entire concept of unifunctional centers is highly questionable. I am, of course, aware of the fact that the species unifunctional centers is perhaps necessitated and certainly furthered by the phenomenon of anti-city. Whether one of these phenomena is the cause and the other effect is about as hard to decide as the eternal question: "Which came first—the chicken or the egg?"

Yet contemplation of the problems of the unifunctional centers have caused me, and I hope also my readers, sufficient concern to give serious thought to the question whether and in which manner the human and economic waste which the development of untold thousands of unifunctional centers cause, could be removed.

5

Figure 5-83 Nordwest Stadt: A part of the center. (See Case Study XIV on page 152.)

THE MULTI-FUNCTIONAL CENTER

INTERMEZZO

Before delving into this chapter, which deals with the multifunctional center and constitutes a turning point in this book, I feel that it is necessary to pause for a moment in order to look backward over the terrain which I have asked my readers to cover so far, and forward, toward the more difficult, steeper landscape which we are now about to traverse.

I feel, as an author who wishes to be taken seriously, and who certainly does not want to be accused of being contradictory or schizophrenic, that I owe my readers a few reassuring words. Though I could claim in my defense that, in the Foreword and in the chapter "Horizons and Restraints," I set up some road signs indicating the overall direction which this book was going to take, I realize that I could still be accused of having, in the foregoing chapters, made certain statements which may possibly appear contradictory. I have, in Chapter 2, celebrated the new building type, "The Regional Shopping Center," especially as manifested in the pioneering centers, as an important breakthrough

in urban planning. I stated in Chapter 3 ("Twenty Years: Shopping Towns International") my awareness of the fact that thousands of shopping centers have been constructed in the last 20 years and that many more will be constructed in the near future. In that chapter I have developed my thoughts on how such "unifunctional" centers could be planned, developed, and designed in a superior manner.

After having done all this, I have in Chapter 4 dealt highly critically with *any* type of unifunctional center, not excepting the regional shopping center and have apparently "thrown cold water" onto everything discussed before, and possibly, so I feel, into the faces of my readers. I therefore have complete and sympathetic understanding for all those who would suspect me of being inconsistent.

However, though I have in the foregoing chapter, expressed strong doubts as to the long-term validity of the concept of any unifunctional center, I am asking my readers to believe that all the words written in appreciation of the unifunctional center, especially as far as they concern the building type regional shopping center are expressed with greatest sincerity. I believe that the opportunity to plan, develop, and design unifunctional centers has offered the first chance to re-experience the activity of planning in an era which suspected planning of being a kind of subversive activity and which saw salvation in unplanned, unfettered growth as an expression of free enterprise. I do maintain, on the one hand, the views expressed in Chapter 4 concerning the downfall of urbanism and the role of the unifunctional center in this development. On the other hand, however, I maintain that without the experiences which have been gained in planning, designing, and developing unifunctional centers, we could not enter the more complex field of planning multifunctional ones and integrating these latter into an overall urban system. As far as my own professional life experience is concerned, I am deeply convinced that my activity in the field of environmental planning, urban planning, and planning for multifunctional centers would have been impossible were it not for two circumstances:

1. That I have always been aware of and deeply concerned with the shaping of the overall human environment, influenced in my youth by men like Le Corbusier and Camillo Sitte and other creative thinkers.
2. That I have, with my overall vision as lodestar, devoted my professional interest to practically every one of the small crystals which must shape the mosaic, from furnishings to dwellings, store fixtures to stores, individual structures to groupings of such structures, store groups to shopping centers, unifunctional centers to multifunctional ones, core revitalization to the design of new cities and to regional planning. This is not to be misunderstood as the great success story of a little boy who started with the design of a chair and ended up with the design of a city. I have always devoted myself and still do, to the limits of my ability, to the single little stones, to the groupings of stones, and to the complete mosaic simultaneously. Whatever wisdom I may have acquired through this simultaneous approach of learning and experiencing is, of course not infallible. I will most certainly confess to the fact that as experience has widened my horizons I have felt that, on the basis of greater insight, I have not only a right but an obligation to modify my views.

The direction which the foregoing chapters of this book have followed and which the next chapters will assume, are reflections of my own development, and the experiences which I have drawn from it.

Motivated by the conviction that interest in and appreciation of environmental "building stones" are essential before we dare to approach their composition into an overall mosaic, this book proceeds from here in the following manner:

This chapter deals with the problems and opportunities of the multifunctional center, as it could now develop within urbanized areas.

Chapter 6 concentrates on the special theme of the reshaping of existing urban cores.

The final chapter, Chapter 7, represents an effort to correlate and unite the context of all foregoing chapters into a system, "The Emerging New Urban Pattern."

WHAT IS A MULTIFUNCTIONAL CENTER?

Though it is my contention that the "multifunctional center" represents a new building type which will attain a world-wide significance to an even higher degree than the regional shopping center, I am fully aware of the fact that it is not a new invention. Just as the regional shopping center concept was built up on the experiences of its ancestry (for example the oriental bazaar and the nineteenth-century gallery), the concept of the multifunctional center does not come out of a vacuum. It represents, in fact, the natural and organic organization pattern which has existed since the founding of human settlements and has expressed itself everywhere as the nomadic hunter turned to the pursuit of agriculture, the activities of craftmanship and of trade.

Thus, in every realm of life, we have to acknowledge the old saying that "nothing is really new in this world." Having acknowledged this undeniable fact, we should not be hesitant about studying and learning from the experiences of urban organization as expressed in the past.

When I refer repeatedly, in this book and especially in this chapter, to those values which I cherish in the old, organically grown town and city, this should not be misunderstood as a sentimental, romantic attachment to the past. I am completely aware of the fact that for reasons of changing sociological conditions and because of the impact of scientific and technological inventiveness, many of the old, organically grown multifunctional centers have assumed the role of tourist attractions because they satisfy a strong underlying human desire for certain "old" ways of life. In other cases, their very existence is threatened, because they do not respond to certain real—and a few imagined—needs of twentieth-century man. In spite of these difficulties, multifunctionality remains operative in central areas of many settlements: in villages and town squares and in centers of large cities.

In Europe, highway signs will direct the driver to the inner city, to the center. In Vienna, Austria, one refers to a visit to the center by saying, "Gehen wir in die Stadt." ("Let's go to the city"). In Spanish-speaking countries, one refers to the center as *intramuros*. In the United States, significantly enough, one refers to the central areas of the city as CBD (Central Business District), acknowledging the fact that at least in the newer cities, even the center has become unifunctional, namely, mostly a place for the employment of white-collar workers. In London, the term "city" is commonly used in a perverted sense, because it refers now only to a huge financial center.

In shaping concepts for the new-type multifunctional center, we must try to profit not only from the positive aspects of multifunctionality which we recognize by studying urban history, but we must also recognize the dangers which threaten the continuous existence of the historic model. We cannot close our eyes to the fact that in nearly every human settlement, from the smallest to the largest, the vitality of the central multifunctional core is diminishing and that though it may appear to be overloaded through the amount of vehicles, both parked and moving, the intensity of its human activities—as measurable by the number of participants—is ebbing away. The physical arrangement (as expressed by the size and shape of its public areas—streets, squares, plazas, lanes, etc.) which was formed during preindustrial epochs is in violent conflict with expressions of contemporary technology. Its structures and facilities, usually of old vintage, no longer fulfill the requirements of "modern living standards."

SELECTIVITY

Because of historic development many of the old city cores grew not just as "multifunctional centers" but as "omnifunctional centers." This was due to the fact that within the confines of the old cities, formerly protected by fortifications, all urban requirements had to be satisfied. This "omnifunctionality" is no longer necessary or attainable.

For each type of multifunctional center, certain standards of selectivity must be established. Certain functions, especially those serving an auxiliary nature will prove unsuitable for inclusion into any central urban structurization. This quality of "nonconformity" may, for example, relate to airports, freight yards, warehouses, military installations, large industrial plants, energy or utility plants. "Center nonconforming" functions are of course represented also by national parks, wildlife preserves, agricultural activities, and large spectator sport facilities.

Selection is often a difficult and painful process.

We cannot, however, escape from it as an obligation if we want to reestablish a strong differentiation between urbanized areas on the one hand and landscape and countryside on the other. As far as individual multifunctional centers are concerned, selectivity must be applied depending upon specific roles within the entire urban organism. Standards of selection must be established relative to the multifunctional center's role as the nucleus of a neighborhood, a village, a borough, a city, or an entire metropolitan area.

This type of selectivity should not be confused with the discrimination which now takes place through the instruments of zoning legislation and its even less respectable offspring which strive to segregate urban functions, and quite especially population groups of different economic, sociological, and ethnic characteristics, from each other.

Thus the new-type multifunctional center cannot be developed with the goal of creating omnifunctional centers. The goal should be rather to combine as many urban functions of the "center conforming" type as possible in a concentrated and land-conserving manner, counteracting the tendencies toward fragmentation, sterility, and waste of time and energy .

AN EMERGING BUILDING-TYPE

In discussing the new multifunctional centers I find myself in a similar position as when I discussed the then new building type, the regional shopping center a dozen years ago. Just as then, there are only a handful of examples either constructed or projected available. Even the few examples with which I am acquainted represent only partial solutions. Some combine only a limited number of functions; other, more ambitious ones, were "cut down to size" during the process of planning or implementation.

There are various reasons for the difficulties with which the planning and implementation of the multifunctional centers are beset. These projects fly in the face of planning legislation and the administration of this legislation through the planning bureaucracy. Both of these are influenced by certain planning principles established by CIAM in the Charte d'Athènes, which was first annunciated in 1933. This thoughtful and at that time revolutionary document, recognizing certain weaknesses of the organically grown city, prescribed the separation of functions as one of the tools to create order and a higher degree of social justice. This document, however, was conceived—under the leadership of Le Corbusier—over 40 years ago, in an era when one sincerely expected that all the impressive developments of technology would turn out to be beneficial to mankind. Now, nearly half a century later, we know that the tools of technology can be used or misused and can potentially create either human progress or the destruction of all biological life, including the human race.

One of the tasks entailed in the creating and shaping of the multifunctional center is therefore to employ the tools which science and technology have given us, to the highest degree but in a discriminating manner, using them to eliminate the deadly conflicts between man and his mechanical slaves, recognizing the fact that these tools are to act as servants but never as tyrants of humanity.

GUIDELINES

On the basis of these general thought processes, there emerge a number of practical guidelines for the planning of multifunctional centers. If it is our aim to reestablish the most important characteristics of urbanity (as enumerated in the foregoing chapter), then we must obviously invent methods which enable us to place a maximum amount of enclosed space serving human activities on a minimum of land. If we achieve this goal, we will shorten the distances between the various functions to such a degree that we will minimize the waste created by enforced mobility. We shall remove those obstacles which exist in a thinly spread out agglomeration and which deter from taking advantage of the existence of multiplicity of choice. But in creating this high utilization of land for productive activities, we must learn to avoid those mistakes which are the cause of the deterioration of historic multifunctional centers. We must preplan a workable pattern of coexistence between mechanical servants and the free expression of human needs, desires and aspirations. For this purpose, we will find that the tools of modern technology—if thoughtfully employed—can be of greatest assistance.

For me personally, the knowledge and experience which I acquired through my involvement in the planning and design of regional shopping centers have established a valuable background for approaching the tasks which are described in this and the following chapters. Nearly everything which I related as a result of my experience in relation to the unifunctional center applies to the planning approach for multifunctional types. I have always, as I pointed out in *Shopping Towns USA,* regarded the development of the regional shopping center on virgin land as an "experimental workshop" for further developments.

In discussing later on in this chapter a number of multifunctional centers, in describing their oppor-

tunities and problems and how these were faced, I will concentrate mainly on those in which I have been personally involved, not because I think that they are the best or most valid examples, but because I have intimate knowledge concerning them. Each of the case studies which I will examine in this chapter in greater detail has, besides its own particular qualities of problems and solutions, important characteristics in common with all representatives of the generic term "multifunctional center."

In all fairness, it must be acknowledged that for the entrepreneur as well as for the planner and the center team, the task of creating a multifunctional center is an infinitely more difficult and complex one than that of creating a unifunctional one. But the difference in the degree of difficultiy is no greater than the one which was overcome when, nearly 20 years ago, the move was first made from the practice of subdividing land for stores to the one of creating a preplanned ensemble in the form of a federation of commercial enterprises. One of the great obstacles which has to be removed in order to approach the task of planning the multifunctional center is specialization.

SPECIALIZATION

Specialization has resulted in our inability to deal simultaneously with the complexity of various facets of knowledge and experience. We are educating and training millions of specialists, and in order to heighten their efficiency, we insist that they should concentrate on their speciality and neither look left nor right, in order not to be "confused by facts." We have millions of people who see the individual tree, but who can no longer see the woods.

In discussing the planning of the regional shopping center, I have already pointed out that it cannot be successfully accomplished without the guiding, inspiring, and coordinating efforts of the generalist. This applies to an even greater degree to the multifunctional center. The center team in this case must not only be aware of the numerous interactions which occur in a unifunctional center but also of the much greater number and subtlety of interactions between an "orchestra" of different urban functions. It would be foolish to underestimate the complexity of such a task, but on the other hand, shortsighted not to recognize the new opportunities which it presents.

The obstacles created by specialization must be partly ascribed to inertia and intellectual laziness. These are human failings which must be overcome before the idea to which everybody seems to agree can be practically applied. I heard over and over again, at the time of the development of the regional centers, from the merchants who had "dared" to take the courageous step of becoming developers, that the "shoemaker should stick to his last." They all claimed that though they had great experience in the field of buying and selling, all the other knowledge necessary for the developing of a center was completely beyond their capabilities. They felt that they were like "newborn babes" when it came to acquiring real estate, dealing and negotiating with the other participants of a center and solving problems of transportation, and of urban design, which involved especially the shaping of public spaces. Once they had taken the initial jump out of the narrowness of their own speciality, however, they proved themselves to be more than an equal match for all the specialists, none of whom on his own, could ever have created a new building-type. It was amusing to observe however, that within a year or two, those men who had broken out of a narrowly defined speciality were honored and celebrated as experts in the "science" of shopping center planning and were earmarked as a new type of specialist.

If we can overcome inertia, mental laziness and a certain inferiority complex which each specialist possesses, we will witness the development of generalists who dare to deal with the complexities of the multifunctional center, and it would not surprise me if after a few years these generalists are referred to as experts on the creation of multifunctionality.

THE TERM "MULTIFUNCTIONAL"

The boundary line between the unifunctional and the multifunctional center cannot be sharply drawn. In discussing the regional shopping center, I mentioned the fact that some centers contain accessory activities which are not directly connected with the buying and selling of merchandise. We find in most of them eating facilities, in some entertainment or even cultural activities, certain public services, for example, post offices, and in rare cases, offices and some other functions. Even in a unifunctional office center there are usually some facilities catering to immediate shopping needs and personal services. Thus it appears that the division line must be drawn in accordance with the consideration of whether a center is, as far as its productive space is concerned, devoted to the highest degree to only one specific function or whether various functions are combined with each other in such a manner that each is strongly represented.

Multifunctionality is already established when just two different urban functions are combined (for example shopping facilities with employment facilities in offices), but the meaningfulness of multifunction-

ality grows when one succeeds in combining a large number of urban functions within one physical framework. The term "multifunctionality" does not, however, embrace only the idea of functional composition. If a center—though composed of more than one function—is planned and placed in such a manner as to exclusively serve only a specific sociological, economic, or ethnic group, then it will obviously be a promoter of compartmentalization and segregation. From the sociological point of view it will have to be regarded as a unifunctional center. Such sociologically unifunctional centers are represented for example, by exclusive clubs which offer a multitude of services, such as residential facilities, eating, drinking, and social facilities, sports facilities, health services, and so on, but only to their selected membership.

LAND USE

Inasmuch as one of the prerequisites for the creation of a meaningful multifunctional center is an intensive usage of land, the concept is plagued by certain obstacles represented by fallacious and superstitious views concerning the term "density." Concentration and cohesiveness can obviously not be created as long as the superstitious belief is perpetuated that low density is virtuous and high density sinful. Both of these statements lack any logical foundation. What is, however, provable is that sprawling and spreading, as an effect of low density, lead unavoidably to pollution of land, air, and water, and to the destruction of all man's biological needs. A pattern of high density is, of course, unacceptable if it interferes with basic human requirements like access to air and light, the need for privacy and restfulness.

The problem which faces the center team is then, simply that of inventing methods which make possible the most intensive use of land, avoiding, however, the disadvantages and dangers commonly associated with the term "high density." In discussing land use in relation to regional shopping centers (Chapter 3), I pointed out that the land use for a center of 1,000,000 square feet varies in existing projects from anywhere between 20 to 100 acres. However, even in the case of the most concentrated unifunctional shopping center, a density ratio of only about 1:1 is achieved.

If it is our aim to create cohesive and concentrated multifunctional centers, then we will have to succeed in changing the relationship between productive surface and land surface considerably. That this aim *can be* attained and how, I will discuss in relationship to the case studies, but I would like to point at this time to one thought-provoking fact. In regional shopping centers, even the largest and best planned ones, the structures containing all productive functions are rarely higher than two floors above ground. In organically grown cities, on the other hand, we find that each structure is multifunctional. In basements, on the ground floors, and often one floor above, there can be found stores, shops, and various institutions. Above them, there are additional floors, varying in number from five to fifty, which contain residences, offices, etc. Sometimes these additional floors are topped by penthouse restaurants, terrace cafés, and other enterprises which profit from breathtaking views. This comparison should give an inkling of the economic wastefulness implied in the unifunctional center.

IMPACT OF TECHNOLOGY

Technology has supplied us with certain tools which have changed the design of certain types of structures from an engineering and architectural point of view. Outstanding in this respect is the progress made in creating conditions of controlled light and air and that made in the field of vertical transportation. Merchants were the first to make full use of the opportunities offered. To the despair of the architect, who found himself robbed of one of the traditional means of styling the facades of a building, they declared that they did not need any windows. They found the conditions which were offered to them by controlled illumination highly preferable to those of natural lighting, which forced them to carry merchandise to the windows for the shopper's judgment. They also found that climatization, which offers not only control of temperature but also of humidity and cleanness of air, was highly preferable to the procedure of opening and closing windows and consequently creating drafts and introducing dust and dirt.

Thus, in principle, the merchants demand a structure without windows and openings. Since the building regulations of many countries have not quite caught up with requirements, there exist in many cities large structures housing stores which, respecting the law, contain a prescribed area of windows. These windows have a solely symbolic value and a short distance behind them, one usually finds a solid wall. The space between the windows and the wall is sacrified purely in order to make window cleaning possible.

All the reasoning which persuaded the merchant that conditions of controlled air and light are preferable for his store can also be applied to a large number of other utilizations of inner space. It certainly applies to large assembly rooms where natural light infiltrating through even the largest of window apertures can penetrate into only a small

strip around the perimeter. This category includes also meeting rooms, conference rooms, cinemas (which of course have to be dark in order to operate), lecture halls, storage rooms (whether for goods or automobiles), restaurants, etc. It is thus possible to establish a listing of urban functions for which conditions of controlled light and air are definitely preferable. There are, on the other hand, a number of functions which could theoretically also operate under conditions of controlled light and air but where psychological considerations outweigh the advantages. I believe this to be generally true for residences, offices, smaller classrooms of schools, etc. In establishing these two categories we might depend sometimes on subjective judgment, sometimes on climatic conditions and sometimes on a slowly changing attitude which progresses at different speeds in various parts of the world. However, the full recognition of the importance of our technological ability to provide conditions of controlled light and air will—as I will later discuss in detail—assist us in utilizing land in a highly intensified manner.

I mentioned as a second tool the development of vertical transportation. Whereas in the field of horizontal movement, all that our "progress" has brought us is a vast increase of individual transportation by motor car, and a decrease of public transportation, the opposite is the case in the field of vertical transportation. Here, technology has to a large degree replaced the individual transportation medium, the climbing of stairs, through highly efficient and speedy public transportation, by means of electronic elevators, escalators, freight elevators, inclined moving ramps, vertical conveyor belt systems, etc. These inventions have made possible the construction of multistoried department stores, multilevel shopping centers and of course, high-rise apartment buildings, office buildings, hospitals, etc. Those who claim that public transportation in our age is condemned to a slow death overlook completely that vertical public transportation has increased a thousandfold. There is no doubt that we are on the threshold of new technological development concerning horizontal public transportation. Dozens of meaningful inventions have been made in this respect, and it is only in their application that we lag behind. In connection with the concept of the multifunctional center, both the already applied technology concerning vertical transportation and the already available but not yet applied technology concerning horizontal transportation will have to play a role.

THE FINANCIAL BURDEN

In the foregoing chapter, I brought to the reader's

attention the financial burdens which the system of a multitude of unifunctional centers entails. One of these burdens is expressed by the fact that each individual unifunctional center has to provide serving facilities which are utilized only during the times the specific function is in full operation. A center devoted to offices, for example, will be in operation only five days a week, less when holidays are also taken into consideration, and only for eight hours a day. A center devoted to shopping may operate anywhere between eight and ten hours a day, but it will be closed on Sundays and holidays. It is an undeniable economic fact that the capital investments and part of the operating expenses for each individual unifunctional center have to be amortized or paid in relation to a comparatively short usage time. (Example: utility services as they are concerned with heating, climatizing and the supply of electric power). Obviously cost could be more easily carried if, through the existence of a variety of urban functions, they were used around the clock and also on Sundays and holidays. An admixture of shopping facilities, office activities, residential quarters, cultural and entertainment functions, would facilitate the achievement of this aim.

Even more obvious is the possibility of lightening the financial burden in the case of all transportation and related facilities. Since the peak hours, as far as automobile traffic is concerned, do not occur at identical times and with identical intensities for different urban functions, the duplicating and triplicating of provision for roadways for trucks and cars, and most of all, for parking, can be avoided. Also, because the inhabitants and those employed within a multifunctional center are also participants in other functions like shopping, entertainment and cultural pursuits, the necessity for enforced mobility is for them completely eliminated since they can fulfill all their needs and requirements within the concentrated multifunctional center by walking or using vertical or horizontal local transportation. Thus a skillfully programmed and designed multifunctional center may contain a multiple of the revenue-producing space of a unifunctional center but be satisfactorily served by the same amount of parking and transportation facilities as a smaller, unifunctional type. In addition, a large multifunctional center establishes those conditions which make public transportation practical and economically feasible.

PARKING

In discussing the unifunctional center, I have conceded that deck parking, though for various reasons extremely desirable, rarely proves economically possible. This situation changes radically in the case of the multifunctional center where the usage of parking space is assured for longer time periods during each day and also for Saturdays, Sundays, and holidays. Such a pattern of continuous usage facilitates the amortizing of the capital investment and the payment of the operating costs.

In those cases where a multifunctional center is mostly dependent on automotive vehicles for its accessibility, it is necessary to take into consideration —through programming of the various functions to be represented—a balancing of the transportation and car storage requirements. The aim of such programming is to create an ensemble which will utilize the road network at various times and in various directions and which will integrate each with the others as far as the usage of storage facilities for cars is concerned. The existence of public transportation widens the possibilities of programming because public transportation characteristically has surplus capacity and a built-in flexibility.

COMMON DENOMINATORS

The multifunctional centers which have been successfully executed, and also those which have been well planned but for extraneous reasons not yet implemented, have had certain common planning methods and characteristics. Because there seems to be a common thread running through most, if not all, of them, I want to discuss these generalities briefly, before describing single projects in greater detail.

PREREQUISITES

As far as prerequisites are concerned, they are similar to those which I have enumerated for the regional shopping center in Chapter 3. If a multifunctional center is very large and if it includes residences as an important function, its dependency on the prerequisite of "supporting population" is not as strongly evident as in the case of the unifunctional center.

The prerequisite of the long-term motivated developer and the complete control of the center team under the leadership of a strong generalist assumes even greater importance in the case of the multifunctional center. Any attempt to bring about a multifunctional center by relying on the efforts of specialized developers and their specialized teams is fraught with dangers and usually condemned to failure. A multifunctional center represents what in the planning and architectural world is sometimes referred to as a "megastructure." This implies that, as large as a complex may be, it has to be regarded as one structure in which all uses, functions, and serving facilities are interdependent and therefore in need of the closest integration.

THREE-DIMENSIONAL PLANNING

The planning of a multifunctional center, as indeed the planning of any urban development, can be successfully accomplished only if planners employ new techniques. Unfortunately the two-dimensional planning approach has become so engrained in the thinking of the planner and the architect that it has become second nature to them. As far as planning documents and programming is concerned, this method is expressed in a purely two-dimensional manner. In the drawings, various urban functions are indicated by placing them side by side, filling up a piece of drafting paper, by indicating, in an appropriately diminished scale, sizes and shapes of specific land parcels, in the form in which they are visualized for the housing of one type of urban function or another. The major roads or other communications are also marked on the land usage plan, but it is assumed that all minor communications and service functions such as secondary roads, parking areas, and space for mechanical equipment will be constructed by the entrepreneurs according to their needs, in the specific land parcel allocated to a specific function. When such a land usage plan is implemented, the effects are similar to the ones which I described in discussing the "dispersed center" in Chapter 4. Structures which contain urban functions of any type are surrounded by roads and parking areas, thus appearing as islands within seas of transportation areas of moving and stored vehicles. In this manner, any effective intimate communication between any one function and all the others, is rendered impossible. The

two-dimensional programming, often expressed in tabulations, simply adds the land requirements for buildings to those necessary for all secondary functions, and the total land requirement is then established in a cumulative manner.

It cannot be denied that this traditional practice of two-dimensional programming is simply and easily expressed on a piece of paper. By employing the T square, the triangle, and simple mathematics which can be efficiently carried out by a computer, it gives, for a time at least, the illusion of easy solutions, doing away with any necessity for complicated intellectual processes. The problem is, this method is *too* simple and naïve if one views it in relation to the tremendously complex task of achieving the characteristics of urbanity. If we want to create meaningful urban communities, if we want to make a significant contribution toward the solution of the environmental crisis, we must stem the tide of sprawl, and fight against compartmentalization and ghettoization of the urban organism. We must create integrated multifunctional centers which will offer us a sense of identification, ease of human communication, the possibility of exchange of goods and ideas—in other words, places which have the virtue of urbanity. These qualities can only be achieved if we also accept the need for multifunctional use of land.

The traditional two-dimensional planning techniques do of course offer the possibility of indicating, by implication, the height of structures, by the simple device of marking certain density ratios on paper, with expressions such as "high-density residential," "medium high residential," or "low-density residential," and so on. What is not possible is the achievement of compactness, ease of human communications, and collective use of all communication and service facilities such as roads, other transportation media, parking areas, and mechan-

Figure 5-1 The traditional two-dimensional land usage plan.

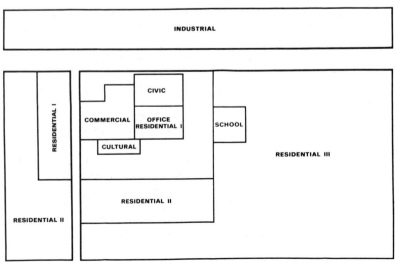

ical plants. The result of two-dimensional planning is unavoidably, the creation of sprawl, lack of homogeneity, and an unnecessary increase in the financial burden for the developer and, above all, for the public (whether federal, state, or municipal government).

The difference which results in land usage alone, depending on whether a two- or three-dimensional planning approach is utilized, is indicated by statistical material concerning university campuses in various parts of the world. The campus, of course, is one of the unifunctional centers to which I am, in principle, opposed. However within the framework of this unifunctional center (a ghetto for the young), amazing variations of land usage are being achieved, depending on whether the planning team approaches the task on a traditional two-dimensional basis, which results in a sprawling, suburban-type development, or a three-dimensional planning approach, whereby they arrive at an "urban" university. The following figures show that the suburban type of university requires fifteen times the land area of an urban type:

University of Santa Cruz, California	13.7	students	per	acre
Philipps Marburg, Germany	16	"	"	"
Scarborough (Toronto) Canada	106	"	"	"
Chicago	189	"	"	"
Forest Park (Georgia)	220	"	"	"

Thus the two-dimensionally planned university requires for 20,000 students 1,500 acres and the three-dimensionally planned university requires for the same number of students, 100 acres.

A listing of opportunities which can be created by the integrated multifunctional center is set down here in brief form, summarizing what has been indicated up to now:

1. An immediate close relationship between a large number of diverse functions, making it possible to shorten distances to such a degree that they can be bridged either by foot or with the assistance of slow-moving pedestrian accessory transportation.
2. A breaking down of the barriers which today separate people of different economic, racial, or sociological groups.
3. A supply of green areas within the urban tissue and within easy access, in order to provide urbanites with clean and oxygen-rich air, and to establish the possibility of an intimate contact with the expressions of nature.
4. A strong sense of identification with the ele-

ments of the urban structure, reaching from the smallest, a neighborhood, to the totality of a city. This identification is needed to counteract the neurosis of "urban loneliness."
5. A possibility of connecting meaningful centers of the urban environment with each other by systems of public transportation and thus making a meaningful contribution to the solution of the traffic crisis with its accompanying phenomena of danger to life, health, and safety.

In order to help us visualize the difference between the methods of two- and three-dimensional planning, I would here like to relate it to a completely different field—that of music. It is possible to indicate the simple placement of sounds and their quantity (duration) in a single melodic line and thus permit the implementation of the musical design through a voice or an instrument, which transmits melody and rhythm. However, when the composer wishes to design a more complex sound structure, he will employ additional means to express his concept. A third dimension is indicated by the employment of a secondary linear system— the bass register. The composer thus achieves, on one piece of paper, an indication of "functions" in the "basement" and of "functions" on the "upper level."

Figure 5-2 Indication of a melody utilizing a two-dimensional planning method.

Figure 5-3 Introduction of a third dimension (the bass register).

Musicians have invented a planning technique which permits the implementation of a music concept for a "hundred specialists," who together form the "team" of a symphony orchestra, on single sheets of two-dimensional paper. This team is then guided and coordinated by a "generalist," in the person of the conductor.

The manner in which the orchestration of a symphony or an opera is transcribed could serve planners as an inspiration. Here we find that the interaction of a large number of specific instruments (functions) which have diverse characteristics are expressed on all levels of the scale as to their exact time, position, strength (quality), and quantity of performance. The manner in which this is done permits the implementation with all specific functions acting "in concert." On one sheet of paper, of course, a composer can express only a small part of the entire planning concept. The score of a work of music consists of a multitude of sheets which are used by the conductor of the team for the implementation of the entire work, or "opus." Besides that, each specialist (the player of each instrument) is furnished with a "detailed drawing" which applies to his specific task. The musical score lists the instruments of expression in a vertical sense (string instruments, wind instruments, percussion instruments, etc.), whereas the exact location, quantity and quality of sounds are indicated in a horizontal manner.

Though architecture has been poetically referred to as "frozen music," we should obviously not let ourselves be carried away by this not-quite-applic-

Figure 5-4 Musical score for a symphonic work indicating the integration of many functions on one sheet of paper.

able simile. Though we can be inspired by certain characteristics of the planning technique employed in music, it is not feasible to slavishly adopt them. If we wish to establish a method by which vertical and horizontal relationships of the manifold urban functions are made visually clear on a single document, we could do this only by using the device of a three-dimensional model, similar to many egg crates

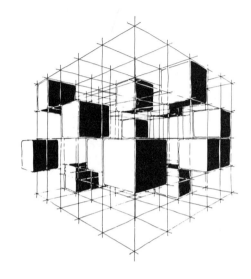

Figure 5-5 Drawing of a space frame for visualization of three-dimensional planning.

stacked on top of each other. We could then place multicolored cubes as an indication of each function, according to the quantity and location of each in the horizontal and vertical sense, within the skeleton of this model.

Though a model of this type might be of visual assistance during the programming and conceptual phase of a project, it would represent too unwieldy a tool for practical use. To achieve the desired results during the programming and conceptual phase of any planning undertaking, we will have to acquire the skill of envisaging vertical and horizontal arrangements simultaneously. We will even be forced to include in our considerations, a fourth dimension, that of *time*, which must be included as a factor because it concerns the scheduling of implementation.

Since the architectural and planning profession is skilled with regard to the placement of functions in the horizontal sense, I strongly recommend that the programming and conceptual process be studied first by concentrating on the much neglected task of establishing vertical relationships. For this purpose, a tabulation which bears a certain resemblance to the musical score of a symphony has proven very suitable.

Before starting the physical programming for any specific project, we should of course have some idea about its "givens." That is, the land area, the type and approximate size of functions contemplated for that area, and any physical characteristics which have to be respected (streets, rights of way, and landscape features or conditions which are inherent characteristics of the land, such as topography, quality of the ground, groundwater, etc.). How such preestablished conditions can be taken into account will be demonstrated in the later discussion of case studies.

The illustrated chart omits all these special considerations, aiming at showing, in a highly schematic form, the general approach. On the left edge of the tabulation are listed the urban functions which, in their composition, are to result in a multifunctional urban center. Along the upper edge of the tabulation are listed the various levels which are normally available for the placement of the func-

tions. Vertical and horizontal lines then form, as in a graph, spaces in which we can indicate by figures, the size of the area which is to be allocated to each one of the urban functions on certain or all levels at our disposal. For the purpose of this model chart, we are listing the functions in accordance with urbanistic principles, but in the case studies we will show that this can also be achieved on the basis of economic considerations. Thus we find three main groups along the left edge of the tabulation:

1. Human functions
2. Human communications
3. Service functions and their communications

In each of the groupings there is a subdivision representing the various "instruments" within that particular group. In the horizontal mode the levels are listed. We have hypothetically assumed that

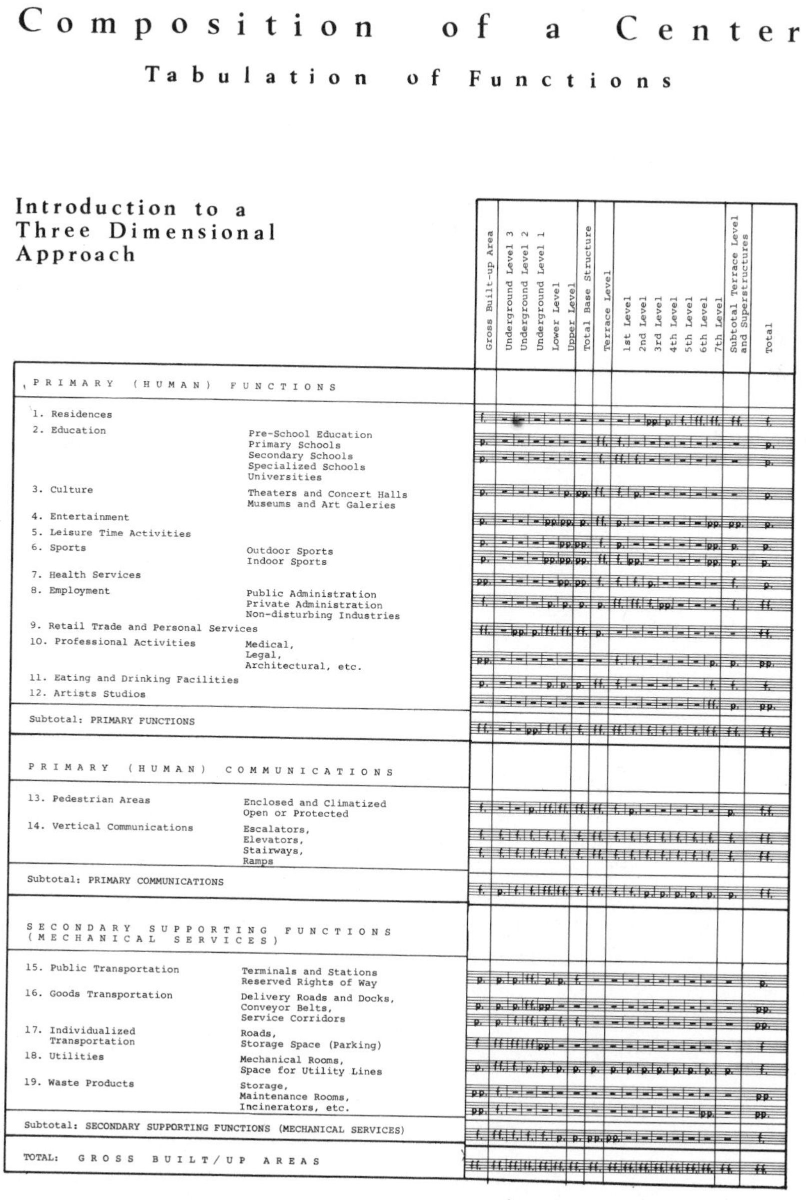

Composition of a Center
Tabulation of Functions

Introduction to a Three Dimensional Approach

Figure 5-6 Three-dimensional chart for a multifunctional center.

there would be three basement levels, a ground level, and an upper level. These together would form a base structure which would house all those functions which either do not demand access to natural light and air or which actually benefit from conditions of controlled light and air. We have then assumed that a terrace level (the roof of the base structure), would be created which would be partly utilized for the construction of enclosed space and partly for urban open space in the form of land-scaped areas and a wide range of outdoor facilities, and that eight additional levels would be at the disposal of the project. As will be seen from considering the case studies, there are cases where, instead of eight such upper levels, there are sixty or even more available.

Inasmuch as I intend to keep this tabulation as abstract as possible, I have refrained from showing any quantity figures but have used instead those symbols which the musician employs to indicate strength or volume (pianissimo (pp), piano (p), forte (f), fortissimo (ff), and in those cases where specific areas are not used for a function, the symbol for a pause.

PLANNING PROBLEMS

If one comes then to the practical application of the planning instrument (the three-dimensional tabulation) it will become evident that a step-by-step procedure which involves the application of "system engineering" is necessary if we are to arrive, after painstaking work, at a meaningful result. Obviously the distribution of various functions on various levels will be influenced by structural considerations which, as a rule, will determine that low levels of the base structure must be of about equal size in order to structurally carry each other and that, on the levels above the platform, sufficient space must be kept free of any structures in order to permit sufficient access to air and light. Through detailed studies of each one of the horizontal levels, the workability of the arrangement and relationship between human functions and communications, and service functions and their communications, will have to be established. The design of the entire system becomes further complicated by economic considerations and also those arrangements which are necessary to ensure superior accessibility and the functioning of interior communications. The problems which confront the creator of the multifunctional center are caused by human failings as exemplified in outdated zoning legislation and the addiction to two-dimensional planning. Another consideration is the fact that multifunctional centers cannot be created by laissez-faire planning, but need "guided" planning.

Even this very rough indication of the problems involved in three-dimensional planning should make it obvious that it engenders a series of tasks which make it infinitely more complex, time-consuming, and therefore more costly than the traditional two-dimensional planning approach. However, the results, whether measured according to purely human values, environmental values, or overall economic benefits, justify the greater effort.

TERMINOLOGY

Since economic considerations play a decisive role in the decision-making process concerning any undertaking, it will facilitate the discussion of work procedure for multifunctional centers if we utilize a terminology which reflects as clearly as possible the "cost-benefit ratio." Being exposed to projects located in various parts of the world, I find that a wide range of terms relating to economic evaluation are used. The terms vary not only from continent to continent and nation to nation, but also differ greatly as to their implications. I am therefore proposing the following terms which can be applied internationally.

1. *Revenue-Producing Building Area.* This term applies to the gross building area of each center element which the developer expects to rent or sell to an individual participant. The conditions under which the sum total of these revenue-producing areas are sold or rented must be such that the amortization of the total capital costs of the project is possible over a reasonable time span and the operating and management costs which accrue to the developer are covered. Beyond that, the income received from the revenue-producing building areas should yield a reasonable profit to the developer.

2. *Income-Producing Building Areas.* This refers to gross building areas which will produce an income, though not necessarily one which will be sufficient to amortize the capital investment or pay for operating costs. This applies, for example, to parking facilities which will create an income through parking charges and possibly through leasing arrangements with gasoline and service stations. However, in most cases it must be expected that this income will not be sufficiently high as to be revenue-producing, for otherwise costs for the utilization of such spaces may be unacceptable to the public and would therefore jeopardize the interests of all individual participants and the multifunctional center as a whole. Into this category also fall those building areas devoted to semipublic facilities such as meeting rooms, auditoriums, public toilets, which may all create some income but not necessarily sufficient to create revenue.

3. *Nonproductive Building Areas.* In this category belong all those building areas which, though absolutely essential for the functioning and enjoyment of the multifunctional center, do not create income. Into this category fall all communication areas such as pedestrian malls, courts, corridors, terraces; also included would be all those areas required in order to provide the necessary services: truck service roads, service towers, loading docks, mechanical equipment rooms, communication for mechanical serving functions, etc.

For the expression of the physical and economic organization of a multifunctional center, these three terms embracing major categories appear sufficient.

In the economic planning of the center, other considerations will have to be included. There are available to the developer some other sources of revenue which do not find expression in the physical plan, for example: renting of advertising space, display vitrines, or small selling kiosks, etc. The developer will also be able to create income, though not necessarily profit, as the provider of public utilities for which he establishes in leasing or sales agreements, certain systems of charges applying to each participant. This refers to charges for supply of climatization (heating, cooling, and filtration), in some cases the supply of electric energy, of hot water, upkeep of landscaping, cleaning of all public spaces, etc.

In order to simplify the graphic charts (or tabulations), shown in connection with the case studies, I am using in all of them, the following terms and abbreviations: R = revenue-producing building areas. I = income-producing building areas. N = nonproductive building areas.

THE MULTIPURPOSE USE OF LAND

As a result of the application of the three-dimensional planning approach, the total available land area and each parcel thereof is utilized on various vertical levels for different functions in an integrated manner. For this reason, the concept of individual land ownership in relation to each participant of a multifunctional center cannot be maintained. An identical piece of land may be used on subsurface levels for technical equipment, for public transportation, for roads, for delivery facilities, for storage areas or productive functions, on two or more of the levels above ground for stores, shops, banks, meeting rooms etc., and on upper levels for apartments, offices, and recreational and cultural facilities.

The legally established principle of ownership of land in most countries of the world, determines that the proprietor of any land parcel, owns the land to the center of the earth and to the limits of the atmosphere. This concept has proven itself, in the light of technological and sociological developments, extremely difficult to maintain. In the case of the multifunctional center, ownership of the land will have to rest with some kind of public, semipublic, or private agency. The owner might be the state, the municipality, a federation of all participants, or a developer. The owner can then, by a variety of methods, establish charges for the utilization of the built-up surface, for each of the individual participants. Some of these methods are in practical use; for example, there are short-term or long-term leasing arrangements which in many cases provide a "minimum guaranteed rent" and an additional "bonus rent" based on percentages of gross income. Long-term leasing arrangements, relating to time spans of up to 99 years, provide that the leased structure reverts to the public or to the private developer at the end of the leasing period.

THE PLATFORM PRINCIPLE

I mentioned earlier the fact that certain functions operate decisively better under conditions of controlled air and light. This opens up the possibility for these functions, together with all service, public transportation, and parking facilities to be combined into a "base structure" which might start two or three levels underground and find its upper limit two or more levels above ground. The base structure, then, constitutes one completely homogenous structure which is to a large extent utilized by revenue-producing uses, and to a smaller extent by income-producing uses and nonproductive service facilities. In order to make all productive elements of the base structure easily and enjoyably accessible, it should contain public communication in the form of pedestrian malls, arcades, plazas, etc., which are shaped and designed along the same principles discussed in Chapter 3 for the public spaces of the regional shopping center. If one considers for purposes of an economic analysis all these public pedestrian areas and all service facilities (with the only exception the garages or parking decks) as nonproductive space, because they do not bring any direct revenue, one will find that in relation to the total building area of the base structure, about 30 percent has to be devoted to this purpose.

The upper limit of the base structure forms a "platform." This platform does not necessarily have to be uniformly flat. It may be organized as a number of terraces which differ by one split or full level from each other. (This, of course, can only be achieved if the upper limit of the base structure is not on a uniform level.) This platform represents nothing else than a duplication of buildable land. Through the platform principle, new, highly desirable building land is being "fabricated." A sufficiently strong ceiling structure for the base structure makes it possible to cover this platform with earth and thus gives a chance to create a richly landscaped pedestrian area. From this garden-like environment buildings can rise serving those functions which for physical or psychological reasons benefit from direct access to air and light. These structures might be residential units of varying heights, office structures, hotels, civic administration buildings, etc. Directly related to the landscaped terraces there might be low structures containing restaurants with outdoor terraces, cafés, sports facilities, exhibit halls, and open air exhibits, open air theaters, botanical and zoological gardens, etc.

Through the skillful combination of the "three-dimensional" planning approach, the "multipurpose use of land," and the "platform principle," large amounts of productive space can be placed on comparatively small land areas. The size of the land area is usually determined by the wish to keep its dimensions within acceptable walking distance. If one succeeds in this limitation of land size, then any mechanical, horizontal transportation becomes unnecessary. Vertical public transportation between the various levels, on the other hand, can be easily and satisfactorily established. Thus, most multifunctional centers can succeed in attaining a ratio between productive space and land which is considerably higher than the ratios which have been demonstrated as achievable in the unifunctional center.

PROBLEMS OF IMPLEMENTATION

Having now enumerated some of the advantages which, by the usage of certain methods and techniques, can be gained through the concept of the multifunctional center, it would only be fair to point out the problems.

It is evident that a "megastructure" has to be planned to the last detail in advance in one single planning phase. It is advantageous to construct it also in one phase, but if economic or other considerations make this absolutely impossible, it is feasible to spread the implementation, especially as far as the superstructures are concerned, over longer time spans. A phasewise implementation of the base structure is somewhat more problematic. However, whether or not the implementation proceeds in one construction phase, it is obviously essential to predetermine the exact location, siting, height, and weight of all superstructures in order to establish

data concerning the foundations, and all vertical connections for mechanical services which must be an intrinsic part of the base structure. This then implies that, for the planning process, the developer and the center team must be ready and prepared to spend considerably more time, effort, and probably more money than for a grouping based on a two-dimensional planning approach. The planning process to which I am referring includes not only the work of architects and engineers but also the efforts of the administrator, the leasing department, the public relations department, and the financing department of the developer.

Another problem is that dealings with all public authorities in order to achieve building permits become more complex. This is especially true in those cases where zoning regulations, building volume restrictions, and height restrictions exist. Thus the courageous developer of a multifunctional center may have a hard battle on his hands which may result in failure or in compromises, and only occasionally in full success. However, this situation is not too different from the ones with which the developers of the pioneering regional shopping centers in the United States were confronted at a time when the planning bureaucracy reacted as people usually do against everything unknown: with open hostility.

It is therefore obvious that the development of a multifunctional center needs courage, perseverance, imagination, and ingenuity. It also needs considerable capital funds. I certainly do not expect that free enterprise will take the risks involved just in order to attain idealistic aims such as the improvement of the urban environment. Valid reasons lie again in the field of economics and specifically in the vastly improved "cost-benefit ratio." Here, I submit, lie the strongest arguments for the multifunctional center, for private enterprise as well as for publicly subsidized, controlled, or owned enterprises.

MISSED OPPORTUNITIES

It is painful to observe the many cases, where the conditions and ingredients necessary for the creation of a meaningful multifunctional center were present but, for reasons sometimes difficult to understand, the opportunity to do so was missed.

From the hundreds of such cases with which I am personally acquainted. I would like to discuss just one. I have chosen it not because it is an especially flagrant case of lack of planning, and I mention it without the slightest intention of accusing any member of the developers and planning team of any wrongdoings. It would be presumptuous to do so, because I am not acquainted with the nature of the difficulties or obstacles which may have prevented the creation of a meaningful multifunctional center.

I am referring to the case of Century City in Los Angeles. Because the name contains the term "city," it seems likely that the intention of creating "urbanity" must, at one time or another, have existed in the minds of the entrepreneurs. Century City also seems to be worthy of our attention because the ingredients needed for the creation of a truly urban multifunctional, important crystallization point within the sprawling Los Angeles region were present to an unusually large measure.

1. The center team had at its disposal a considerable land area (180 acres) formerly used by a major movie-making company and therefore under one ownership.

2. The land area, made vacant due to the discontinuation of its former use, is located in the midst of a fully developed area and specifically close to residential developments inhabited by people representing nearly all economic strata, with an especially strong emphasis, however, on middle class and very high income groups.

3. The interest of potential participants was great and varied. It existed with regard to residences, hotels, major shopping facilities, banking, and other institutions and a number of other functions. This interest was so strong that the achieving of high quality represented no problem.

4. Accordingly, there existed no serious problems as far as the availability of financial funds was concerned. It was in this case therefore possible to provide for underground or garage

Figure 5-7 Location of Century City in relation to the region, indicating the downtown area of Los Angeles and residential developments surrounding the site. (Upper income groups are served especially by the developments of Westwood, Beverly Hills, Bel Air, Brentwood etc.).

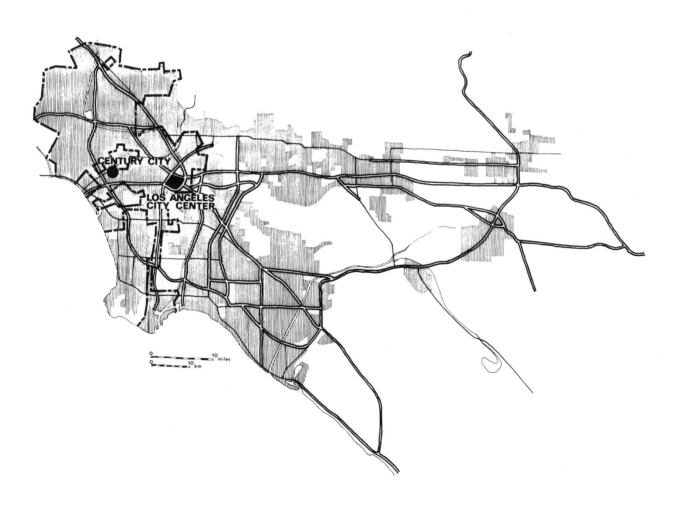

parking for the greater part of the buildings and for superior architectural design and quality of individual structures. It should therefore not come as a surprise that from the financial point of view, the project moves along in a highly successful manner.

An article which appeared in the *Los Angeles Times* on June 7, 1971, stated: "Century City, a vacant area a decade ago, is fast becoming the 'uptown' for Los Angeles."

Development Research Associates have established that Los Angeles is now polarized around two strong business areas, the central busines district on the one hand, and Century City on the other. Thus it is concluded that Century City points the way to a new pattern for urban development, with a series of high-rise centers, instead of just one major core.

The concept for the polycentric structuring of the city and region of Los Angeles has been brought into definite form by the City Planning Department of Los Angeles (discussed in Chapter 7). The new centers which are proposed by the City Planning Department, however, are based on the concepts of three-dimensional design, compactness, multipurpose use of land and the separation of traffic and other serving functions from human functions.

The fact that these tools have not been utilized in the planning of Century City becomes evident if one views the master plan. Here, an obvious two-dimensional approach and a compartmentalization of the entire site for various functions is discernible. The existing road pattern is improved, but no attempt has been made to subordinate it to a lower level and thus to prevent the road grids from dividing the entire development into separated parcels. Each parcel now represents a unifunctional development. We find in the extreme left corner of the master plan, a large regional shopping center, adjoined on the right by a hotel development. Other parcels on the left side of the plan are devoted to office buildings and other commercial developments. Land parcels to the right side of Olympic Boulevard are earmarked for residential structures.

A real integration between differing urban functions is not accomplished. This is partly due to the distances which result from the shape of the site, (the longer dimension of the rectangle is about 4,800 feet) and partly by the fact that strong auto-

Figure 5-8 Century City, land usage master plan.

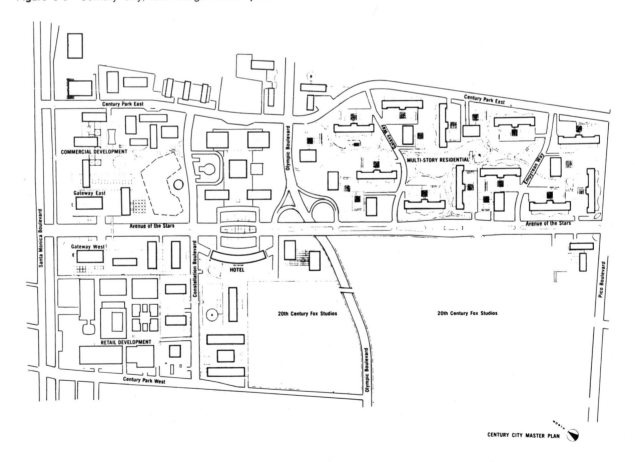

mobile movement on the surface streets makes walking or the utilization of any kind of pedestrian accessory transportation impossible. The result is that in spite of the fact that a large number of high structures are located within the project area, communications between all these structures, serving different urban functions, is only possible by means of the private automobile.

Though it must be concluded that Century City does not live up to the term "city" as far as qualities of urbanity are concerned, it does constitute an impressive private real estate development along traditional planning principles, excelling as far as quantity and quality of individual structures are concerned.

CASE STUDIES

The environmental and economic opportunities and also the problems which are inherent in the creation of a multifunctional center planned in accordance with the three-dimensional approach will become apparent as we turn to the discussion of some specific representatives of this species.

Figure 5-9 Century City: The impressive character of the development on one specific parcel is illustrated by "Century Tower" the central building of which rises to over 50 stories.

Figure 5-10 Century City: A view of the model (which does not reflect all latest developments) transmits an impression of its general character.

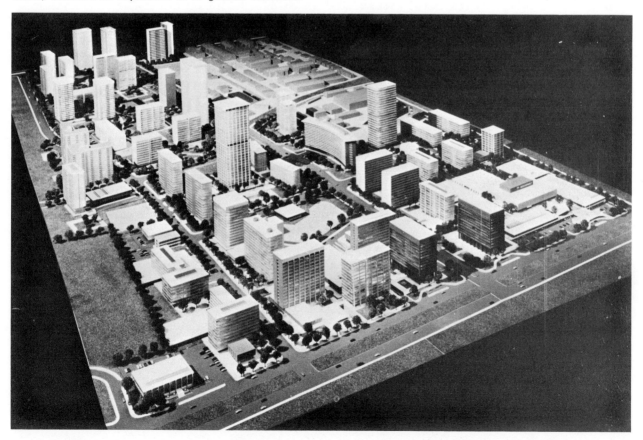

CASE STUDY I

Name of Project: Valencia City Center

Location: The new satellite town of Valencia, in the Los Angeles metropolitan area.

Architects: Victor Gruen Associates

Developers: California Land Company

The development of the satellite town of Valencia, with a projected population of 250,000 is proceeding in phases. The city center site is still vacant, the general strategy being to service the needs of the growing population through the village centers which are constructed simultaneously with the construction of each urban subunit and to proceed with the development of the satellite town center only when a sufficiently strong demand has been created.

Although it was developed in 1963, the Valencia City Center project expresses the methods of three-dimensional planning, multifunctionality, and the platform principle in pure form. The triangular-shaped site covers about 93 acres. The development program lists the following revenue-producing and public uses:

	Square feet
Retail	2,500,000
Offices	4,500,000
Apartments	6,000,000
Governmental buildings	150,000
Cultural functions	200,000
Entertainment functions	100,000
Hotels	100,000
Institutional uses	600,000
Total	**14,150,000**

The ratio between revenue-producing functions and land area which could be achieved on the basis of this program and the preliminary plans would be 3.5:1.

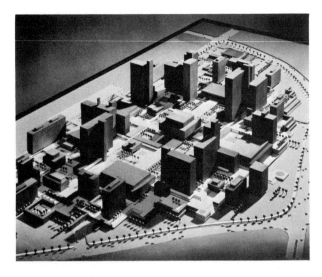

Figure 5-11 Valencia: Model of the projected town center. Only the superstructures are visible on this model, the entire base structure containing all commercial facilities, all serving facilities and all parking, is concealed.

Figure 5-12 Valencia: Part of an already developed village in which separation of automobile and pedestrian traffic is realized. (The footpath system is also used by minibuses.)

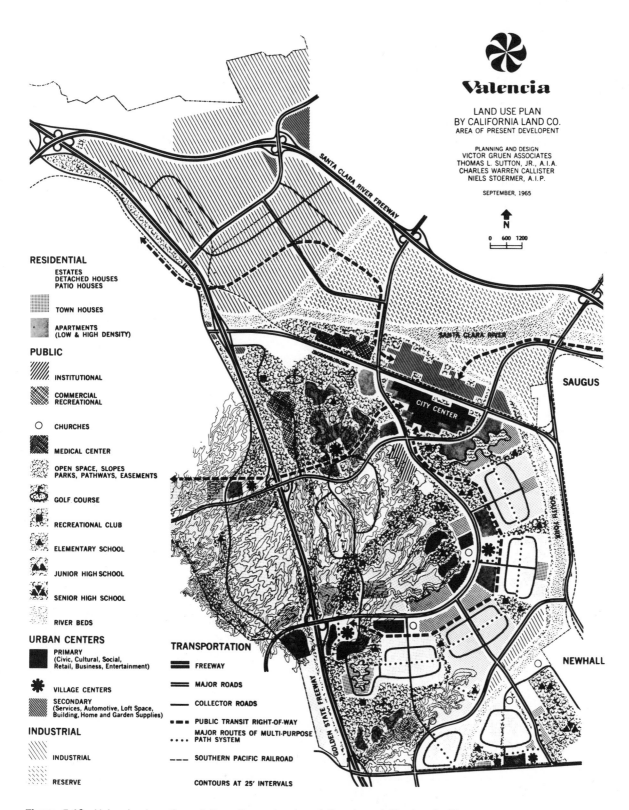

Valencia

LAND USE PLAN
BY CALIFORNIA LAND CO.
AREA OF PRESENT DEVELOPMENT

PLANNING AND DESIGN
VICTOR GRUEN ASSOCIATES
THOMAS L. SUTTON, JR., A.I.A.
CHARLES WARREN CALLISTER
NIELS STOERMER, A.I.P.

SEPTEMBER, 1965

N

0   600   1200

RESIDENTIAL

ESTATES
DETACHED HOUSES
PATIO HOUSES

TOWN HOUSES

APARTMENTS
(LOW & HIGH DENSITY)

PUBLIC

INSTITUTIONAL

COMMERCIAL
RECREATIONAL

CHURCHES

MEDICAL CENTER

OPEN SPACE, SLOPES
PARKS, PATHWAYS, EASEMENTS

GOLF COURSE

RECREATIONAL CLUB

ELEMENTARY SCHOOL

JUNIOR HIGH SCHOOL

SENIOR HIGH SCHOOL

RIVER BEDS

URBAN CENTERS

PRIMARY
(Civic, Cultural, Social,
Retail, Business, Entertainment)

VILLAGE CENTERS

SECONDARY
(Services, Automotive, Loft Space,
Building, Home and Garden Supplies)

INDUSTRIAL

INDUSTRIAL

RESERVE

TRANSPORTATION

FREEWAY

MAJOR ROADS

COLLECTOR ROADS

PUBLIC TRANSIT RIGHT-OF-WAY

MAJOR ROUTES OF MULTI-PURPOSE
PATH SYSTEM

SOUTHERN PACIFIC RAILROAD

CONTOURS AT 25' INTERVALS

Figure 5-13 Valencia: Location of the city center in relation to neighborhood villages, public transportation lines and the highway system.

CASE STUDY II

Name of Project: Barbican Development

Location: City of London, England

Architects: Chamberlin, Powell and Bon

Developers: City of London Corporation

This project, which is being constructed on a site within the old limits of the City of London, is named after Barbican street, which runs across the development site from east to west. "Barbican" actually means a projecting watchtower over the gate of a fortified town, and parts of the Roman Wall which used to enclose and protect the City and which gave the street its name, have been pre-

served within this new multifunctional center. The only other original structure which has been preserved on the site is Saint Giles, an old Church of historic value which is believed to date back to the twelfth century.

The 35 acres which this project covers were previously an almost completely devastated area, having been badly damaged in World War II. The site was prepared by clearing all existing structures (both devastated and intact)—with the exception of St. Giles—and by removing all existent utility lines.

The development represents an attempt to create an urban environment which offers the best and avoids the worst aspects of urban life.

Pedestrian and automobile traffic are strictly separated, the pedestrian being moved to a "podium" level, which is about 20 feet above ground level, and all mechanized

Figure 5-14 Land usage plan of the Barbican Site.

traffic and servicing facilities being located below this platform.

A complete new system of public utility services and 23 acres of underground parking space for about 2,500 cars and access and delivery roads have been constructed.

Rising from the platform level are structures containing the following functions:

1. Residential: about 2,100 units in the form of flats, maisonettes, and houses.
2. A 200-room hostel for young people.
3. A retail area to cater to the needs of the inhabitants.
4. 300,000 square feet of office space.
5. A public school for girls—including a swimming pool.
6. New structures for the Guildhall School of Music and Drama.
7. A cultural center including: a lending library; an art gallery; a theater; a concert hall; a cinema.

All of these functions (of which a major part are already constructed) are laid out around water gardens, landscaped areas, and open public spaces, resulting in an extremely pleasant environment for the inhabitants (of which 6,000 are projected), employees, and visitors to the center.

Figure 5-15 The Barbican Development: A rendering of the main part of the development.

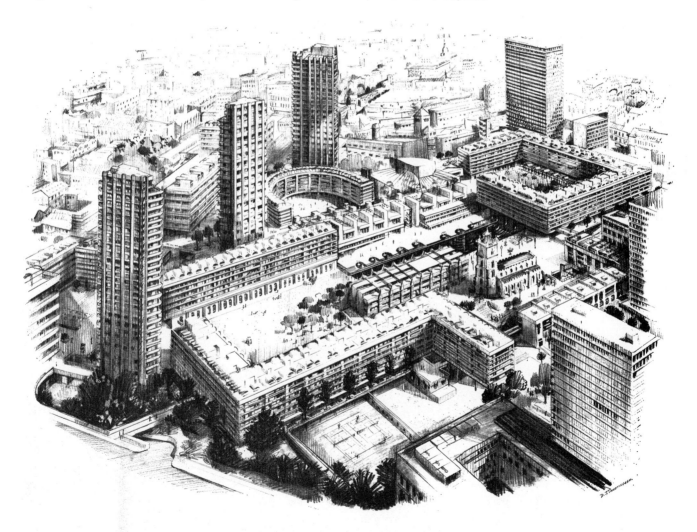

CASE STUDY III

Name of Project: Houston Center

Location: Adjoining the existing downtown area of Houston, Texas

Master Planners and Architects: William L. Pereira Associates

Project Managers: Brown and Root Inc., engineering and construction firm

Developer: Texas Eastern Transmission Corporation

This project covers 75 acres, directly adjoining the existing CBD area of the city of Houston. It is planned to include offices, hotels, retail stores, apartments, and cultural and recreational facilities, which together will provide 23,000,000 square feet of revenue-producing area. The residential function, with 5,000 units in apartments and town houses, will be strongly represented.

The project—which will be lifted off the ground—includes provision for 40,000 parking spaces. These parking facilities, together with all communication functions, will be located below the platform level, which provides a pedestrian area from which all major structures will rise. The superstructures will be clustered around plazas and promenades, some open and some enclosed. The highly developed internal transportation system will consist of elevators, escalators, moving sidewalks and high-speed "people-movers."

Figure 5-16 Houston Center: Aerial photograph of downtown Houston. Boundaries of the project are indicated by the white line.

Figure 5-17 Houston Center: Model showing the projected first phase.

Figure 5-18 Houston Center: Rendering illustrating a partial section. The base structure and the utilization of the platform above, are indicated.

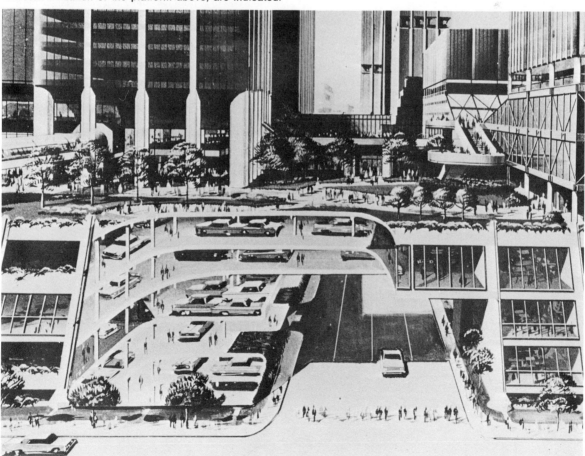

CASE STUDY IV

Name of Project: The City

Location: Orange County, California

Architect: Minoru Yamasaki and Associates

Associated Architects: Naramore, Baine Brady and Johnson

Economic Consultants: Economic Research Associates

Developer: City Management Corporation, Orange

A land area of approximately 200 acres has been set aside for a multifunctional center which will serve the large surrounding suburbanized areas, including the communities of Garden Grove, Santa Ana, and Orange.

This project has a long history which began in the late 1950s. It appears that many difficulties and problems had to be overcome and that even now the planning of the entire concept is still in a state of flux. The execution is planned to occur in a number of phases. The first phase, consisting of a large office building and a shopping center, opened in May 1970. In the meantime, a second department store has been constructed, 441 apartment units in 8 3-story buildings have been completed, a twin movie theater is under construction (as part of a projected entertainment center), and a medical clinic has been erected. A 6-story hotel is in operation.

If all the intentions of the developers and master planners can be carried out, the following functions should be strongly represented:

1. Retail shopping facilities.
2. Living quarters (1,650 units).

3. Entertainment facilities.
4. Medical facilities.
5. Office buildings (including a financial center).

The program for phase 1 is described in a document by the master planning architect as follows:

Gross built-up area = 3,810,325 square feet.
Parking space for approximately 14,700 cars. (Surface utilized for parking, which is to be partly on the ground and partly in structures, is 4,839,120 square feet.)
Separately mentioned in the program outline are the apartment buildings which during phase 1 and phase 2 will provide approximately 1,124,500 square feet of built-up area. An additional 1,700 parking spaces are foreseen for these apartment units.

On the basis of this information, it would appear that (using the terminology which I have set up and by including the apartment buildings), a total of about 6,000,000 square feet of revenue-producing area is to be provided. If one considers this figure in relation to the land area, a building density of about 0.70:1 between revenue-producing surfaces and land area results.

This signifies a higher land use than the one found in traditional unifunctional centers, but, due to the fact that parking is partly on the ground and only partly in two-level structures, it is considerably lower than that found in other multifunctional centers discussed. It can thus be stated that although The City project does constitute a multifunctional center, it cannot, probably due to the fact that it has to be developed in various phases, be characterized as an integrated multifunctional center. In this project, the tools of three-dimensional planning and the platform principle have not been employed.

Figure 5-19 "The City": Location of project.

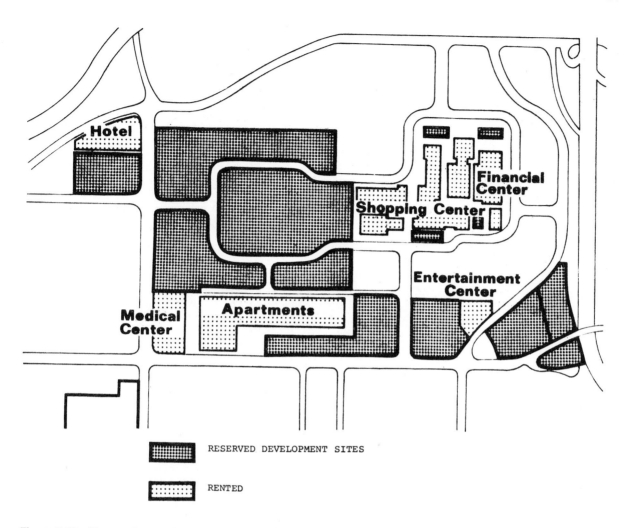

RESERVED DEVELOPMENT SITES

RENTED

Figure 5-20 Master plan of "The City."

Figure 5-21 "The City": Status of the project as at the opening of phase 1.

CASE STUDY V

Name of Project: Gateway, Newark

Location: Newark, New Jersey. A blighted area located between the Pennsylvania Railroad Station and the existing CBD area of Newark.

Architect: Gruen Associates

Developer: Gateway Urban Renewal Corporation (a joint venture of Food Fair Properties Incorporated of Philadelphia and Gene A. Genola, Asbury Park, New Jersey)

The total Gateway plan envisages the replanning of the entire urban renewal area, creating a complete air con-

ditioned environment for shoppers and office workers, and connecting the upper level of the Penn Central Railroad Station with Mulberry Street.

The elements of Gateway I and II, the first phases of this project are either completed or under construction. They are: a 30-story office building; a 10-story, 260-room hotel; retail space along a mall; and an 18-story office building. The total built-up area of these buildings is approximately 1,300,000 square feet.

In future stages, additional office buildings, apartment buildings, and other urban functions will be added.

Separation of pedestrian and automobile traffic is achieved by bridges connecting Penn Central Station with the project and the various elements of the project with each other.

Figure 5-22 Gateway, Newark: General location of the site.

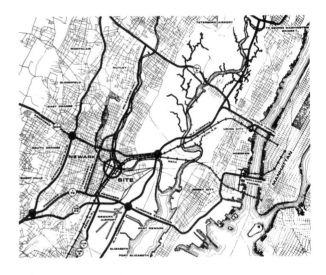

Figure 5-23 Gateway, Newark: Rendering indicating the now nearly completed first phase of the project.

CASE STUDY VI

Name of Project: Golden Gateway Center

Location: Downtown San Francisco, California

Architects: Wurster, Bernardi and Emmons; DeMars and Wells; Anshen and Allen; Skidmore, Owings and Merrill

Developer: Redevelopment Agency of the City and County of San Francisco

The area in which the project is constructed was formerly a blighted produce-marketing district. Construction is being carried out in phases which began in 1962. The project is multifunctional: it includes 2,600 living units, which are partly located in 8 high-rise buildings and partly in town houses, and office buildings, retail stores, restaurants, and sports and health facilities.

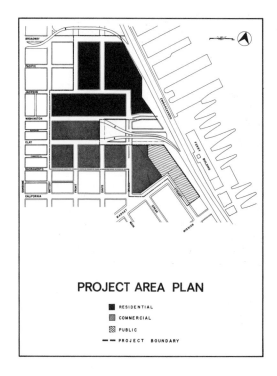

PROJECT AREA PLAN

■ RESIDENTIAL
▨ COMMERCIAL
▧ PUBLIC
-- PROJECT BOUNDARY

Figure 5-24 Golden Gateway Center: General view of the development.

CASE STUDY VII

Name of Project: Center of the New Town of Perlach

Location: In the Region of Munich, Germany

Architects & Planners: Planungsgruppe Zentrum Perlach, Berndt Lauter, Horst Mauder, Hans Maurer, Paolo Nestler, Manfred Zimmer

Developer: Neue Heimat, Bavaria

Munich is one of the fastest growing cities in the Federal Republic of Germany (population growth over the last 16 years—400,000). An attempt is being made to accommodate the population growth in a number of new towns. The largest of these towns is Perlach, constructed on a land area of approximately 2,470 acres. The project encompasses 25,000 dwelling units, for a population of about 80,000. The population density is about 91 persons per acre. Also included in the project are: a multifunctional town center, a number of multifunctional neighborhood centers, and offices, laboratories and industry, supplying about 14,300 employment places.

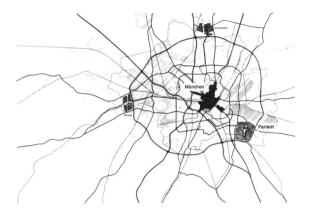

Figure 5-25 Zentrum Perlach: Location of the new town of Perlach, in relation to Munich and the region.

Figure 5-26 Zentrum Perlach: Plan of the central zone.

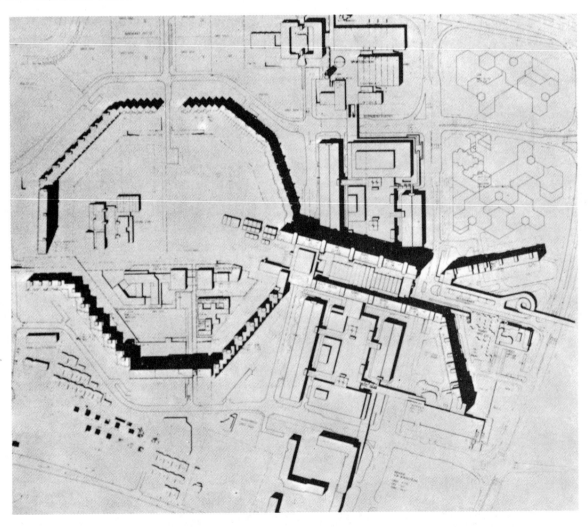

The main town center will have, especially as far as its commercial facilities are concerned, an influence area far beyond the boundaries of the new town, corresponding to a population of about 400,000. It is situated within a central urban zone, developed in a compact manner. The central core represents a multifunctional center developed according to the principles of three-dimensional planning and the platform principle. It encompasses the following functions:

1. Retail
2. Offices
3. Residences

4. Cultural, entertainment and community facilities
5. Sports facilities
6. Health and educational facilities

It also forms the hub of all transportation media (subway, regional bus terminal, parking in multilevel garages, and the crossing point of pedestrian ways establishing connections with other parts of the new town).

Status of the Project: The development of the new town is now in part completed. Plans for the central zone and the core have been developed and approved.

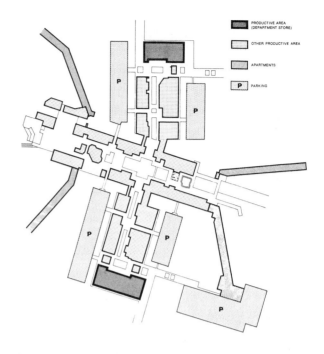

Figure 5-27   Zentrum Perlach: Plan of central zone core.

Figure 5-28   Zentrum Perlach: Model of the central zone with the central core in the foreground.

Figure 5-29   Zentrum Perlach: Section. Note: from left to right: Young people's leisure time activities center, parking garages, Art Court, restaurant and café, community center with delivery street below, storage and technical rooms. On lowest level, central hall, cinema, subway tunnel and station, and regional bus terminal. The structure shown in elevation above, contains offices, apartments and a hotel.

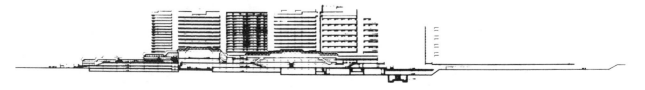

CASE STUDY VIII

Name of Project: Lancaster Square

Location: An urban renewal project in downtown Lancaster, Pennsylvania

Architects: Gruen Associates

A multifunctional development within an existing core area. Functions are: a hotel; a 900-seat theater; a department store; an apartment building with 288 units; offices; retail stores.
The major functions are arranged around a square providing a number of public amenities. Pedestrian circulation is provided on three levels overlooking the square.

Status of Project: Completed in September 1971.

Figure 5-30 Lancaster Square: View over the completed square.

Figure 5-31 Plan and section of the project of Lancaster Square.

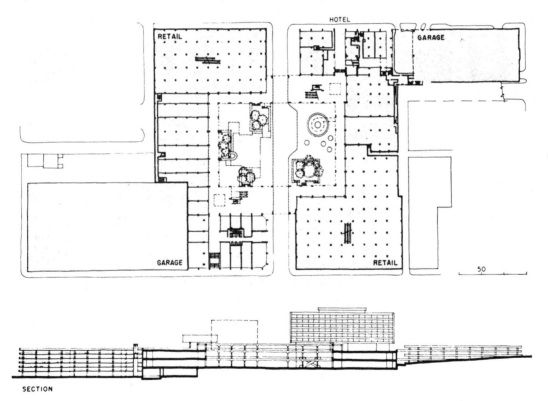

CASE STUDY IX

Name of Project: Midtown Plaza

Location: In the core area of Rochester, New York

Developer: The Midtown Holdings Corporation. (Established by two department stores: McCurdy & Company and B. Foreman Company.)

Center Team: Planners and architects, Victor Gruen Associates; planning consultant to the city, Ladislas Segoe; economic consultant, Larry Smith & Company; traffic consultants, Wilbur Smith & Associates; supervising architects for the city, Bohacket & Flynn.

Background for Planning: In 1956, the owners of two large department stores, concerned about the future of their enterprises located within a slowly deteriorating core area, called on Victor Gruen Associates for guidance. It was obvious that they had two choices. Either to follow the general trend and establish branches in outlying districts which would undoubtedly lead to further deterioration of business in the core area and finally to the closing of their central stores, or to strengthen their central locations. However, they realized that the latter could only be successful if, through a combination of public and private efforts, a revitalization of the entire core area could be achieved.

On investigating the situation, we found that a progressive city administration had, with the help of federal funds, projected and started a number of measures directed toward the revitalization of the core area. We therefore recommended discussing the individual problems of the two department stores with the municipal authorities, and to attempt to bring about an integration.

In order to win the support of the city government, it was necessary to prove that Midtown Plaza could be effectively coordinated with the overall planning concept of the city and that it could form a logical part of a future, larger central development project.

In April 1957, we submitted a schematic plan which took its departure from the already projected belt highways. This plan recommended that in order to save land, an underground garage should be constructed instead of the multilevel parking structures already projected in the vicinity of Midtown Plaza. We also stated that the Midtown Plaza project could only be executed if the city were willing to cooperate with regard to the following:

1. Immediate construction of the first link of the projected inner loop road.
2. Permission to close two traffic congested streets and to convert them into pedestrian ways.
3. Readiness of the city, to build a multilevel underground parking garage below the land owned by the developers. (The developers would put the underground rights at the disposal of the city).

Thanks to the energetic and enthusiastic assistance of the mayor, agreement was reached in a comparatively short time. (One of the additional conditions which the city insisted upon was that the public streets which would be converted into pedestrian ways would remain municipal property).

On the basis of this overall agreement, the owners decided to proceed with the project. They did this in spite of the findings of the economic consultant who pointed out that land costs within the core area were very high compared to those in suburban areas, and that it was doubtful whether one could attract tenants willing to pay an adequate rent. The economist also pointed out that there was a large supply of unrented office and store space in the core, available at low rents. He concluded that as a real estate venture, the project entailed great risks. The owners based their decision to proceed on their strong belief in the future of their city and on their wish to contribute something toward the revitalization of its core area and by so doing, assure the future of their stores.

Figure 5-32 Midtown Plaza: Plan of downtown area of Rochester, indicating loop road, projected inner loop road and projected pedestrian system within inner loop road. The location of Midtown Plaza is marked with an asterisk.

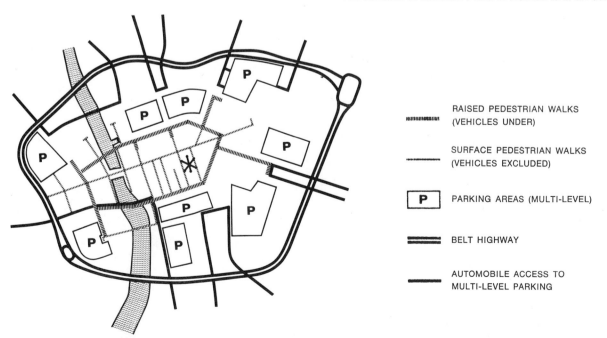

RAISED PEDESTRIAN WALKS (VEHICLES UNDER)

SURFACE PEDESTRIAN WALKS (VEHICLES EXCLUDED)

P PARKING AREAS (MULTI-LEVEL)

BELT HIGHWAY

AUTOMOBILE ACCESS TO MULTI-LEVEL PARKING

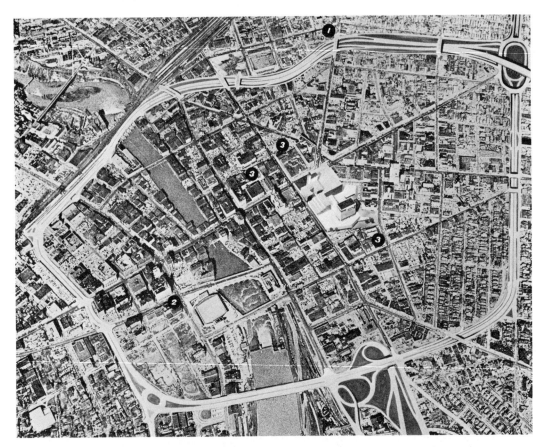

Figure 5-33 Midtown Plaza: Aerial photograph showing completed outer loop road (1), the enlarged civic center (2), municipal parking garages (3), and in the center of the picture, the Midtown Plaza.

Figure 5-34 Midtown Plaza: Plan of the typical basement floor. The garage was at that time, the first fully automatically controlled by an ultrasonic detection system. At the beginning of each lane, a sonar device located in the ceiling, emits sound waves and registers passage of each car, transmitting this information to central control where it is stored in a computer. Thus all cars entering or leaving the garage are counted. A device activates lighted traffic signals which inform motorists of nearest available space and the quickest route to it. This eliminates all searching and recirculation by motorists.

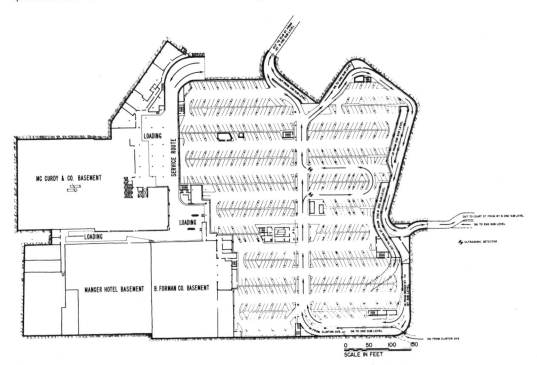

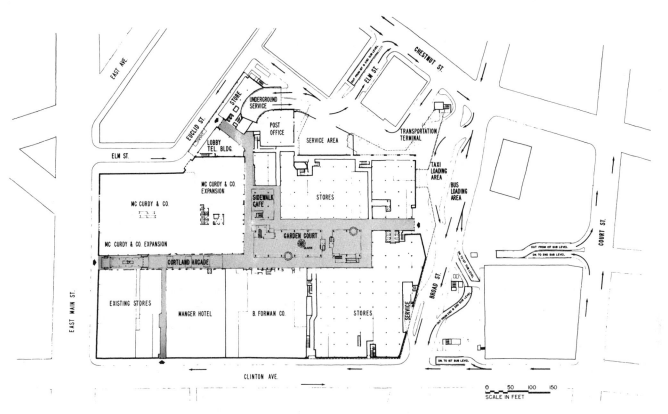

Figure 5-35 Midtown Plaza: Plan of the lower activity area (plan for upper activity area is similar).

Figure 5-36 Midtown Plaza: Plan of major superstructures rising from the roof of the platform level. (Not indicated are the upper floors of the two large department stores and the upper floors of the existing hotel and office building.)

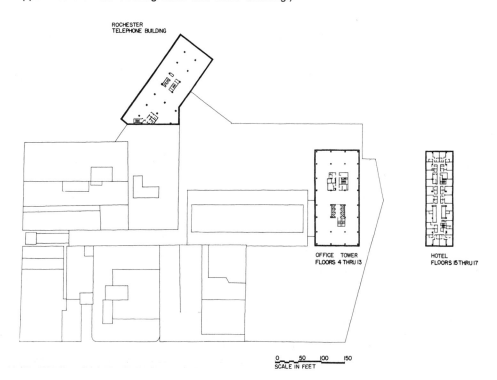

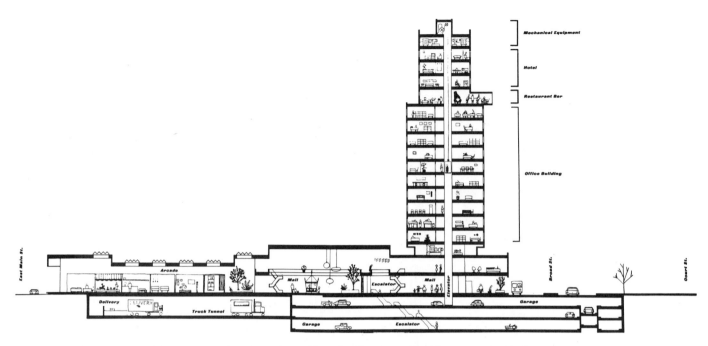

Figure 5-37 Midtown Plaza: A schematic section showing use of subterranean levels for garages, delivery roads, loading facilities and storage. Two levels of the base structure above ground level for retail and other related facilities, surrounding a spacious garden court. From the roof of the base structure, rise superstructures, of which only one is shown on this section. This building contains, on the lower levels, offices, on the middle level, a public restaurant and bar, on the upper levels, a hotel, and on the top level, mechanical equipment.

Figure 5-38 Midtown Plaza: Three-dimensional chart listing functions and their locations on various levels.

Midtown Plaza	Description	BASE STRUCTURE					SUPER-STRUCTURES LEVELS 1-17	Total
		Sublevels			Ground Levels			
		3	2	1	Lower Level	Upper Level		
R REVENUE PRODUCING BUILDING AREAS	MAJOR RETAIL			8,260 m2 89,000 sq. ft.	9,660 m2 104,000 sq. ft.	9,660 m2 104,000 sq. ft.	32,790 m2 353,000 sq. ft.	60,370 m2 650,000 sq. ft.
	SMALLER RETAIL				12,540 m2 135,000 sq. ft.	11,610 m2 125,000 sq. ft.		24,150 m2 260,000 sq. ft.
	OFFICES			920 m2 10,000 sq. ft.	460 m2 5,000 sq. ft.	1,850 m2 20,000 sq. ft.	28,330 m2 305,000 sq. ft.	31,560 m2 340,000 sq. ft.
	HOTEL AND RESTAURANTS			2,570 m2 27,750 sq. ft.	2,570 m2 27,750 sq. ft.	2,570 m2 27,750 sq. ft.	19,950 m2 214,750 sq. ft.	27,660 m2 298,000 sq. ft.
SUBTOTAL				11,750 m2 126,750 sq. ft.	25,230 m2 271,750 sq. ft.	25,690 m2 276,750 sq. ft.	81,070 m2 872,750 sq. ft.	143,740 m2 1,548,000 sq. ft.
I INCOME PRODUCING BUILDING AREAS	GARAGES	23,680 m2 255,000 sq. ft.	23,680 m2 255,000 sq. ft.	26,940 m2 290,000 sq. ft.				74,300 m2 800,000 sq. ft.
SUBTOTAL		23,680 m2 255,000 sq. ft.	23,680 m2 255,000 sq. ft.	26,940 m2 290,000 sq. ft.				74,300 m2 800,000 sq. ft.
N NON-PRODUCTIVE BUILDING AREAS	PEDESTRIAN AREAS				4,180 m2 45,000 sq. ft.	2,780 m2 30,000 sq. ft.		6,960 m2 75,000 sq. ft.
	TECHNICAL ROOMS		1,390 m2 15,000 sq. ft.				1,110 m2 12,000 sq. ft.	2,500 m2 27,000 sq. ft.
SUBTOTAL			1,390 m2 15,000 sq. ft.		4,180 m2 45,000 sq. ft.	2,780 m2 30,000 sq. ft.	1,110 m2 12,000 sq. ft.	9,460 m2 102,000 sq. ft.
TOTAL	BUILT-UP AREA	23,680 m2 255,000 sq. ft.	25,070 m2 270,000 sq. ft.	38,690 m2 416,750 sq. ft.	29,410 m2 316,750 sq. ft.	28,470 m2 306,750 sq. ft.	82,180 m2 884,750 sq. ft.	227,500 m2 2,450,000 sq. ft.

The superior motivational quality of the developer led to the decision to establish an efficient center team under the guidance of the architects. Victor Gruen Associates not only took care of master planning and architectural and engineering design for the developer, but also for the city. They also planned the enlargement and remodeling of the two department stores.

Planning Approach: Having assured coordination with all other elements of revitalization planning with the city authorities, a project site was determined. This site was partly occupied by minor structures (warehouses, garages, repair shops, etc.) which had to be acquired by the developer, and partly by major buildings; the two department stores, a hotel, and an office structure. These buildings were integrated into the overall development plan.

For the execution of the plan, three dimensional planning, multipurpose land usage and the platform principle were employed. Those functions which benefit from conditions of controlled light and air were combined into a base structure consisting of three subterranean levels containing a garage with space for 2,000 cars, mechanical facilities, delivery roads, and loading docks, basement sales areas for the two department stores, and storage areas, and two levels above ground which are utilized for retail sales, a regional bus terminal, restaurants, cafés,

banks, private schools, service enterprises, a post office, and also for the lobbies of office and hotel buildings.

Within the base structure (which contains a total built up area of 1,460,000 square feet) all urban functions are arranged around a large garden court which is accessible from the city street system by arcades.

From the base structure rise superstructures with a combined built up area of 980,000 square feet, which contain offices, hotel facilities, the upper floors of the department stores and the upper floors of the previously existing buildings.

Although not containing residential facilities, Midtown Plaza does constitute a multifunctional center. As far as cultural and entertainment facilities are concerned, these are served by the events which are held in the garden court. This public space has become, de facto, the town square, and has held, on occasion, more than 10,000 people. It is used regularly for symphony concerts, balls, art exhibitions, festivals, and political meetings. Its varied usage is encouraged by the fact that it provides full weather protection and by its festive character, created by tree groups, flower beds, lighting and works of art. One of the great attractions of the garden court is the centrally located "Clock of the Nations" which, on its 12 revolving arms, carries cylindrical forms which on the strike of each

Figure 5-39 Midtown Plaza: An exterior view as seen from Broad Street. On the right of the photograph, the bus terminal.

Figure 5-40   Midtown Plaza: The garden court during a normal shopping day, at a time when the "Clock of the Nations" is in operation.

hour, open to display dancing puppets. Though some purists have smiled about this romantic feature, it has lodged itself so firmly in the hearts of the citizens that on the rare occasions when it is not functioning, the news is related in the Rochester newspapers. This clock which caused many worries and considerable expense, has proved convincingly that it is desirable to give humanist features the same consideration which is given to practical aspects.

Status of Project: Since its opening in 1962, Midtown Plaza has operated with surprising success. All provided space, which, in contrast to the space in the old existing buildings, could offer prestige and modern amenities, was rented during construction time. The municipal program has progressed. The outer loop road is completed, other road improvements have been made and the efficiency of the public transportation system has been increased. The existing civic center has been greatly enlarged and a new congress hall has been constructed. Though the plan for the revitalization of the entire area and for the creation of additional pedestrian areas has not yet been carried out, the opening of Midtown Plaza drastically changed the image of the city core and after 25 years of downgrading,

the new project became a symbol of hope and optimism. The city core has regained its role as a major attraction point of the whole region. This change brought about practical repercussions. A large industrial firm which had contemplated constructing a headquarters building in the suburbs, revised its plans and constructed a handsome headquarter building adjacent and connected to Midtown Plaza. Other construction developed around Midtown Plaza.

This renaissance of building activity after 25 years stagnation is significant evidence to the fact that one courageous act can start a chain of reaction of unexpected scope. It is also proud testimony to the courage of the owners and the city government.

Figure 5-41 Midtown Plaza: Map showing the location of nine new buildings, nine modernized, and four enlarged structures. Most important are: 30 story office headquarter building for Xerox, completed in 1968, 12 story office building for Blue Cross, completed in 1970, a 13 story Security Trust Bank and office building completed in 1965, a 20 story Marine Midland Bank and office building completed in 1970, a 240 room hotel with restaurant, completed in 1964.

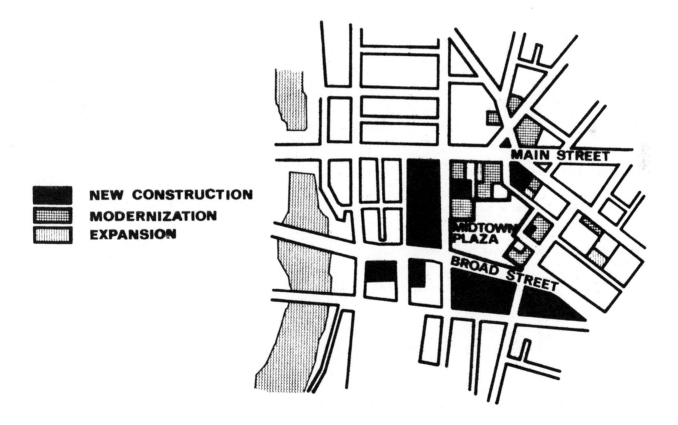

NEW CONSTRUCTION
MODERNIZATION
EXPANSION

CASE STUDY X

Name of Project: Tête Défense

Location: Paris, France. Part of the La Défense development, to the west of Paris. Situated at a central point between zones A and B of the La Défense project.

Developer: EPAD (Etablissement Public pour l'Aménagement de la Défense)

Planning Team: Planners and architects, Victor Gruen Planning and Architecture; technical staff of EPAD; transportational consultants, Freeman, Fox, Wilbur Smith; economic consultants, Larry Smith and Company.

Background for Planning: The Tête Défense project, although in itself of impressive size, must be regarded as an

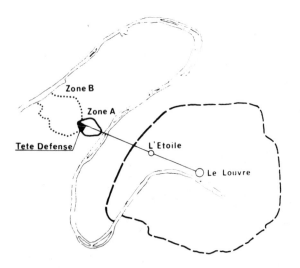

Figure 5-42 Tête Défense: Location of project La Défense zones A and B in relation to the city boundaries of Paris, the Seine, Le Louvre, and the Etoile. The location of the project Tête Défense is marked in black.

Figure 5-43 Tête Défense: Schematic section clarifying names of levels.

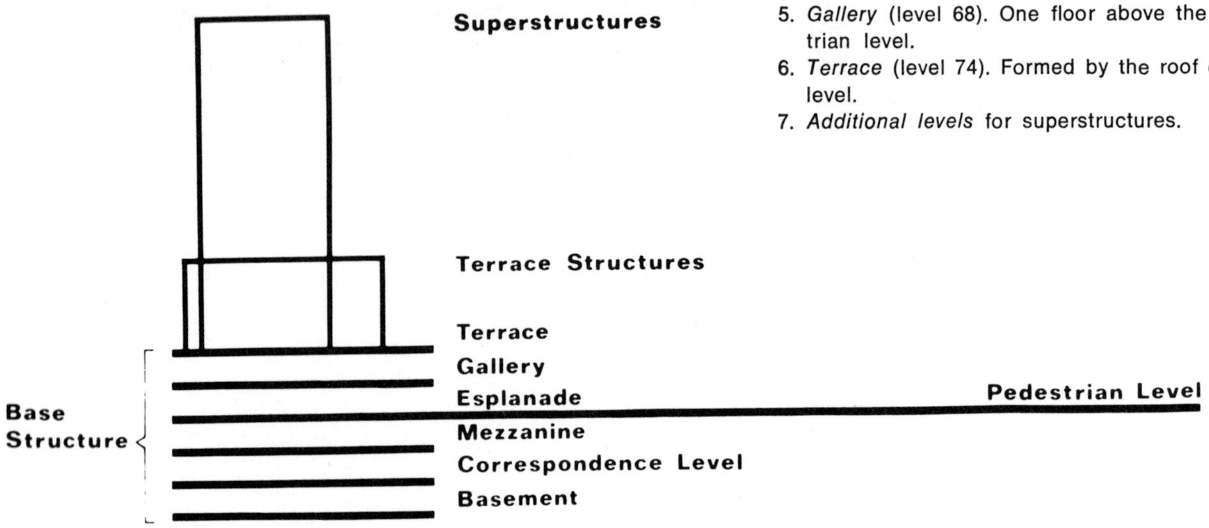

integral part of the entire undertaking of the La Défense development.

The infrastructure of zone A of the La Défense development is completely planned and to the largest degree constructed. Of the buildings projected for this zone, 60 percent have been constructed.

The site of the Tête Défense project is particularly favored in respect to accessibility by public and private transportation. Within the site there are stations of the regional metro network, the commuter railroad system, the urban metro system, and local bus routes. There is also a regional bus terminal. Individual traffic will be served by a system of freeway-type roads, partly underground, of which some are already constructed and the remainder projected.

Planning Goals: Because of its strategic location, the land is to be intensively utilized as a multifunctional center. Functions served will be shopping facilities, offices, one or two large hotels, cultural and entertainment functions and all necessary service amenities such as parking garages, delivery roads, and technical services, both for the above-mentioned urban functions and for the already existing CNIT exhibition hall.

Residential functions which are represented in zone A and planned to an even higher degree for zone B, are not projected for the Tête Défense area.

As configuration and continuity of the site differ from level to level, the underground levels being cut by transportation routes and utility lines, it was necessary to plan the location of functions in accordance to their need for intimate communication with each other. Only those functions which could operate without contiguity could be placed on lower levels. Above the projected main pedestrian level, the site is contiguous.

The following terminology was established for the various levels:

1. *Basement* (level 46)
2. *Correspondence* (level 51). The main arrival points of all public transportation are situated on this level.
3. *Mezzanine* (level 56.75). Accessible from local bus and taxi routes.
4. *Esplanade* (level 62). Pedestrian circulation and accessory pedestrian transportation will be available on this level.
5. *Gallery* (level 68). One floor above the main pedestrian level.
6. *Terrace* (level 74). Formed by the roof of the gallery level.
7. *Additional levels* for superstructures.

Superstructures

Terrace Structures

Terrace
Gallery
Esplanade   **Pedestrian Level**
Base Structure < Mezzanine
Correspondence Level
Basement

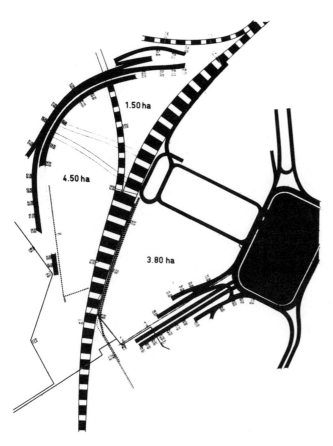

Figure 5-44 Tête Défense: levels 56.75 to 62. Land available on these levels, which are typical of the lower levels, is cut into small parcels by roads and railroads.

Figure 5-45 Tête Défense: Above level 62, the site appears for the first time, undivided, with a total surface of 27.6 acres.

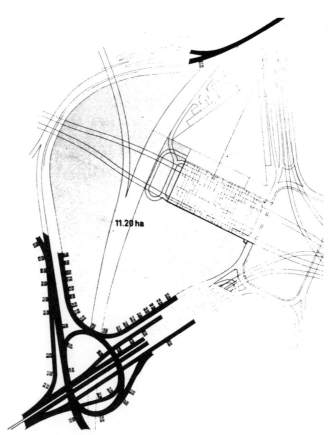

The basement, correspondence, mezzanine, esplanade and gallery together form the base structure. The terrace is used for cultural, entertainment and leisure time amenities both enclosed and open air. Levels above the terrace are utilized for high-rise buildings serving private and public administration and hotels.

The three-dimensional chart (Figure 5-55), shows in the last column on the right, the area provided for each function, and along the various horizontal columns, the location of functions. Approximately 5,700,000 square feet of revenue-producing enclosed space and about 200,000 square feet of revenue-producing open space (the latter not shown on the chart) are provided. Further, approximately 3,200,-000 square feet of income-producing space (parking) is available, and there is approximately 790,000 square feet of nonproductive space. This results in a total built-up area of approximately 9,700,000 square feet which produces the following densities: revenue-producing space to land, 5:1, revenue-producing and income-producing space to land, 8:1, revenue and income-producing and nonproductive space to land, 10:1.

It is due to the outstanding quality of accessibility by public transportation and pedestrian ways that these exceptionally high densities could be achieved. In spite of these high densities, public areas in the base structure are very generously dimensioned and the superstructures are so arranged as to permit maximum access to natural light and air and to offer attractive vistas.

Parking: The amount of parking to be provided was calculated on the basis of the open traffic capacity of the immediate and regional road network. This provision of parking space was also influenced by the fact that the multifunctional character of the center with the consequential varying peak hours of the different functions, would permit parking to be used by a number of functions at different times.

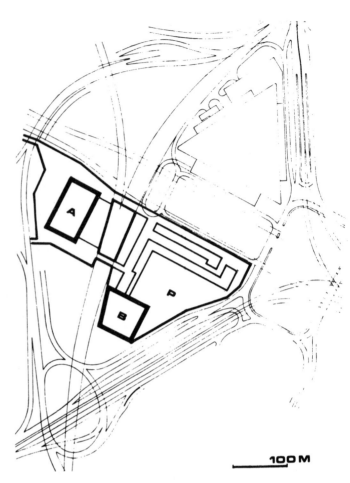

100 M

Figure 5-46 Tête Défense: Schematic plan of basement level containing storage facilities of department stores A and B and of tenant stores and parking area for employees. (Note: the triangular building is the existing CNIT exhibition hall.)

Figure 5-47 Tête Défense: Schematic section parallel to the esplanade. On the right hand side, the relation of parking decks to activity levels is indicated.

Figure 5-48 Tête Défense: Cross section. On the right hand side, section through the existing exhibition building of the CNIT, in the center, station of the regional metro. On the left hand side, the relation of parking decks to activity levels is illustrated.

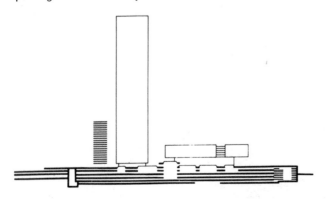

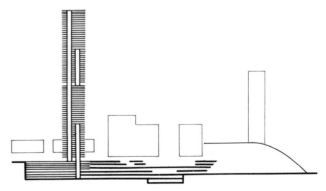

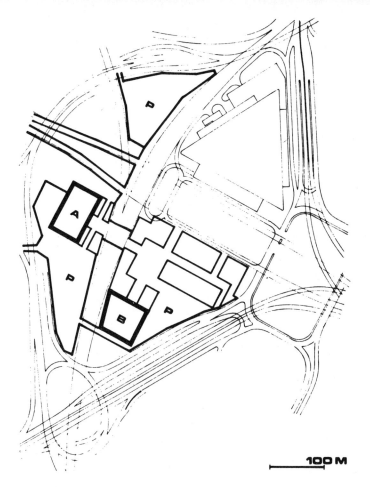

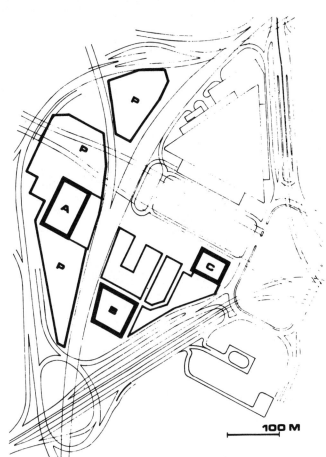

Figure 5-49 Tête Défense: Correspondence level containing retail sales facilities, parking for customers, and for office employees (upper edge of plan).

Figure 5-50 Tête Défense: Mezzanine. Sales and storage areas of department stores A, B, and C, and of tenant stores, and parking decks.

Figure 5-51 Tête Défense: Esplanade. Sales areas of department stores A, B and C, and of tenant stores, parking decks, and (shown in black) service areas of hotel.

Figure 5-52 Tête Défense: Gallery. Sales area of department stores, A, B, and C, and of tenant stores, entrance hall of hotel (in black), and parking areas.

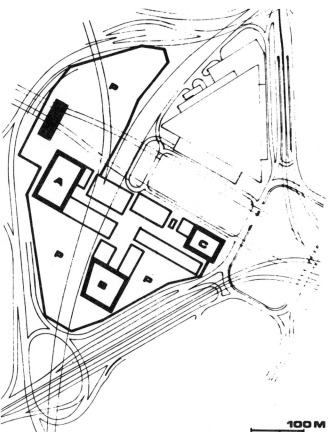

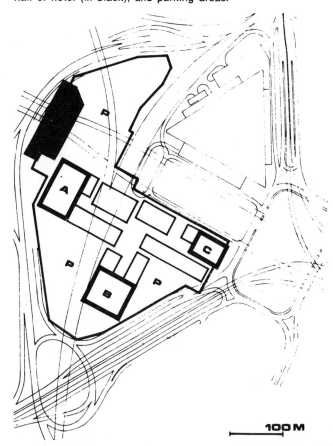

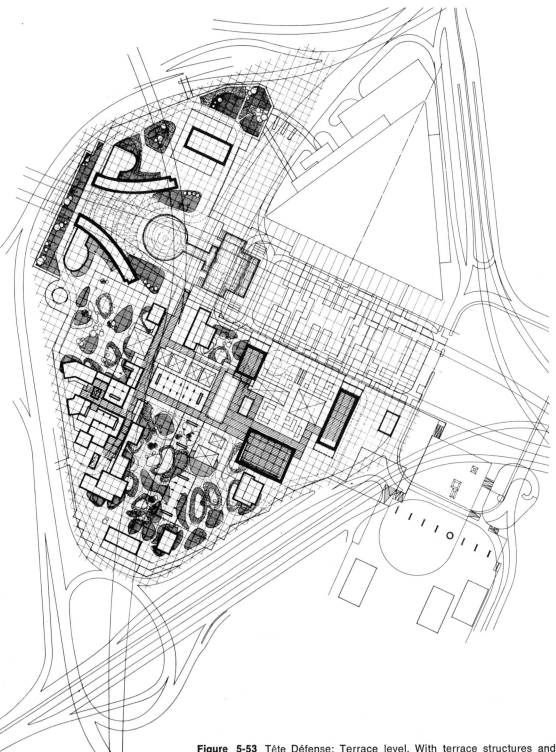

Figure 5-53 Tête Défense: Terrace level. With terrace structures and the base of super-structures. Terrace structures contain theaters, restaurants, sports facilities and entertainment. The open terrace area is used for a botanical garden, a zoological garden, green areas, open air eating facilities. Within the pedestrian esplanade are fountains and ponds.

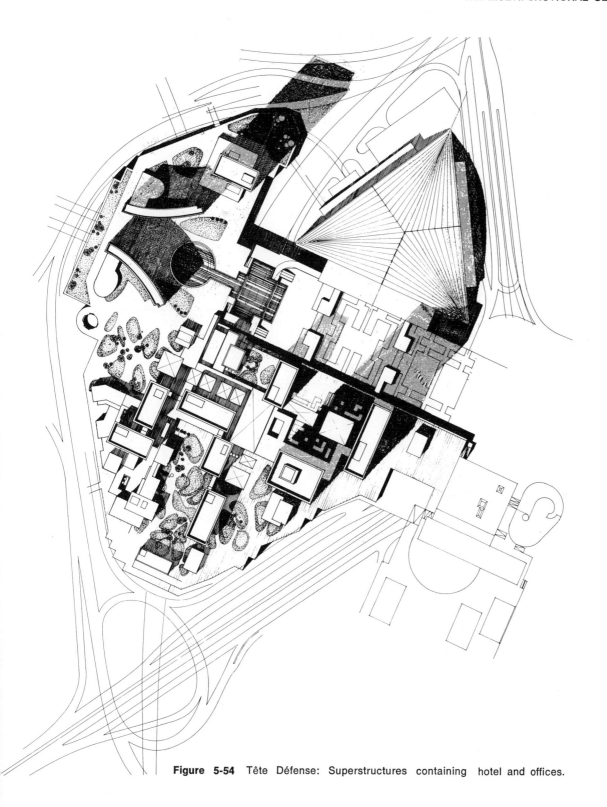

Figure 5-54 Tête Défense: Superstructures containing hotel and offices.

Tête Défense	Description	BASE STRUCTURE					TERRACE LEVEL	SUPER-STRUCTURES	Total
		Sublevels			Above Ground				
		Basement 3	Correspondence (Public Transport. Distr. Level) 2	Mezzanine 1	Esplanade Lower Level	Gallery Upper Level			
R REVENUE PRODUCING BUILDING AREAS	MAJOR RETAIL	11,400 m2 122,700 sq. ft.	11,400 m2 122,700 sq. ft.	14,470 m2 155,700 sq. ft.	14,470 m2 155,700 sq. ft.	14,980 m2 161,200 sq. ft.	11,910 m2 128,200 sq. ft.		78,630 m2 846,200 sq. ft.
	SMALLER RETAIL	11,340 m2 122,000 sq. ft.	16,890 m2 181,800 sq. ft.	9,480 m2 102,000 sq. ft.	16,360 m2 176,100 sq. ft.	15,640 m2 168,300 sq. ft.			69,710 m2 750,200 sq. ft.
	VITRINES		1,600 m2 17,200 sq. ft.		1,020 m2 10,900 sq. ft.				2,620 m2 28,100 sq. ft.
	CULTURAL, RECREATIONAL, SPORTS FUNCTIONS						14,800 m2 159,300 sq. ft.		14,800 m2 159,300 sq. ft.
	OFFICES							290,000 m2 3,121,600 sq. ft.	290,000 m2 3,121,600 sq. ft.
	HOTEL	450 m2 4,800 sq. ft.	390 m2 4,100 sq. ft.	1,730 m2 18,600 sq. ft.	1,730 m2 18,600 sq. ft.	7,600 m2 81,800 sq. ft.	1,540 m2 16,500 sq. ft.	52,500 m2 565,100 sq. ft.	65,940 m2 709,500 sq. ft.
	SERVICES			7,460 m2 80,300 sq. ft.					7,460 m2 80,300 sq. ft.
SUBTOTAL		23,190 m2 249,500 sq. ft.	30,280 m2 325,800 sq. ft.	33,140 m2 356,600 sq. ft.	33,580 m2 361,300 sq. ft.	38,220 m2 411,300 sq. ft.	28,250 m2 304,000 sq. ft.	342,500 m2 3,686,700 sq. ft.	529,160 m2 5,695,200 sq. ft.
I INCOME PRODUCING BUILDING AREAS	GARAGES	31,760 m2 341,800 sq. ft.	29,400 m2 316,400 sq. ft.	49,350 m2 531,200 sq. ft.	84,250 m2 906,800 sq. ft.	99,000 m2 1,065,600 sq. ft.			293,760 m2 3,161,800 sq. ft.
SUBTOTAL		31,760 m2 341,800 sq. ft.	29,400 m2 316,400 sq. ft.	49,350 m2 531,200 sq. ft.	84,250 m2 906,800 sq. ft.	99,000 m2 1,065,600 sq. ft.			293,760 m2 3,161,800 sq. ft.
N NON-PRODUCTIVE BUILDING AREAS	PEDESTRIAN AREAS		8,010 m2 86,200 sq. ft.	1,560 m2 16,700 sq. ft.	7,400 m2 79,600 sq. ft.	8,300 m2 89,300 sq. ft.			25,270 m2 271,800 sq. ft.
	SERVICE AREAS	2,260 m2 24,300 sq. ft.	1,350 m2 14,500 sq. ft.	820 m2 8,800 sq. ft.	1,460 m2 15,700 sq. ft.	1,460 m2 15,700 sq. ft.			7,350 m2 79,000 sq. ft.
	TECHNICAL ROOMS	16,480 m2 177,300 sq. ft.	1,890 m2 20,300 sq. ft.	16,700 m2 179,700 sq. ft.	5,300 m2 57,000 sq. ft.	770 m2 8,200 sq. ft.			41,140 m2 442,500 sq. ft.
SUBTOTAL		18,740 m2 201,600 sq. ft.	11,250 m2 121,000 sq. ft.	19,080 m2 205,200 sq. ft.	14,160 m2 152,300 sq. ft.	10,530 m2 113,200 sq. ft.			73,760 m2 793,300 sq. ft.
TOTAL	BUILT-UP AREA	73,690 m2 792,900 sq. ft.	70,930 m2 763,200 sq. ft.	101,570 m2 1,093,000 sq. ft.	131,990 m2 1,420,400 sq. ft.	147,750 m2 1,590,100 sq. ft.	28,250 m2 304,000 sq. ft.	342,500 m2 3,686,700 sq. ft.	896,680 m2 9,650,300 sq. ft.

Figure 5-55 Tête Défense: Three dimensional chart listing functions and their locations on various levels.

Recommendations for Implementation: The master planning document which was completed in four months also contained recommendations for implementation. It stated that the project had to be treated as an integrated megastructure, and therefore the overall development of the total structure should be undertaken by the developer (EPAD) who should have complete control over planning, construction and operation. This complex task could only be mastered by an efficient center team under the leadership of EPAD and a single architect/planner. Individual elements of the megastructure could be constructed by a number of individual sub-developers, under the condition that the overall plan was respected.

It was recommended that in order to achieve full control, building rights should not be sold as is usual in France,but rather leased on a long term basis. The entire base structure should be built in one phase and must contain all structural and mechanical elements necessary for terrace structures and superstructures which could then be constructed in a number of phases.

Status of Project: In January, 1970, I was informed by the President of EPAD, Mr. Jean Millier, that our master plan was in principle accepted and that interested sub-developers were available, even beyond the framework of the master plan. At that time, Mr. Millier expressed the intention of entrusting us with the planning task which would proceed in close cooperation with the technical staff of EPAD and engineering organizations.

Shortly thereafter however, the largest potential subdeveloper who was willing to construct all superstructures, expressed the wish that his own architect (I.M.Pei and Partners of New York) participate in the planning effort. Submitting to this wish, Mr. Millier asked us to cooperate with I.M.Pei and Partners in the planning effort, stipulating that we should be mostly concerned with the base structure, and I.M.Pei and Partners with the superstructures.

In spite of best efforts on both sides, this division of planning responsibility was not successful. At the time of writing (April 1972) disagreements caused partly by the divergent wishes of the clients for the office functions, and partly by a different architectural philosophy, have not been settled. A decision by the developer which would permit construction work to commence is still awaited, however, it seems certain that, due to its strategic position, the Tête Défense project will be implemented in one form or another.

Figure 5-56 Tête Défense: Photograph of the model. From left to right: exhibit hall of the CNIT, one of the office buildings, the two curved buildings of the hotel, various terrace structures and smaller office buildings, in the background, high office structures, in the foreground, the loop road system.

CASE STUDY XI

Name of Project: Center Glatt

Location: In the region of Zurich, Switzerland

Developer: AG Einkaufszentrum Glatt-Zürich. (Stockholders are three large merchandising concerns: Jelmoli AG, Globus Department Store, and Migros Organization).

Center Team: Planning and architecture: Victor Gruen, Planning and Architecture AG; Engineering: Elektrowatt Engineering Services Ltd. The planning staffs of the three participating merchandising organizations.

Background for Planning: Zurich, the largest Swiss city, is experiencing a dynamic population and economic growth, and the city core, which is restricted in size both by natural boundaries and historic characteristics, can no longer serve all needs and desires of a steadily growing population.

Zurich's main role is to serve as an international financial and business center. This has led to the tendency of continuous expansion of the tertiary sector of the economy in the city center, while pushing out residential and other non-commercial functions.

Increasingly high living standards and widespread automobile ownership have encouraged the spreading of residential areas. To counteract automobile domination, impressive improvements in public transportation have been planned, but implementation will take considerable time.

The three founding retail enterprises based their decision to plan and construct a center at a strategic point within the region on the fact that their existing facilities in the core could not be further enlarged, and could no longer cope with the demands of an increasingly large and affluent population.

The site was purchased in 1965 but implementation of the undertaking had to await the completion of public works which would assure accessibility. It was also necessary to reach agreement with developers of surrounding land parcels with regard to the creation of a pathway system connecting the new center with the surrounding residential areas and the nearby town of Wallisellen which is the location of an important commuter railroad station.

The site, which actually represents an island surrounded by existing or projected roads, covers an area of only 5.6 acres. In addition, its utilization is restricted by a height limit imposed due to aviation needs, and by a density restriction which determines that the total built-up area must be kept within a ratio to the open land of 1.4:1. This restriction is however eased by the fact that storage basements, technical rooms, and the air-raid shelter (which is a legal necessity in Switzerland) are not considered as built-up area. It was later agreed that parking garages could also be added to this list of exceptions.

Figure 5-57 Center Glatt: Zurich and its region, indicating the location of Center Glatt in relation to the city core of Zurich.

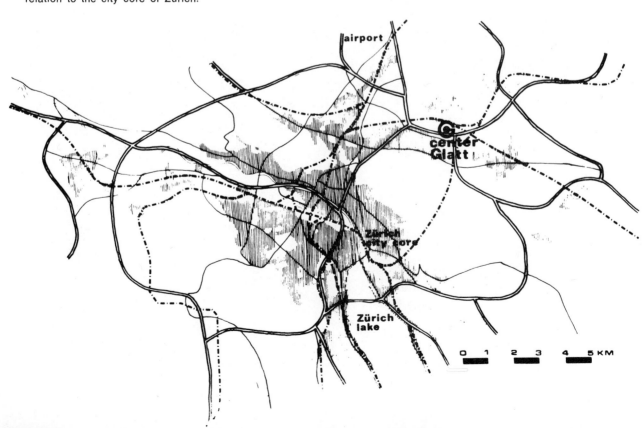

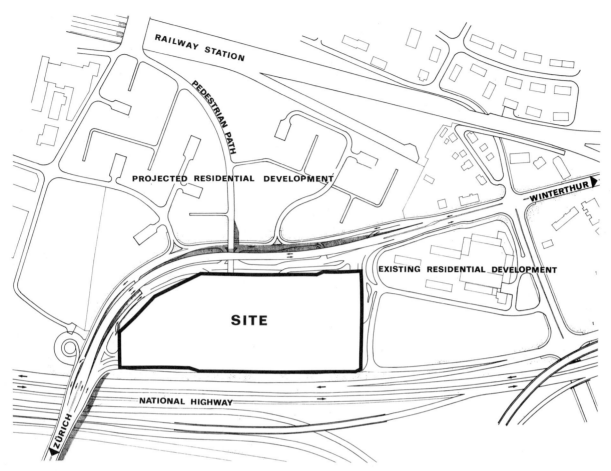

Figure 5-58 Center Glatt: Site Plan. The site of 13.1 acres actually constitutes a traffic island between major roadways. Indicated is the location of the community of Wallisellen and its railroad station which is important for commuter traffic. Between the community of Wallisellen and the location of the center, lies an area for which a major housing development is projected. The railroad station and the center are connected by a pathway system for pedestrians, bicycles, and electric minibuses.

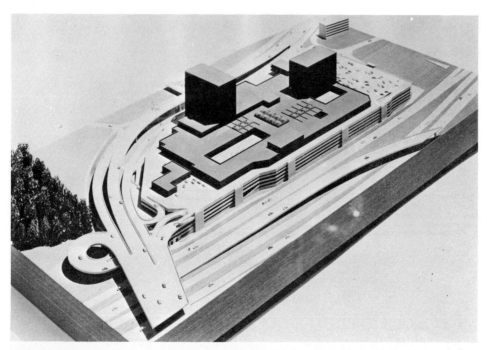

Figure 5-59 Model of Center Glatt.

Center Glatt	Description	BASE STRUCTURE				TERRACE LEVEL	SUPER-STRUCTURES LEVELS 1-9	Total
		Sublevels		Above Ground				
		2	1	Lower Level	Upper Level			
R REVENUE PRODUCING BUILDING AREAS	MAJOR RETAIL	10,615 m2 114,200 sq. ft.	10,651 m2 114,200 sq. ft.	10,168 m2 109,400 sq. ft.		4,008 m2 43,100 sq. ft.	3,025 m2 32,500 sq. ft.	38,467 m2 413,400 sq. ft.
	SMALLER RETAIL	4,099 m2 44,100 sq. ft.	4,218 m2 45,400 sq. ft.	4,056 m2 43,600 sq. ft.		9,874 m2 106,200 sq. ft.	996 m2 10,700 sq. ft.	23,243 m2 250,000 sq. ft.
	SERVICES			913 m2 9,800 sq. ft.	726 m2 7,800 sq. ft.			1,639 m2 17,600 sq. ft.
	OFFICES						13,429 m2 144,500 sq. ft.	13,429 m2 144,500 sq. ft.
	DWELLINGS						598 m2 6,400 sq. ft.	598 m2 6,400 sq. ft.
SUBTOTAL		14,714 m2 158,300 sq. ft.	15,782 m2 169,400 sq. ft.	14,950 m2 160,800 sq. ft.		13,882 m2 149,300 sq. ft.	18,048 m2 194,100 sq. ft.	77,376 m2 831,900 sq. ft.
I INCOME PRODUCING BUILDING AREAS	GARAGES	8,158 m2 87,800 sq. ft.	22,360 m2 240,600 sq. ft.	40,571 m2 436,700 sq. ft.	41,431 m2 445,900 sq. ft.			112,520 m2 1,211,000 sq. ft.
SUBTOTAL		8,158 m2 87,800 sq. ft.	22,360 m2 240,600 sq. ft.	40,571 m2 436,700 sq. ft.	41,432 m2 445,900 sq. ft.			112,520 m2 1,211,000 sq. ft.
N NON-PRODUCTIVE BUILDING AREAS	TECHNICAL ROOMS	12,956 m2 139,400 sq. ft.	2,023 m2 21,700 sq. ft.	562 m2 6,000 sq. ft.	562 m2 6,000 sq. ft.	553 m2 5,900 sq. ft.	3,131 m2 33,700 sq. ft.	19,787 m2 212,700 sq. ft.
	SERVICE CORES, TOILETS, ADMINISTRATION	261 m2 2,800 sq. ft.	1,773 m2 19,000 sq. ft.	1,127 m2 12,100 sq. ft.	1,467 m2 15,700 sq. ft.	780 m2 8,300 sq. ft.	3,211 m2 34,500 sq. ft.	8,619 m2 92,400 sq. ft.
	PEDESTRIAN AREAS (CLIMATIZED)			2,854 m2 30,700 sq. ft.	1,908 m2 20,500 sq. ft.	1,282 m2 13,700 sq. ft.		6,044 m2 64,900 sq. ft.
	PEDESTRIAN AREAS (NON-CLIMATIZED)			564 m2 6,000 sq. ft.	268 m2 2,800 sq. ft.			832 m2 8,800 sq. ft.
	DELIVERY ROAD		3,671 m2 39,500 sq. ft.					3,671 m2 39,500 sq. ft.
	AIR-RAID SHELTER	3,384 m2 36,400 sq. ft.						3,384 m2 36,400 sq. ft.
SUBTOTAL		16,601 m2 178,600 sq. ft.	7,467 m2 80,200 sq. ft.	5,107 m2 54,800 sq. ft.	4,205 m2 45,000 sq. ft.	2,615 m2 27,900 sq. ft.	6,342 m2 68,200 sq. ft.	42,337 m2 454,700 sq. ft.
TOTAL	BUILT-UP AREA	24,759 m2 266,400 sq. ft.	44,541 m2 479,100 sq. ft.	61,460 m2 660,900 sq. ft.	60,586 m2 651,700 sq. ft.	16,497 m2 177,200 sq. ft.	24,390 m2 262,300 sq. ft.	232,233 m2 2,497,600 sq. ft.

Figure 5-60 Center Glatt: Three-dimensional chart listing functions and their locations on various levels.

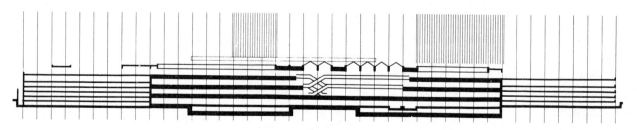

Figure 5-61 Center Glatt: Longitudinal section showing relationship of parking decks to activity levels.

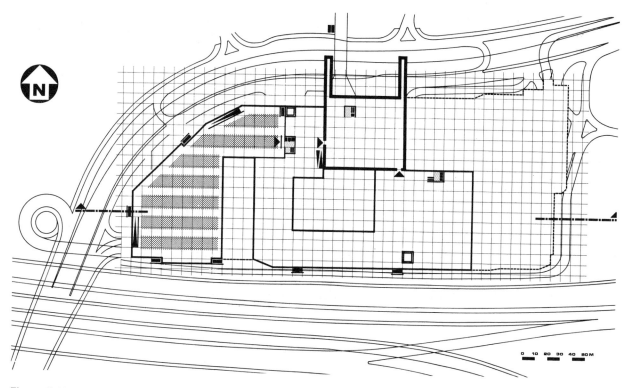

Figure 5-62 Center Glatt: Plan of 2nd basement containing air raid shelter and employees parking.

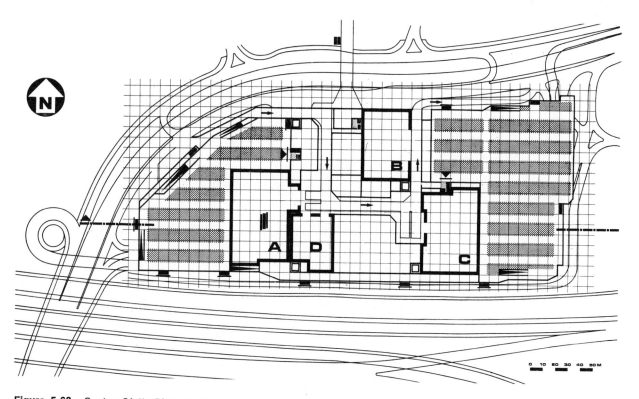

Figure 5-63 Center Glatt: Plan of first basement containing sales and storage areas of retail establishments, delivery road, and deck parking.

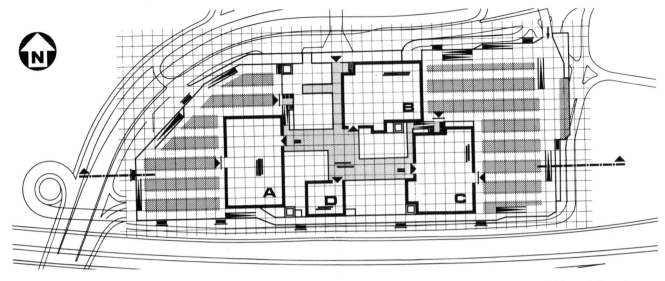

Figure 5-64 Center Glatt: Plan of lower sales level containing sales activities of department stores A, B, and C, junior department store D, tenant stores. Indicated on the upper edge, the bus station and deck parking.

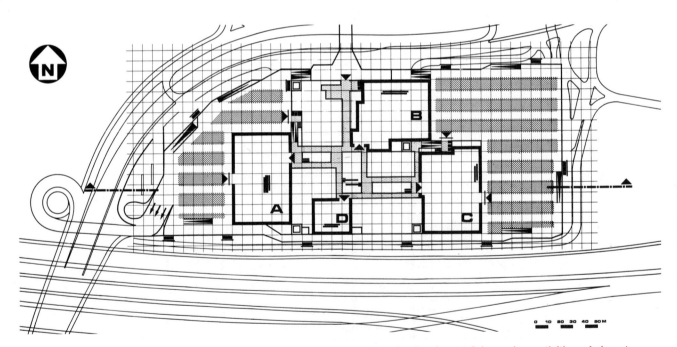

Figure 5-65 Center Glatt: Plan of upper sales level containing sales activities of department stores A, B and C and junior department store D, and of tenant stores. On the upper edge is a bridge connecting to the footpath system. On both sides are parking decks.

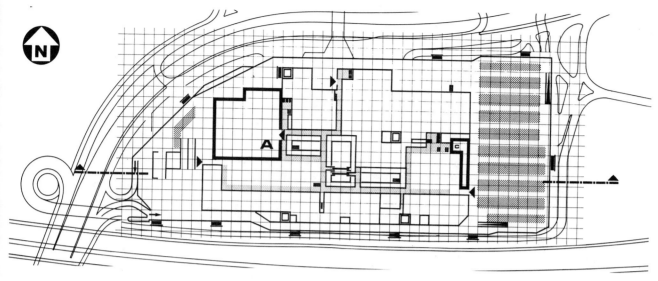

Figure 5-66 Center Glatt: Plan of terrace level containing upper level of department store A, restaurants, exhibit rooms, health center, etc. On the left side, service station, with car wash, on the right side, parking deck.

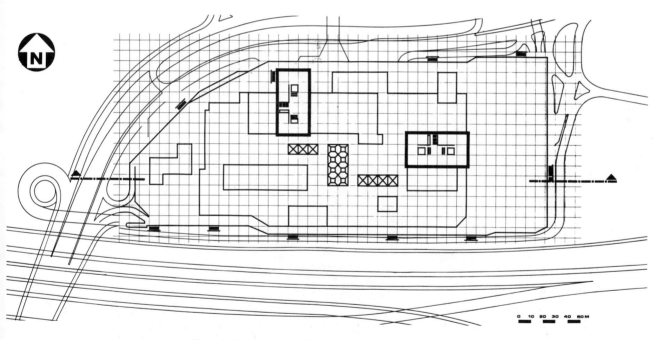

Figure 5-67 Center Glatt: Superstructures containing offices and apartments.

Planning Approach: In order to produce a sufficient amount of revenue-producing structures to offset land costs (which are extremely high as compared to the United States), and the costs of parking structures, it was essential to employ three-dimensional planning, multipurpose land usage, and the platform principle.

The base structure consists of two basement levels and two major activity levels. It is surrounded by a multilevel parking structure. These parking facilities are arranged in such a way that shoppers' traffic is equitably distributed to all revenue-producing functions on all levels.

The roof of the base structure forms a landscaped pedestrian terrace on which are placed restaurants, showrooms, sports facilities, a health center, and a limited number of residences etc. Two superstructures providing office space, rise from the terrace.

Vertical connection between all levels is achieved by escalators, stairways and high speed elevators.

Because of the multifunctional character of the center, which ensures round the clock usage of transportation media and parking, and because of the extensive public transportation and pedestrian facilities, it was possible to limit the total number of parking spaces to 3,600, thereby avoiding the possibility of overloading the regional road network.

Status of the Project: Because building permits for this project were attained before the general building stop which has now been imposed in Switzerland, took effect, the developers have been able to acquire permission to commence construction in July 1972. Completion is projected for 1975.

Figure 5-68 Model of the interior of the main court of Center Glatt.

CASE STUDY XII

Name of Project: Place Bonaventure

Location: Montreal, Canada. This multifunctional center is situated in the center of Montreal, immediately south of Place Ville Marie and the CNR Block which contains the Queen Elizabeth Hotel and the CNR headquarters building.

Planning Team: Architects: Affleck, Desbarats, Dimakopoulos, Lebensold, Sise. Structural consultants: R. R. Nicolet & Associates; Valois, Lamarre, Valois & Associates. Mechanical and Electrical consultants: Jas. P. Keith & Associates, Contractor: Concordia Estates Ltd.

Planning Approach: Quote from "Architecture Canada", July 1967:
"An attempt was made, in the design of Place Bonaventure, to develop an architecture based on patterns of human behaviour rather than on tenets of formal composition".

Land Available: Six acres but with certain underground restrictions because the site is situated directly over Canadian National Railway (CNR) lines and platform. (18 lines and platforms).

Description: This project was developed as a multifunctional seventeen-story urban complex, containing the following functions:

1. Retail shopping center (two levels).
2. Cinema.
3. "Better Living Center" (permanent exhibition of building materials).
4. Exhibition Hall for short term exhibitions such as "Boat Show."
5. "Merchandise Mart" (permanent wholesale rooms).
6. Office space and international "mart."
7. 400-room hotel.

Supporting functions:

a. car garage for approximately 1,000 cars
b. public open space of approximately 50,000 square feet

The design of Place Bonaventure also entailed the design of an underground interchange for the future east-west expressway which will lead to the entire complex.

Place Bonaventure is extremely well served by public transportation (commuter trains, subway and railroad) and is also linked to the existing underground pedestrian system of the core area.

The two-level shopping concourse of which one level is on the subway communications level, covers approximately 150,000 square feet and contains major stores, boutiques, and the 700-seat cinema.

Above the retail shopping levels is the Convention and Exhibition Hall, covering approximately 250,000 square feet and with a seating capacity of 17,000. This is designed to accommodate large, short duration shows. Two large mezzanines along the south and north sides of the hall are designed to provide ancillary facilities. The south mezzanine is equipped to handle meetings of various sizes, and the north mezzanine contains a large selection of eating and drinking facilities which overlook the main space.

On the levels above, there is one million square feet, spread over five levels, which comprises the "Merchandising Mart," a series of Canadian wholesalers's showrooms.

Above this, there is office accomodation of approximately 100,000 square feet, and on the same level an international trade center, supplying exhibit and office space for the principal trading nations of the world.

On the roof of the building is the hotel with 400 rooms. This deserves special attention, having succeeded in supplying an extremely agreeable environment for its visitors, giving them restfulness, fresh air, and green surroundings in an abundance unique in Montreal. The hotel rooms are situated around and overlooking a winter garden, which is laid out in the manner of a Japanese landscape. The public rooms such as restaurant, and recreation facilities are in the center of the garden, with the effect that wherever one is in the hotel, there is a feeling of fresh air and nature all round. When the weather is not good enough to allow guests to circulate from one part of the hotel to another, through the garden, glazed bridges from which the gardens can be viewed may be utilized. There is also a street level landscaped plaza. This has been developed over the parking area in the west part of the building, and from this plaza there is an off-the-street hotel entrance which is linked to the roof-level lobby with express elevators. This plaza constitutes a significant public open space for downtown Montreal.

Figure 5-69 Place Bonaventure: Exterior view.

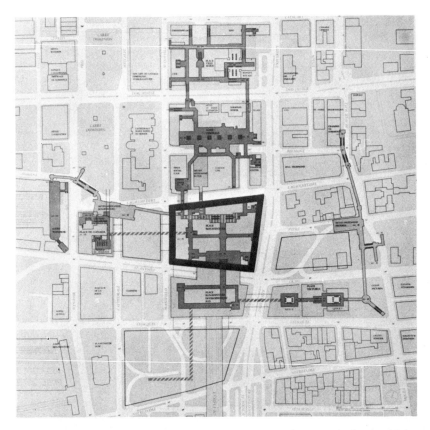

Figure 5-70 Place Bonaventure: Map of downtown Montreal, indicating the underground system of pedestrian pathways connecting major projects. The boundaries of the Place Bonaventure project are marked with a heavy line.

Figure 5-71 Place Bonaventure: Schematic section. Note subway on the lower edge of the picture and railroad line on the basement level.

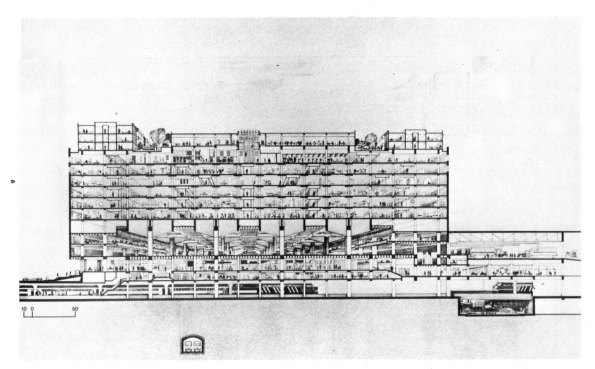

CASE STUDY XIII

Name of Project: Alster Zentrum

Location: City core of Hamburg, Germany

Developer: Neue Heimat, Städtebau, Hamburg

Center Team: Planning and architecture: Staff of Neue Heimat under the leadership of Hans Konwiarz, architect. Consultation: (particularly with regard to the base structure) Victor Gruen

Background for Planning: The site for this project, which was foreseen as the redevelopment of an overaged portion of the core area (St. Georg), adjoins the Hamburg Hauptbahnhof (central railroad station), neighbors major business areas, and borders on the Außer Alster, a lake-like water body. The land area of the site covers approximately 45 acres.

The aim of the developers was to contribute to the revitalization of the city core by establishing a multifunctional center which would provide a large amount of highly desirable residential quarters, integrated with cultural, educational and commercial functions.

Description of the Project: This project is based on the principles of three-dimensional planning, multipurpose land usage and the platform principle, and achieves a high land utilization with a ratio between built-up area and land of approximately 5:1.

The base structure, which is comprised of three main levels, contains public transportation terminals, approximately 10,000 parking spaces, arrival and distribution points for goods, revenue-producing functions such as shopping facilities, entertainment and cultural functions, office space and other employment facilities, and storage space for all functions. The revenue-producing area of the base structure is about 6,500,000 square feet.

Superstructures arranged in a wide curve rise from the terrace level which is formed by the roof of the base structure. These superstructures, which contain 6,500 apartments, vary in height from 30 to 60 floors. By means of setbacks, the apartments are provided with generous terraces and enjoy attractive views.

Status of Project: This well-conceived project has, surprisingly, not been constructed in spite of the fact that the necessary prerequisites (an excellent location, a developer led by long term motivations, a pressing demand for space, and the necessary financial backing), were present. This is a case where the enthusiasm of private enterprise was not fully shared by city government. The authorities feel that the density of the project is excessive in relation to uncertainties concerning development of the core which is influenced by the existence of a large number of satellite towns.

It is therefore envisaged that a smaller project on a limited area be projected and that for this purpose, an architectural competition should be arranged.

Personally, I feel that these restraints will interfere with the potential impact of the development. The injection of 20,000 inhabitants as was envisaged, would have made a considerable contribution to the economic, cultural and social health of the city core, and the multifunctional character of the project would have assisted in easing the problems of automobile congestion and encouraged the use of public transportation.

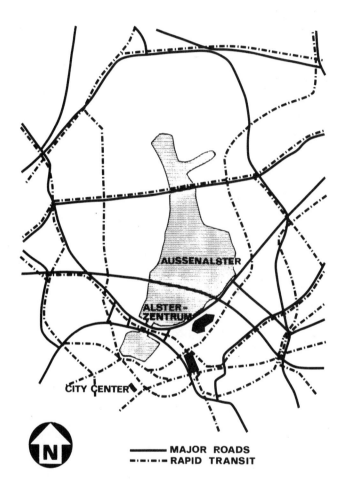

━━━━━ **MAJOR ROADS**
▪—▪—▪— **RAPID TRANSIT**

Figure 5-72 Alster Zentrum: Location of the project.

Figure 5-73 Alster Zentrum.

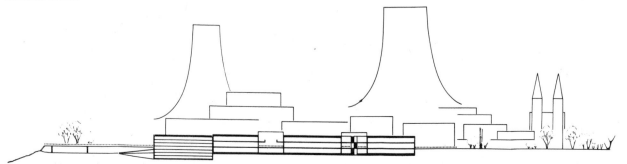

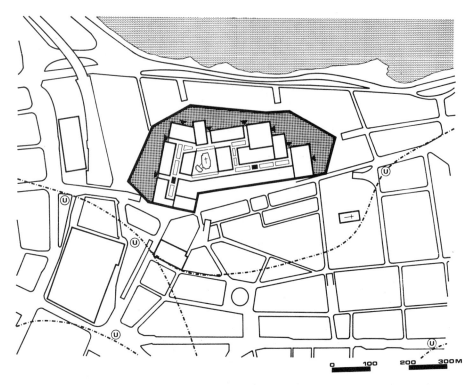

Figure 5-74 Alster Zentrum: Schematic plan of main activity level with a court around existing church, parking areas surrounding retail and related activities. The letter U denotes subway stations.

Figure 5-75 Alster Zentrum: Schematic plan of terrace level with buildings serving various functions grouped around a landscaped pedestrian terrace.

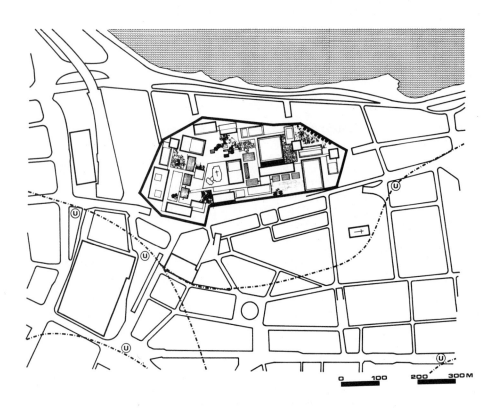

Figure 5-76 Alster Zentrum: Bird's eye view of the model of the project.

Figure 5-77 Alster Zentrum: Model showing relationship to Alster and skyline of Hamburg.

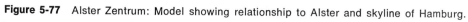

CASE STUDY XIV

Name of Project: Center of Nordwest Stadt, Frankfurt

Location: About four miles north of the core of Frankfurt-am-Main, Germany

Developer: Gewerbebauträger GmbH, Hamburg, in collaboration with numerous public and private developers.

Center Team: Many architects and planners under the guidance of Dr. Hans Kampffmeyer, City Planner of the Department of City Planning, Frankfurt.

Referring to this center, Dr. Kampffmeyer said: "The Nordwest area of Frankfurt has its city." Although I personally feel that the term "city" does not fully apply in this case, it can certainly be said that Nordwest Stadt, a well-planned and reasonably dense new satellite town is now structured around a compact multifunctional center, in the design of which, advantage was taken of three-dimensional planning, multipurpose land usage and the platform principle. Table 5-79 gives an idea of the multifunctional character and land utilization of this project. From this tabulation it can be seen that the total built-up area is almost three times the land area and the ratio of revenue-producing area to open land is about 1.30:1.

Generally speaking, the base structure below terrace level is devoted to public and private transportation, delivery roads, technical equipment rooms, and storage areas for productive functions, however, there are also a large public bath with swimming and health facilities, a number of shops and restaurants, and cultural, educational and social facilities, located around large, open-air courts.

The terrace level, which is the main pedestrian level, offers main access to the superstructures rising from it, which contain residential, office and educational facilities etc., and to terrace structures which contain stores, services, and educational, cultural and public facilities.

Figure 5-78 Nordwest Stadt: Map showing location of project in relation to the center of Frankfurt.

Figure 5-79 Nordwest Stadt: Land usage tabulation.

	Square feet	Acres
Land Area	753,000	17.30
Urban Usage Area		
1. Commerce	409,000	9.40
2. Professional offices, medical, etc.	16,100	0.37
3. Administrative offices	26,900	0.62
4. Apartments	107,600	2.47
5. Public Services	279,800	6.40
6. Education	182,900	4.20
	1,022,300	23.46
For Human Communications	279,800	6.40
Auxiliary Facilities		
1. Service Roads	290,600	6.70
2. Parking Area	710,400	16.30
	1,001,000	23.00
Grand Total	2,303,100	52.86

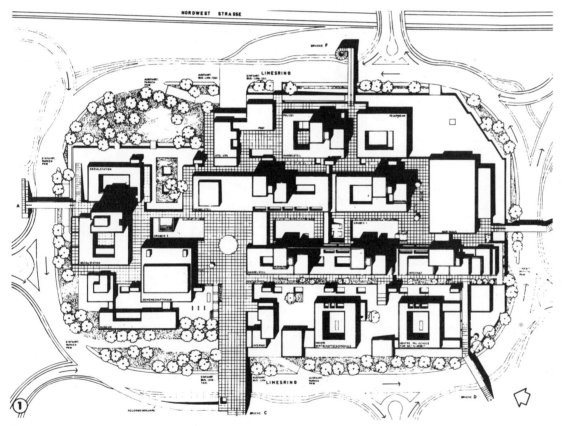

Figure 5-80 Nordwest Stadt: Floor plan of the main pedestrian level (which is one of the four main levels), indicating the following functions: three department stores, a community center, a public bath, social services, specialized educational facilities, and various pedestrian bridges crossing the loop road and leading to pedestrian ways to the surrounding town development. (Various other functions such as parking, delivery facilities, etc. are on a lower level.)

Figure 5-81 Nordwest Stadt: A typical section.

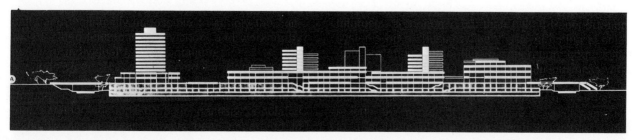

Figure 5-82 Nordwest Stadt: Air view of center and surrounding area.

Figure 5-84   Nordwest Stadt: A part of the center.

6

Figure 6-48 A view of the pedestrian area in Hartford, Connecticut. Here, a pedestrian system was created as part of a redevelopment project.

URBAN CORES

ARE URBAN CORES NECESSARY?

In approaching the discussion of urban cores and what, if anything should be done about them, some soul-searching questions have to be raised. Are urban centers essential?—Desirable?—Possible? Or is their role, under the impact of contemporary sociological and technological change, diminished to such a degree that we should just write them off as a hopeless and outdated species.

The latter view, which we hear especially often expressed in the United States is exemplified in an article written by Eugene Raskin, which appeared in the *New York Times* of May 2, 1971. In this article, Mr. Raskin suggested that any effort to improve the functioning of big city cores such as Manhattan is comparable to the act of beating a dead horse:

They are physically obsolete, financially unworkable, crime-ridden, garbage-strewn, polluted, torn by racial conflicts, wallowing in welfare unemployment, despair and official corruption. As they exist at present they are unsalvageable, destined to join the dinosaur in deserved extinction. Urban planners and others who come up with

temporary patchwork schemes and gimmicks to keep the cities going another year or two or three are as pathetic as the officers of the Titanic charting tomorrow's course while the water rises above their ears.

In my view, Mr. Raskin is judging and sentencing Manhattan, in the same way as, according to the Bible, the Lord judged and sentenced Sodom and Gomorrah. Because of the sinfulness evident in these two cities, they were destroyed by divine power, the city and especially its core, being held responsible for all human misdemeanors and the resulting crises. Whenever, throughout history, power structures of an empire deteriorated, this necessarily expressed itself in the most forceful manner in those places where large population concentrations existed and of course, most formidably in the cores which contain the quintessence of urban civilization.

Those who condemn cities generally and their cores specifically, as being the cesspools of humanity, have ample supporting material for their wrath. They just forget that the city reflects, as in a magnifying mirror, all human qualities, instincts, virtues, and sins, in the most concentrated and easily recognizable and exposed form. The identical vices and virtues exist, of course, also in a rural hamlet though obviously not in such quantities, and therefore not subject to broadcasting through the mass media. Antisocial behavior by the human animal is in evidence wherever members of the human race congregate. The larger the group is, the more notice is taken of such aberrations, because they disturb a greater number of people. On the other hand, the measures which are taken, or should be taken, against them are also more intense. Those who talk about the dissolution of the cities and especially of the evacuation of their cores, are escapists who believe that sin can be done away with if one just spreads it out. Their hope is that human misbehavior will be less noticed and the public conscience therefore eased if one decentralizes wrongdoing. The advocates of dispersement of the population by scattering it all over the globe still owe us an answer to the question of how we could then preserve the last vestiges of natural life which form the foundation for the biological existence of Man. Thus, though fully acknowledging that we have acted preposterously in the way we have managed our urban environment, we are forced to acknowledge that there is no alternative to urbanity, for, as I have already said, any attempt by man to run away from his cities, is as futile as an attempt to escape from himself.

On the same page of the *New York Times* as Raskin's article, another writer, Samuel Tenenbaum sings a hymn of praise celebrating the virtues and values of urbanity and especially of Manhattan as an example of a dynamic core. He overlooks, however, that we have unfortunately destroyed, in most of our urban cores, the conditions under which the advantages of urbanity can flourish. When large numbers of people live together they recognize that they will have to accept certain personal sacrifices in order to attain certain benefits. Whenever the sacrifices outweigh the benefits, the city finds itself in a critical condition. We have cities which are, by the majority of their population, loved, others which are hated, and yet others—and maybe these constitute the most serious cases—which evoke no emotional reaction and where, therefore, those revolutionary movements for improvement evident in the hated city are missing.

Generally, cities, like any human creation, have their ups and downs, depending on political and economic developments and on the balance between sacrifices and benefits which the inhabitants experience. Rome, the "eternal city," shrank after the downfall of the Roman Empire, to an insignificant town of 17,000 inhabitants, only to regain its importance later in its history. Like Rome, other cities seem to have an inherent power of resurrection,

even after the worst periods of deterioration. Cities which were completely wiped out in World War II in Europe and Asia have risen like phoenixes out of the ashes. Thus I for one believe fervently in the city. I do so, not on the basis of dreamy optimism, expecting a richer flow of the milk of human kindness, but on the basis of the realistic cognizance that the city is necessary and irreplaceable. If it is each individual's longing to make the most of his life, so it must be the aim of humanity to make the most out of our cities. It is, in my opinion, a healthy sign that in our epoch, loud criticism of all the detestable qualities of city life are aired. This criticism represents one half of the equation that has to be formulated in order to find the solution. The other part of the equation, however, which outlines avenues of action, is not yet receiving sufficient attention.

SAVE OUR CITIES

We have, however, achieved, in nearly all parts of the world, a growing awareness of the importance of the city core and of the fact that "something must be done." The SOS alarms are heard in the new world and in the old and in the cities of every continent. "Save our cities," "Save our downtown," "Revitalize the city core" are slogans heard in most cities of the world. In some cases they are concretely expressed through "programs" like slum clearance, urban redevelopment, restoration, "pedestrian precincts," traffic improvements, and so on. The special attention which is being paid to the core is justified by the preeminence of its role, within the entire urban organism. It represents its heart, its brain, and its soul. Every town, every city, every metropolis of the world, possesses a core. Their sizes, their history, their functioning pattern, however, are of such variance that any all-encompassing recommendations for measures to improve their conditions would be meaningless. A clinical examination concerning the health of the tens of thousands of cores would yield widely varying results and the diagnoses could reveal either conditions of basic organic health and great power of resistance or, at the other extreme, one of hopeless, terminal disease. In accordance with such varying diagnoses, the necessary treatment may indicate greatest attention to the conservation of existing values; or the necessity of complete elimination of the diseased elements, and therefore rebuilding from scratch. Between these two extreme actions lie a multitude of possibilities: of employing preventive medicine; of various types of cures; of partial regeneration; and, where unavoidable, of surgery.

It would be a self-delusion to believe that in one

chapter of this book I could deal with the avalanche of problems and with the vast range of measures necessary to solve them. This is a task which has employed and, over generations to come, will employ the minds of untold numbers of planners and writers. I will attempt, in all humbleness, to make a small contribution by highlighting those qualities and characteristics which I feel a city core should be endowed with and then, by presenting case studies related to projects in which I have been personally involved, discuss attempts which have been and are being made to gain or recapture at least some of those essential qualities of urbanity.

I am taking my reader a long way, from the discussion of the regional shopping center, over the discussion of the multifunctional center, to the emphatic expression of my belief that the key to a continuation of urban culture and therefore human civilization lies within our city cores. I previously raised this point in the book *Shopping Towns USA* in 1960, when I stated:

So far as central business districts are concerned, the feeling is constantly growing that something must be done to revitalize them. . . . The real need is for improvement of the entire quality of the urban core and an integrated attack on all problems.

So long as people deliberately avoid the downtown district, the core area will continue to deteriorate. . . . The solution calls for an understanding of what people need and want in their daily lives; but as Edgardo Contini, speaking at the Aspen Design Conference in 1955 stated, "Not being manufacturable, environment has seldom been the subject of organized effort."

Nevertheless, it is safe to assume that within the next 20 years the importance of environmental planning for downtown will receive greater recognition and understanding from those who are in a position to act, and that out of the present despair will be born the will and the wherewithal to accomplish the reshaping of our city cores.

The lesson learned and the experience gained in the planning of regional shopping centers will contribute immeasurably to the successful carrying out of this task.

BODY, MIND, AND SOUL

The city, like the human being, possesses a body, a mind, and a soul. The body is measurable in all its qualities and it therefore provides a happy hunting ground for an army of statisticians. It is possible, through counting and measuring, to quantify those factors which permit conclusions to be reached concerning economic and functioning characteristics relating to the body of the city. It is immeasurably more difficult to determine what can be done about the state of the mind of the city. This is represented by the intensity, vigor, and freedom of intellectual and artistic expression. Efforts to improve the mind of the city, solely by promotional activities and through the construction of cultural and civic

centers, may have disappointing results.

Even more puzzling are problems connected with the "soul." We have never managed to determine the meaning of the term "soul" in relation to the individual human being; yet the word appears in every language and has been glorified in poetry, religion, and through every expression of art. It is the cities with a soul which are the destination of pilgrimages by millions of tourists. This undefinable term which in public relations lingo is referred to as the "image" is also the one force which, more than any other, ties together the inhabitants in an emotional attachment or love for their city. Though we are unable to define what establishes the existence of a soul in a city, we know that there are certain ingredients which seem to be indicative: natural settings within and around the city—rivers, lakes, hills, or forests, and the climate and the manner in which all this has been integrated into the urban form; historical heritage as expressed by specific buildings, streets, and squares; outstanding structures utilized for significant functions, and which become landmarks, attaining symbolic value.

Travel posters give a clue to the essence of the soul of a city. Just by illustrating one feature they manage to convey immediate recognition of the product they are advertising: for Paris the Eiffel Tower; for New York the Statue of Liberty; for Athens the Parthenon; for London Big Ben; for Pisa, the Leaning Tower; for Vienna, St. Stephan's Cathedral; for Rome, the Colosseum; for Washington, the Washington Monument obelisk. Poster designers get into difficulties when faced with the task of communicating, by a symbol, cities with a poorly

Figure 6-1

developed soul such as Los Angeles, Düsseldorf, or Johannesburg. Thus even if we are unable to determine exactly what the meaning of the intangible term "soul" is, the quality seems to exist. We should therefore conclude that a humanly desirable urban organism should be healthy and vigorous of body and mind and should have a soul, and further, that these conditions should be most forcibly expressed within the heart of the city—its core. In the city core then must be represented all the most essential urban qualities and functions which, through outstanding characteristics and qualities rather than through impressive quantity, express the essence of urbanity. Because the city core can fulfill its task of achieving human communications between a large variety of functions only if it is compact, it is necessary to use the limited space available with wisdom and through selectivity.

SELECTIVITY

The procedure of selectivity, discussed in the foregoing chapter, when applied to the city core requires demanding and sensitive discernment. Urban, regional, national, and international significance; exceptionality and symbolic values; an emphasis on quality rather than on quantity—all these form decisive selection criteria. Certain functions however, are characterized by an insufficiently low ratio between their space demands and their human experience value. These cannot be organically fitted into a compact core and must be categorized as "core-nonconforming." Into this category also belong all those functions which are creators of irremovable disturbances and those which have to be classified as auxiliary serving facilities. In an attempt to clarify the nature of "core-conforming" and "core-non-conforming" uses, I will catalog various functions, attempting to indicate the methods of selectivity involved.

1. *Residences.* A city core which is not populated becomes a ghost town outside of working and business hours. It is obvious, however, that it would be neither physically possible nor desirable for all to live in the city core. The ideal core population is formed by those who, due to their work or interests, are potentially the most enthusiastic participators in city life. This may include students, artists, intellectuals, scientists, writers, those who love sociability and active participation and those who appreciate living near their place of employment. This characterization of the core residents then, obviously cuts across all socioeconomic boundaries and all separations by age or ethnic origin. Those cities which have either ceased to have a city core population or those which through economic structuring

have reserved the core exclusively for the poorest or the richest are not living up to the tenet of urban selectivity.

2. *Government.* The central and representational functions of municipal, state, or national governments should be present in the core but not necessarily all administrative offices or those government offices which serve local interests and are therefore better located in multifunctional centers of the urban subunits.

3. *Private Business Administration.* The central headquarter offices of national and international organizations should be in the core, but not necessarily general clerical services, computer departments, etc.

4. *Trade.* Those stores which offer merchandise of exceptional quality or who offer an unusually large range of choice should be represented. The stores will appeal to the entire regional population for the supply of goods for specific festive occasions and for the satisfaction of needs which are not of the everyday type. Stores offering goods required for daily or weekly needs should be represented only to the degree necessary to serve the population of the core. Trade in the central area must be geared to the demands of the total city and regional and possibly international clientele, for goods of exceptional character and quality.

5. *Culture and Art.* The major museums, concert halls, theaters, movie houses catering to a selective clientele should all be located in the city core.

This catalog could be continued to include every facet of human interest as expressed in spiritual life, entertainment, tourism, leisure activities, and through eating places, recreation parks, financial institutions, etc.

This approach to selectivity indicates that for certain urban functions separation should occur between sections which can be termed "representational" or "top management" and those operations which are devoted to routine activities, or those which function better on the local level. In the private sector of the economy, this has, to a large degree, already found expression. Large stores and other private enterprises find the space which they occupy in the core too valuable to sacrifice to "non-central activities." They have very often moved their storage facilities, administration offices, and statistical departments out of the center. The fact that, not only in the United States but also in some European cities, some public and private agencies have gone overboard and moved totally to the countryside is due to the poor quality of the urban scene. In a well-structured urban organism, they would find a suitable place in the multitude of centers of a polycentrically organized urban pattern. Thus the city core would contain all of those functions which can successfully operate only in a central location of an entire urban region where they can draw on hundreds of thousands or even millions of people and where, because of their uniqueness, they in turn make the city core a place of exceptional human experiences. A city core composed of such functions undoubtedly achieves the "power of attraction."

POWER OF ATTRACTION

But a power of attraction based on the impact of functions will not suffice if the possibilities to participate in these functions in an enjoyable manner and without undue sacrifice are not established by fullest attention to the following conditions.

1. *Environmental Conditions.* The urban environment must be safe, healthy, and inviting. Also in this respect, the core must be an expression of the highest quality. Its air should be free of pollution; the sense of hearing should not be offended by unpleasant mechanical noise; the eye should not be insulted by disorder, dirt, or ugliness; the nose should not be offended by unpleasant smells. Human senses should rather be flattered and inspired by the impressions they receive from the man-made environment.

2. *Accessibility.* Even if attractiveness is achieved, it cannot be utilized if the core is not made accessible from all areas of the city and the region, the nation, even the world, by means of speedy, comfortable, and reasonably priced transportation. The main burden of this accessibility will have to be carried by public transportation because it is physically and technically impossible to supply the centrally located functions with visitors and workers by means of individual travel containers.

3. *Public Open Spaces Reserved for Human Functions.* This basic principle has been adhered to throughout history as a trademark of urban civilization. Serving functions have, in densely populated or highly active areas, always been separated in the vertical sense from human functions. Sewers and drainage lines were relegated to complex canalization systems; electricity and telephone wires which in primitive cities dangled from masts over the city streets have been installed underground. A similar procedure has been followed with regard to waterlines, heating lines, gas pipes, pneumatic tubes for postal delivery, public transportation which crisscrosses the city underground, etc.

Strangely enough, this principle has not been applied to one specific type of transportation; that of individually operated vehicles, whether they are used for the transportation of people or of goods. This one omission has in many cases proved itself capable of unleashing a destructive force of unparalleled magnitude. It is one of the basic physical laws (Archimedes' displacement theory) that two masses cannot occupy the same space. If all public space is usurped by moving or stationary automotive vehicles, then evidently this mass must force out another mass which in the case of an animated urban center is the human being. Even if a public awareness concerning the polluting qualities of the automotive vehicle should bring about, within the next 15 or 20 years, technological improvements, the tremendous space consumption by an evidently nonconforming urban function would remain unchanged. Thus, separation of all mechanical functions from human life expressions must be extended to include all means of individual transportation for people and goods.

PUBLIC TRANSPORTATION

Urban transportation is generally experiencing an era of deterioration. Yet in all those cities which have conserved some remnants of true urbanity, public transportation had to be kept going because otherwise the entire functioning pattern of economic life would collapse. Thus we find that, in most large cities of the world, public transportation is subsidized by means of taxpayers' money. This subsidization is, however, granted in a hesitating and extremely stingy fashion and results in a kind of vegetating of the public transportation system, giving it too much to allow it to die, but too little to keep it vigorously healthy. Most cities have, in the interests of economy, put their public transportation systems on a "businesslike" basis, creating special transportation authorities or operation companies which are directed to rationalize their business with the aim of keeping the need for subsidies to a minimum. Whether this policy is wise, or whether it results in municipal expenditures which amount to a multiple of the sums saved by economizing on public transportation, is to be questioned.

I experienced one expression of a healthy behavior pattern concerning public transportation when I discussed the newly constructed *tunnelbana* (subway) with representatives of the city of Stockholm. Upon my questioning them as to whether the income created by the sale of tickets was sufficient to pay for the operating costs, and if any provision toward the amortization of the capital investment had been made, they looked blankly at me and said: "We have never given any thought to that question and we have not the slightest idea of the answer. We obviously needed the tunnelbana and it is therefore completely irrelevant whether it results in profit or loss." This seems to me the only sensible attitude to take concerning public transportation in general. It cannot and should not be regarded as an isolated element of city politics or city finances. There exists a strong interdependence between urban planning, the functioning of a city, and above all between private and public economics and public transportation. The importance of the latter should therefore range on equal terms with other public services such as schools, hospitals, law enforcement, etc. If one fully appreciates the public service role of mass transportation, then the concept of permitting its usage free of charge, which is discussed in many cities of the world and experimented with in some, would appear highly logical. The power of the argument for the so-called "zero tariff" becomes even greater when one realizes that those procedures which are connected with the printing and selling of tickets, controlling the possession of valid tickets, collection of the fare money, as well as safeguarding, transporting, and counting it are so costly that they reduce the so-called "gross income" to a minimal figure and sometimes to nothing. Since a large part of the total expenditure is in any case covered by income from taxes, a small increase in such taxes may prove sufficient to make it possible to allow the usage of all public transportation free of charge, and to improve the system both quantitatively and qualitatively. Besides the concept of the zero tariff, there are others which are being studied or experimented with, for example, the distributing of passes or "ridership licences" similar in form to a credit card or a driving license. Payments for such passes are made through check on a monthly or yearly basis. Possession of a pass or license, entitles the holder to use *all* public transportation. Controls to ensure that passengers possess a license are then carried out only on a "spot check" basis. Those cities who prefer the pass or ridership license system claim that it would be more popular than the raising of taxes because the purchaser of a pass is given the feeling that he is gaining a privilege.

There are probably additional ideas, in the direction of encouraging the use of public transportation and of simplifying the charging system. They all deserve highest consideration, it being evident that the presently used systems are antisocial, penalizing that part of the population who for one reason or another cannot use the private automobile. Conversely, by putting public transportation on a starvation diet, municipal authorities encourage the utilization of the private car for routine trips and in this manner necessitate the expenditure of a multiple of any possible savings made in the field of public transportation for the accommodation of individual transport.

THE WAR BETWEEN THE CITY AND THE AUTOMOBILE

In our society, the automobile has assumed an importance of such dimensions that I will deal with this phenomenon at some length, facing the danger that I will be accused of having an unreasonable phobia against this unique product of human inventiveness. My arguments are not directed against the existence of the vehicle as such, but against its misapplied usage within areas and for purposes for which it is not suitable. I am fully aware of the fact that I am dealing here with a touchy problem, because the possession and operation of an automobile usually involves emotions. Far beyond its importance as a machine for propulsion, it has become a status symbol, a sign of male virility, a financial statement on four wheels, a beloved object which is washed, polished, and otherwise pampered, a personal companion. Nations regard it as an indicator of national prosperity and progress, and even communist countries which believe in collectivism have, in their blind desire to achieve technological equality with the capitalistic West, abandoned their original concentration of efforts on good public transportation. Russia especially, receives financial help from the West for the developing of its automobile industry. (It has at least been rumored that an American Secretary of Defense favored the aid as constituting a secret weapon by which the communist countries would be forced to spend a great deal of their national product on the building of all the paraphanalia necessary for mass traffic by automobiles and thus would not have enough financing strength left over to keep up the armaments race!)

On the other hand, it appears that in the United States, where the automobile population grows at a faster rate than the human one, the popular mood shows signs of change. *Fortune* magazine reported, in an issue devoted to the future of the American automobile industry, in April 1971: "Ominous from the automobile industry's point of view, are signs that Americans, having almost stopped loving their cars, may begin to hate them." There have been cases of popular rebellions which have sabotaged the building of urban freeways in San Francisco and New Orleans. Members of the younger generation have buried automobiles as a symbolic gesture. Man, though still schizophrenic in his attitude toward the car, has started to become conscious of its dangers and has commenced defensive actions. There are many signs in the wind that "birth control" measures will have to be applied by governments to the automobile population. Public concern regarding pollution and danger to safety have caused legislative measures, as exemplified by the stringent standards established in laws passed by the American Congress in 1971.

Wilfred Owens of the Brookings Institute, a transportation expert, pronounced as early as 1957: "Our attempt to be urbanized and motorized at the same time has been less than a complete success." There are undeniable proofs which establish the reasons for the failure of this attempt.

THE INSATIABLE SPACE DEMANDS OF ANY INDIVIDUAL MOBILITY INSTRUMENT

Any individual automobile occupies large quantities of space for its movement and for its storage, even during the time of its birth (assembly plants) and after its death (automobile cemeteries). If this space demand is fulfilled, it preempts all the available land area within an urban organism and therefore must indisputably lead to the withering away of human urban functions or to their widespread dispersement, resulting in the "anti-city." Evidence for this statement can be found by applying simple mathematics:

A Motor Car Needs:

1. *For Storage:*

    1 parking space at residence

    1 parking space at place of employment

    2 to 3 parking spaces at various other points of destination

    Total of 4½ parking places, which, if one considers exit and entrance ways, each occupy .... 500 square feet

    Therefore: 4½ x 500 ... 2,250 square feet

2. *For Movement:*
    Assuming that a car is not being operated all the time, one can conservatively estimate that the space required for movement is about equal to that required for storage, i.e. .... 2,250 square feet

3. *For salesrooms,* repair shops, filling stations, automobile cemeteries, and production space; conservatively estimated at .... 1,000 square feet

    Thus the total space demand per vehicle is: ... 5,500 square feet

If we apply this figure to a hypothetical city of 500,000 inhabitants and assume that one automotive vehicle would be operated for every family unit of three persons, this would mean that the automobile population would be 166,000. The urban space demanded by these vehicles would then be:

$$166,000 \times 5,500 \text{ square feet} = 913,000,000 \text{ square feet}$$

$$\text{or (in acres)} = 21,000 \text{ acres}$$

As a comparison we might mention that the space which the human inhabitants need for their place of residence is, on an average, 300 square feet per person, which for 500,000 inhabitants amounts to 150,000 square feet, or approximately 3,445 acres.

This living space is of course in an urban organism, arranged on many levels, so that the actual land utilization of 3,445 acres would, in a compactly organized urban organism, be more than sufficient for the placement of all other urban functions serving employment, administration, trade, education, and cultural and leisure time activities.

Even if we were ready to considerably enlarge the total land area to be devoted to human functions, there would remain a disproportionate relationship between the land which we seem willing to sacrifice for our transportation slaves (which in fact have become our masters) and the land for human beings. The more highly organized any part of the urban environment becomes the more bizarre becomes the space relationship. The most active, animated, and significant parts of our cities, namely the cores, cannot even by the widest stretch of the imagination and by utilizing all palliatives, such as multilevel parking structures, underground garages, urban freeways, computerized signal systems, be adjusted to this disproportionate use of land without being destroyed. All those road builders who are so busily engaged in sacrificing urbanity to traffic are only building "dead-end" roads. I certainly do not claim any right of authorship or special originality for the expression of this conviction. What I have stated sounds quite moderate in comparison to a paragraph in the article written by Mr. Raskin in the *New York Times* of May 2, 1971, which reads:

Every plan to "ease" traffic congestion by building more and wider approaches, underpasses, overpasses and similar anti-personnel devices must be scotched instantly, the proposers summarily shot and their estates used to help build blockades to keep autos out of the city.

COUNTERMEASURES

The phenomenon of the voracity of the private automobile is being recognized in nearly every large city of the world, though mostly on the basis of bitter experience rather than wisdom. Measures which are being taken are still generally of a half-hearted nature. Some cities restrict the use of the automobile in certain streets to certain times (for example, New York, Fifth Avenue and Madison Avenue, and Tokyo, the Ginza); others attempt to create localized, peaceful coexistence by either forcing people to move on to higher levels in the form of elevated sidewalks and bridges, or condemning them to a mole-like existence in tunnels, subways and basement concourses (for example Minneapolis is experimenting with a bridge approach for pedestrians; Montreal, in Canada, favors the underground solution). There are also by now hundreds of cities which have created pedestrian streets or pedestrian zones on a temporary or permanent basis. In most of these cases, however, only isolated pedestrian ways have resulted and a systematic approach is still rather exceptional. All measures which have been taken, though to a certain degree constructive and effective, have still the character of a "strategic retreat" from an overpowering enemy force. A force which will have to be dealt with on a broader scale and much more firmly in the future.

INCOMPATIBILITY OF HUMANS AND CARS

In documenting the incompatibility of human activities and those of the automobile population, I have refrained from mentioning the dangers created through the use of "gas warfare" and "terrorism through noise."

As far as terrorism through noise is concerned, though automotive vehicles (cars, motorcycles, and trucks) are by no means alone responsible for disturbing noise, they do make an appreciable contribution. They create noise when starting, through the screeching of brakes, when accelerating, by rolling over the pavement and horn-blowing (even though this is in many cities *officially* forbidden except in case of emergency). Scientists are alarmed. In a meeting of the International Organization for Setting Up Standards in Geneva in June 1971, it was stated that research had shown that the noise levels in cities grow each year at the rate of 1 decibel. This is sufficient to create a noise level in about 20 years' time which would lead to the complete deafness of all city dwellers. The city of Frankfurt, West Germany, has reacted to this noise problem in a rather humorous fashion. Loudspeakers have been installed in the city center which

transmit "pleasant noise," such as the sound of waves breaking on the seashore and birdsong, sufficiently loud to camouflage and drown out the mechanical noises of the city.

Medical science has called worldwide attention to the dangers which are created by the emission of poison gases, the consumption of oxygen, the cancer-promoting dust particles resulting from the wearing process of brakes and tires, etc. Though it is by now common knowledge based on the personal experience of all urbanites who are plagued by smog and unpleasant smells that these are manifestations ascribable to the use of the automotive vehicle, I have not stressed them. It now seems possible that these disturbing characteristics may be controlled, if not eliminated, by the automobile and oil industries, under the pressure brought to bear by governments. But even if we should succeed within the next 20 years, in constructing and utilizing exclusively electric automobiles this would not alleviate the insupportable space demand which I have listed as my main argument.

HOPEFUL SIGNS

Yet there are some signs on the horizon that an overall solution can be found. It is a fact that the automobile as a species has built-in, self-devouring qualities. The greater their number becomes, the more questionable becomes the usefulness of their positive qualities. The quality of attaining great speeds is made meaningless through speed restrictions and even more so through congestion. The ability of the owner of an automobile to use his individual travel machine to drive from the door of his housing unit to the door of his destination is already turning out to be an illusion, because the place in front of the door is either prohibited as to parking or is already occupied by somebody else's car. It has been established that, within central city areas, the average walking distance from a parked car to the desired destination is around 800 to 1,200 feet.

Though the cost of the automobile itself has been, thanks to mass-production techniques, only slowly rising, the cost of operating it has skyrocketed. Higher prices for gasoline, for repairs, for insurance, and for parking fees are responsible for this. Within urbanized areas, the use of the automobile for routine travel purposes is being slowly priced out of the market. Thus all those who, especially in Europe, follow fascinatedly the straight-line projections of automobile registration numbers since the end of World War II, and who are basing programs for road building and garage constructions on a consideration of this straight-line projection, will probably be bitterly disappointed. The saturation

Figure 6-2 (a)   Normal conditions of The Ginza.

Figure 6-2 (a) (b)   Temporary closing of major retail street, The Ginza, in Tokyo, Japan.

Figure 6-2 (b)   Appearance of The Ginza on days when automobile traffic is excluded.

Figure 6-3 A permanent pedestrian street in Norwich, England.

Figure 6-4 A permanent pedestrian street in Riverside, California, U.S.A.

Figure 6-5 A permanent pedestrian zone in the historic center of Rouen, France.

Figure 6-6 Pedestrian shopping street in Essen, West Germany.

Figure 6-7 Pedestrian shopping street, in Hong Kong. Note: Sign at entrance to street reads: PROHIBITED UNLESS AUTHORISED IN WRITING BY THE COMMISSIONER OF POLICE FOR ACCESS TO PREMISES IN THE ROAD.

points have already been reached in most urbanized areas, though the recognition of this fact usually lags behind by a few years. Considering all the counter-trends which I have touched upon, it must logically be assumed that the number of automobiles, and even more certainly, the daily mileage use of the automobile, will be reduced sharply in the next 10 to 20 years.

DO WE NEED MORE PARKING SPACE?

Whenever or wherever the representatives of free enterprise in a city conclude that traffic congestion interferes seriously with their activities, they respond to this by demanding more parking space, justifying this demand by the correct observation that moving traffic is brought to a standstill by the parked cars which occupy, legally and illegally, a considerable portion of the streets. Under the pressure of business interest, governments then proceed to subsidize or at least to promote the construction of multilevel parking structures or underground garages and to pass legislation by which the owner of a building has to provide parking space on his own ground. This entails great financial sacrifices

and also the loss of the few remaining green spots and parks, which are paved over to serve this purpose. However, the long-range effects are that the actions designed to save the cities actually contribute to their final doom. The reasons for this disappointing result are the following:

1. An increase of parking facilities causes, automatically, a greater influx of cars into central areas.
2. Those people who rent living or working space in a building which is forced to provide parking garages have also to pay the rent for a garage, and therefore feel that they are wasting their money unless they buy an automobile to occupy the garage.

Thus the quantity of automobiles and their usage for routine purposes are artificially enlarged. A vicious circle becomes operative. The greater the number of parking facilities, the more space must be sacrificed for moving cars in and out of these. If a city manages, which is rarely the case, to improve the street system in relation to the then existing number of automobiles, traffic conditions ease and even more people are encouraged to purchase and operate cars. The possession of a car is a persuasive factor in encouraging the population to move further away from the unbearably traffic-congested urban areas. A cancer-like growth of inhabited areas appears, spreading more and more as each of the suburban expectation areas become themselves victims of "autorosis." At the same time, and to the same degree as the utilization of the automobile for routine purposes grows, public transportation loses its ridership and is forced to decrease its efficiency until finally it has to be entirely subsidized or completely abandoned. As the quality of public transportation deteriorates and its tariffs are raised, a new spur for purchasing and using more and more automobiles is injected and so it goes on in a never-ending spiral.

We must then conclude that all legislation which forces property owners to provide parking space on their own grounds causes, especially in highly urbanized areas, considerably more damage than benefit. It also robs the pedestrian of his last refuge, the sidewalk, which is steadily violated by entering and exiting vehicles. It is further evident that the indiscriminate provision of garages within a tightly woven urban tissue can in the best cases be only a short-term palliative, but on a long-term basis must result in urban catastrophe. I would like in this connection, just to mention the case of the

city center of Detroit, where public agencies responded splendidly to the demands of business, and supplied an abundance of parking space within the city center. The results were that multilevel garages usurped space which was formerly used for urban functions and that the widening of existing and routing of new roads within the city center reduced the space for urban functions to such a degree that downtown Detroit today has the character of one monumental parking facility. As an effect, business activities decreased. Of four department stores which originally existed, only one survived. An exodus of all other types of enterprise took place and the beautiful garages are now rarely used to their full capacity, due to the reduced number of reasons for visiting the city center. How far paradoxical thought can deviate from human considerations is exemplified by the following remark expressed by a speaker on the occasion of the Traffic Engineers Convention in Los Angeles in April 1969: "The only impediment to free and efficient traffic circulation in downtown Los Angeles is the pedestrian."

RENAISSANCE OF PUBLIC TRANSPORTATION

Slowly the conviction grows that the answer to the wish for urban dynamism can only be the revival

Figure 6-8 City devours countryside!

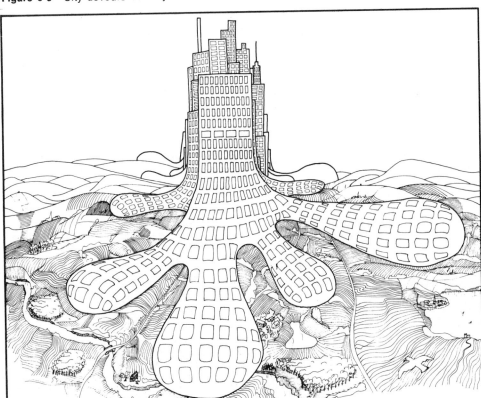

of urban public transportation. Such transportation, which has been pronounced dying or dead for about the last 30 years, is experiencing a surprisingly strong comeback. Even passengers' railroad traffic, which in the United States had been so effectively murdered by the railroad companies, is being revived by public action. The list of cities constructing new subway systems or enlarging existing ones and modernizing their commuter systems, is impressive. It is certainly symptomatic that the automobile industry itself, as well as the electric industry, is engaged in research and development of new types of mass transportation.

SCHIZOPHRENIA

At the present time, however, most city governments and city planners are acting in a schizophrenic manner. They are using huge amounts of the taxpayers' money for construction of facilities which are in direct competition with each other. Paris, France, for example, is engaged in a monumental program of enlarging the *métro* system and of building one of the finest new public transportation systems, the regional *métro* (RER), and at the same time is spending equal or even greater sums for the construction of urban freeways, underpasses, overpasses, and public garages. One of the two undertakings must necessarily go bankrupt. I am mentioning Paris as an example because the efforts in both directions are of such impressive size and quality. The same schizophrenic attitude prevails in every city of the world. From a fiscal point of view, such massive expenditures for two completely competitive undertakings, each of which cancels out the effectiveness of the other, must be ruinous. Sooner or later, a choice will have to be made. Faced with the undeniable proof that transportation within an urban area cannot be resolved by individualized transportation, and that its promotion runs counter to the interests of all qualities of urbanity, the choice should not be too difficult.

NO PERFECT ANSWERS YET

Before presenting some case studies, I must call attention to the fact that none of the solutions described in them provides complete answers. This is partly due to the fact that in the reshaping of an existing environmental element, certain measures which can be applied to a brand-new, yet-to-be constructed center, are, for physical, financial, or conservation reasons, not applicable. All proposed measures for city revitalization, if they are to result in any meaningful political action, must be geared to comparatively short time spans of 10 to 15 years. Thus certain parameters of realism have to be established which take into account the polit-

ical feasibilities within a democratic society which directly or indirectly is influenced by the voters.

To achieve any worthwhile results, it is, in a democratic society, necessary to get a concensus of public opinion. Great efforts concerning the spreading of information in the direction of convincing individual interests that they must subordinate certain personal desires to the well-being of urban society are imperative. Whenever energetic efforts in the direction of public awareness of problems and possible solutions are not made, when some popular prejudices are not overcome, the resulting measures must necessarily be of half-hearted character. The results then amount to symbolic gestures such as experimental pedestrian malls or pedestrian zones of insufficient scale; these carry the seeds of failure in them and often result in a setback for effective planning measures for decades.

UTOPIAS

Thus in attempting to cure the heart of the city, two types of utopia must be avoided:

Utopia 1. To proceed with dangerous "heart operations" or the "implanting of a new heart," which involve mortal dangers. This implies that in the case of most cities, we cannot fully utilize those physical measures which I have enumerated for new multifunctional centers.

Utopia 2. To believe that it is possible to treat an organic disease effectively with palliatives and cosmetics, such as the introduction of one-way streets, the imposing of parking and stopping regulations (which never prove enforceable), computerized signal systems, and even temporary or small-sized pedestrian reservations.

The difficulties which planners and public authorities encounter vary greatly from city to city. Generally, it can be stated that city cores of great, historically based tradition are the ones where physical changes are more damaging than beneficial, but that they on the other hand offer the greatest opportunity for revitalization because they possess the strongest powers of resistance against deterioration. Those cities, however, which have developed quickly over shorter time periods and in accordance with materialistic motivations rather than on the basis of civic pride are less sensitive to physical change. However, they will need the application of superior efforts and skills to establish a spirit of urbanity which previously existed only to a minor degree. I will attempt to highlight the difference in the necessary approaches by discussing two extremes: (1) A European city with a long and solidly established urban tradition. (2) Two comparatively young American cities.

CASE STUDY I

Case Study: Core area of Vienna, Austria

Client: The Planning Department of the City of Vienna

Location: The first municipal district of Vienna

Planning Team: Victor Gruen International, Vienna, in cooperation with the municipal planning department and its various technical and economic sub-divisions.

Assignment to the Consultant: A study, to be completed in 26 months (November 1969 to December 1971), devoted to existing conditions, diagnosis concerning physical, economic and sociological health, and development of a concept which would delineate measures to increase the dynamism of the city core with respect to all urban functions.

Background for Planning

History: As an encouragement to all those who believe that every crisis which develops in their specific city is an indication not only of its ultimate doom, but also the end of urbanism generally, I would like to briefly recall the ups and downs of Vienna.

Signs of the existence of this city reach back into the Stone Age. A certain high level of culture had been reached by the Illyrians, but the city was then destroyed around 400 B.C. by the Celts. The Romans founded a new city around a military camp called Vindobona in the first century A.D. This was destroyed by the Markomanns and rebuilt under the Roman Emperor Marcus Aurelius. During the era of the Great Migration, the city was repeatedly occupied, destroyed and rebuilt. In the history of the Goth, it is mentioned as Vindomina, later it is called Wenia and still later, Wiennis. In 1131 the city of Wien was finally raised to the rank of "civitas." It became the residence of the Babenbergs around 1160 and in 1278 was established as the residence of the counts of Habsburg. From then on, its fate was closely connected with the Habsburgs, and it developed from the capital of a Duchy to that of an Arch-Duchy and finally, in 1804, to the capital of the Austrian-Hungarian Empire. As such, it flourished economically and culturally, drawing immigrants from all parts of the widespread empire and thus becoming, similar to Manhattan, the home of a multitude of ethnic groups and a babble of languages. When, in 1918, World War I ended with the dissolution of the Habsburg Empire, Vienna had to readjust itself to its new role as capital of a little republic of 6,000,000 inhabitants. At that time its doom was prophesied, yet between 1918 and

Figure 6-9 Historic etching of Vienna: K & K Haupt und Residenz Stadt Wien. (Imperial and Royal capital and residence city of Vienna in the 18th century.)

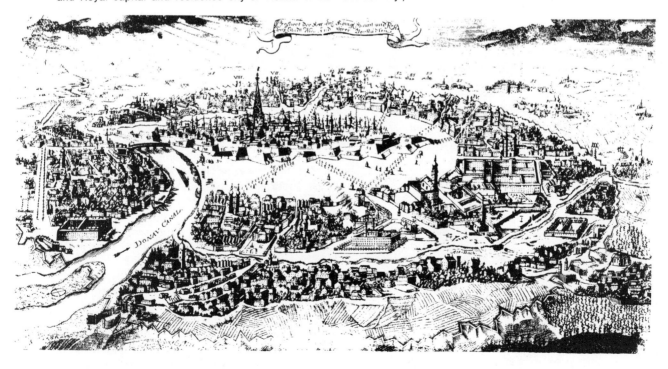

Figure 6-10 Historic etching showing Vienna during the siege by the Turkish armies in 1683.

1938, Vienna remained a center of intellectual and cultural life and was regarded as a shining example of social progress as exemplified by large public housing programs and important achievements in public health and welfare.

With the Anchluss to Hilter-Germany, the city was degraded from the capital of a free country, to a provincial city of Hitler's 1000 Year Reich. Through the driving out of

Jews, socialists, liberals and anti-Nazi catholics, and later on through the ravages of World War II, the city lost hundreds of thousands of its most active citizens. At the end of World War II Vienna was a heap of rubble. This catastrophe was followed by the occupation by Allied troops.

During this occupation, Vienna was divided. Each dis-

Figure 6-11 Vienna's position as center of the Austro-Hungarian Empire (shaded area) until 1918.

trict was occupied by one of the four allied powers, with the exception of the core of the city which was jointly administered. In this manner, the outstanding importance of the core area was, perhaps for the first time in history, recognized by political arrangements.

Reconstruction started during the occupation years with the assistance of the Marshall Plan. Significantly, the first efforts were directed toward reestablishing the "soul of the city." Financial means for the rebuilding of Saint Stephan's cathedral and the State Opera House were partly obtained through public collections in which all political parties, including the communists, participated. Speed of reconstruction increased after the signing of the 1955 peace treaty which ended the occupation.

However, even now, if one applies the usual rules of economics, Vienna has no right to exist. Its population is over-large in relation to the total population of the republic. Geographically, it is located on the extreme end of the nation, only 16 miles distant from the Iron Curtain but very far from those countries with which it has its main trading ties. Thus the phenomenon that the city not only still exists but flourishes and is engaged in ambitious civic undertakings, can only be explained by the inherent power of resistance of its urbanism.

Existing Conditions: Though the city core still plays a major role in relation to the entire city and its region, a number of trends which are traceable to developments which occur outside of the core threaten its continued

vitality. Almost all construction in the last ten years has taken place in the peripheral areas, quite especially outside of the political boundaries. Because of the tie-up between the health of the core and development occurring outside of the political boundaries, we devoted part of our study to an analysis of concept proposals for city-wide and regional measures which are necessary as prerequisites for the revitalization of the city core. These measures are discussed in Chapter 7.

Though the city of Vienna is not subject to population explosion (the regional population is stable at about two million) all other forces (increasing space demands for each urban function, mass transportation by automobile as a consequence of higher incomes and technical progress) are also apparent in the development of Vienna.

Figure 6-12 Vienna's position in Europe. Note line indicating Iron Curtain.

```
■■■    THE IRON CURTAIN
▒▒▒    THE REPUBLIC OF AUSTRIA
```

A	—	ALBANIA		
B	—	BELGIUM		
BU	—	BULGARIA		
CZ	—	CZECHOSLOVAKIA		
D	—	DENMARK		
F	—	FRANCE		
FI	—	FINLAND		
GB	—	GREAT BRITAIN		
GDR	—	GERMAN DEMOCRATIC REPUBLIC		
GFR	—	GERMAN FEDERAL REPUBLIC		
GR	—	GREECE		
H	—	HUNGARY		
I	—	ITALY		
IR	—	REPUBLIC OF IRELAND		

N	—	NORWAY
NL	—	NETHERLANDS
P	—	PORTUGAL
PO	—	POLAND
R	—	ROUMANIA
S	—	SWEDEN
SP	—	SPAIN
SU	—	SOVIET UNION
SW	—	SWITZERLAND
T	—	TURKEY
YU	—	YUGOSLAVIA

The Structure of the City Core: The city core itself is synonymous with the first district. It covers a surface of 690 acres and is located centrally in relation to the municipality and its region. The first district constitutes a central activity area and the historic center of the city.

The structure is differentiated as the result of historic developments. Originally, the core area was surrounded by fortifications and the Glacis (an open green area necessary for military actions). Around 1860 the city walls were removed and one of the largest urban redevelopment projects was undertaken. The land which had been occupied by the Glacis was utilized for the construction of an excellent loop road system (Ring, Kai, Lastenstraße) and adjoining it, public buildings of eclectic style, spacious squares, parks, monuments, fountains, and elegant apartment buildings. The straight-line, grid-iron street pattern of this area, and its buildings, constructed between 1860 and 1890, contrast markedly with the intricate street system of the central portion (which stems from the middle ages), and its buildings, some of which derive from the Romanesque, Gothic, Renaissance, and Baroque periods.

The multifunctional character of these two structurally different areas is also different. The central area contains a very small-grained functional admixture while the nine-teenth-century area is characterized by a much larger-grained admixture.

The historical area, which can be viewed as the heart of the city, has a diameter of about 4,600 feet and contains small and medium-sized enterprises, integrated in an intimate fashion in the horizontal as well as in the vertical sense.

Analyzing the character and size of urban functions contained within the first district and relating the findings to the remaining area of the city, we found that the greatest concentration and variety occurs within the boundaries of the core area. Here we find the most important facets of public administration, cultural, spiritual and educational facilities, many hotels, eating facilities of all types, entertainment facilities, an abundant supply of retail establishments, private administration, professional and other services, and residences housing 25,000.

The average day-time population of the core area is about 240,000 of which 25,000 are inhabitants, 135,000 employees and 80,000 visitors. Of these 215,000 employees and visitors, 60 percent travel to and from the core by public transportation, 24 percent on foot, and 16 percent by automobile.

Most public transportation halts at the loop road. Within

Figure 6-13 First district of Vienna. Note the medieval street pattern within the core, grid pattern along the periphery of the first district.

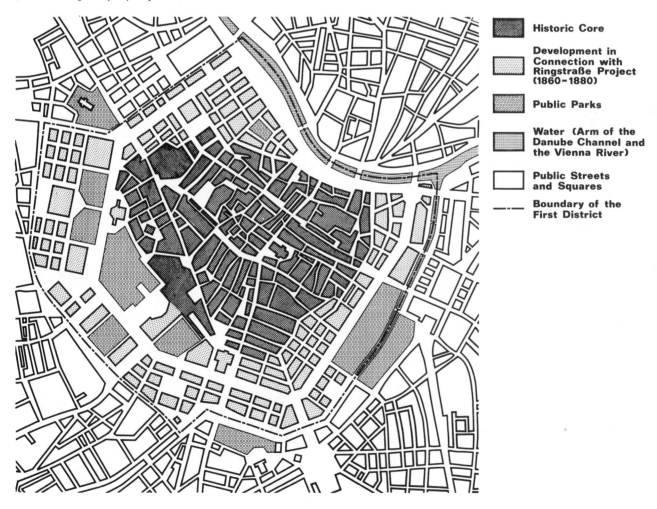

■ **Historic Core**

▒ **Development in Connection with Ringstraße Project (1860–1880)**

▓ **Public Parks**

▨ **Water (Arm of the Danube Channel and the Vienna River)**

□ **Public Streets and Squares**

— ‧ — **Boundary of the First District**

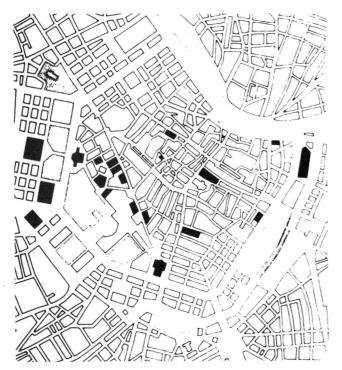

Representation of the Republic, the Government of the Province of Lower Austria, and of the City.

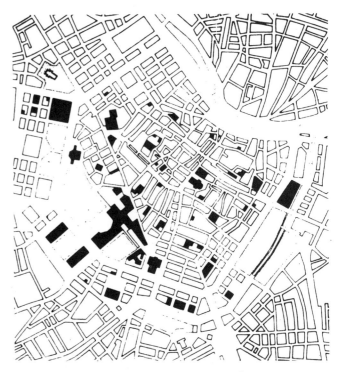

Cultural, spiritual and educational functions

Residential

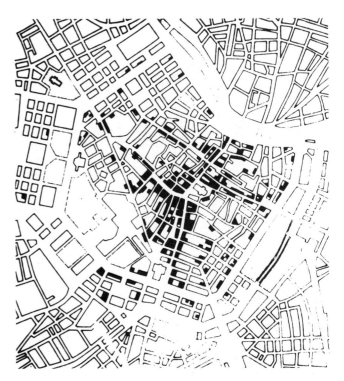

Trade

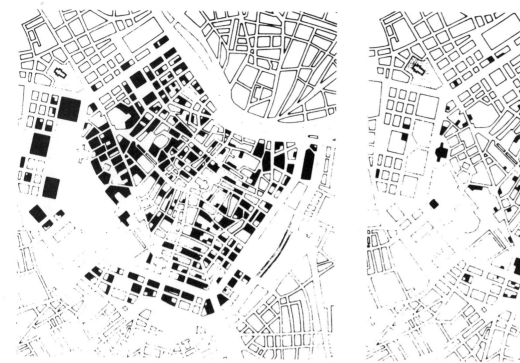

Public and private administration (offices)   Tourism, entertainment, and eating places

Figure 6-14 These six maps try to convey the multifunctional character of the core. Only the main functions are indicated:

Figure 6-15 Methods of transportation used by those entering or leaving the core area of Vienna.

Figure 6-16 Schematic plan for locations of underground garages.

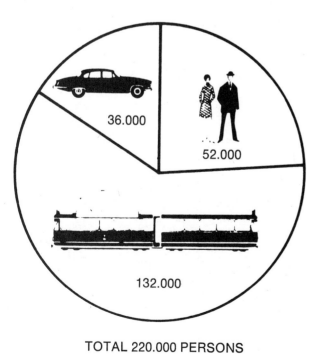

TOTAL 220.000 PERSONS

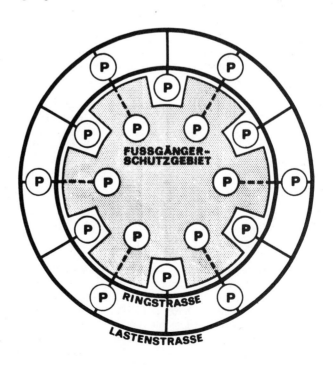

the heart of the city, the only available public transportation is an internal bus system which serves an insignificant number of passengers (16,000) daily.

Diagnosis: Although the city core is basically healthy, there are some functions in the core area which should be considered "non-compatible" because they either create environmental disturbances or are of low productivity in relation to their space demands. These functions would be better located in sub-centers within the highly built-up city area or even on the periphery.

There is also a tendency toward a diluting of the multi-functional character. The number of inhabitants for example, is steadily decreasing. Around 1800 the population of the core was 100,000. It has now dwindled to 25,000. This is partly due to the increased space devoted to public and private administration and partly to the undesirable environmental conditions within the core. A certain lethargy is also recognizable with respect to trade, culture, and social and entertainment activities.

Accessibility by public and individual transportation is not satisfactory. Traffic congestion, air pollution, unbearable noise, and dangers to life and health are typical for the core. This poor performance of secondary serving functions diminishes the vitality of the human functions and could cause serious deterioration if corrective measures are not taken.

Planning Approach: We divided our recommendations into three parts; the functional concept, the urban design concept and the economic concept. These three planning measures are interdependent, and the main thrust of the overall planning approach is directed toward an improvement of the environment with a simultaneous, radical improvement in operation of all serving functions.

Functional Concept: Great attention was paid to the functional concept because only through it could the prerequisites necessary for the other two planning concepts be established.

Accessibility: A significant improvement of public transportation had been ensured in advance of our planning study by the city's decision to construct a subway system, the main lines of which will converge at the very center of the city core.

For this very ambitious and costly undertaking to be a full success however, its highest possible utilization must be assured, which can only be done if the attractive power of the core is considerably enhanced. The transportation capability of the new subway system together with the existing street car and bus systems and existing and projected commuter train connections, is sufficiently great to assure a superior accessibility to the city core.

With regard to accessibility by individual transportation, a number of facts have to be taken into consideration. The total capacity of the radial and circumferential roads serving the core area is restricted and indicates that a maximum of 20,000 parking spaces could be served. The medieval, spider's web-like street pattern of the heart area is unsuitable for automobile traffic, but the existence of a loop road system (Ring, Kai, Lastentraße) establishes the possibility of diverting automobile traffic around the core. This loop road system should be regarded as the last and impenetrable defense line and no private automobiles

would be allowed to travel beyond it, into the core area. In order to make this defense system effective, the circumferential road system must be improved and underground garages for automobiles constructed in locations directly accessible from the loop road system. The plan recommends the construction of these garages under the available generously-dimensioned public squares. These garages would supply approximately 20,000 parking spaces. This is an improvement over the present 16,000 parking spaces especially when one takes into consideration the fact that the majority of the 16,000 are on the surface of public areas.

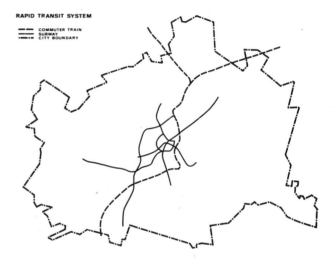

Figure 6-17 The new basic rapid transit system now in construction. It consists of a subway (black line) and a commuter train line (broken line).

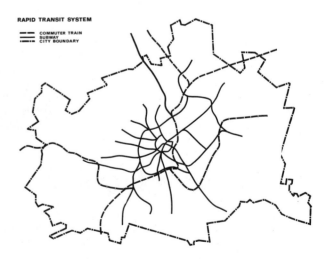

Figure 6-18 Proposed complete network of the rapid transit system.

Figure 6-19 If the automobile were to be given freedom of the city of Vienna, a freeway through Saint Stephan's cathedral might be required.

Figure 6-20 To provide sufficient parking space in the city of Vienna, demolition of all structures might be required. (For sentimental reasons, Saint Stephan's cathedral might be spared.)

Accessibility for pedestrians who stream into the core from adjoining districts is to be improved by the provision of grade-separated pedestrian gates at all important points where the loop roads have to be crossed. These gates are projected partly as underpasses and partly as overpasses, to be utilized also by accessory transportation vehicles.

To improve accessibility for goods and services, two measures are proposed. Firstly, improvement by introducing grade-separation. This can be achieved by utilizing the subway lines during night and early morning hours for the transportation of goods, which could then be temporarily stored in large underground depots adjoining subway stations. Similar depots would also be constructed along the periphery of the core, directly accessible from the loop road system. The second improvement could be made by rationalizing the present goods-moving handling. Goods-moving services should be taken care of by a cooperatively organized company, which would supply services by messengers on foot, tricycle, and with small- and medium-sized electric trucks. All services would be attainable by radio or telephone call. In this way, the thousands of individual poorly utilized goods transportation vehicles would be replaced by a few hundred efficiently used, environmentally friendly vehicles.

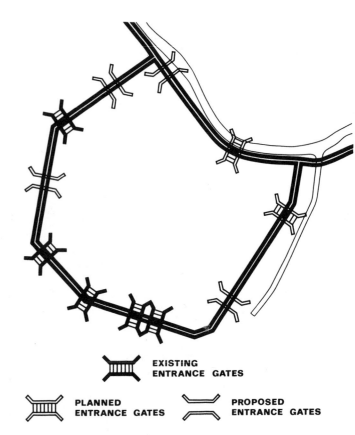

EXISTING ENTRANCE GATES

PLANNED ENTRANCE GATES

PROPOSED ENTRANCE GATES

Figure 6-21 Schematic map of pedestrian gates, existing, projected or proposed. All these gates are grade-separated.

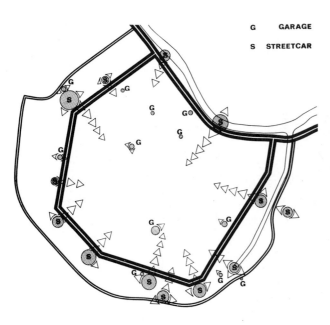

G GARAGE

S STREETCAR

Figure 6-22 Origin and strength of pedestrian streams presently.

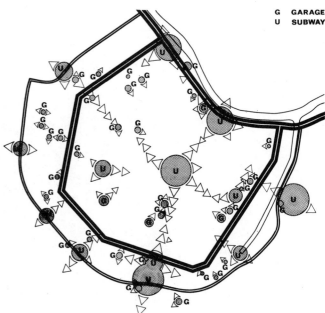

G GARAGE
U SUBWAY

Figure 6-23 Origin and strength of pedestrian streams after completion of the concept.

Figure 6-24 Map illustrating the role of the basic network of the subway as freight carrier. Stations on the outside, establish direct communication with railroads or freeways. The circles indicate significant places for underground goods depots.

Figure 6-25 Mass produced electric truck. (One of the types of vehicles recommended for the goods transportation company.)

Movements within the City Core: At the present time, movement by automobile, by truck or on foot is extremely time consuming. The available land area of the core within the Ring is utilized to an unusually high degree by buildings and parks. This area can in no way provide sufficient space for movement of all types. Counts have shown that at any given moment of a high activity hour, the limited public space of the core is filled with 16,000 vehicles, moving or parked. The utilization of streets and squares by vehicles is so intense that movement space for public transportation and pedestrians is insufficient.

Disturbances caused by vehicular traffic and the dangers to life and limb created by it, are mainly responsible for the extremely poor environmental conditions. The measures we have recommended have two aims.

1. To radically reduce the quantity of surface movement by vehicles.
2. To improve the quality of the remaining traffic by regulations which aim at achieving a peaceful coexistence between human and mechanical service-functions, and at a radical reduction in air pollution, noise, and danger.

All permitted vehicles in the core are classed as accessory transportation and as such must have a number of qualities in common. Restricted in size and weight, and powered either electrically or by liquid gas, they will be subject to a speed limit of 7.5 mph and controls concerning permissible noise levels. For transportation of people within the core, a mini-bus system has been proposed.

This would establish connections with all important arrival points along the loop road system. A bus has been especially designed for this purpose, and a prototype has now been constructed (Manufacturers Steyr-Daimler-Puch). This bus, which was designed to specifications of the municipal transportational authority, will carry 20 passengers. It will be operated at two minute intervals during normal times, one minute intervals during peak hours, and at longer intervals during off-peak hours.

In addition, a limited number of electric or liquid gas operated taxis (300 liquid gas operated taxis are already in operation in Vienna), will be allowed in the core. Special electric vehicles for hotels and tourism, the characteristic Viennese Fiaker, (a rubber-tired carriage drawn by two horses), emergency vehicles for fire protection, health services, municipal services, etc., and electrically operated goods-moving vehicles, will also be permitted. With the exception of the emergency vehicles, all will be subject to the restrictions as imposed on accessory transportation.

Calculations have shown that the amount of traffic within the core area can in this manner be reduced from the present 16,000 during one moment of a high activity period, to about 800, or 5 percent of the present quantity. Because these remaining vehicles will be subject to all aforementioned regulations, those phenomena which interfere with human functions will be eradicated and an absolute priority for human functions will be established.

The aim of the functional concept to create an environmental oasis by eliminating conflicts between primary human functions and secondary serving functions can thus be attained. Simultaneously an improvement of the functioning of all serving functions will be achieved.

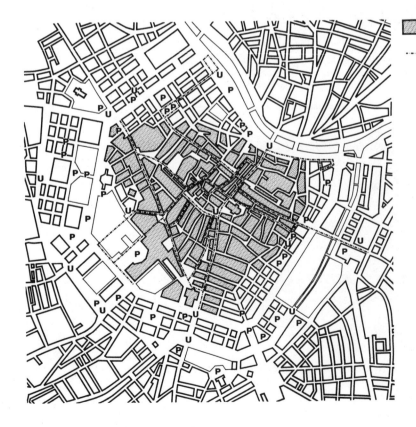

	ENVIRONMENTAL OASIS
-------	MINIBUS ROUTES
U	SUBWAY STATIONS
P	PARKING GARAGES

Figure 6-26 Proposed network for minibuses.

Figure 6-27 Photograph of minibus prototype.

Figure 6-28 The Viennese Fiaker.

Pedestrian Malls versus Environmental Oases: It will be noted that the creation of a limited number of pedestrian streets or so-called malls, has not been envisaged. In spite of the fact that this method which has been utilized in centers of cities all over the world also has its advocates in Vienna, we regard the concept of creating a limited number of pedestrian malls as generally undesirable for the effective enlivenment of an urban area and in relation to Vienna, particularly unsuitable.

The pedestrian mall has proved successful in suburban regional shopping centers where it is possible to achieve grade-separated delivery traffic and horizontally separated transportational parking areas, and where only one function (shopping) is served. The blind imitation of this method within a multifunctional, organically grown core area can only be regarded as an attempt to suburbanize the heart of the city.

When pedestrian malls are created in central areas, along those streets where a concentration of retail trade is located, it is necessary to create space for the needed transportational requirements along parallel adjoining streets. Garages, delivery roads and traffic ways have to be arranged in areas which are poorly equipped to handle the load which has been excluded from the main streets. Although the retail streets may benefit economically from their new status as pedestrian malls, in other parts of the

Figure 6-29 If one street is made into a "pedestrian paradise," the adjoining streets become "hell"!

Figure 6-30 The Kärntner Strasse now.

core, where residences, cultural and artistic functions, and smaller enterprises are located, environmental conditions deteriorate and the functions located in these areas are endangered.

With regard to the particular unsuitability of pedestrian malls for the core area of Vienna, this is partly due to the fact that the concentration of large merchandising operations which is found in the center of most cities, does not exist in Vienna. In fact, the smaller enterprises which form the bulk of trade facilities in the core, are fairly evenly distributed, in interesting and architecturally important side streets and small squares. In addition, due to the intricate and irregular street pattern of the core, parallel side streets to major shopping streets, do not exist. Believing that the city must be regarded as an organic entity we concluded that only a systematic approach could achieve a marked improvement of environmental conditions and an improvement of the functioning of the service facilities.

Urban Design Concept: Our report establishes guidelines for approaches to urban design without however, engaging in any detailed design activity which we believe should in the interests of variety and individuality, be put in the hands of many creative professionals.

The liberation of public space from unnecessary quantities of surface traffic and the regulations to which all other traffic is subject, will assure the dominance of the pedestrian and provide new space for additional urban expressions. The aim of the guidelines was to propose ways and means in which this newly liberated space could be used to best advantage. The guidelines recommended that:

1. Level difference between sidewalks and driving lanes be eliminated.
2. Pavements should be varied and designed to enhance the pleasure of walking.

Figure 6-31 Kärntner Strasse after completion of the concept.

3. Street lighting, up to now designed for the needs of vast hordes of fast moving automobiles, should be redesigned according to human scale. Depending on the character and size of the street it could be of festive or intimate character.

4. Weather protection should be provided along store fronts by means of canopies, arcades or colonnades.

5. The liberated public urban space should be enlivened by tree groups, flower beds, sculptures, fountains, rest benches and children's playgrounds.

6. In squares and broader streets, the liberated open space should be used for side-walk cafés, markets, music pavilions, stage platforms, etc.

7. Existing buildings of outstanding architectural or emotional character and assemblies of such buildings should be protected, and enhanced in their appearance. In order to make protection effective however, it will be necessary to encourage productive use of these structures. At the same time regulations should be enforced which would discourage demolition or neglect of significant structures. A number of measures which are possible within the legal framework have been proposed.

Economic Concept: The Municipal Department for economic coordination expressed the belief that the measures proposed in the functional and urban design concepts would be so successful that a considerably increased space demand would be created. Reacting to this assumption, we established a land and space inventory (with the

Figure 6-32 The Graben now.

Figure 6-33 The Graben after completion of the concept.

assistance of the Geographical Institute of Vienna and the economic organization WIST), and outlined possibilities for meeting an additional space demand. We established that increased space demands could be met in the following ways:

1. Through intensification of existing utilization (higher sales per measuring unit of retail space, fuller utilization of existing built-up space, a more rational utilization of office space).
2. By increasing revenue-producing space by utilizing unused land and under-used building substance and the space now occupied by non-conforming functions (warehousing, technical equipment, industry, etc.)

3. By the creation of new building substance by means of redevelopment of certain fringe areas in which outdated buildings of no historic or architectural value exist.
4. By enlargement of the core area in those directions where an integration with the environmental functioning pattern would be easily achieved. This particularly concerns those areas now occupied by two large military barracks and other areas which are occupied by over-aged structures.

Summarizing, it was possible to prove that the reserves necessary for an expanded economic potential are fully available without the need to interfere with the historic skyline of Vienna by the construction of skyscrapers.

Figure 6-34 The Neue Markt now.

Figure 6-35 Typical markets, as they existed in many of the public squares of the Vienna core area until the outbreak of the automobile age, can be reintroduced.

Figure 6-36 The Neue market after completion of the concept. (Note: the vehicles shown represent service vehicles, which will be permitted.)

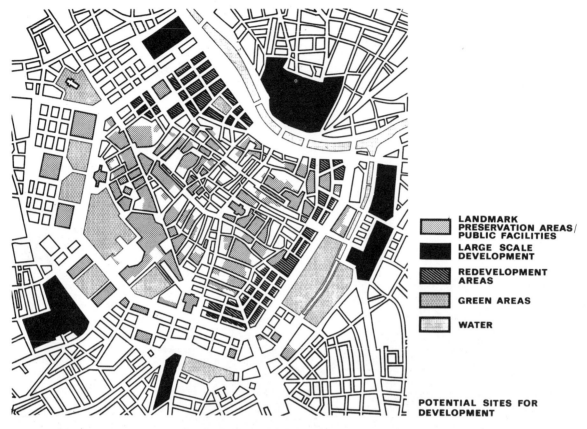

LANDMARK
PRESERVATION AREAS/
PUBLIC FACILITIES

LARGE SCALE
DEVELOPMENT

REDEVELOPMENT
AREAS

GREEN AREAS

WATER

POTENTIAL SITES FOR
DEVELOPMENT

Figure 6-37 Redevelopment areas: map indicating (a) preservation areas, (b) large scale development areas outside the Ring, (c) development areas within the heart area in places where neither the building substance nor the street pattern are of historic interest.

Figure 6-38 The Graben: View of part of Vienna's temporary pedestrian area.

Status of Project: Our study proceeded in steady cooperation with the planning department of the city of Vienna and was submitted in final form in December 1971. It is now being studied by various municipal departments and it is hoped that political decisions can be made in 1972. However, a number of elements of the overall concept have already been decided upon.

1. The construction of the subway system is underway. The main station of this system, in the center of the core area (near Saint Stephan's cathedral) is located in the middle of a square, thus anticipating a pedestrian area.
2. A number of the projected fringe garages are under construction, or have already been completed, others are in advanced planning stages.
3. The improvement of the loop road system is underway.
4. During the Christmas 1971 season, an experimental traffic-free area was created in order to test public reaction. This experiment was so successful that it was decided to enlarge the area and to make the arrangement permanent.
5. Revitalization of the core area and the concepts which we have proposed have become a matter of public interest, reflected in lively discussions through all mass media.

Figure 6-39 Rendering of the main subway station in front of Saint Stephan's Cathedral, located within an area free of surface traffic (with the exception of minibuses and emergency vehicles). Architects, commissioned by the Planning Department of Vienna, Wolfgang and Traude Windbrechtinger.

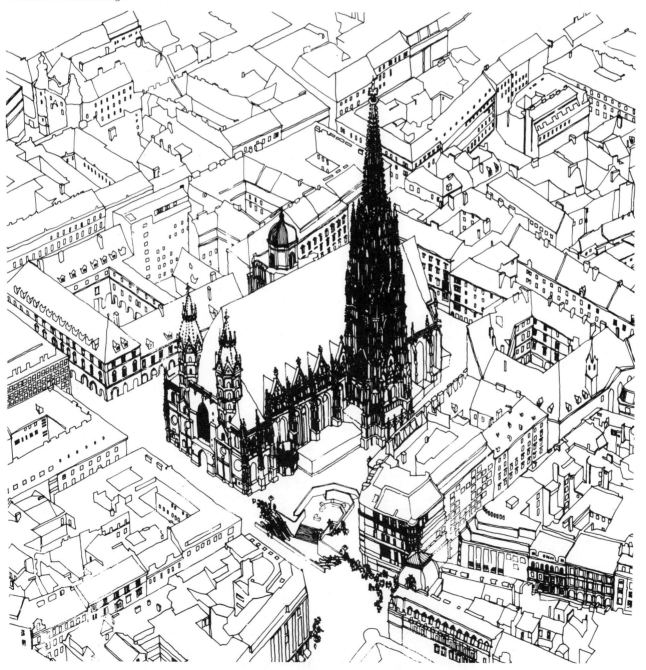

CASE STUDY II

Name of Project: Revitalization Plan for Fort Worth

Location: Core area of Fort Worth, Texas

Client: The Texas General Electric Company

Planners: Victor Gruen Associates

Background for Planning: The leading spirit behind the master plan for Fort Worth was a private business organization, and in particular the man who was then its President, Mr. J. B. Thomas.

Mr. Thomas' interest was aroused by an article which I had written for the Harvard Business Review in 1954, shortly after the opening of Northland Center. In this article, I had stated my opinion that the experiences gained in the planning of regional shopping centers could and should be transferred to the revitalization of existing downtown cores. Mr. Thomas felt that it was in the interests of his company, the General Electric Company of Texas, to achieve a revitalization of the core area of Fort Worth because of the heavy investments which had been made in this area in order to serve its population.

15 years and 5,000 miles lie between the study for the core area of Vienna and the one for Fort Worth (presented in 1956), however, although Vienna is an organically grown, old city, and Fort Worth a comparatively new town, founded and operated in the interests of trade, there are similarities in the problems which were to be solved, which resulted in a similar planning approach.

The revitalization plan for Fort Worth is unique in that it was the first ever developed for a major American city. Its basic principles and the planning approaches employed, significantly influenced all similar undertakings on which I have since worked, and also revitalization projects undertaken by others, throughout the United States and in other countries. This, in spite of the fact that the plan was never fully executed. This phenomenon is illustrated by a remark made by the City Planning Director of Philadelphia, Mr. Edward Bacon, who said: "The Fort Worth plan is, as far as I know, the only unborn child who has produced hundreds of grandchildren."

From the aerial view of Fort Worth (Figure 6-43), it can be seen that the core area is marked by small herds of skyscrapers which are utilized for administration and trade. This small, high density area is surrounded by an under-utilized "gray area" which is cut into ribbons by a mechanically laid out road pattern. Only beyond this neglected gray area do the residential suburban zones begin.

In order to revitalize the core, we recommended steps which would achieve the following:

1. Improvement in accessibility, especially by means of public transportation.
2. Exclusion of the private automobile, and radical reduction of all other surface traffic within the core, with the remaining traffic operated either electrically or by some other environmental-friendly method.
3. Creation of a loop road around the core area by rerouting the already projected freeway (then destined to cut *through* the core).

4. Provision of garages and bus terminals directly accessible from the new loop road.
5. Encouragement of multifunctionality. (Achievable because of the superior environment which the core would possess).
6. Creation of new urban features and landscaping in the urban space liberated from automotive traffic.
7. Establishment of an underground goods-moving system beneath the existing service alleys.

In this way, the core area could be converted into an environmental oasis.

Description of Plan: The projected multilevel parking garages providing 60,000 parking spaces were to be so arranged that they would reach like fingers into the downtown areas, thereby reducing walking distances between the pedestrian exits of the parking garages and the center of town, to between two and four minutes. It was proposed that the pedestrian areas be served by accessory transportation in the form of slow-moving electrically-powered buses.

A new system of express buses connecting the region with the city core was proposed. To achieve highest possible utilization of the land within the core, it was proposed that the built-up area of existing functions be increased and added to by means of new building substance. To enhance and enliven the sterile, grid-iron street pattern, visual interruptions such as new structures around plazas, and landscaped squares were proposed.

The major effects for which the plan was striving, are best described by an excerpt from the book *The Exploding Metropolis*, written by the great crusader for human values in urbanism, Jane Jacobs who wrote:

The plan by Victor Gruen Associates for Fort Worth . . . has been publicized chiefly for its arrangements to provide enormous perimeter parking garages and convert downtown into a pedestrian island, but its main purpose is to enliven the streets with variety and detail. . . . To these ends, the excellent Gruen plan includes in its street treatment, sidewalk arcades, poster columns, flags, flower beds, and special lighting effects. Street concerts, dances and exhibits are to be fostered. The whole point is to make the streets more surprising, more compact, more variegated and busier than before, not less so.

Status of the Project: Although the plan was adopted by the City Authorities, only certain features of it were executed. Thus for example, our proposal to reroute the freeway and to convert it into a loop road around the core, was implemented.

Although discussion concerning the project has never ceased, the opposition, coming mostly from the parking lot and garage operators, has up to now prevented its further execution.

Judging with the benefit of hindsight, I believe that the reasons for this non-action are that the city and state authorities resented the fact that the plan was developed by private enterprise, that the project was far ahead of its time, and that federal assistance for urban redevelopment was not at that time available.

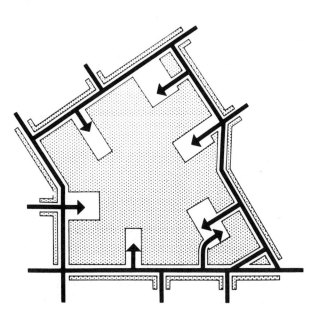

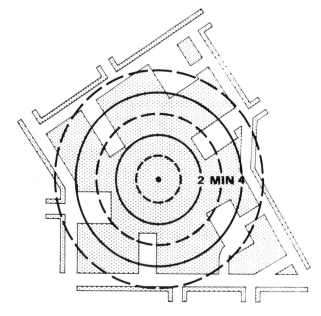

Figure 6-40 Fort Worth: Schematic plan showing proposed loop road with accesses to the perimeter garages.

Figure 6-41 Fort Worth: Schematic diagram with walking time distances from the perimeter garages to various points in the heart area.

Figure 6-42 Fort Worth: Bird's-eye view of a portion of the central area as foreseen in the concept.

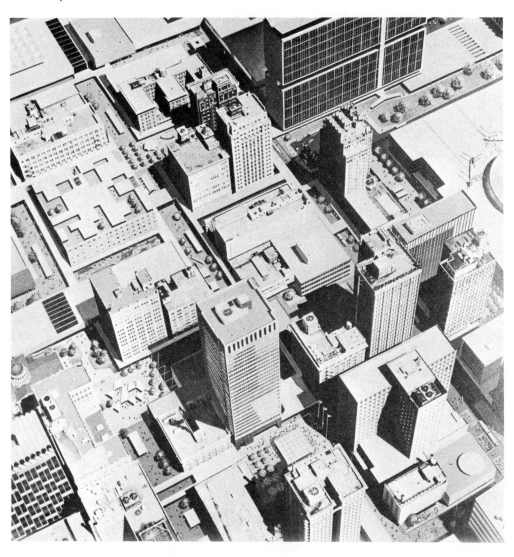

Figure 6-43   Aerial view of Fort Worth showing conditions as they were around 1955.

Figure 6-44 Fort Worth: Bird's-eye view of the proposed revitalization project. (The heart area of Forth Worth.)

CASE STUDY III

Name of Project: Core area of Fresno

Location: Fresno, California

Client: The Federal Urban Redevelopment Agency, the city government, and a private citizens' association. (The Hundred Percenters).

Planning Team: Planners and architects, Victor Gruen Associates, landscape architects, Eckbo, Dean and Williams.

Background for Planning: The revitalization project for the core area of Fresno, of which a significant part was accomplished by September 1964 when a pedestrian area in the center of the core was opened, was part of a city redevelopment project on which I and the partners and staff of Victor Gruen Associates had been engaged since 1958.

Fresno is strategically located in the St. Joaquin Valley, approximately halfway between Los Angeles and San Francisco. It is a young city, with a steadily growing population which in 1960 had reached about 200,000. Unhampered by any physical boundaries, the inhabited area of Fresno has spread in all directions in a typical suburban pattern, with the result that this sprawling area could be realistically served only by private automobile and truck. The central area, plagued by traffic congestion and pollution, deteriorated.

Description of Plan:

1. Projected freeway alignments were redesigned to provide a loop road a considerable distance from the core, connected by arterial roads, to a proposed inner loop road directly surrounding the core area.
2. It was proposed that garages and bus terminals be located along this inner loop.
3. Within the central area, an automobile-free environment was to be created which however, would be served by accessory transportation (small buses) and, during certain hours, by goods-moving vehicles.
4. Multifunctionality was to be encouraged, especially through the construction of new residential quarters, a convention center and new hotels.
5. Urban design efforts and landscaping which would

create an attractive atmosphere in the core, were proposed.

The effects of these measures are perhaps best described if I let an objective observer give testimony. Bernard Taper wrote in the October 1966 issue of *Reader's Digest:*

As I write this, I am sitting contentedly, a cool drink at my elbow, right in the middle of Fulton Street—the main street of downtown Fresno, California, but nobody gives me a second glance. Two and a half years ago, I would have been run over, arrested or firmly led away to have my head examined. What I am doing now is simply part of the new pattern of life this bustling city has adopted: one starting from the premise that downtown is for people.

Fresno has boldly banished all automobiles from the heart of its business district, converting an area six blocks long by three blocks wide into an attractive pedestrian area. Ultimately, nine more blocks will be added. Where there once were traffic jams, fumes, and the standard ugliness of an American city's downtown, there are now gardens, fountains, pools and numerous pieces of handsome sculpture. For the children, there are imaginative playgrounds. And for the elderly or leisurely, benches shaded by grape arbors are placed near fountains and pools.

Status of Project: All proposed measures were implemented and during the first years after the completion of the project, it appeared that this courageous venture would be a full success. In recent years however, developments of the overall plan have slowed down and certain critical situations have arisen which, if not met, may threaten the efforts and financial investments which have gone into this project.

It is particularly disappointing to note that department stores and other retail establishments which it was intended should be integrated into the new core, moved instead into large regional shopping areas, located beyond the boundaries of the area controlled by the city authorities. In addition, and perhaps even less understandable, suburban locations were chosen for certain federally financed urban functions which could have been constructed in the core area. Thus the admirable cooperative effort of citizens and authorities to revitalize Fresno's core, is seriously threatened due to the schizophrenic attitude of the government, the lack of redevelopment funds, and the nonexistence of overall regional planning.

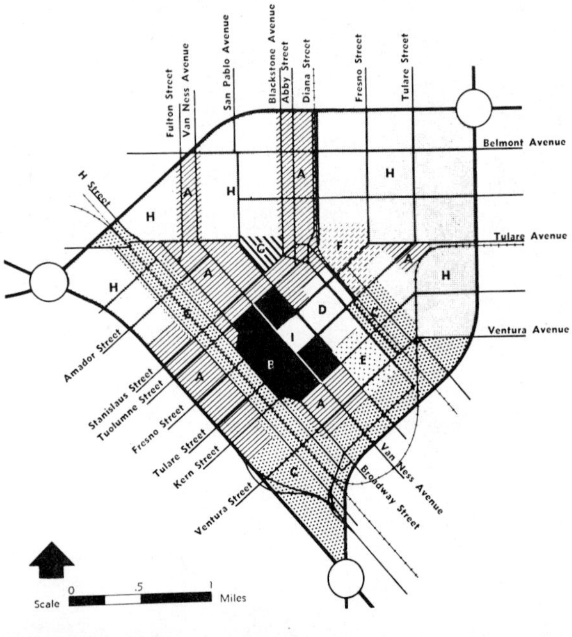

Schematic Land Use
A Outer Commercial
B Inner Commerical
C Industrial, Wholesaling, and Warehousing
D Civic Center
E Convention Hall
F Medical Complex
G Institutional Complex
H Residential
I County Park

Figure 6-45 Fresno: Schematic land usage plan.

Figure 6-46 The new Fresno.

Figure 6-47 This illustration, together with that on the facing page, shows the arrangement of pedestrian streets and zones in 20 cities. All are drawn to the same scale.

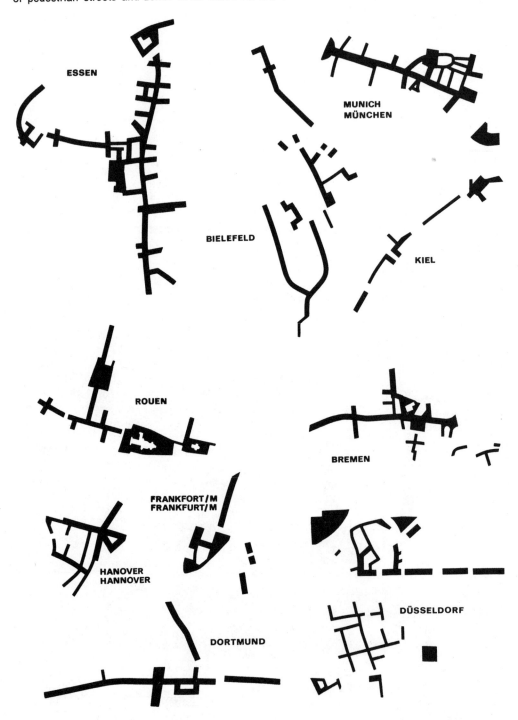

SUMMARY

Efforts to save city cores: The number of cities in which efforts have been undertaken to revitalize the core areas is considerable. The OECD (Organization for Economic Cooperation and Development) has collected data on 160 such cities just in their member states (14 European countries, United States, and Japan), but unfortunately, the majority of these projects are restricted to the conversion of a number

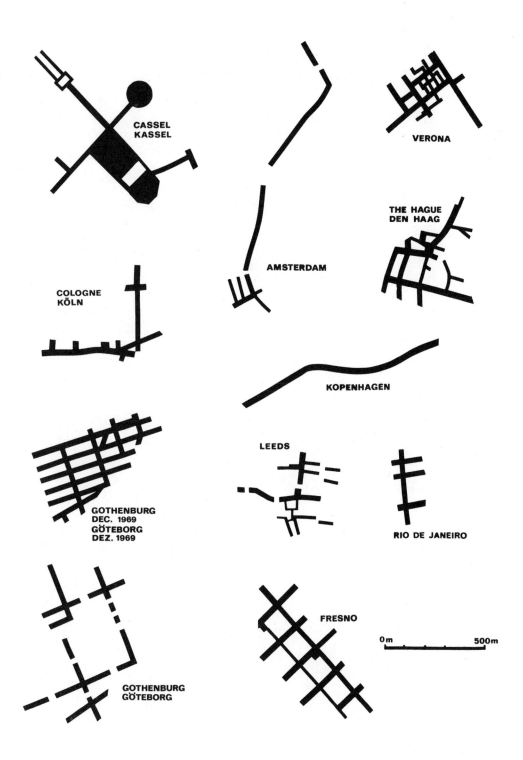

CASSEL
KASSEL

VERONA

AMSTERDAM

THE HAGUE
DEN HAAG

COLOGNE
KÖLN

KOPENHAGEN

LEEDS

GOTHENBURG
DEC. 1969
GÖTEBORG
DEZ. 1969

RIO DE JANEIRO

FRESNO

0 m   500 m

GOTHENBURG
GÖTEBORG

of main business streets to malls or pedestrian streets. The case studies in this chapter are, in contrast, all directed toward the creation of a contiguous, large area with a radically improved environment.

If the achievement of multifunctionality, safety and a systematic improvement of servicing functions is to be considered as the way to revitalize city cores, then I submit that only a systematic approach can be of avail.

7

Figure 7-43 The organically-grown city as source of inspiration for the new urban pattern. (See Case Study III, Region of Vienna, page 244.) This historical map of Vienna was drawn in 1766 by Daniel Huber.

THE EMERGING NEW URBAN PATTERN

THE SPACE SQUEEZE

The title of this chapter indicates a certain optimism as to the emergence of a new urban pattern. This optimism is not based on the belief that radical changes will occur because of a sudden wave of wisdom and benevolence as expressed by individuals or groups organizing themselves into large corporations in the free enterprise system or into collectives or combines in authoritarian, communist countries. It is grounded in my conviction that dire necessity will force us to take decisive countermeasures in the face of a phenomenon which I will call the "space squeeze."

The "space squeeze" is caused by countervailing forces. The existence of the growing strength of these forces, which push from two different directions, creates a trap which will prove inescapable if we do not find ways and means to take countermeasures.

What then are these countervailing forces? They could be compared to two armies, one of which is on the offensive, and another forced into a defensive position.

The offensive forces are those which increase the demand for urban space and, as aggressors, tend to steadily widen what Hitler used to call the lebensraum and which we can also express as the "elbowroom" or the living space of urbanized humanity. However, just as Hitler had the sad experience of finding that his overambitiousness in the extension of the lebensraum of the German nation all over Europe had to collapse because of overextended communications, so we have found that, by extending the "breathing space," we are running out of air suitable for breathing. We may thus be forced to recognize, in the near future, that we have to employ, on a municipal, national, and international basis, a strategy which will permit us to channel our growing urban space demands into new forms which will conserve land and all those nature-given substances establishing the basis for biological life on this planet; instead of just growing, we shall have to learn how to *grow up*. This implies inner and vertical growth instead of horizontal sprawl.

In developing an overall strategy, we have to face frankly the existence of those undeniable factors which are increasing the demand for urban space:

1. Human population explosion.
2. The increasing desire of humans to settle in urban areas.
3. The increasing space demand for each individual living unit.
4. The growing space demand for working quarters in the tertiary structure of the economy (office space).
5. Increasing consumption, therefore greater space demands for distribution, warehouses, and selling facilities.
6. The increase of waste products.
7. Increasing demands for communication corridors for the moving of people and goods.
8. An increased demand for space for leisure-time activities of all types.

The pressure of the aggressive forces differ from continent to continent, from country to country, and from one urban conglomeration to another. However, we can observe some typical phenomena:

1. Large conurbations grow most rapidly.
2. Small towns grow at a lesser rate or even retreat.
3. Rural areas are depopulated.

Within large conurbations we find:

i. Central areas lose population.
ii. Older suburban areas remain stable.
iii. New suburban areas (metropolitan regions) grow explosively.

The most critical situations, which occur as a result of the pressure for more urban space, develop in large conurbations where the suburbs of one city grow together with those of the adjacent ones, resulting in a shapeless, poorly served, and in every respect, "under-developed" megalopolis.

Operating in the opposite direction from the easily recognizable space-demanding forces, the elemental powers of nature which, though they have been pressed into a defensive role, demonstrate their overwhelming strength by proving to us in an ever more convincing way that any future aggression against them must result in the self-destruction of the aggressor. Their "miracle weapons" are convincingly effective. They threaten a total blockade, cutting off urbanized areas from supply of air, water, and food, and all contact with the expressions of nature which man needs to reload his physical and psychological batteries, and a growing impossibility to escape through the blockade into the remaining areas in which man could spend his leisure time. The effects of such a blockade are so powerful that they would bring about physical and psychological starvation of urbanized man. This implies starvation of the totality of the human race, with the exception of those few who might outlive the holocaust, protected as hermits in the pollution-proof shelter of an isolated spot within natural environments. The existence of the "space squeeze" is undeniable, as is also the existence of those forces which increase the demand for urban space. Urbanized man can escape from the squeeze only if a "new urban pattern" emerges.

We extricate ourselves from the trap sprung by the "space squeeze" only if we conserve the nature-given assets with greatest wisdom and economy.

A BLUEPRINT FOR THE MANAGEMENT OF OUR PLANET'S SURFACE

The "Global Environmental Chart" (Figure 7-1) attempts to illustrate a sketchy outline for the utilization of our planet's surface. The term "surface" concerns the thin layer of the planet's crust and atmosphere which man is inhabiting or exploiting.

In this chart, three categories of environment are established:

A. The man-made environment.
B. The man-influenced environment.
C. The natural environment.

If we want to safeguard the biological and ecological balance, then our paramount goal must obviously be to control category A (man-made environment) stringently, as far as size and location are concerned, in order to minimize adverse influences on nature-given assets.

Category B (man-influenced environment) is the one in which, by a synthesis of man's efforts and nature's blessings, our food supply and our requirement of wood and its by-products are produced. With regard to this area, controls must be created and maintained to safeguard long-range highest possible productivity without permitting interference with natural assets.

Figure 7-1 Global Environmental chart: Utilization of our planet's surface.

Types of Environment	Goals	Functions	Means	Land Use Criteria	Land Use Methods
A. THE MAN-MADE ENVIRONMENT					
a. Cityscape	urban amenity, protection from natural and man-made hostile forces	1. habitation	dwellings	compactness, strictly defined boundaries, cellular organization	confined and defined
		2. production	light industry plants		
		3. distribution	stores, eating places		
		4. services	facilities for professionals and crafts		
		5. education and research	schools and institutes		
		6. public + private administration	government buildings and offices		
		7. health care	medical facilities + hospitals		
		8. recreation			
		a. physical	sports facilities, parks + greenbelts		
		b. psychological	entertainment places		
		9. human experiences			
		a. cultural	theaters, concert houses, galleries		
		b. social	meeting places, hotels		
		c. spiritual	places for introspection		
		d. artistic	studios		
b. Technoscape	provision of basic resources, basic production, primary communication	1. extraction of minerals and fossil oils	mines, quarries, oil fields	restricted as to size and location	location to be chosen with respect to protecting A.a., B,C from disturbances through emissions of noise. gases, fumes, dust, vibration location to be chosen with respect to accessibility from areas A.a. distribution net system in areas A.a. subterranean. in areas B,C strictly controlled
		2. production of energy	energy plants		
		3. conditioning + storage of water	reservoirs, filtration plants		
		4. climate management (heating, air conditioning)	heating and air-conditioning plants		
		5. production of primary goods	plants for heavy industry		
		6. storage and reprocessing of waste products	incinerators, sewage treatment plants chemical plants		
		7. large scale protection from hostile forces (natural + human)	flood control, avalanche control, fire control, security force camps		
		8. primary distribution net for 1,2,3,4,5,6,7	railroads, pipelines, aviation facilities, cables, roads, harbors telecommunication, outer-space navigation		
		9. mass storage for 1 and 5			
B. THE MAN-INFLUENCED ENVIRONMENT Landscape Waterscape	growing of natural products	agriculture	fields	best suitable surfaces should be utilized	low density, restricting land use to structures which serve directly the function of supplying natural products, controls concerning preservation of natural assets
		forestry	forests		
		cattle raising	pastures		
		fishing	fishing grounds		
C. THE NATURAL ENVIRONMENT					
a. Nature parks	linkage between man and nature, air and water conservation	recreation, achievement of physical and mental fitness	path-way system, bridle-paths, camping grounds, hostelries	generous setting aside of areas of scenic interest	large number of sufficient size, partly in easy accessibility of cityscape, partly further remote but with good accessibility
b. Nature preserves	preservation of nature and natural species to safeguard biological balance	research or natural sciences	extremely limited access	select relatively unspoiled natural areas of considerable size	no structures of any type permitted, although scientific recording equipment such as a weather recording station would be allowed

Finally, category C (the natural environment) should be carefully guarded against any slopping over of the land uses which are permitted in categories A and B. Areas belonging to category C should be well distributed. They should be as numerous, large and contiguous as feasible.

Taking time as a factor, it may prove necessary to set aside certain parts of the natural environment for future development. These areas should be selected in accordance to the following considerations:

1. They should be of comparatively little value as far as benefits of nature are concerned.
2. They should be remote from existing elements of the man-made environment.
3. They should not encroach on areas needed for category B.
4. They should be utilized only if our ability to intensify the land use for cityscape and technoscape by highest usage of land assigned to them has been completely exhausted.

I submit that we have by no means reached this point and that, quite to the contrary, we have been splurging indiscriminately and irresponsibly with respect to the use of surfaces for the man-made environment. We have done so without consideration to the obvious scarcity of supply of natural assets and to the simple truth that land cannot be manufactured.

I would therefore like to concentrate now on:

Utilization of Urban Land

For this purpose, I have developed an "abstract urbanization model" in which I attempt to furnish proof of the practical feasibility of containing the man-made environment on reasonably limited surfaces. This abstract model is based on realistic assumptions. It utilizes technological tools which are already available; densities which are lower than those one finds in some existent cities. It is conceived with the aim of creating human amenities superior to the ones which are offered by the conurbation pattern today.

There is no doubt that through progress of technology, a considerably greater intensification of land use can be achieved. Even the conservative approach, as illustrated through the "abstract model," however, demonstrates that compared with land use practices now applied, a substantial saving of surfaces for the man-made environment could be achieved.

On the Global Environmental Chart I have subdivided the man-made environment into two parts: (a) Cityscape; (b) Technoscape.

Cityscape is devoted to the functions listed on this chart. In order to create the greatest amount of amenities and opportunities for the urbanite, it must be protected from hostile forces, whether created by nature or through man's technology.

Urban technoscape serves only certain of the functions listed on the global chart. In the interest of urban amenity, it must be separated from cityscape. That part of the technological environment which for employment reasons must be located close to cityscape must be organized in a land-conserving fashion, in compact clusters, with due regard to prevailing winds and accessibility but with that amount of isolation which, in relation to disturbance factors appears necessary.

The abstract model relates to an urban organism with a population of two million persons. However, the principles expounded could be applied to much smaller settlements (maybe down to a few hundred inhabitants) and, of course, to much larger ones also.

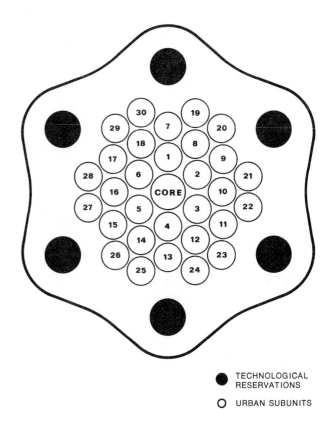

Figure 7-2 Abstract model of an urban organism with a population of 2 million persons.

Figure 7-3 determines three distinct areas, all located within the incorporated boundaries of a metropolis.

The metropolitan area covers 85,500 acres. The central portion of this metropolitan area is occupied by cityscape of 24,700 acres. The remaining peripheral area is devoted to six "technological reservations," each of 1,310 acres, together 7,860 acres and an urban green belt of 52,940 acres.

Cityscape itself is composed of urban subunits in accordance to a cellular organization pattern. The subunits are 30 towns gravitating around a metropolitan core. Each one of these units consists of a nucleus and a surrounding green area. The latter effectuates the separation of one urban environmental unit from another and furnishes the space needed for subsurface, urban communications.

The sizes of these urban subunits are:

Metropolitan core	1,210 acres	
30 towns each 783 acres	23,490 acres	

Each town consists of three districts of 247 acres each and one town center of 42 acres—together 783 acres. Each district is composed of three communities of 74.1 acres each, together, 222.3 acres; and one district center of 24.7 acres.

Each community is composed of three neighborhoods of 22.2 acres each and one community center of 7.5 acres.

Each of the neighborhoods is provided with a small center.

Demographically, the total urban population is assumed to be 2,000,000, with the population of the core 50,000, of each town 65,000, of each district 20,000, of each community 6,000, and of each neighborhood 1,900.

The population of the multifunctional centers is, for each town center, 5,000 for each district center, 2,000, and for each community center, 300.

(For the organization of each town into urban subunits, see Figure 7-4.)

metropolitan core

centers of urban subunits

urban subcenters

green belts

technological reservations

Figure 7-3 Abstract model of an urban organism.

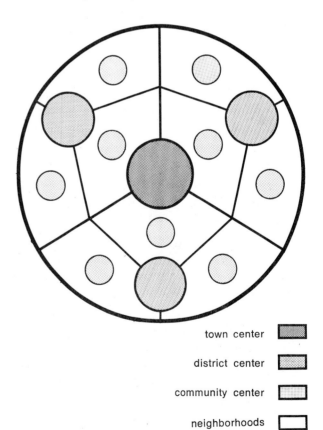

town center

district center

community center

neighborhoods

Figure 7-4 Abstract models of an urban organism: Organization of a typical urban subunit.

If we consider the division of population between centers and neighborhoods, we arrive at the following figures:

Metropolitan core	50,000
Town centers (30) each with 5,000	150,000
District centers (90) each with 2,000	180,000
Community centers (270) each with 300	81,000
Total center population	461,000
Neighborhoods (810) each with 1,900	1,539,000
Total population	2,000,000

On the basis of the area sizes and population figures, we then arrive at the following average densities:

In relation to cityscape:
2,000,000 people on 24,700 acres = 81 persons per acre

In relation to the entire incorporated metropolitan area:
2,000,000 people on 85,500 acres = 23.4 persons per acre.

The recreational area located in the outer green belt alone, as related to the total population, offers 1,153 square feet per inhabitant.

Before going any further, I would like to examine the population density figures arrived at for this abstract model, in relation to some existing cities and some projected ones.

Example 1: Paris
2,600,000 inhabitants on 10,000 hectares (24,711 acres) = 260 persons per hectare (105 persons per acre)

Example 2: Vienna
1,700,000 inhabitants on 41,000 hectares (101,315 acres) = 41.5 persons per hectare (16.8 persons per acre)

(Here it has to be taken into consideration that Vienna's population was once 2,000,000 and that very large parts of the incorporated city area are still utilized for agricultural pursuits and serve as reserve areas.)

Example 3: Project of Louvain (first case study, this chapter)
50,000 persons on 690 hectares (1,760 acres) = 72.5 persons per hectare (29.5 persons per acre)

The case study of Louvain also furnishes proof that an abstract model, after it is modified in relation to shape of land, topography, and other given conditions, can remain a valid tool for the development

of a master plan. Validity can, however, be maintained only if the salient points of the abstract model are reflected in the process of transposition to actual conditions. These salient points are:

1. *The urban organism* as a man-made artifact is strictly defined and clearly separated from "man influenced" and "natural environment." The slopping over of cityscape into countryside or landscape, the diluting of the urban structure along ragged edges, leads to the destruction of natural assets on the one hand and the loss of the qualities of urbanity on the other. The abstract model implies an end to the phenomenon of suburbia and to the practices of sprawl and spread. It also means the end to the rape of landscape or nature by shanty towns, commercial strips, uncontrolled industrial sprawl, etc.

2. *The cellular organism* of the total urban organization provides for identification of each inhabitant with his neighborhood, his community, his district, his town, and finally, his metropolitan core.

3. Inasmuch as each one of the *urban subunits* is grouped around its own multifunctional center, the need for unifunctional centers is eliminated. To describe the role of each of the centers in the simplest terms:

   a. The neighborhood center serves immediate needs.
   b. The community center serves daily needs.
   c. The district center serves weekly needs.
   d. The town center serves standard requirements.
   e. The metropolitan center serves exceptional requirements.

The cellular structure and the provision of multifunctional centers for each one of the urban subunits facilitates human communications and cuts to a minimum "enforced mobility." Each one of the urban subunits represents, in fact, an environmental oasis, completely freed from any surface or above surface expressions of technological and transportation disturbances. Yet, speedy communication between all parts of the urban environment and toward the outside are attained.

ABSTRACT TRANSPORTATIONAL MODEL

Figure 7-5 establishes a pattern for public transportation: Outside the urbanized area, public transportation is accomplished by railroads, shipping, and aviation. Inside the boundaries, urban underground transportation takes over. The abstract scheme for public transportation illustrates how public transportation coming from the outside is distributed along the boundaries of the urban area by a circumferential system, and how primary urban transportation connects all town centers with each other, with the "metropolitan core," with the "technological reservations," and with the "green belt."

Secondary public transportation would consist of accessory transportation for people and goods, conforming to strict standards concerning environment protection, and to low speed limits of about 12 kph (7.5 mph). Concrete proposals for accessory transportation are described in the case study of Vienna in Chapter 6.

Figure 7-5 Abstract model of an urban organism: Public transportation.

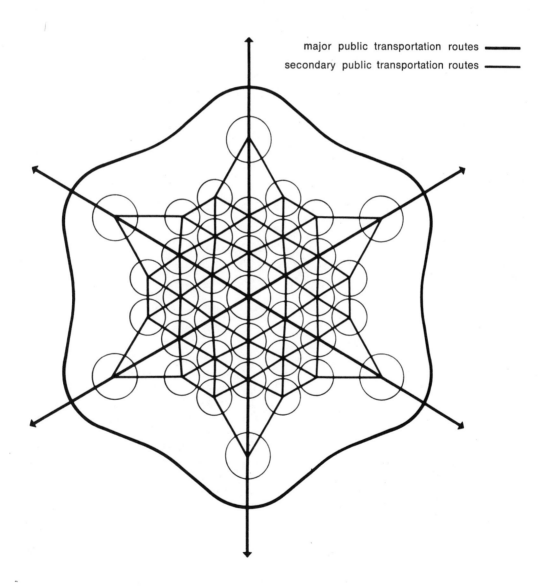

major public transportation routes ━━━
secondary public transportation routes ━━━

Figure 7-6 relates to arrangements for individual transportation. In contrast to public transportation, which increases in intensity as it approaches the metropolitan core, the opposite applies to individual transportation.

Individual transportation approaches the urbanized area from the outside over freeways and national highways, until it reaches a circumferential major loop system, along the boundary of the entire metropolitan area. This outer loop road system forms the extreme outer defense line against the flooding of the urbanized areas with individual vehicles (automobiles and trucks).

The second defense line is constituted by a loop road system surrounding cityscape.

The third one appears on the outer limit of the six inner towns, and the last, impenetrable one is represented by a loop road around the metropolitan core.

Along these defense lines occurs the transfer from individual transportation of people and goods to the urban transport system (consisting of underground lines for people, and underground freight-moving equipment in the form of railroads or conveyor belts.)

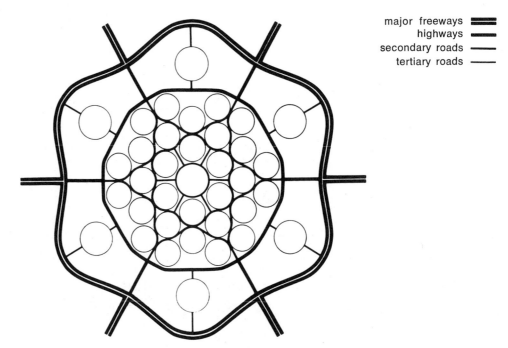

major freeways ══
highways ━━
secondary roads ──
tertiary roads ──

Figure 7-6 Abstract model of an urban organism: Individual transportation media.

Figure 7-7 indicates the possible transfer points in accordance to their size and importance, at those spots where individual transportation and public transportation routes cross. The transfer from individual to public transportation is encouraged by a tariff policy which favors transfer points (garages or goods depots) on the periphery, and penalizes the users of those which are located along the inner defense rings. The transfer is further promoted by the fact that public transportation becomes an increasingly better and faster alternative as one moves into the vicinity of the metropolitan core. To illustrate the tariff policy, we may assume that parking charges along defense ring I would be equal to 1, along defense ring II equal to 2, along defense ring III equal

to 4, and along defense ring IV equal to 8. The use of public transportation would be further promoted by high speed and comfort. The use of individual transportation within the urbanized area on the other hand, would be discouraged by increasingly stringent speed limits.

Assuming that public express transportation would move with an average speed of 50 kph (31 mph) (considering stopping times at stations), the following travel time distances would result:

1. Between the centers of towns 19 to 30 and the metropolitan core—8 minutes.
2. Between the centers of towns 7 to 18 and the metropolitan core—5 minutes.
3. Between the centers of towns 1 to 6 and the metropolitan core—3 minutes.
4. Between the metropolitan core and the "technological reservations"—10 minutes.

Figure 7-8 shows the relationship between green areas and urban subunits as well as between green areas and "technological reservations." Not indicated on this plan are urban green areas which would occur within each one of the urban subunits in the form of parks, small sports areas, tree groupings, etc.

Figure 7-7 Abstract model of an urban organism. Transfer points between individual and public transportational media, for people and goods.

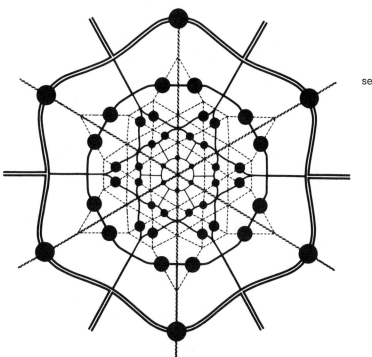

major freeways ▬▬
highways ───
secondary roads ───
tertiary roads ───
major public transportation routes ∿∿∿
secondary public transportation routes ------
transfer points ●

GREEN AREAS ▨

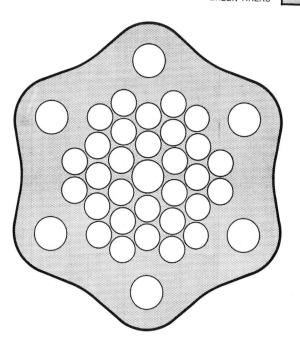

Figure 7-8 Abstract model of an urban organism: Relationship between green areas and urban subunits.

ENVIRONMENTAL PLANNING LEGISLATION

The now existing planning legislation and its administration and application represent unsuitable tools for the concepts which have been discussed concerning the utilization of our planet's surface and with regard to the creation of urban organisms corresponding to the one illustrated by the "urban abstract model." Our planning legislation interferes, restricts, hampers and restrains individual action, in a haphazard manner, with damaging effects. It creates and abets urban sprawl, land wastage, the destruction of natural assets, compartmentalization and ghettoism, economic and ethnic segregation, and enforced mobility.

The arsenal of planning legislation is certainly sufficiently great to bring a more meaningful order about. Laws and regulations and their application will, however, have to be modified in order to comply with environmental planning goals. Generally it can be stated that the environmental planning legislation could be considerably more permissive as far as cityscape is concerned, but would have to be more restrictive in the areas of "technoscape," the "man-influenced," and the "natural" environment.

Within the urbanized area, the practice of prescribing that certain parcels can be used only for certain urban functions, can and should be completely abandoned and all land should be, in principle, permitted for multifunctional use. Multifunctionality, in fact, should be enforced by ensuring that certain urban functions, including employment facilities, should be available within walking distance from residential functions, others within a distance which can be easily mastered by the use of accessory transportation, and yet others which can be easily reached by means of public transportation.

As far as density regulations are concerned, these are now mostly directed toward prescribing a "maximum density." The directive thrust of these laws should be reversed and a "minimum urban density" which may be modified in accordance to the size of the settlement should be prescribed. No absolute ceiling for density should be established, but rather a performance standard which would guarantee the achievement of human amenities.

All planning legislation and related measures (such as taxes, subsidies, land-usage plans) should be utilized with the aim of bringing about greatest possible diversity and a small-grained mixing of urban uses and functions on a sociological, ecological, and ethnic basis.

Summarizing, one can then say that with respect to major urban functions and uses, the presently existing restrictive type of planning legislation should change into an extremely liberal and permissive one. In contrast to this, would be the character of all legislation concerning the natural environment, the man-influenced environment, and technoscape. In green belt areas, around and within the urbanized area, construction activity would be highly restricted, to serve only buildings such as sports facilities, resting places and eating places, which enhance the usage of these areas. In the man-influenced environment (landscape), only structures as necessary for agricultural and cattle-raising activities would be permitted.

In the natural environment, we might make a distinction between nature preservation areas, which serve the preservation of fauna and flora and which should remain completely undisturbed, and natural parks which, in order to further man's communication with nature, could contain the necessary hostelries, path systems, etc.

As far as disturbing functions of our technological apparatus are concerned, legislation should be designed in such a manner as to achieve compactness and a clear delineation of technological reservations. With regard to technological communication lines (this includes transportation of all types), graduated restrictions would have to be imposed which should be reasonably permissive within the man-influenced environment, severe within the natural environment, and extremely severe within the man-made environment. With respect to the last, all communication lines, pipes, cables, public and individual transportation should be relegated to subsurface areas. (An exception would be accessory transportation.) The restrictions on using surface land for mechanical services would also be applied to parking. The present parking rules which prevail in so many countries and which prescribe that every property owner is obliged to supply a certain amount of parking space on his own land, would be totally reversed by prohibiting the storage of vehicles on any individual land parcel. Storage spaces for vehicles would instead be arranged on a communal basis and located in direct adjacency to major roads within a reasonable walking distance from urban functions (residential or otherwise), which might form the points of origin or destination.

Two types of measures which are missing in most planning legislation would have to be added.

1. Provisions which would, especially with regard to residences, eliminate the possibility of being overlooked from neighboring living units.
2. Provisions which would protect effectively from the creation or transmission of disturbing noises. Building ordinances would have to be brought up-to-date to protect from internal noises caused by water and heating installations within housing units.

Without such environmentally oriented planning legislation the human race will not succeed in escaping the trap of the space squeeze. Individual or even localized action is obviously impotent in a battle against forces which do not recognize fences, walls, city boundaries, or even national boundaries.

THE CONCEPT OF PRIVATE LAND OWNERSHIP

If one considers the magnitude of the problems we are facing and of the opportunities which a rational use of land could bring about, the question arises of whether our feudal concepts of the holiness of private land ownership can be maintained. This concept was completely strange to the original inhabitants of the American continent, the Indians. When the white people wanted to buy land, they encountered a sense of complete bewilderment on the part of the Indians. The warrior chief Tecumseh, when approached by white people who wanted to buy land said: "Sell the country? Why not sell the air, the clouds, the great sea?" Land as a property to be bought and sold appeared to the Indians as an absurd proposition, and they often fought for their belief to the death. They maintained that man was not standing outside of nature, but was part of it. They maintained that unborn generations had an equal claim to the land, that it was man's need to learn from nature, and to replenish his spirit in frequent contact with animals and countryside.

I may be accused of being subversive in proposing that all land should be owned by government and one day, hopefully, by a united government of mankind, but I could claim in my defense that in Great Britain, for example, nearly all land is owned by the Crown (which is in fact the state) and only leased on long-term arrangements to individuals or organizations. As long as each parcel of land is theoretically owned, "to the center of the globe and to the boundaries of the atmosphere" by individuals, the undeniable danger exists that all efforts which are now expended on city planning, regional planning, state planning, might produce mountains of paper but molehills of action. In the light of the critical situation caused by the space squeeze, we cannot permit a situation to endure which gambles with the fate of humanity by endangering it through actions of individual caprice, acquisitiveness, and avarice, or the unending striving for growth of our technological bureaucracy.

PUBLIC PLANNING AND LAND OWNERSHIP

Those who view with trepidation any kind of public interference will be forced to realize that the real values of individual freedom, personal initiative, and the sanctity of personal liberty can only be safeguarded if the basic prerequisites for human well-being and survival are established by public action. The recognition that piecemeal planning can become meaningless if the pieces around us are planned in a manner incompatible with our own aims impresses itself forcefully on all those who try to create a tiny oasis within a dangerous wilderness. Large-scale planning, on the other hand, is proven to be ineffective and abortive when those who inspire or conceive the plan do not possess the power to implement it. This power, however, can only be attained through ownership as a weapon against land speculation or obstructionism.

SUBORDINATION

It is implied in the task of planning for any human undertaking that it is necessary to distinguish between goals of lasting values to society and other less essential ones, which must be subordinated.

Subordination always involved certain sacrifices. Subordination is practiced by people who plan for their old age, for the education of their children, for sickness or economic setbacks. The practice of subordinating certain short-term and inessential desires to long-term needs must of course be expressed in the strongest manner when the fate of a whole city, of a nation and in fact of the entire human race is involved. Those who consciously or subconsciously conclude that major efforts in the direction of environmental and urban planning could abruptly end a happy era of freewheeling heroic pioneering, live in a world of self-delusion. The days of the great wild west romantic adventures or of discovering continents are actually long gone and only kept alive for us on the television screen. It should also not be forgotten that in nearly every developed country, governmental action already influences our present life and fortunes to an increasing degree, though it must be confessed, mostly on a hit-or-miss basis. It is interesting to note that the stoutest fighters for completely free enterprise are characteristically the ones most eager to take fullest advantage of opportunities triggered off by governmental planning or public subsidies. The value of private property can skyrocket solely as a result of "happenings" caused by public action. A new railroad line, the placement of a subway station or a freeway interchange, the installation of an airport, the regulation of a river, the construction of a missile-launching site, the re-zoning of an area, and thousands of other steps can create for the lucky ones, without the slightest effort on their own part, tremendous "windfall gains." The same measures, however, can create for others, who happen to own land in the wrong spot, considerable losses. It is only in these cases that vehement protests are voiced in the name of "individual freedom."

AN EXAMPLE OF THE "HIT-AND-MISS" PHENOMENON

To illustrate the aforesaid, I would like to relate one rather bizarre case on which I was asked to give advice as an arbiter. In the New England area of the United States, there existed an important state road establishing a much-traveled communication between a number of cities and towns. Enterprising businessmen had swiftly taken advantage of the existence of this public installation by buying up land parcels on both sides of the road and constructing there, hundreds of stores, eating places, gas stations, motels, nightclubs, etc. Their enterprise was rewarded by thriving business, rising land values, and huge profits. Some years after, it became obvious that the primary function of the road, namely that of serving as communications link, was seriously affected—by the traffic attracted to the enterprises on both sides of the road; by trucks delivering merchandise; by cars parking on the road; by those who entered and left parking lots; by shoppers who crossed the road on foot; etc. The government found itself in a dilemma. On the one hand, it was anxious not to interfere with the rights of property owners; on the other hand, it was obliged to safeguard reasonably good communications. Thus the decision was made to invest public (taxpayers') money in constructing, as a replacement for the road which had become obsolete, a new bypass road. Having learned from bitter experience, the land on both sides of the road was also purchased by the government. Once the new road was opened, an uneven split of traffic occurred. Those primarily interested in speedy communication used the new road, and only those who were primarily customers of the roadside developments remained faithful to the old road. As a result, business along the old road diminished. Faced with this development, the property owners along the old road organized and protested against the authoritarian planning. They demanded public assistance through a "redevelopment project" and governmental subsidies. Government, being very sensitive to any organized effort, asked me, as a consultant, to investigate whether a redevelopment was possible and whether governmental funds should be utilized to assist the property owners along the old road. I submitted at that time my opinion that no need for governmental assistance was indicated. It was one of those cases where the "hit-or-miss" effects of governmental

planning had, for a long time brought windfall profits to private property owners and where now, for a change, another governmental action, necessitated by the "enterprise" of these businessmen, had brought a loss to the same people. I also pointed out that the construction of the new road did not interfere with the success of the retail trade in the area generally, but only shifted the business volume from the "pirating" roadside business back to the merchants in those towns which were made more easily accessible by the new road.

THE RISKS OF "PUBLIC PLANNING"

The overall national ownership of land and overall planning would not increase the influence of public action on individual enterprise but it would eliminate the injustice of creating windfall profits for some and undeserved damage to others.

Overall planning, however, does entail certain dangers which we must face and against which we must take countermeasures. If in a plan for a new town, a new city, or a new region, certain locations are reserved for urban activity centers, this necessarily implies that such central functions cannot take place in other locations. Thus certain monopoly locations may be created which could be misused by those who lease land for the construction of buildings serving urban functions within city centers. The monopoly situation could bring about exceptionally high rents for users of apartment buildings or office buildings or high prices and poor service in stores. Thus public planning necessarily involves the development of measures of all types which will prevent the taking of unfair advantage as an effect of providing monopoly locations.

SUPPORTING EVIDENCE

The California Tomorrow Plan

It is symptomatic that in the richest state of the richest country, problems have arisen which create such an impasse that a group of responsible citizens (California Tomorrow, a nonprofit educational organization) found itself moved to develop and publicize a thoughtful document called "The California Tomorrow Plan—A First Sketch for the Future of California, Its Land, Its Cities and Its People."

The document starts with a statement of existing conditions entitled "The Hard Truth." I am quoting briefly:

We are misusing ourselves and our environment to the point where amenities are rapidly disappearing, life itself is threatened, order gives way to anarchy, and a relatively healthy social order becomes bankrupt, economically and morally.

Figure 7-9 lists the major disruptions causing misuse of our environmental resources and misuse of human resources. As an approach to action, the report states: "Amenity—the pleasantness and attractiveness of our environment—becomes essential to public policy. Mere survival is not enough."

The typical existing problems concerning the misuse of land, air, and water are enumerated. Some of the most significant are:

a. *Energy Resources:* California's electric power demands double every nine years. Most hydroelectric sources have been tapped. New plans include construction of 15 potentially hazardous nuclear "burner" plants along the coast before the year 2000 even though there is no assurance that supplies of the necessary fuel (Uranium-235) will not be used up before all the plants are completed. Supplies of natural gas are limited and could be exhausted sometime after 2010. To date, no effective "breeder" reactor (which would convert more plentiful materials into increasing amounts of nuclear fuel) has been designed.

b. *Soil:* California loses tens of millions of cubic yards of topsoil every year unnecessarily. Among the causes of this loss are logging and watershed management practices in many watersheds; forest fires; cuts and fills from housing and road construction and bad farming practices.

c. *Agricultural Land:* Originally there were almost 8.7 million acres of prime agricultural lands. Over two million acres of these lands have been urbanized. By 1980 another 650,000 acres of California's prime lands will be urbanized.

d. *Recreational Land:* Potential recreational land, especially near urban areas but also in unpopulated sections, is constantly subject to subdivision and development. There is no adequate state program to identify and protect such lands.

e. *Species:* Since California became a state, six animal species have become extinct and forty animal species are now classed as rare or endangered.

f. *Natural Disaster Areas:* Enormous areas of California are subject to fires, floods, slides or earthquakes. Fires in metropolitan areas are virtually annual summer occurrences. In the fall of 1970 for example, more than 100,000 acres burned in Los Angeles County. In 1969, over 200,000 acres of California lands were flooded. Extensive building continues on land especially subject to earthquake damage. An earthquake of the magnitude of San Francisco's in 1906 could kill tens of thousands.

g. *Air:* Smog is now found in almost every populous area in California. This is true of all settlements of over 40,000 and in some cases of rural areas as far as 70 miles from cities. In Los Angeles County, the state's nominal standards for certain pollutants are exceeded more than half the time. More than 30 percent of the

Figure 7-9 The California Tomorrow Plan: Tabulation of major disruptions.

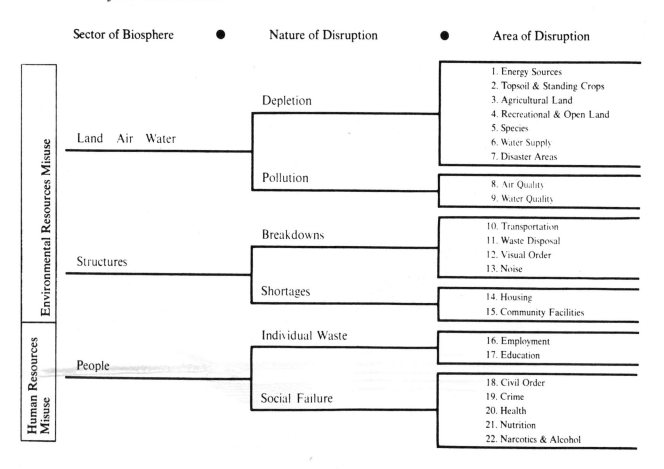

MAJOR DISRUPTIONS

state's population suffers eye and respiratory irritation and aggravated allergies. Automobile exhaust is a major contributor to smog. While efforts are being made to reduce emissions through exhaust control devices, substitutions of alternative forms of transit have been blocked by gasoline manufacturers, truckers, automobile clubs and others associated with the "Freeway Establishment."

h. *Water:* Virtually all major rivers, bays and estuaries are polluted. Oil spills and oil-well blow-outs have developed as major pollution threats to our bays, beaches and offshore waters.

i. *Population:* California's population has historically doubled every twenty years. Current projections show that in 1990, the population will reach about 30 million.

Having presented this rather alarming picture of prevailing conditions and problems, the "California Tomorrow Plan" proposes some policies:

1. *Basic State Responsibility:*
The state assumes and declares its responsibility to protect the land, air and water of California from destructive or wasteful use, and to maintain the beauty and productivity of the natural environment.

2. *State Zones:*
State zones are established according to the adopted California plan. They define, in general, which areas may be built upon and which may not. They protect the state's most valuable open lands, including prime agricultural soils and effectively check urban sprawl. There are four state zoning categories. The four categories are:
Agricultural: Classified as non-buildable or conditionally buildable at a density no higher than one unit per 25 acres. This zone is administered by the state through its environmental protection agency.
Conservation: The conservation zone includes lands which are ecologically, scenically, or historically impor-

tant recreational areas of exceptional quality, or the preserves of threatened or unique, animal or plant species. Conservation lands are state-administered and protected mainly by zoning, but also by outright purchase.
Urban: The zone includes lands which do not fall in either of the first two categories and that are either suitable for urban development or have already been urbanized. Lands in this zone are administered by the regional governments, according to state standards and their own respective regional plans.
Regional Reserves: Lands which do not fall within any of the first three categories are zoned as regional reserves. They are administered by the region and are a key to flexibility and variety in regional development. Within the standards of the California Plan, the regions may plan to develop them at high densities, keep them largely as open space, or use them for a variety of public and private purposes.

3. *California Standards:*
California standards are state-wide amenity standards which control the use of land, air and water so as to guarantee not only a safe but also a thoroughly enjoyable environment.

On the basis of these principal aims, the "California Tomorrow Plan" continues to discuss specific problems and solutions and comes to conclusions concerning compactness of urbanity and preference for public transportation which are nearly identical to the ones I have expounded.

The Paris Region

The force inherent in the demand for increased urban space was brought into focus in a thoughtful speech made by the Prefect of the Region of Paris, Maurice Doublet, at a meeting which I had the privilege of attending in March 1971. I would like to quote from this address as follows:

A double paradox plagues the Parisian region. The beauty of yesterday faces the ugliness of today and today's rigidity is threatened by powerful forces which will model it irreversibly between now and the year 2000. Our task is to acknowledge the Paris of today, perpetuate the Paris of yesterday and integrate both in the Paris of tomorrow.

Figure 7-10 The California Tomorrow Plan: A view of the future. "The old established cities are sprawled out, but not much more than they were in 1970. They come to a dead stop right at their boundaries, at the edge of the urban zone, and beyond that there is farm land or the hills."

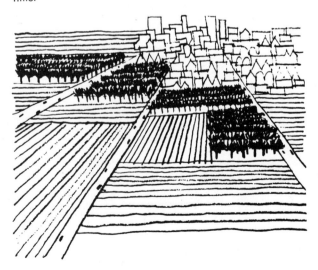

Figure 7-11 The California Tomorrow Plan: A view of the future: "A new town leaves the valley free for agriculture."

Forty years from today, the demand for space for office employment and for living units will have doubled and the number of rooms will have tripled. The population of the region will have grown by two thirds. The number of individual cars, if the present trends continue, will have quadrupled and the purchasing power will be five times as high as today. Today our suburbs are under-equipped, housing developments devour open spaces, the historic center becomes increasingly congested and ruined by the aggressor —modern technology. Old and poor quarters are renewed at a rhythm which is much too slow, open spaces are eaten up by demands for parking space, and pollution grows.

These are just some of the aspects which are known to us and which the government of the region has denounced. The task is immense, but to quote Malraux: "History needs the type of courage which wins and not the type which just comforts."

The population of the Paris region has grown between 1962 and 1968 by 800,000 to reach a figure of 9,200,000 inhabitants. Compared with other countries, this concentration within the largest conurbation is not monstrous. The Paris region contains 16% of the national population, the one of London, 15% and the one of Tokyo 10%. In spite of the spread of the Paris region, it is still more dense than the regions of other agglomerations in the world, with the exception of Tokyo. Thus, though the population of London is 10% larger than the one of the Paris region, the land area of Greater London is 50% larger than that of the region of Paris. On the other hand, there is a much greater contrast as far as national population density is concerned. France has a national density of 80 inhabitants per square kilometer and the Netherlands have one of 360 inhabitants per square kilometer. The total urban population of France is considerably lower than that of other countries. 63% of the total population are urbanized in France, compared with 70% in the USA, 75% in West Germany and 80% in England. The great difference between Paris and other world metropolises is that the French capital exists isolated, whereas other large cities are part of a megalopolitan structure. Our present situation is one of unbalances: an unbalance between housing and equipment; an unbalance between housing and employment; an unbalance between population and health, leisure and cultural activities; an unbalance between demographic development within Paris which has lost 200,000 inhabitants and the population of the older suburbs which has just slightly increased and the population of the outer suburbs which has exploded; an unbalance in transportation: public transportation has decreased, private transportation has increased enormously, yet 80% of trips from work to the home are now taken through public transportation. Knowing that the number of these trips will double within thirty years, it is certainly necessary to adopt a policy.

I will discuss the strategy of the policy mentioned in this speech, which is clearly expressed by the "Plan Directeur," in one of the case studies.

The Tale of Two Cities

In support of my expressed view that we are squandering land in certain urban agglomerations irresponsibly, let us just consider two extreme cases of land economics:

The city of Paris (within the city boundaries) has a population of 2,600,000 (in 1954 it was 2,900,000) on approximately 21,250 acres. If one includes into the city area the large natural reserves of the Bois de Vincennes and the Bois de Boulogne, then the area is approximately 24,700 acres which results in a density of about 105 persons per acre.

In Los Angeles, the city boundary encompasses 290,000 acres. This results in a density of approximately 8.5 persons per acre, since the population within the city boundary was, in 1968, about 2,480,000. The difference between the two cities is also evident if one considers the size of the region and its population in both cases. (Los Angeles region: Population— 6,750,000, size—3,100,000 acres, density—2.2 persons per acre. Paris region: Population—7,400,000, size— 360,000 acres, density—20.5 persons per acre.) Los Angeles, based on the principle of low density resulting from a majority of single family homes surrounded by gardens, has spilled over into a large number of suburban developments of neighboring cities and thus an inescapable megalopolis reaching from the Mexican border to Santa Barbara and from the Pacific Ocean to the San Bernadino Mountains has developed, wiping out orchards, vineyards, and all other vestiges of nature. Paris, on the other hand, in spite of the growth of its region, has still managed to preserve large forest and green areas within the regional fabric and has held its growth within distances which can be overcome by means of public transportation.

Los Angeles, in contrast to this, has to rely nearly completely on individual means of transportation for which a technically admirable but humanly monstrous urban freeway system has been constructed and has to be steadily enlarged. Los Angeles, of course, fulfills to a much larger degree the individual desire for "one's own little house with one's own little garden." Paris, even in the new peripheral developments is utilizing, to the highest degree, the concept of apartments in rentable units, sometimes of considerable height. Two questions can be raised if one considers the two completely different approaches:

1. In which of the two city types does the individual enjoy the greatest sense of life fulfillment, of privacy, and of free time?
2. Which of these two methods is more likely to give us a direction for finding a response to the problems of the urban space squeeze?

The answer to the second question is, I believe, obvious. In fact, it is provable that the type of density pattern which exists not only in Los Angeles, but in most American cities, is only feasible in a large, comparatively thinly populated country. The same pattern juxtaposed into a densely populated Euro-

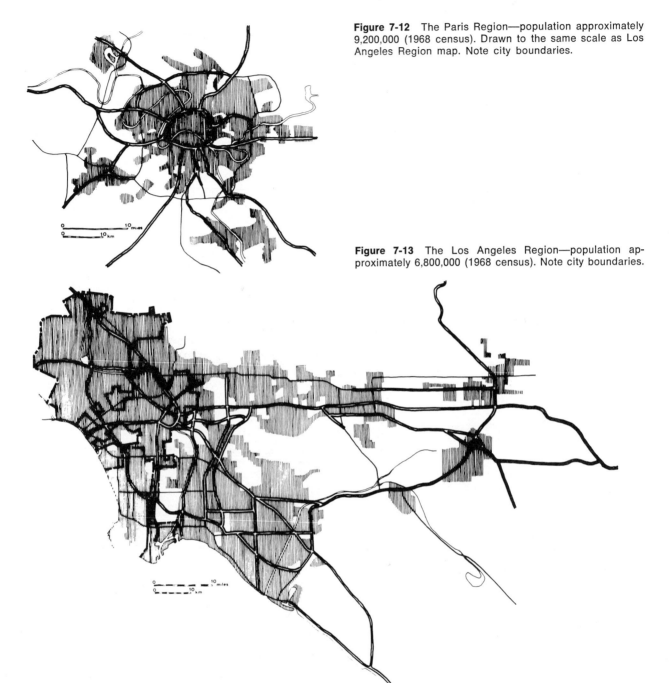

Figure 7-12 The Paris Region—population approximately 9,200,000 (1968 census). Drawn to the same scale as Los Angeles Region map. Note city boundaries.

Figure 7-13 The Los Angeles Region—population approximately 6,800,000 (1968 census). Note city boundaries.

pean country would lead to the complete disappearance of all agricultural land, nature, and most of the land needed for industrial activity. As to the first question, there are some general answers. Los Angelenos are becoming disenchanted with the "blessings" of suburban life. The relationship of building permits for single homes and multiple apartment structures gives an inkling of this. In 1941, 64 percent of all permits concerned single dwellings and 36 percent apartments. In 1962, permits given for single family dwellings amounted to 25 percent and for apartments and other multiple dwellings, 75 percent. The reasons for this change of popular attitude are: long distances and time losses involved in going to work, shopping, or participating in other urban activities; lack of household help, in particular gardeners; the higher security offered in apartment houses; preference for air-conditioned apartments in place of smog-polluted gardens.

I can, additionally, give some answers based on

my own experience. I am a resident of Los Angeles; I also have an apartment near the city core of Vienna, a small apartment in connection with an office in a densely built-up area of Paris, and at various times I have lived in apartments in the Greenwich Village section of Manhattan and in a suburban area of Detroit. In each case, the choice of location was up to me. I found it undesirable to have an apartment in downtown Los Angeles and I am there a typical suburbanite. I found it unimaginable to have a residence in Vienna, Paris, or New York anywhere else than in the center of the city. In Los Angeles I have to confess that I belong to the land wasters. My house and garden cover three-quarters of an acre, that is approximately 32,670 square feet. With about the same amount of living space—though without the garden and swimming pool—I occupy in Vienna (taking into consideration that the building in which my apartment is housed is six stories high) a *land* area of approximately 345 square feet.

To justify the large area of land which I occupy in Los Angeles, one would have to conclude that, occupying one hundred times more land in Los Angeles than in Vienna, I should be one hundred times happier there. In fact, the varying land areas do not express a different quantity of life fulfillment, but rather a completely different style of living. In Los Angeles, I enjoy my swimming pool and my wife enjoys tending a beautiful garden. Both of us drive a car, which she needs for many hours of the day in order to do her shopping and which I need in order to get to the office or to visit clients. In Los Angeles we are hesitant to leave our sheltered home in order to visit friends or to participate in cultural or entertainment events because every such outing involves a major investment of time and nervous strain in driving long distances. The enjoyment of the garden is somewhat diminished by the occurrence of smog and by the incessant mechanical noises caused by automobiles rushing by and jet planes flying over. In Vienna, I miss the garden, but I have from my window a breathtaking view of a public park with a fountain and I actually enjoy more quietude and privacy than on the large piece of land in Los Angeles. I can walk to my office in twelve minutes, or I can drive there in three, I can also take a streetcar, which takes me about six minutes. In Vienna we are persuaded to go out often because we are within easy walking distance of two concert halls, the opera, a number of theaters, and a variety of restaurants, cafés, and shops. Seeing friends does not have to be a prearranged affair as in Los Angeles, and more often than not, one bumps into them on the street or in a café.

There are undoubtedly advantages for me in both of these residences. It depends on personal tastes

and preferences, on moods and age, which one should be rated higher. I personally, am inclined to prefer the urban atmosphere I enjoy in Vienna and Paris and which I did enjoy thoroughly in Manhattan. But quite aside from the mode of living within the conurbation, there is one decisive advantage for the inhabitants of the compact city. The Viennese, for example, can, by investing between thirty minutes and one hour in traveling time, by streetcar, railroad, bus, or automobile, reach unspoiled countryside which surrounds the city in every direction, and they make abundant use of this opportunity. However, disregarding individual tastes concerning a choice between urban and suburban living, the decisive fact remains that only through compact urbanity can we create tools to resolve the dilemma of the urban space squeeze.

Concurrence from London

It is always gratifying when one finds confirmation of one's own thoughts in statements of others. A newly published book, written by Ivor de Wolfe and entitled *Civilia: The End of the Sub Urban Man*, parts of which can be found in an article in the *Architectural Review* of June 1971, depicts the plans for a new city "Civilia," by means of photomontages which create the visual impression of a truly urban environment, and states the following:

Aided by Geddes, Mumford, Doxiadis and certain more specialised and contemporary advisers, official policy underwent a change of heart: in the form of a regional take-over under which the city becomes a city-region, becomes open, becomes open-ended, becomes bereft of its "wall" whether real or imagined, in an exercise designed to get the citizens to spread themselves over the surrounding country-side in "Sectors of Growth."

The dreadful consequence of Lewis Mumford should now be clear. Fairer perhaps to say the dreadful consequences of Patrick Geddes, for he, after all, was the earliest prophet of the city-region concept, the meaning of which, let the layman be in no doubt, is the city-*into*-region (or, more credibly, region-*into*-city).

The need today is not to expand but to contract urban development, in such a way as to multiply its potential and thus its hospitality to overspill. And this, because our forefathers indulged in conspicuous waste on a gigantic scale, can indisputably be done.

Far from being a collection of cities, the conurbations consist in fact of deglomerations of sprawl, and if the need to find new centers for resettlement is great, isn't it commonsense of the most elementary kind to bring the old sprawl which needs a new center into contact with the new center which can digest the old sprawl, and so provide homes where the work is, conserve land, revitalise the industrial scene . . .

Sprawl pinpoints a world emergency as pressing for the New World as for the Old, for the East as for the West.

Three such cities as "Civilia" would occupy 48 square

Figure 7-14 Civilia: A typical view of the imaginary city of Civilia. In the background, general view of the "citadel."

miles, a frightening figure to any normal mind not yet acclimatised to the fantasies of planners in their current state of Angelenic fixation. The population of Los Angeles is in fact the equal of three such Civilias and occupies not 48 square miles but 5000, two thirds of which consists of roads and their services and carparks. With moreover, certain other incalculable advantages, starting with a cloud of smog that travels 85 miles to the mountains by lunchtime and by the tea-break veils them in 10,000 tons of pollutants which are already gnawing at over a million trees in the vicinity, most of which will be dead in 10 years.

The real benefits of advanced technology will only be manifest when we are prepared to live together.

NEW CITIES

What are the practical means and ways by which we can either create new cities, giving us the advantages of compactness and urbanity but free of the conflicts with technological apparatus from which present densely populated cities suffer, or reshape the existing regional agglomerations, which presently deserve the term "slurbs?" I do not believe that the present vogue for the construction of new towns or satellite towns or, as the Germans call them, *Entlastung Städte* (literally translated unloading towns), represent a solution. Even the best

of them result in only a slightly improved organization of suburbia. Yet, historically seen, as experimental workshops, they are as important and significant as the regional shopping center was for the development of multifunctional centers. Inasmuch as we are faced with an overall growth of human population and, quite specifically, with the growth of urban population, the obvious answer is that we need new cities, ones which are of considerable size for, let us say, a population of one to three million, which are self-dependent and do not just serve as "unloading" places or "dumps" for existing large cities. This is basically the proposition made by the planners of "Civilia." This was also the point made in a report which I and my partner, Edgardo Contini, wrote in 1966 for the Department of Housing and Urban Development in Washington which was entitled *New Cities USA* (discussed in detail later). This is also, to a certain extent at least, the spirit of the planning for seven cities in the region of Paris, each of which is projected for a population of 500,000.

In those cases where spreading suburban regions exist, powerful new urban centers could be injected, providing focal points for existing parts of the region and at the same time creating, over a small area, densities of such impact that other areas could be freed from the brushwork of little houses

Figure 7-15 Civilia: Part of the university (student housing).

and could be utilized as public green areas, oxygen reservoirs, and for leisure time activities.

New Cities USA

In the summer of 1966, Victor Gruen Associates submitted to the United States Department of Housing and Urban Development (HUD), a report entitled *New Cities USA—A Statement of Purpose and Program.*

The aim of this report was to present, in a clear-cut form, the reasons for a national commitment to a program of development of new cities. The term "new cities" in the context of that report indicated new urban entities of metropolitan scale, located at significant distances from existent conurbations, and established, planned, and developed by intent.

The report was submitted upon the request of Dr. Charles Haar of Harvard University, who was for a time, a member of President Johnson's Advisory

Year	U.S. Population	Population Inside S.M.S.A.	% of Total	Population Outside S.M.S.A.	% of Total
1940	132,165,000	72,834,000	55.1	59,331,000	44.9
1950	151,326,000	89,317,000	59.0	62,009,000	41.0
1960	179,323,000	112,885,000	63.0	66,438,000	37.0
1965	192,185,000	123,813,000	64.4	68,372,000	35.6
1970	208,249,000	137,444,000	66.0	70,805,000	34.0
1980	244,566,000	168,751,000	69.0	75,815,000	31.0
1990	287,472,000	206,980,000	72.0	80,492,000	28.0
2000	337,472,000	253,104,000	75.0	84,368,000	25.0

Figure 7-16 Tabulation indicating U.S. population from 1940 to 1970 and projections to the year 2000, inside and outside of the Standard Metropolitan Statistical Areas.

Committee on Urban Affairs and who later became Assistant Secretary for Metropolitan Development in the Department of Housing and Urban Development.

Before writing the actual report, it had been discussed by us with several members of the administration and of Congress, in particular with the Secretary of the Interior, Stewart Udall, with Vice-President Humphrey, and with Senator Joseph Tydings of Maryland. During the time of the Johnson administration, this concept did receive considerable attention; on the other hand, we have no knowledge to which degree the interest widened into action during the Johnson administration, and during the present administration of President Richard Nixon.

The enormity of the task which urban population growth presents was brought into focus by a statement made by President Johnson:

In the next thirty-five years we must literally build a second America—putting in place as many houses, schools, apartments, parks and offices as we have built through all the time since the Pilgrims arrived on these shores.

The tabulation (Figure 7-16) traces the growth of the total United States population and that of the urban population within the Standard Metropolitan Statistical Areas (SMSA) between the years 1940 and 1965, and projects the population figures for the future on the basis of straight-line projections (which need not necessarily be correct) until the year 2000. The tabulation thus indicates that between 1965 and 2000 (the 35 years to which President Johnson was referring) urban population will more than double, increasing from 125,000,000 to 253,000,000.

We then stated:

Since the rate of population growth has to be accepted as an established fact, the only variable remaining is the location of urban growth. As far as location is concerned,

we are faced with two alternatives: either to continue the operating trends, in which case two-thirds of the U.S. population would be concentrated in about a dozen clusters of urbanization (megalopolises) each with a population of between 15 and 20 million, or, as an alternative, to embark as a matter of national policy on a program of creation of new cities. "New" in that they must be viewed as urban organizations, conceived with imagination and responsive to human needs and aspirations. "Cities" in that unlike the so-called "new towns" clustered next to and dependent upon an existing conurbation, they are to be programmed from the beginning as full-fledged urban structures, accommodating populations of metropolitan scale, and located at a substantial distance from existing urban concentrations.

We then pointed out that in the chronological sense, all cities in the United States are "new cities" if one compares them with the long-established European and Far Eastern urban centers. Even the city of New York had, at the beginning of the nineteenth century, a population of less than 100,000. However, from the point of view of government initiative, only the city of Washington D.C. and the atomic research communities in New Mexico and Tennessee can be considered as cities generated or effected by expressed national policy. All the others reflect, as far as their locations and population concentrations are concerned, the nation's classic government posture of noninterference with private initiative and the workings of the free market.

In many areas however, the "hands off" policy of government has had to be modified due to the pressing demands of sociological progress, technological advancement, and the complexity of the national economy. Government has accepted steadily expanding responsibility, going so far as to prescribe safety and operational standards for private automobiles. Only in the field of urban settlements has the "hands off" policy of non-programming prevailed to this day, despite the contribution of thought and ideas from individuals, private groups, and educational organizations, which has been extensive.

The report then examined the reasons why historical urban settlements did develop in the United States in the past.

At first, in a predominantly agricultural country, as market places at the crossings of rural paths, later at harbor locations or along navigable rivers; in the age of industrialism in the proximity of deposits and sources of energy (coal, oil or of raw materials) or along transcontinental railroad routes, sometimes from no other motivation than that of locating a station next to a convenient spring to refill the boilers. Thus, until recent times, the sequence of motivations has been constant and clear: the city developed where the economic opportunity emerged and people were drawn in increasing numbers to the city.

There is now ample evidence that this historical pattern is losing its validity and that motivations other than obvious preexisting economic opportunities may justify the location of urban settlements. For the first time in the history of mankind, a vast majority—rather than a small, privileged class is in reach of affluence. One direct result of this is the increase of leisure time and recreational demands. Thus the selection of residence is no longer solely affected by employment opportunity, but balanced by other factors of human chioce, such as climate, proximity to natural surrroundings etc. Furthermore, technological and transportation developments (synthesis rather than extraction of materials, atomic or electric power rather than dependency on coal, air transportation) all tend to expand the choice for locations of urban settlements, liberating us from certain historical limitations of the past. The reasons for the location of the major existing metropolitan regions were founded in criteria that have become obsolete. It would therefore be tragically shortsighted if we were to allow all the future urban growth to gravitate around the existing urban conurbations.

We are now in a position to reverse the sequence. The choice of locations for new urban settlements could be determined on the basis of optimum factors such as climate characteristics and recreational opportunities and then industry and other employment opportunities could be induced to follow such urban settlements. Thus we proposed a thorough reassessment of our land inventory: "We must take a second look at all the territory that, in our explosive westward expansion, was bypassed or ignored, and evaluate them on the basis of rational criteria." In conferences with the Department of the Interior, it was found that a considerable number of sites suitable for the development of large new cities was available on land owned by the federal government.

The report then discussed the opportunity for innovations in the areas of education and health, of political administration, of urban economics, of planning and urban design. We pointed to the catalytic effects which the planning of new cities could have on existing cities. At the end of the report, we expressed, in summarizing, the hope that the case for a positive set of answers to the question, "Why new cities?" had been convincingly presented. We proposed, by way of classical proof, to formulate the question as a negative statement:

Why *Not* New Cities in the United States? Why should the United States with its tremendous resources of undeveloped regions not start new cities? Why, after having successfully started new cities until about 100 years ago, have we suddenly stopped, and not built a single one in the last century? Why, as we are destined to become an urbanized nation should we compress our population just into a few locations? Why should the United States as pioneers in so many aspects of science, technology and social innovation, retain an unimaginative laissez faire policy with respect to the living environment? *Why should we engage in the exploration of outer space and not explore the possibilities of better urban space within the United States?*

CONCLUSION

If we want to create a new urban pattern of compactness, which appears to be essential, we will have to apply those techniques of three-dimensional planning, the mutipurpose use of land, and the platform principle which I discussed in the chapter "Multifunctional Centers."

We will also have to develop methods by which all mechanical serving facilities, including all types of transportation, can be as completely as possible separated from human activities. Beyond that, we will have to structure the urban organism in such a manner that enforced mobility is cut to a minimum.

This aim will only be achieved by relating all compatible types of urban functions in the most intimate manner with each other, within urban subunits of a size which establishes desirable walkability. In this manner we can hope to cut the need for the use of mechanical transportation to a minimum and thus save vast areas of land now required for all types of communication lines and car storage space. Planning approaches demonstrating how we can move in this direction, though by no means claiming to be final answers, are discussed in the following four case studies which have been selected with the intention of demonstrating that the principles of the "new urban pattern," as discussed in the framework of this chapter and illustrated by the abstract models for "utilization of urban land" and "transportation," possess validity for dealing with distinctly different situations.

The case studies concern:

1. A new, planned city (Louvain, Belgium).
2. A sprawling agglomeration (Los Angeles, California).
3. An expanding region around an old city in Europe (Vienna, Austria).
4. A rapidly expanding region of a European metropolis (Paris, France).

CASE STUDY I

Name of Project: University Town for the Catholic University of Louvain

Location: Near Ottignies, Belgium

In order to avoid any misunderstandings, I should actually entitle this study "The University Town which Could Have Been." It could have been because all the basic prerequisites existed, not one but two master plans proving economic feasibility were developed and a government which had forced the establishment of a new university was obliged to support it. Nevertheless, whether or not this university town will come into being in a manner which fulfills the original intentions of the Academic Council is, at the time of writing, uncertain, for reasons which I will later discuss.

Background for Planning: Due to a governmental decision to succumb to Flemish demands and separate Belgium into two distinct areas, one Flemish-speaking and one French-speaking, it became necessary to separate the bilingual, Catholic University of Louvain (which, founded in 1425 is one of the oldest universities in Europe), into two parts. As the original buildings lie in a Flemish-speaking area, a new section for the French-speaking part of the university had to be created. Because of political pressure, fast action was demanded, and it was decreed that the first 2,000 students should be in the new university by 1971, the entire move to be completed by the year 2000.

The division of such a large, tradition-rich university poses untold problems and hardships. The difficulties which arose in attempting to divide a large university library into two, is just an example. A second problem was posed by the insistence of students and faculty of safeguarding for the new university, the values which had been experienced in Louvain, where university and city formed an integrated entity. Thus the principal decision was made that the French section of the university should not lose the benefits of integration with a city, and that under no circumstances would an isolated university campus be constructed. As a result of this decision, the Chief Administrator in charge of the creation of the new university visited the United States in 1967 and asked me to point out examples of truly integrated new university towns in the United States, so that he could learn from their experience. Unfortunately, after considerable research I discovered that even in those cases where university and town development had proceeded at the same time, for example, Irvine Ranch in Los Angeles, strong compartmentalization was evident between university campus and surrounding real estate development.

On the basis of an exchange of opinions as to how the aims of the French section of the university could be achieved, I was asked to act as consultant to establish land demand and assist the university in finding a suitable site. This assignment proceeded with great speed and efficiency, and by the end of 1967, the site had been determined and purchase of land had proceeded.

I was then asked to develop, with the assistance of staff members of Victor Gruen International, and representatives of the university, a master planning approach for the new city. This concept was submitted to the Academic Council

Figure 7-17 Map of Belgium with language boundaries, indicating the location of the new city in relation to Louvain, Brussels, and other major cities in Belgium.

in September 1968. It was basically accepted as a guiding document for further efforts. Though it dealt with the overall problem only in conceptual form, it is my firm belief that it established a realistic and implementable approach, and represented a valid answer to the demand for complete integration of "town and gown" and for a spirit of urbanity. Later events necessitated major changes to this first concept, and many ideas expressed in it are irretrievably lost. However, I would like to describe its main features because of my conviction that this original plan contained many answers to the problems which I have termed the "urban space squeeze."

FIRST MASTER PLAN

Major Aims and Goals:
1. A university closely integrated with the new town.
2. A spirit of urbanity and compactness.

The latter is only attainable if the principles of three-dimensional planning, multipurpose land usage and the method of platform structures which results in the "fabrication" of additional land are used.

In order to achieve a measuring stick for the term "compactness," a comparison between Louvain (including an incompleted university campus at Heverlee) and the plan for the new university town was made. Louvain covers an area of 1,270 acres and has a population density of 46.5 persons per acre. The plan for the new university town at Ottignies proposed that approximately 865 acres of land be acquired for a population of 70,000, which would have resulted in a density of 80.9 persons per acre.

The master planning study evolved from an abstract model, (Figure 7-19) which provided for an urbanized area with a diameter of approximately 4,000 feet, consisting of an urban core with a diameter of approximately 1,300 feet and four quartiers; further, a peripheral area, or fringe mainly used as a green belt and for certain "nonurban" functions. This abstract model was then further developed taking site conditions into consideration. The quartiers were visualized as compact, multifunctional megastructures, separated by open spaces partially utilized for somewhat less dense housing, in the form of neighborhoods. Each of the quartiers were to be partly devoted to university, and partly to civilian functions.

Figure 7-23, an aerial view of the model, indicates the various land usages; the central quartier, the four additional quartiers, separated by green belts and neighborhoods, and a number of peripherally located automotive

COMPARISON OF COMPACTNESS

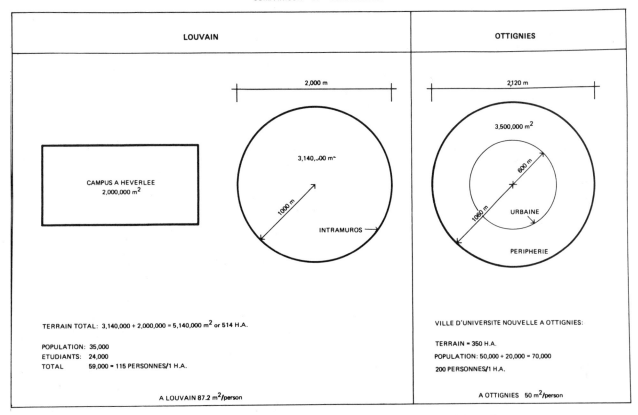

Figure 7-18 Louvain: Comparison of compactness between the old university town of Louvain and the projected new university town near Ottignies.

Figure 7-19 Louvain: The abstract model.

Figure 7-20 Louvain: Evolution of the abstract model.

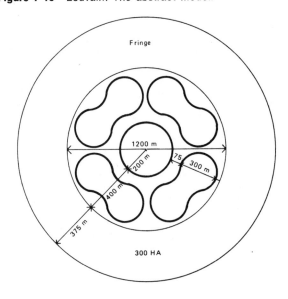

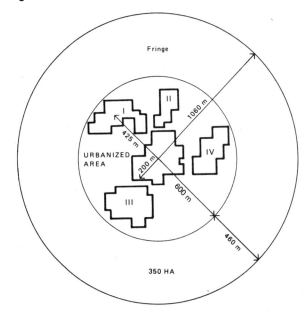

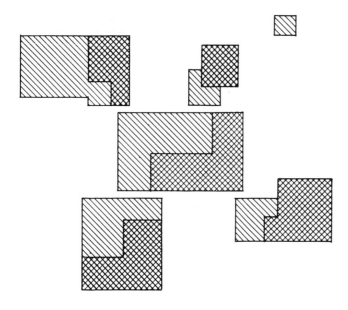

 University

Town

Figure 7-21 Louvain: Schematic pattern of integration.

TYPICAL SECTION THROUGH BASE STRUCTURE OF TOWN CORE

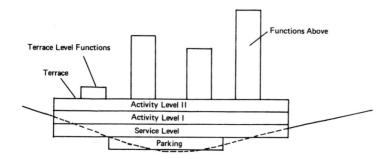

Figure 7-22 Louvain: Schematic section through the base structure of the town core.

centers which serve all needs connected with automobile usage. These automotive centers were foreseen as platform structures, the area above the platform being utilized for sports facilities, restaurants, etc. Figure 7-24 indicates on the same model, the projected public transportation network consisting of the train connection with Brussels, and an inner urban system.

Figure 7-25 represents an attempt to arrive at a three-dimensional chart for an entire town, similar to those we developed for multifunctional centers. In the vertical sense, the building area needed for each function has been allocated to various levels, a strict division being made between those accommodated within base structures and those located on top or adjacent to them. In the last column of the chart, it can be seen that 9,823,500 square feet of gross building area is located within the base structures and 25,029,100 square feet on top and adjacent to them. By placing this total building volume over a large number of levels, it was possible to prove that a land area of between 740 and 865 acres would suffice for the entire town development, including green areas etc.

We concluded our report by summarizing our findings:

1. It is feasible to plan and construct a new university town for a final student enrollment of 20,000, an urban population of 50,000, and all universitary and urban institutions required, on the site selected, within the main road network, on a contiguous parcel of land between 740 and 865 acres. This assumes that additional land will be either owned or controlled by the university in order to provide space for all public service functions, employment facilities (mostly laboratories research institutions, light non-disturbing industry etc.), for housing that part of the faculty desirous of living according to the suburban mode of life, and for secondary functions such as cemeteries, prisons, experimental farms etc.
2. It is feasible to develop the highly urbanized core area on about one third of the project site, so as to limit the distance from one extreme end to the other to about 3,940 feet.
3. It is feasible to develop the university town center on about 35 acres with an average diameter of 1,180 feet.
4. A form of integration between the university and urbia can be found which, though providing for closest interrelationship and adjacency, will not interfere with future changes or growth.
5. It will be possible to conserve significant and important natural assets and some of the man-made assets which exist on the site.
6. By means of multipurpose land usage, it will be possible to endow all urban and academic functions for which access to natural light and air is desirable, with qualities of airiness far superior to those found in the conventional city.

At the time the first master plan was submitted, it was still doubtful whether the university would be able to acquire the specified land area. However, during the months following our submission, about 2,220 acres of contiguous land was acquired, at a lower capital investment than originally visualized. This success is certainly

Figure 7-23 Louvain: Aerial view of the model.

Figure 7-24 Louvain: Photograph of the model with indication of major public and individual transportational routes.

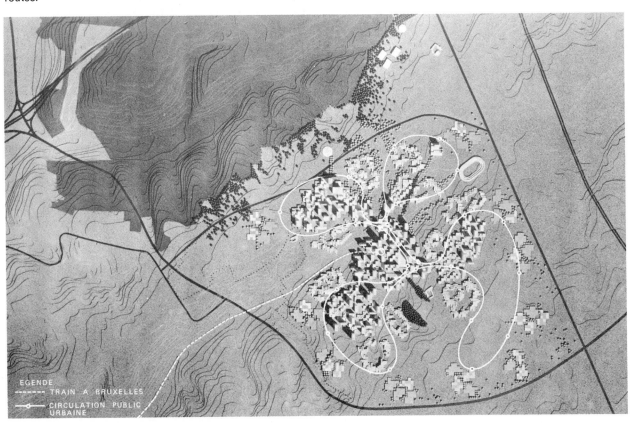

REPARTITION HORIZONTAL ET VERTICALE DES SURFACES DE PLANCHER BRUTES PAR FONCTION

ALLOCATION OF GROSS BUILDING FLOOR AREAS BY FONCTION TO LEVELS AND LOCATION

A L'EXCLUSION DU PARKING ET DES ACTIVITES SITUEES DANS LA ZONE PERIPHERIQUE
EXCLUDING PARKING AND ACTIVITIES WITHIN FRINGE AREA

FONCTIONS / ACTIVITIES			SURFACE DE PLANCHER BRUTE TOTALE EN m² / TOTAL m² GROSS FLOOR AREA	CENTRE DE LA VILLE / TOWN CORE				CENTRE DES QUARTIERS / QUARTIER CORES			SURFACE TOTALE SOUS PLATEFORME EN m² / TOTAL m² WITHIN BASE STRUCTURE
				NIVEAU DES SERVICES / SERVICE LEVEL	NIVEAU D'ACTIVITE I / ACTIVITY LEVEL I	NIVEAU D'ACTIVITE II / ACTIVITY LEVEL II	SOUS-TOTAL / SUB TOTAL	NIVEAU DES SERVICES / SERVICE LEVEL	NIVEAU D'ACTIVITE / ACTIVITY LEVEL	SOUS TOTAL / SUB TOTAL	
FONCTIONS UNIVERSITAIRES / UNIVERSITY ACTIVITIES	FONCTIONS ACADEMIQUES / ACADEMIC ACTIVITIES	AUDITOIRES ET SALLES DE SEMINAIRE / CLASS AND SEMINAR ROOMS	43,100	2,500	20,300	20,300	43,100	–	–	–	43,100
		LABORATOIRES D'ENSEIGNEMENT / TEACHING LABORATORIES	60,100	–	–	–	–	12,000	22,000	34,000	34,000
		LABORATORIES DE RECHERCHE / RESEARCH LABORATORIES	184,500	–	–	–	–	84,500	100,000	184,000	184,500
		BUREAUX DE FACULTES / DEPARTMENTAL OFFICES	123,600	600	7,500	7,500	15,600	22,000	47,000	69,000	84,600
		SALLES DE REUNION / MEETING ROOMS	18,000	1,000	3,500	3,500	8,000	–	8,000	8,000	16,000
		BIBLIOTHEQUE SPECIALISEES / SPECIAL LIBRARIES	44,000	–	–	–	–	3,000	28,000	31,000	31,000
		BIBLIOTHEQUE CENTRALE / CENTRAL LIBRARY	88,000	9,000	20,000	20,000	49,000				49,000
	AUTRES FONCTIONS UNIVERSITAIRES / OTHER UNIVERSITY ACTIVITIES	ADMINISTRATION CENTRALE / CENTRAL ADMINISTRATION	12,800	400	1,800	4,300	6,500				6,500
		INSTALLATIONS SPORTIVES COUVERTES / INDOOR SPORTS	10,200	2,000	1,500	1,500	5,000	1,300	2,400	3,700	8,700
		SERVICES ETUDIANTS / STUDENT SERVICES	17,000	–	–	–	–	2,000	12,000	14,000	–
		LOGEMENTS POUR ETUDIANTS / RESIDENCE HALLS	176,000	–	–	–	–	6,000	10,000	16,000	16,000
		RESTAURANTS	22,000	1,200	1,900	1,900	5,000	2,200	8,800	11,000	16,000
		LOGEMENTS POUR ETUDIANTS MARIES / HOUSING FOR MARRIED STUDENTS	54,000	1,600	800	800	3,200	1,200	1,200	2,400	5,600
		AUTRES LOGEMENTS FOURNIS PAR L'UCL / OTHER HOUSING PROVIDED BY UCL	104,000	3,400	6,600	4,100	14,100	2,100	4,000	6,100	20,200
	TOTAL DES FONCTIONS UNIVERSITAIRES / TOTAL UNIVERSITY ACTIVITIES		957,300	21,700	63,900	63,900	149,500	136,300	243,400	379,700	529,200
	HOSPITAL NON COMPRIS / NOT INCLUDING HOSPITAL 100,000										
FONCTIONS URBAINES / URBAN ACTIVITIES	LOGEMENT / HOUSING		1,872,000	11,000	7,000	7,000	25,000	32,000	33,000	65,000	90,000
	ECOLES / SCHOOLS		118,000	4,000	15,000	15,000	34,000	7,500	48,500	56,000	90,000
	EQUIPEMENTS SANITAIRES / HEALTH		27,000	2,500	5,000	5,000	12,500	2,500	8,000	10,500	23,000
	INSTALLATIONS SPORTIVES COUVERTES		6,000	500	500	500	1,500	800	1,700	2,500	4,000
	EQUIPEMENTS CULTURELS ET RELIGIEUX / CULTURAL AND RELIGIOUS	EGLISES / CHURCHES	28,000	500	2,000	2,000	4,500	1,000	5,000	6,000	10,500
		BIBLIOTHEQUES / LIBRARIES	9,400	1,000	1,500	1,500	4,000	800	2,700	3,500	7,500
		EXPOSITIONS / EXHIBITIONS	2,200	300	600	600	1,500	50	150	200	1,700
		SPECTACLES / ENTERTAINMENT	2,200	200	900	900	2,000	–	–	–	2,000
		CLUBS	2,200	100	700	700	1,500	100	600	700	2,200
	COMMERCE / RETAIL SHOPPING		148,500	20,600	38,700	38,700	98,000	6,000	30,000	36,000	134,000
	BUREAUX / OFFICES		50,000	4,500	3,500	3,500	11,500	–	–	–	11,500
	SERVICES PUBLICS / PUBLIC SERVICES	ADMINISTRATION LOCALE / LOCAL ADMINISTRATION	10,500	900	950	950	2,800	–	–	–	2,800
		POLICE	1,500	100	400	400	900	100	400	500	1,400
		POST AND TELEGRAPH	3,000	600	600	600	1,800	600	400	1,000	2,800
	TOTAL DES FONCTIONS URBAINES / TOTAL URBAN ACTIVITIES		2,280,500	46,800	77,350	77,350	201,500	51,450	130,450	181,900	383,400
	FONCTIONS UNIVERSITAIRES ET URBAINES / ACADEMIC AND URBAN ACTIVITIES		3,237,800	68,500	141,250	141,250	351,000	187,750	373,850	561,600	912,600

SURFACES DE PLANCHER SOUS PLATEFORMES / FLOOR AREAS WITHIN THE BASE STRUCTURES

	SURFACES DE PLANCHER DU SOMMET OU EN DEHORS DES PLATEFORMES / FLOOR AREAS AT TOP AND ADJACENT TO BASE STRUCTURE								
CENTRE DE LA VILLE / TOWN CORE				CENTRE DES QUARTIERS / QUARTIER CORES					TOTAL DES SURFACES AU SOMMET OU EN DEHORS DES PLATEFORMES
NIVEAU DE LA PLATEFORME / TERRACE LEVEL	NIVEAU DES SERVICES ABOVE		SOUS-TOTAL / SUB-TOTAL	NIVEAU DE LA PLATEFORMES / TERRACE LEVEL	NIVEAU DES SERVICES ABOVE		EN DEHORS DES PLATEFORMES / ADJACENT	SOUS TOTAL / SUB-TOTAL	TOTAL m² ON TOP AND ADJACENT
	SURFACE AREA	NOMBRE DE NIVEAUX / NO. LEVELS			SURFACE AREA	NOMBRE DE NIVEAUX / NO. LEVELS			
–	–	–	–	–	–	–	–	–	
–	–	–	–	4,100	22,000	5	–	26,100	26,100
–	–	–	–	–	–	–	–	–	
3,000	12,000	4	15,000	4,000	20,000	5		24,000	39,000
1,000	–	–	1,000	1,000	–	–		1,000	2,000
–	–	–	–	2,600	10,400	4		13,000	13,000
3,000	36,000	12	39,000	–	–	–	–	–	39,000
1,500	4,800	4	6,300	–	–	–		–	6,300
500	–	–	500	1,000	–	–		1,000	1,500
–	–	–	–	3,000	–	–	–	3,000	3,000
–	–	–	–	20,000	140,000	7		160,000	160,000
–	–	–	–	3,000	3,000	1		6,000	6,000
2,600	26,000	10	28,600	1,800	18,000	10	–	19,800	48,400
6,900	44,000	7	50,900	4,100	28,800	7	–	32,900	83,800
18,500	122,800	–	141,300	44,600	242,200	–	–	286,800	428,100
21,000	252,000	12	273,000	108,000	648,000	6	753,000	1,509,000	1,782,000
8,000	–	–	8,000	20,000	–		–	20,000	28,000
2,000	–	–	2,000	2,000				2,000	4,000
500	–	–	500	1,500	–			1,500	2,000
3,500	–	–	3,500	6,000	–		8,000	14,000	17,500
1,000	–	–	1,000	900				900	1,900
500	–	–	500	–				–	500
200	–	–	200	–				–	200
–	–	–	–	–				–	
10,000	–	–	10,000	4,500				4,500	14,500
3,500	35,000	10	38,500			–			38,500
700	7,000	10	7,700						7,700
100	–	–	100						100
200	–	–	200			–			200
51,200	294,000	–	345,200	142,900	648,000	–	761,000	1,551,900	1,897,100
69,700	416,800	–	486,500	187,500	890,200	–	761,000	1,838,700	2,325,200

Figure 7-25 Louvain: Three-dimensional chart for the entire university town.

one of the reasons for the client's wish to have a less compact town, thereby necessitating a second master plan.

THE SECOND MASTER PLAN

In 1968 we were informed that for reasons of "national sensitivity" the further developments of the plan would have to be carried out by a Belgian group of architects and urbanists. However, I was asked to act as consultant to the university and in a guiding and coordinating capacity to the Belgian team. This "cooperative venture" lasted for about one and a half years and it proved, to put it bluntly, a failure.

During the long time in which we battled in order to reach a common denominator, the Belgian team was emotionally involved in an attitude of urban planning which I termed "romantic planning." In contrast to "technocratic planning" which in blind admiration of the achievements of modern technology is willing to subordinate the expressions of human life to the functioning of machinery, "romantic planning" is based on an admiration of the past. It considers the manifestations of modern society to a large extent vulgar and believes that for the urban environment to become desirable, the examples of the past must be slavishly followed.

We did find some common ground as regards our attitudes toward the automobile and other infringements of modern technology upon the urban environment. However, there was a great difference with regard to the actions derived from these attitudes. The romanticist tries to solve the problems caused by these technological facets of life by denying the fact that they exist, thus not paying any attention to their demands and needs, with the foreseeable end effect that reality, infringing upon the dream, may convert it into a nightmare. The attitude concerning all other "unpleasant" facts of life is similar. The sociological problem is solved by declaring that the town will be reserved for "nice people with high incomes." Unpleasant matters such as garbage collection and utility lines are pushed aside with an elegant gesture. Expressions of "materialistic vulgarity" such as department stores, would not be permitted in the new town, but would be asked to settle somewhere on the outside.

The Belgian team presented their counter master plan in the form of model photos and skillfully drawn perspective bird's eye views. The reaction was most favorable. Many of the professors sighed a breath of relief. They had accepted our first master plan under certain emotional duress because it stated in an unmistakable fashion that in order to achieve the overall goal of a compact, integrated university town, certain personal sacrifices would have to be accepted. Not all faculty buildings would enjoy views of unspoiled countryside, and even professors might have to live in multiple dwelling units instead of spacious single houses with gardens. The new plan proved to them that they could have a town and yet live in splendid rustic isolation.

However, after making a study of this new plan, we confronted the Academic Council with dry, mathematical calculations which proved that the aims of settling a population of 50,000, creating an automobile-free environment, and creating a practical, implementable plan

had not been even partially met. Faced with the dilemma that the "romantic" plan which they emotionally liked would not produce what they required, and having certain strong feelings, preconceived notions and prejudices which had in the meantime hardened, against features of the first master plan, we were asked to develop a new master plan within a three month period. We were warned however, that this new plan could only be accepted if we took into consideration strongly entrenched objections to certain features of the first master plan. Further we had to submit to certain decisions made due to the pressure of time with regard to the move of the first academic groupings. Thus the location of certain important structures could not be again altered. Purely specialized interests concerning the operation of academic facilities further eroded the original idea of complete integration. Academic facilities had to be concentrated into two major campuses and one minor one. The original term "integration" had to give way to a new term of "coordination." The only element of integration which could still be saved was expressed in a willingness to place in the city center, in close proximity to each other, the central facilities of the university and the major structures required by the "civilian" town. The new plan which was submitted in September 1970, deviates from the original one in some important respects. The concept of three-dimensional planning with multipurpose land usage and platform structures had to be greatly curtailed and expressed to its full extent only in the town center. Because of this, considerably more land than originally previsioned had to be devoted to urbanization. The request by the Academic Council that the majority of housing units be privately owned and not exceed three stories in height, complicated the task further. Realizing that these changes necessitated a reduction in the program, the university reduced the projected total population to 50,000.

The new master plan fully considered the directives of the client. In spite of this, it achieves certain characteristics which represent important progress in the direction of a superior urban environment. The master plan consisted of three parts: a 91 page report, a technical supplement and graphic documents depicting the master plan with respect to its major elements, supporting graphs, tabulations and visual material.

As far as the visual material is concerned, we imposed on ourselves certain conditions which we set forth in the main report. These conditions were, that although we had not dealt with the problems of precise urban design or architecture in our report, we had submitted certain documents which were meant to illustrate that the necessary population densities were achievable, and to help in the visualization of the plan. These documents were submitted with the proviso that they should not be taken as attempts to determine design or architecture. We also explained that due to our belief that bird's eye views did not serve any purpose because very few people would ever be in a position to see the town from the sky, we excluded them and concentrated on showing views which could actually be experienced.

Program Questioned: The report also contains certain critical observations concerning the overall program as given to us. The new programmed population figure seemed to us insufficient as, if one excludes single and married residential students from this figure, a civilian population of only about 34,000 remains. The original program would have resulted in a population of between 65,000 and 70,000 and we felt that this was more adequate because the new figure was not sufficient to offer housing even to those who would be employed directly in the city. Thus a good percentage of them would have to live outside of the town, which would lead to the artificial creation of suburbia. We called attention to the fact that it was essential the university influence planning beyond the land actually owned, and that the execution of the master plan might prove difficult without the full cooperation of regional as well as national authorities. The plan would be meaningful only if fully integrated into long-range regional development plans at the earliest possible time.

Psychological Prerequisites for the Execution of the Master Plan: We pointed out that the university's approach to the undertaking appeared overly pessimistic. The second plan was already conservative, and to approach it in fear and trepidation could only result in complete failure. The university had after all, created unparalleled opportunities and potentials and should therefore be confident of success.

Potentials:
1. The university had been able to assemble 2,220 acres of suitable contiguous land.
2. Good conditions of accessibility for both public and private transportation had been achieved.
3. The university had developed a definitive plan for the implementation of a major university and started construction of the first buildings.
4. Through a comparatively modest promotional effort, the university has been able to attract a large number of laboratories and industrial enterprises to the Parc Scientifique.
5. The university had directed that through the master plan, an urban organism much superior to the existing Belgian urban environment should be created.

The attractive power of this unparalleled combination of conditions in an area only 25 kilometers from the spreading conurbation of Brussels could only be underestimated.

Background for Planning: This is determined by pre-established conditions such as location, land area, topography etc. It is further influenced by deliberately established preconditions.

Programming: Of special importance are the calculations which establish a land inventory, and land requirements. A distinction is made between urbanized area which contains all urban functions, and the peripheral area, which is reserved for non-urban functions, for a green belt, certain serving facilities etc. In no way does this peripheral area represent the character of "suburbia." Generally speaking, the plan utilized about 712 acres, or 32 percent of the total for the urbanized area, while the balance was reserved for peripheral uses (See Figure 7-27 on p. 230).

Density: The most time-consuming discussions between us, the Belgian team and the clients were devoted to the question of density, a term open to various interpretations.

We therefore devoted a specific paragraph to this question.

(From original report) "Density is not a result of the master plan, but rather a given requirement established by the land available for the urban functions and the directives received from the client, not to use certain parcels of land which, in principle, would be suitable for urban functions, but which are more remote than others. *Thus population density was not designed through the master plan, but rather established as an inescapable fact if the program is to be adhered to.* Mathematical calculations have shown that:

1. The population density emerging from existing conditions is sufficiently high to create a truly urban environment.
2. This population density could be accommodated and a basically superior environment created even taking into consideration the various restrictions imposed by the clients, although this will necessitate certain urban design measures which are:
   (a) The creation of a non-automobile dominated environment, thereby avoiding undue wastage of land for roads and parking.
   (b) The creation of walkways and other urban spaces to provide diversity and variety.
   (c) Selection of housing types which avoid undue wastage of land. This therefore excludes the single-story one-family house with garden.
   (d) Special arrangements for storage of vehicles to minimize loss of land for this function.
   (e) Regulations regarding minimum levels allowed for residential structures. It has been calculated that in order to house the programmed population, one-story housing would have to be avoided, but that with a majority of two-and three-story structures, and a small number of high-rise buildings—exact number to be determined by mathematical calculations—the population could be accommodated.

All these findings result from calculations based on given conditions. The master plan proposes those planning and urbanistic arrangements which would provide a desirable urban environment, respect all given conditions and produce a realizable project with regard to economics and marketability."

The Goals and Objectives: (From original report) "The conceptual goals on which this plan has been based are; provision of a maximum of urbanity, livability, flexibility, and the creation of a master plan which is fully capable of being implemented and is both compatible with and complementary to external areas and conditions."

All conceptual goals were described in the master planning report. I want to cite here just those two regarding which I have found the greatest uncertainty exists: urbanity and livability.

Urbanity
1. Ease of all direct human communications in order to promote the exchange of ideas and goods and the fullest development of human qualities and human interrelations.

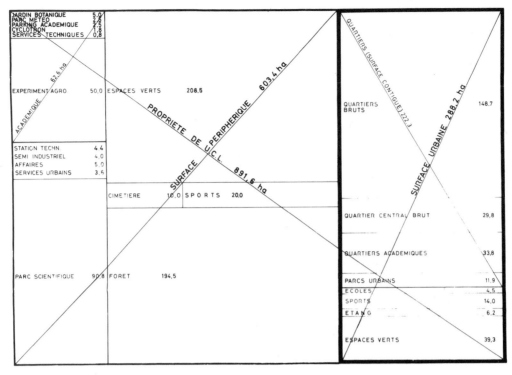

Figure 7-26 Louvain: Schematic graph indicating allocation of total land area for various functions. On the right side of the graph, allocation of land for urban functions.

Figure 7-27 Louvain: Plan of land areas controlled by the university.
A.1 through A.7 = forested areas.
B = artificial lake.
C = remotely located land area to be reserved for future development.
D.1 & D.2 = Land cut off by freeway to be reserved for future utilization.
E.1/E.2/E.3 = Land reserved for the Parc Scientifique (light industries and laboratories).
F = Major utility plants.
G = Academic surface already in construction.
H.1/H.2 = Residential developments already in construction.

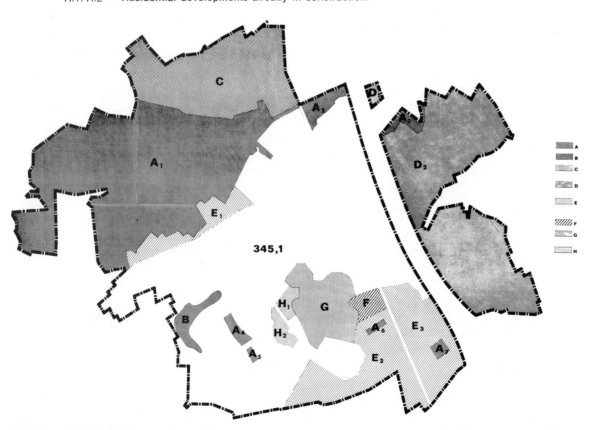

2. A high degree of self-sufficiency achieved by the presence of all desirable and necessary urban functions.
3. A truly urban fabric in which all urban functions are interwoven and closely coordinated.
4. Provision of choices concerning all aspects of life.
5. Sufficient animation and vitality to avoid urban monotony and sterility.
6. Sufficient population to support the facilities needed and sufficient intimacy of urban development to provide for a maximum of interaction and mingling.

Livability: Achieving of superior conditions for life and enjoyment of an urban organism. Livability can be achieved if man, his needs and desires, are regarded as the center of all planning considerations.

The quality of livability can be created if scientifically provable facts concerning physical health, and the biologically based emotional and sensual needs of the human being are considered. The planner of a new urban organism must take into consideration the provable characteristics of livability and the intuitively felt psychological characteristics as can be expected to be acceptable to the majority. As to all those questions concerning individual taste, the planner must contribute by creating opportunities for their expression.

Research is steadily increasing the provable characteristics of livability. To enumerate some of the most obvious: One urban environment is more livable than another if:
1. It provides a better quality of breathable air and drinkable water.
2. It avoids dangers to life and limb as created by the indiscriminate mixing of moving machines and human beings.
3. It reduces noise and unpleasant smells.

Beyond that, it has been proven that human health is endangered if physical exercise as expressed by walking is replaced to a high degree by sitting in "travel containers."

It is provable that man needs a connection with nature which cannot be fully satisfied by small gardens and terraces, although these are desirable as long as they do not negatively effect the creation of a not-machine-dominated environment, and an adequate urban density.

Physical health depends on those measures which prevent pollution of air and water.

The human senses are consciously or subconsciously offended by disorder, mechanical noise, unpleasant odors etc.

The human sense of touch has been dwarfed in our times, yet many are still susceptible to it and react subconsciously, for example to the texture and hardness of the pavement on which we walk.

If we turn to the field of psychological reaction of man to his environment, the area of provability is reduced, yet there are strong indications of what the majority of an urban population psychologically requires.

Monotony—Sterility: There is a strong prevailing tendency to create monotony and sterility, psychologically as well as urbanistically, by departmentalizing the urban environment. (In a meeting entitled "Citizen and City in the Year 2000" which was held in Rotterdam in May 1970, by the Fondation Européenne de la Culture," one of the resolutions passed unanimously was that diversity and variety are the main goals planners should strive to achieve).

Landmarks: Toward the aim of achieving diversity and variety, the master plan did not contain any indication of specific density areas, but rather created focal points. The "coeurs" were to be enriched by means of residential high-rise buildings, placed in order to form landmarks at points deserving recognition. The lower levels of these structures could be utilized for a variety of non-residential functions.

Identification—Adventure: Man is in need of identification with his immediate surroundings, his home, his family, his neighbors, and his quartier, but he also longs for adventure, moving at his will to other quartiers, to the town center, and to the surrounding countryside. Both of these needs were taken into consideration when the plan was formulated.

Though in establishing the master plan, an attempt was made to meet the psychological needs of man, we are fully aware of the fact that a new, planned city can never in our times, fully achieve the qualities of the old, organically grown one. What has organically developed over hundreds of years can obviously not be achieved in a city created by design. Gone are the landmarks which give special interest to old cities, the cathedrals, palaces, castles etc. In a democratized society, these structures are no longer decisive parts of the urban vocabulary and an effort to imitate a historic city would be unrealistic and foolish.

The Organically Grown City as Source of Inspiration: However, this is not to say that we cannot learn important lessons from the organically grown urban communities of the past. By wisely using the tools of modern technology, we can recreate the intricate street pattern and at least partly, the variety and diversity which irregularity provides. The master plan indicates how this can be achieved with a path system which follows the contours of the land wherever possible, steadily changing in width and character. It considers the climate by developing a system of covered paths, and it leads the comparatively narrow paths into wide open spaces in the coeurs, particularly in the coeur of the quartier central. It is this change from intimate to large, well-defined open spaces which accounts for much of the charm of the older European cities.

The open spaces are represented partly by public parks and partly by urban spaces. Pavements of varied texture would dominate in those spaces located on terrace surfaces above parking or other structures in the coeurs. Animation could be furthered by the introduction of planted areas, fountains, works of art, rest benches etc. Taking the climate of the new town into consideration, weather-protected urban spaces in the form of colonnades, covered sitting terraces, and arcades were projected.

Objectives: The following were the objectives of the master plan:

1. Widest possible choice to meet needs and expectations of a diverse and heterogeneous population.
2. Provision of a sense of identification, sense of adventure, and sense of freedom, to satisfy man's psychological needs.

3. A strong connection with nature and a sense of nature.
4. Privacy and sense of quietude in design and location of housing.
5. Satisfaction of the human senses.
6. Physical and psychological security and safety.
7. A proper sociological balance.
8. A non-automobile-dominated city for people.
9. Scale of development sufficiently intimate to create an atmosphere in which pedestrians are comfortable.
10. Sense of convenience in living style, ease of transportation, of access, and availability of needed goods and services.

The Organigram of the New Town: Figure 7-28 represents an attempt to develop in an abstract manner, a pattern in which the planning goals and objectives could be achieved.

The concept is based on a series of interconnecting hexagons, each with a diameter of 2,220 feet, enclosing an area of approximately 74 acres. The model is organized around a central hexagon (quartier central) containing the major commercial and community facilities. Grouped around it are a total of six hexagons, each representing a quartier. The concept is based on hexagons because this form produces the tightest and most efficient spatial arrangement. A diameter of 2,220 feet was chosen since this is generally considered to be the largest possible size which permits full pedestrian orientation without undue distances or inconveniences. The greatest distance from the perimeter to the center is 1,110 feet and a full 90 percent of the area is within 980 feet of the midpoint.

Each quartier is organized into a series of smaller parts. At the center of each is the Coeur du Quartier containing the major commercial and community facilities. In addition, each quartier contains three neighborhoods and at the center of each neighborhood is a "centre du voisinage" containing very limited commercial and community facilities.

In this abstraction, the Quartier Central is designed to house a total population of 10,000 while each of the six remaining quartiers would house approximately 6,600. Thus abstractly, each neighborhood would accommodate approximately 1,650 persons or 500 to 600 dwelling units.

The arrows from hexagon to hexagon indicate the strong linkage between parts of the new town. Each part is physically interdependent on each of the others, so that the town functions as one urban organism rather than as a series of loosely connected elements. Major public transportation linkages and the pathway system tie together all parts of the town, and no road penetrates the entire community, emphasizing the fact that while the community is composed of many parts, it functions as a unified and cohesive organism.

The abstract model related to reality with respect to the size of the available urbanized area. Using this as a point of departure, we proceeded step by step to adjust it to the site, the land requirements of the academic functions, transportation requirements etc., thereby arriving at the final master plan. Though this evolution necessitated changing from geometric forms to forms which would harmonize with all given conditions, we were able to safeguard all those principles of the "organigram" which are of decisive importance for the creation of a superior urban environment.

One of the longest sections of the report is entitled "Guide to Implementation of the Master Plan." It contains recommendations concerning the forming of a development corporation as an instrument for implementation, the phasing over a time span of about 20 years, and construction cost estimates.

As far as phasing is concerned, the following principles were established: (From original report)

1. "A master plan for a community which necessarily has to grow organically over ten to twenty years, must reflect the organic qualities of the new town. It must be additive in character, foreseeing the estab-

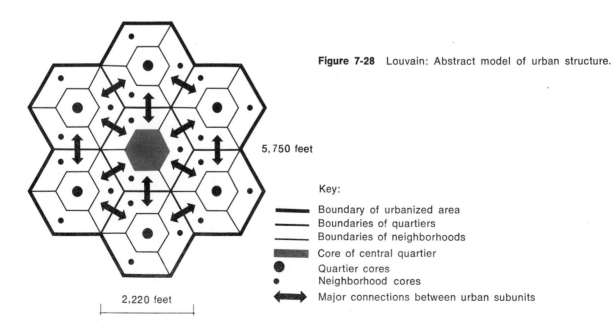

Figure 7-28 Louvain: Abstract model of urban structure.

5,750 feet

2,220 feet

Key:

—— Boundary of urbanized area
—— Boundaries of quartiers
—— Boundaries of neighborhoods
▆ Core of central quartier
● Quartier cores
• Neighborhood cores
⬌ Major connections between urban subunits

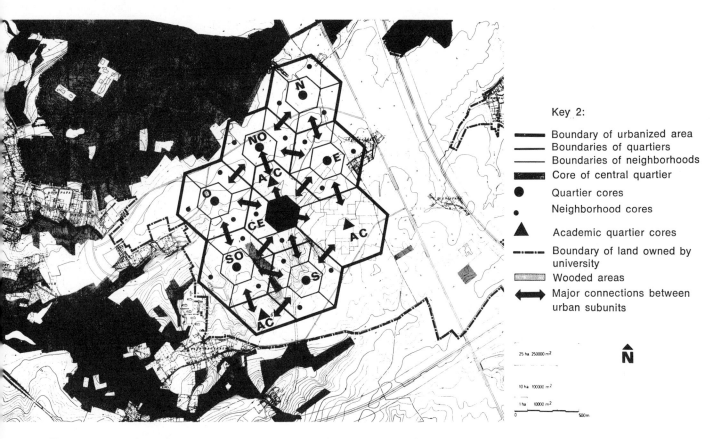

Key 2:

—————— Boundary of urbanized area
———————— Boundaries of quartiers
———————— Boundaries of neighborhoods
■■■■■ Core of central quartier
● Quartier cores
• Neighborhood cores

▲ Academic quartier cores

—·—·—·— Boundary of land owned by university
▨▨▨ Wooded areas
◀▬▶ Major connections between urban subunits

25 ha 250000 m²
10 ha 100000 m²
1 ha 10000 m²
0 500m

N

Figure 7-29 Louvain: Evolution of the abstract model (2nd step), adjusted to the configuration of the site and its topography.
Key 1: AC = Academic CE = central S = South S.O. = South-West N.O. = Northwest
N = North E = East.

Figure 7-30 Louvain: Evolution of the abstract model. After a number of further refinements, the final master plan was developed.

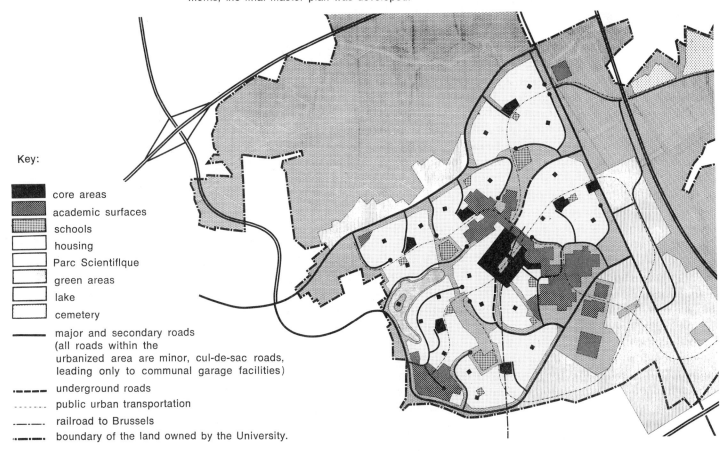

Key:

■ core areas
▨ academic surfaces
▦ schools
☐ housing
☐ Parc Scientiflque
☐ green areas
☐ lake
☐ cemetery

—————— major and secondary roads
(all roads within the urbanized area are minor, cul-de-sac roads, leading only to communal garage facilities)

— — — — underground roads
· · · · · · public urban transportation
—··—··— railroad to Brussels
—·—·—· boundary of the land owned by the University.

lishment of urban units and subunits which can be constructed one after the other until the final size is reached.

2. Since such a plan now exists, it is possible to follow these rules:

   (a) Each phase shall be self-contained and in every respect a completed unit.

   (b) Users and inhabitants of the completed unit shall from the beginning enjoy all environmental qualities which the final town will contain.

   (c) All public facilities such as arrangements for parking, public transportation, deliveries etc. shall be reflected in final form from the beginning. This implies that a switching from ground parking to parking decks later to be constructed, shall not be contemplated.

   (d) Areas foreseen as landscaped areas shall under no circumstances be used temporarily for other functions (for example parking). Landscaping grows slowly and should be one of the first actions to be brought to realization.

Development in a rational, additive manner will reduce the problems associated with living in a "building site" to the absolute minimum."

Cost Estimates: The cost estimates were based on the following assumptions:

1. The university would construct all academic facilities, university facilities, single student housing, and one half of the married student housing.

2. A development corporation would be formed which would undertake the construction of all urban functions (including one half of the married students' quarters), the parking facilities for all urban functions, and the general land development including the entire pathway system and minor local roads. It would operate in accordance with private enterprise methods with the expectation of amortizing all its investments and making a profit within 20 to 25 years. Thus the basic investment would not have to come from university funds or from governmental sources.

3. The urban public transportation including its terminal facilities, rolling stock, etc., may be executed either by the development corporation or a special transportation authority. Once the entire town is developed, it should be possible to operate the public transportation network at a profit and even amortize the capital cost. However, the typical problem with any kind of public transportation network is that it has to be at least partially prebuilt for future demand. It therefore seems logical to ask for public assistance in the form of a grant from the Transportation Ministry. Such a grant would be justified by the fact that this is a pioneering project which would demonstrate to all Belgium, new ways to solve the serious traffic problems from which all cities suffer.

4. Utility plants and major utility lines. This concerns sewage, water system, central heating, garbage collection etc. The utility system could be constructed and financed through a special utility company which would be able to recuperate its expenses by charges to households and other urban functions. This would

be a semi-public institution, which might not be extremely profitable but which should, in the long run, be able to amortize its capital cost. However, some assistance should be requested from government for the initial installations. No estimates of the cost of the utility system were made, because of the absence of meaningful information.

5. Public facilities. Those which we would expect the government to provide. In this category fall, for example, the railroad linking Brussels and the new town, all major highways and roads, schools, churches, hospitals, cemeteries, park development, etc.

6. Miscellaneous facilities. In this category fall all those items for which a cost estimate was not possible at that time, either because it was unclear what the size or complexity of the facilities would be, or who would undertake the construction. Other items would probably have been added to this category as the plans became more detailed. To summarize the findings of the cost estimates:

   (a) University constructed facilities—as detailed in 1 —$245,500,000.

   (b) Facilities to be constructed by a development corporation—as detailed in 2—$342,000,000.

   (c) The internal transportation system including rights of way, central transportation terminal, stations, repair and maintenance facilities, and rolling stock—$5,000,000.

   (d) Utility plants and lines—as detailed in 4—no cost estimates possible at such an early stage.

   (e) Publicly constructed facilities—as detailed in 5— could be only partly calculated at that time (estimated at about 70 to 80 million dollars).

Additionally, the costs of the following would have to be considered:

1. Amenities for the forest reserve in order to make it a meaningful recreation area.

2. The railway communication with the new town, already under construction, with cost assumed by the federal government.

3. Miscellaneous facilities such as botanical garden, observatory, and the 125 acre agronomy experimentation area.

Central Core: A specific section of the master plan deals with the central core. This core will not only have to serve the highest expressions of urban needs for the new city itself, but will also have to act as an urban cultural and commercial center for the existing regional population of about 150,000 which is growing steadily. Thus the accessibility of the central core had to be assured. For this purpose there are, the new railroad communication with main station in the center, a regional bus terminal, and a large number of parking spaces arranged in multilevel parking decks. The features of the topography are fully utilized to create pedestrian platforms on several levels.

Three-dimensional planning, multipurpose land usage and the platform principle were utilized. The location of the center was to form a link between the two most significant academic areas—the Human Sciences Department and the Applied Sciences Department. At the point of

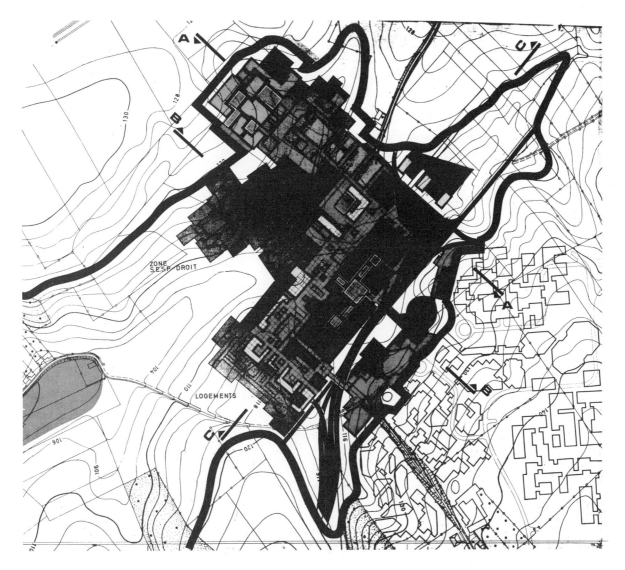

Figure 7-31 Louvain: Plan of upper activity level of central core. In the lower right hand corner, Faculty of Applied Sciences, in the upper left hand corner, Faculty of Human Sciences. The contour lines are indicated, with contour 20 indicated with a thick line. On this level can be seen the main station of the municipal public transportation system (which on levels above is covered).

This level contains:

- academic surfaces
- cultural facilities
- commercial facilities
- administration
- housing
- gardens and other green areas
- ponds
- lake
- vertical service cores
- covered, climatized pedestrian areas
- non-climatized pedestrian areas
- public transportation and bus terminal
- building surfaces below this level

0   50   100 m

N

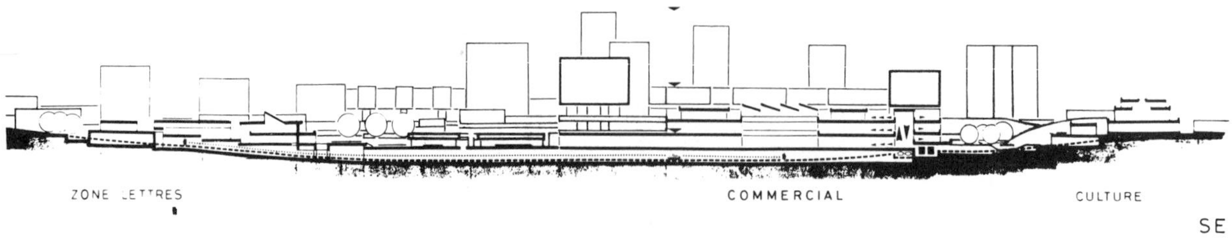

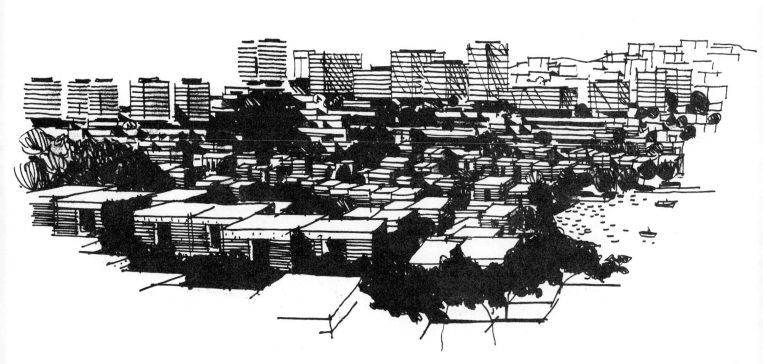

ZONE LETTRES   COMMERCIAL   CULTURE

SE

Figure 7-32 Louvain: Central core section BB. Shown are, from left, academic structures of the Human Science Faculty, library—the central zones with, on the lowest level—transportation; on intermediate levels—commerce, and on the upper levels—academic, public and private administration, and cultural facilities. Further to the right, on the lowest level—the railroad tunnel and on the extreme right—academic and cultural facilities.

Figure 7-33 Louvain: General view of the core of the central quartier. In the foreground—housing of the central quartier, in the background—superstructures of the central core.

linkage, major central facilities of the university were projected in close relationship with major central urban facilities.

Detailed Studies: Recognizing that to be of practical value the master plan had to be sold as well as drawn up, we undertook detailed studies. In order to prove the correctness of the basic assumptions, a detailed study was made of the following housing types (1) a two-story patio, or attached town house, (2) a three-story attached town house, (3) terraced housing which would wrap around those parking structures reserved for the residential development (and its visitors) of each quartier, (4) a 12-story elevator apartment building with luxury duplex apartments, (5) a 20-story apartment structure containing triplex apartments.

The residential densities were calculated not simply according to the space occupied by the buildings, but also to the space required around the buildings in order to safeguard at least a 45 degree angle for access to air and light. Resulting densities were: (1) 155 persons per acre. (2) 178 persons per acre. (3) 150 persons per acre. (4) 289 persons per acre. (5) 465 persons per acre.

Utilization of Urban Space: The land inventory had shown that about 395 acres were available for residential purposes. Since 50,000 persons were to be accommodated, the result was 126 persons net per residential acre, or,

assuming 3.3 persons per dwelling unit, 38 dwelling units per acre. The tabulation proves that even two-story or patio houses achieve a higher density than the one programmed, but it is necessary to reduce the theoretical density figure by at least 25 to 30 percent in order to take into account topography, urbanistic variations, the introduction of schools, parks and other urban functions, and the possibility of a lower number of persons per dwelling unit, due to the expected high number of single persons. Thus we concluded that it would not be possible to accommodate the entire population in two- or three-story attached houses and that it would be necessary to introduce a limited number of high-rise buildings which might have to accommodate about one quarter of the total residential population. In order to prove the correctness of our mathematical calculations, we translated them into an actual plan for one quartier.

The Quartier Sud: The Quartier Sud, covering 93 acres is one of the largest and most difficult of the quartiers. The topography is relatively steep and the configuration of the land irregular. In addition, the railroad line passes directly beneath much of this section as it approaches the station of the Coeur du Quartier Central. In short, this quartier was selected for additional study in the belief that if the planning concept worked well here, it would work at least as well in the other quartiers.

Figure 7-34 Louvain: Partial view of a quartier core. Note that the lower levels of highrise buildings are used for stores and offices.

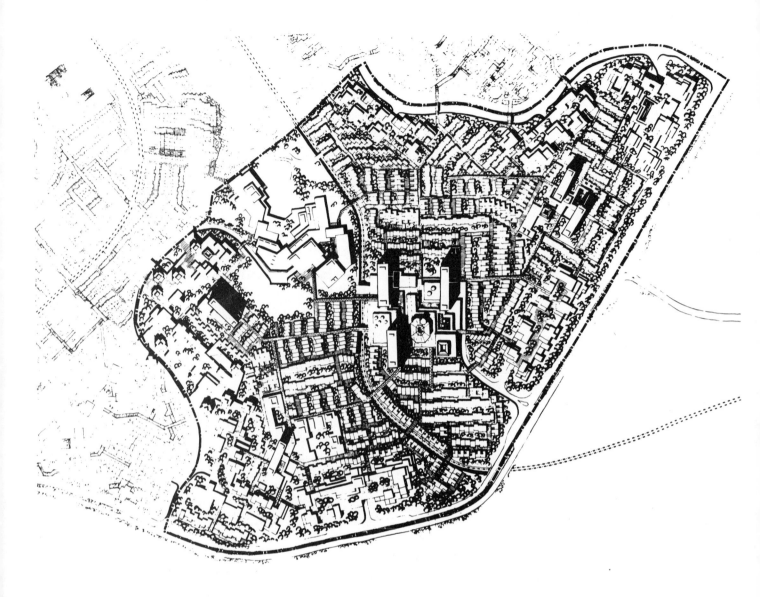

Figure 7-35 Louvain: Plan of the Quartier Sud, showing also adjoining quartiers. In the center of the plan, the quartier core indicated by three high structures. The neighborhood centers are indicated by either one or two high structures. Near the upper edge is a large education establishment, and adjoining it, a major park which continues to the north.

Parking: The client was convinced that our proposals to provide constructed parking throughout would create an unreasonably high capital investment. We therefore prepared a report comparing total development costs for two hypotheses:

Alternative A: Structured parking throughout.

Alternative B: All parking, with the exception of that for the central core, on the ground.

We had of course, to call attention to the fact that alternative B—because of the tremendous land need which parking on the ground requires—would result in an expansion of the entire urban organism and necessitate the use of practically all land owned or controlled by the university thus preempting the possibility of green belts, natural areas, reserve areas etc. Such spreading would also make the introduction of public transportation highly problematic.

Both hypotheses were based on the assumption that all parking would be communal. Comparison between the two hypotheses as far as land usage and costs were concerned was made in a painstaking manner. Land costs were considered on the basis of comparable existing land values within the city of Louvain.

Land Requirement: For alternative A (the system proposed by the master plan), 20 acres. For alternative B 350 acres would be required for the same purpose, a difference of 330 acres which would be expressed in a spreading of the urbanized areas and in higher costs for the capital investment and operating expenses of public transportation.

Construction and Land Costs:

Alternative A: The total costs for construction of structured parking, servicing roads and the land occupied by these is $67.5 million.

Alternative B: Total costs composed of the same elements would be $299.8 million. In addition, the higher capital expense for public transportation and the increased operating costs of ground parking (due to the higher maintenance and repair costs of the larger amount of road surface and the need for widespread lighting, policing and signalizing) is not included in the latter figure.

Present Status of Project: Our master plan was accepted in principle by the Academic Council. The Belgian team, assisted by various consultants and university-connected agencies, was directed to undertake its further development. All development land has been cleared and, surprisingly, large progress has been made in attracting "clean" industry for the industrial area. The railroad is under construction, the major freeway and the loop road system are either in advance planning or in construction, the first buildings of the Human Sciences Department are in construction and a cyclotron is near completion.

Thanks to the kindness of the Academic Council, we have from time to time received information concerning facets of the master plan. Regrettably, though the verbally stated program was in harmony with our ideas, some changes in the physical planning approach have been made which seriously endanger the possibility of living up to the original aims. The most alarming expression of these physical changes is that individual parking is being provided for each dwelling and all other buildings. This of course excludes the possibility of creating a non-automobile dominated environment and it forces land wastage by necessitating traffic areas. My remark at the beginning of this case study, to the effect that it should perhaps be entitled "The University Town which Could Have Been," is thereby explained.

Figure 7-36   Louvain: Terrace housing above and around the communal parking facilities.

CASE STUDY II

Name of Project: Concept for a New Urban Pattern for Los Angeles

Location: Los Angeles, California

Planning Team: Los Angeles Department of City Planning under the leadership of its director Calvin S. Hamilton

Background for Planning: Many derogatory statements, some of them contained in this book, have been made about Los Angeles. However, Los Angeles cannot be grouped with those cities in which government and citizenry take no interest in improvement; it is rather one where the danger is recognized that unless long-range plans for a restructuring of the city are decided upon and carried through, the positive, nature-given assets, (enviable climate, proximity of the Pacific and the mountains) could be destroyed.

In January 1970, after a long and intensive study period, the Department of City Planning submitted a report entitled "The Concept for the Los Angeles General Plan." In the preface of this report, it is explained that the presented concept is intended to be imaginative and far-reaching, looking to the attainment of the full potential of Los Angeles. It is designed to meet the needs of a future city of five million people, within a metropolitan area of eleven million. It seeks to restructure the city in order to eliminate or alleviate current problems and anticipate and deal with future issues. The need for a far-seeing, planning concept was underlined in the report by describing some of the problems presently experienced in Los Angeles.

As the population of Los Angeles now approaches three million, (in a metropolitan area of seven million) the city's amenities are increasingly offset by emerging social, economic and physical disturbances. The most critical, such as air pollution, traffic congestion, and inadequate public transportation are regional in nature. To solve them, concerted action by Los Angeles County, the 77 cities in the county and the State and Federal governments will be required.

Certain problems, such as substandard housing, high unemployment, and limited opportunities for higher education, lock many of the poor, aged, and minority population into a physical and spiritual ghetto. Elimination of poverty, poor housing and limited opportunities must therefore be a top concern.

The present development trends point to an intensification rather than a solution of current problems. If public policies are not changed additional large areas will be used for traffic purposes, and the remaining open space for single-family residences. Adequate public transportation services cannot be provided for the sprawling conditions which would result. Smog will remain a problem even if technology succeeds in reducing automobile emissions, the effect of any such improvement being largely offset by the increasing number of automobiles.

Planning Approach: The following proposals were among those submitted:

1. Continued growth, though permitted, should not be promoted, but rather guided by a comprehensive planning system.

2. The establishment of a rapid transit system is recommended. In order to make this operatively possible, the construction of multifunctional centers is specified as a prerequisite.
3. An open space program, utilizing the rights of public acquisition, and land-use controls, should be formulated and implemented.

Description of Plan: The plan proposes 48 highly developed multifunctional centers within the metropolitan area, 29 of them to be situated in Los Angeles proper. These centers would vary as to size, shape and density. Each would have a core of highest intensity in which a station of the rapid transit system would be located. The core area would extend about a quarter of a mile in all directions from this station.

The designs for the cores follow the three-dimensional planning approach and make use of air rights to permit development over streets. Housing will in many cases occupy the upper floors of multifunctional structures, and landscaped, open spaces, some of which would be used as grounds for schools and other public facilities located on upper levels, would be developed on the rooftops of base structures.

From the tabulation (Figure 7-40) it can be seen how the dwelling units for the population of five million are projected. It indicates that about two-thirds of the housing units would be in apartment buildings, and only one-third in single-family houses. Of the total population, 1,860,000 would reside in centers and cores, and 3,140,000 in areas surrounding the cores.

Figure 7-37 Los Angeles: The concept for the Los Angeles plan indicates (in black) the existing downtown area and (with circles) the 48 centers within the region, of which 29 are situated within the city boundaries.

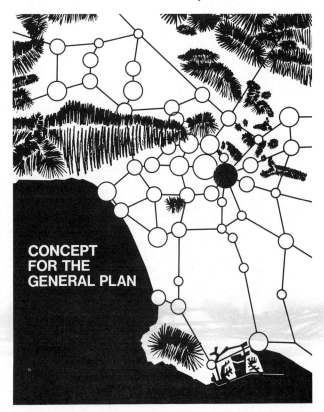

CONCEPT FOR THE GENERAL PLAN

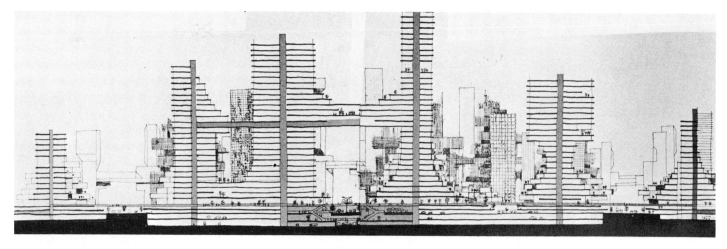

Figure 7-38 Los Angeles: Schematic section through a center core.

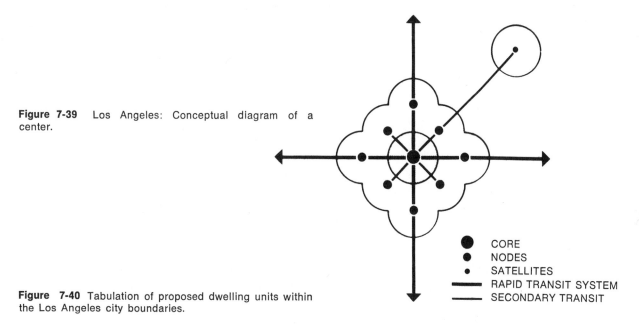

Figure 7-39 Los Angeles: Conceptual diagram of a center.

- ● CORE
- ⁝ NODES
- · SATELLITES
- ▬ RAPID TRANSIT SYSTEM
- — SECONDARY TRANSIT

Figure 7-40 Tabulation of proposed dwelling units within the Los Angeles city boundaries.

Location	OCCUPIED DWELLING UNITS		Population
	Multiple Family	Single Family	
CENTRAL LOS ANGELES			
Centers, in Regional Core	330,000		700,000
Centers, other	145,000		345,000
Suburbs, Regional Core	50,000	40,000	225,000
Suburbs, other	80,000	200,000	830,000
WESTERN LOS ANGELES			
Centers	90,000		210,000
Suburbs	88,000	85,000	490,000
SOUTHERN LOS ANGELES			
Centers	15,000		35,000
Suburbs	42,000	30,000	215,000
SAN FERNANDO VALLEY			
Centers	225,000		570,000
Suburbs	135,000	310,000	1,380,000
TOTAL, CENTERS	805,000		1,860,000
TOTAL, SUBURBS	395,000	665,000	3,140,000
GRAND TOTAL	1,200,000	665,000	5,000,000

Figure 7-41 Master plan for the Los Angeles area, with an indication of centers of various size and the rapid transit lines and stations as well as the existing freeway system.

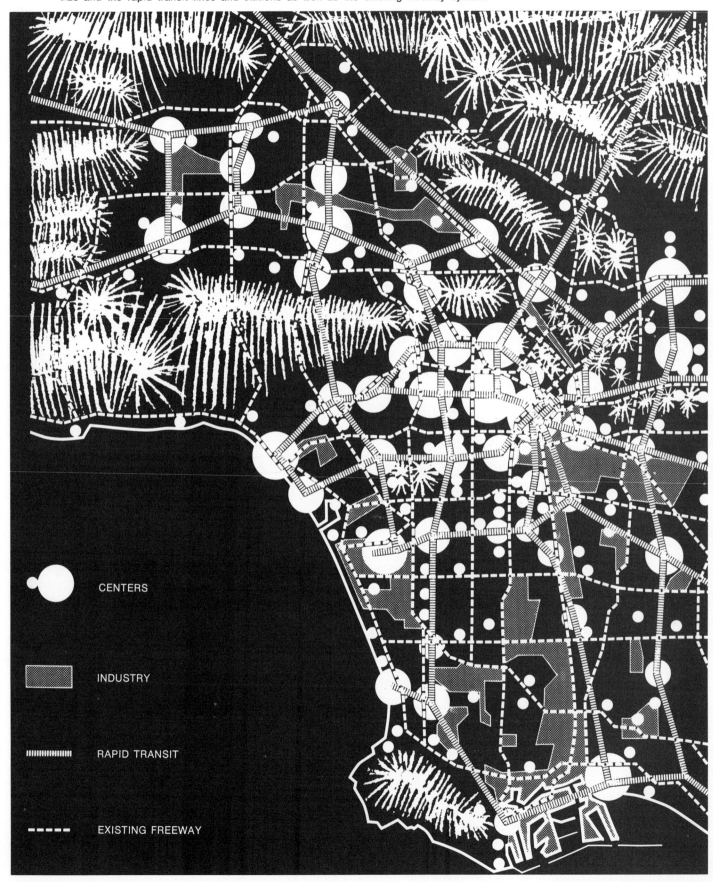

CENTERS

INDUSTRY

RAPID TRANSIT

EXISTING FREEWAY

The overall plan (Figure 7-41) indicates the proposed centers by white circles, the sizes of which vary according to the importance of the center. "Nodes" (local concentrations within the centers) and "satellites" (concentrations which are distinctly separate from the centers) are also indicated. Open spaces which are to be protected are shown, as are also the major and secondary rapid transit lines, and the existing freeway system.

History and Status of Project: The concept for the Los Angeles General Plan must be evaluated as one which realistically reflects those goals and measures which are politically and economically attainable. Before this concept was proposed, three possible alternative approaches were developed and examined as to their possible short-term and long-term advantages and disadvantages. One of them, the "Corridor Concept" arranged development in a linear fashion, a second one, the "Dispersion Concept" distributed population and functions evenly over the whole area, and a third one, the "Low-Density Concept" would preserve the present pattern of Los Angeles. Anal-

ysis revealed that the "Low-Density Concept" would have to be rejected because it could in no way accommodate the projected population. The "Dispersion Concept" was ruled out because per 1000 residents, it could provide only 6 acres of land for parks and recreation, and 3 acres for open space and nature preserve. (In contrast the "Center Concept" provides for 8 acres per 1000 for both parks and recreation, and open space and nature preserves). In neither the Low-Density Concept nor the Dispersion Concept, could public transportation be introduced. Although a public transportation system was projected in the Corridor Concept, it would have been able to serve only those living along the corridors.

Thus the Center Concept was regarded as the optimal solution and as such was submitted for adoption and implementation to the elected officials of the city, with the request that the future nature and form of Los Angeles be determined by the representatives of the citizens and not by special interests, whether public or private. The concept is now being seriously considered by the authorities.

Figure 7-42 Los Angeles: Sketch showing the physical form of a typical center.

CASE STUDY III

Name of Project: The Region of Vienna

Location: The Vienna city area outside of the core, and the region of Vienna.

Client: The Planning Department of the City of Vienna.

Planning Team: Victor Gruen International, in cooperation with the Municipal Planning Department and its various technical and economic subdivisions.

In Chapter 6, I discussed the revitalization of the core of Vienna. Here I would like to describe those measures which were proposed with regard to other parts of the city and its surrounding area.

Vienna, an old organically grown city possesses a superior urban structure which is revealed by the historical map (Figure 7-43 on p. 200) drawn by Daniel Huber in 1766. In a planning study published in 1963, Professor Roland Rainer, the well-known architect commented on this map as follows:

"In this bird's eye view, the Vienna of the baroque almost represents the modern concept of an organized metropolis. Around the center city are grouped the units of satellite towns, separated from the center by the broad green area of the "Glacis." Other green belts separate the satellite towns from each other. Here we see a functionally clearly organized, yet lively, nature-connected urban organism."

In the 200 years which have elapsed since Daniel Huber's drawing was produced, the city's population has grown and its political boundaries have widened to encompass former satellite towns. These changes are illustrated in Figures 7-44, 45 and 46. The demographic changes which occurred between 1910 and 1971 and those predicted up to the year 1980, are shown in Figure 7-47.

In spite of the fact that Vienna has not been exposed to a population explosion (total regional population has been stable since 1910), individual space requirements have grown and thus periphery areas had to be developed. Nearly a quarter of the total population now lives outside of the city boundaries. This move to areas beyond the political boundaries of the city results in a loss of city income derived from taxation. This situation is made more acute by the fact that due to a growing demand for urban facilities, municipal expenditures are increasing rapidly.

Urban Environment: The famously good water, clean air and easy access to landscape and nature which the inhabitants of Vienna enjoyed until the beginning of the automobile age have now all deteriorated. Water consumption has increased to such an extent that the alpine spring water has to be supplemented by treated Danube water. The air has been polluted by industry and the exhaust gases of about 400,000 motor vehicles. Access to nature has become more difficult and time-consuming because many of those areas once used for agriculture or covered by woods and meadows, have now been urbanized. The advantages of urbanity have also become elusive as the population has moved toward the periphery and region. The public transportation system which is well-developed only in the highly built-up area steadily loses passengers and has to be heavily subsidized.

Figure 7-44 Vienna in the "Horse and Buggy" age.

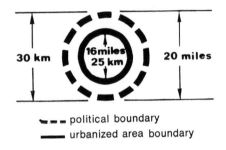

Figure 7-45 Vienna in the "Public Transportation" age.

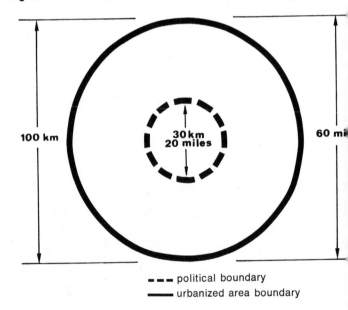

Figure 7-46 Vienna in the "Automobile" age.

Figure 7-47 Demographic development of Vienna.

Year	Total Population	Division of Population			In Percentages		
		A Dense Urban Area	B Periphery within City Boundaries	C Region outside of City Boundaries	A	B	C
1910	2,150,000	1,950,000	100,000	100,000	90.8	4.6	4.6
1934	2,057,000	1,765,000	110,000	182,000	85.9	5.3	8.8
1961	2,064,000	1,250,000	377,000	437,000	60.5	18.3	21.2
1971	2,075,000	1,100,000	503,000	472,000	53.1	24.2	22.7
1981	2,149,000	968,000	671,000	510,000	45.1	31.2	23.7

Vienna's Defense System Against Environmental Deterioration: In the fight against water pollution, the city and federal governments act in concert with regard to the quality of river water (mainly with regard to the Danube). Significant flood control projects are also underway, one of which—through the construction of a second arm of the Danube—will result in the creation of a new 12-mile-long island which is to be mainly devoted to recreational uses. The supply of drinking water is to be increased by tapping additional alpine springs. A protected forest and meadow belt located partly within city boundaries and partly in the adjoining province of Lower Austria (the famous Vienna Woods), provides a defense against air pollution. However, this green belt forms only a partial arc to the west and southwest of the city,, and should be extended.

A system of concentric loop roads (established in the second half of the 19th century) accomplishes distribution of traffic. Aside from the inner defense line (Ring, Kai and Lastenstrasse), there is also an outer loop road called the Gürtel (belt). A third defense ring, a freeway loop along the boundary of the city, is now under construction. Although these defense rings proved highly efficient until the outbreak of the automobile age, it is obvious that they now urgently need reinforcement.

Urban Land Use Policy: Since 1920 (with an interruption during World War II and the postwar years), most housing construction has been carried out either directly by the municipality, or with the help of government subsidies. Between 1918 and 1938, this construction took place within the densely built-up areas, thus utilizing the existing infrastructure. However, because so many housing units were destroyed during World War II, a very large number of dwellings were built from 1950 on, and in order to avoid demolition of existing housing substance, open land, available only along the periphery had to be developed. Thus, encouraged by the planning directives which were at that time internationally accepted: "loosen the urban fabric," "ease the load of the central areas," and "separate functions," decentralization got underway.

The effect of this land usage policy has been that the core, core frame and core fringe have lost population, which has been gained by the periphery and region (see Figure 7-50). The built-up area around the core is depopulated to such an extent that it threatens to become a gray zone, both quantitatively and qualitatively. Our report therefore recommended a complete reversal of policy, from city enlargement to city renewal and redevelopment. This recommendation has in principle been accepted by the city government, however to carry it through, new redevelopment legislation is needed. Such a law is now before parliament. Once this legislation is in effect, large contiguous areas now containing outdated building substance, can be cleared and converted into high-density, multifunctional, environmental oases. All historically valuable building substance would however, be preserved and renovated. Land located in the periphery area could then be used for a widening and strengthening of the green belt, thereby achieving not only adequate air resevoirs, and recreational areas, but also a means for definite distinction between the city and its surroundings.

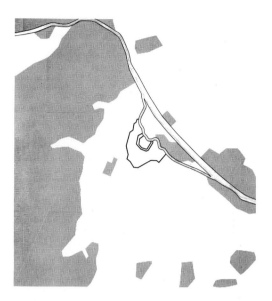

Figure 7-48 Schematic plan of Vienna with defense system consisting of forest belt, major parks and concentric loop roads.

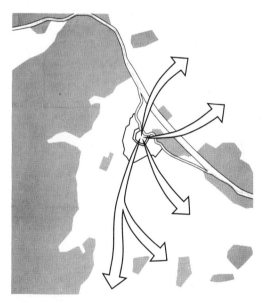

Figure 7-49 Vienna during the automobile age. The defense lines are pierced by urban expansion.

Figure 7-50 Vienna: Schematic plan of the urban structure consisting of core, core frame and core fringe, which together form the densely built-up urbanized area, and the urban periphery which has been developed only since the end of World War II. Population has steadily diminished in areas 1, 2, and 3 and gradually increased in area 4.

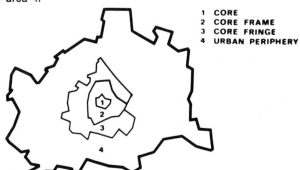

1 CORE
2 CORE FRAME
3 CORE FRINGE
4 URBAN PERIPHERY

Transportation: The principles of the general abstract model for public and individual transportation (page 207) were applied to an abstract model developed specifically for the city of Vienna. (Figure 7-51). Figure 7-52 shows the plan after the minor modifications which were necessary to bring the system into harmony with the existing municipal transportation master plan, had been made.

The system consists of an outer freeway loop forming a bypass within the region, (not completely shown on the plan) a partial freeway loop which forms a distribution road along the boundaries of the densely built-up area, an important surface road located on the boundary between core frame and core fringe, and the final impenetrable defense ring surrounding the core of the city.

The projected primary lines for urban transportation (the subway) and the transfer points between individual and public transportation are also indicated.

Figure 7-51 Abstract model for public and individual transportation superimposed on a map of the city of Vienna: Key: (a) freeways, (b) major roads, (c) secondary roads, (d) municipal subway, (e) regional commuter trains, (f) circles denote transfer points between individual and public transportation media.

Figure 7-52 Vienna: The abstract model adjusted to the actually existing or projected primary road system and public transportation network.

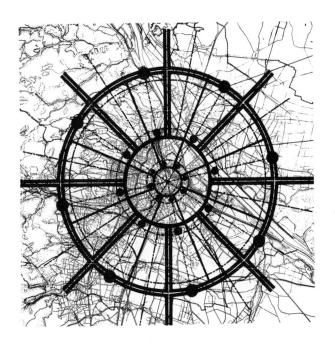

- **Freeways**
- **Major roads**
- **Secondary roads**
- **Municipal subway**
- **Regional commuter trains**
- **Transfer points between individual and public transportation media**

Defense Against Air Pollution: In order to eliminate dirt and poisonous fumes resulting from inefficient heating methods, the city has commenced construction of a series of central heating plants in outlying areas. These plants, which will also be used as incinerators for waste products, are to be connected by pipeline to all parts of the city. The use of electricity for heating is also encouraged, and measures for controlling industrial air pollution are under study. Pollution created by the exhaust fumes of motor vehicles will be limited by discouraging automobile traffic and encouraging the use of public transportation. The utilization of electrical vehicles and liquid-gas-operated vehicles, will also be encouraged.

Status of Project: The measures discussed and many others, were published in a document entitled Guidelines for Urban Development, issued by the Municipal Planning Department, in February 1972. Copies of this document were distributed in tens of thousands to encourage public discussion.

Though there is little doubt that the political powers are desirous of taking the necessary measures, and even engaged in the undertaking of certain of them, the awakening of public awareness and willingness to accept actions, are, as in any democratic state, a prerequisite for full implementation. In addition, close cooperation with the adjoining provinces and communities is absolutely essential for a full success.

However, I feel that the chances are good, that the qualities which I have described as the "emerging new urban pattern," are also achievable in the case of this old, organically grown city.

Figure 7-53 Map of Vienna showing degrees of pollution in the various districts. (Pollution is highest in the historic city.)

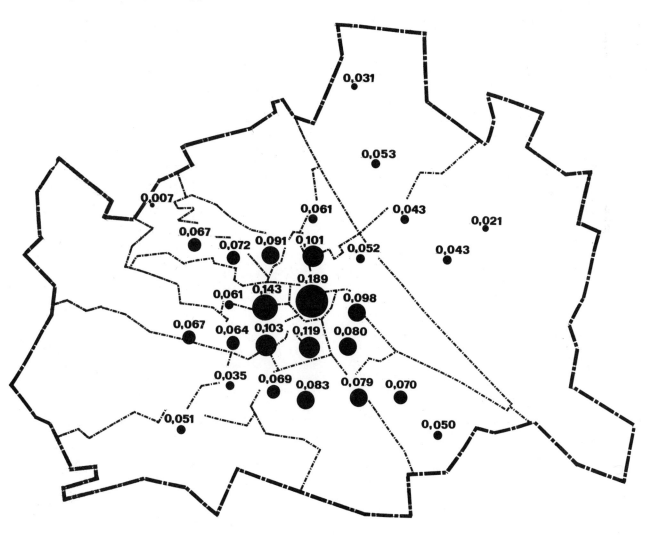

CASE STUDY IV

Name of Project: The Paris Region

Location: The land area surrounding Paris, which is under the jurisdiction of the Prefect of the Region of Paris.

Client: L'Institute d'Amènagement de la Région Parisienne

Background for Planning:
The following summary is based on a report which was put at my disposal by Mr. Serge Goldberg, Director General of the Mission for the new town of St. Quentin-en-Yvelines. Mr. Goldberg has been involved in a leading capacity, with the Institute d'Amènagement de la Région Parisienne (IAURP) since 1960.

"**History:**
August 2nd 1961: Law passed establishing the district of La Région Parisienne.

October 31st, 1961: Decree outlining the powers of a "General Delegate" who would be entrusted with the task of proposing a policy for the development of the Paris Region. He would be assisted by the IAURP.

End 1961: Appointment of Mr. Delouvrier as General Delegate. He entrusted IAURP with the task of producing the development plan for the region, directed toward the year 2000. After completion of this study and following discussions, a goal and projection were agreed upon: 14 million inhabitants for the Paris Region, by the year 2000.

February 23rd, 1963: White book "Advance Project of a Duodecennial Program" submitted to the Administrative Council of the District.

End of 1964: Completion of plan and submission to government.

December 30th, 1967: Passing of the Land Orientation Law, for the development and urbanization of the region. It was stipulated that this still had to be approved by various ministries. Although this approval has not so far been forthcoming, the plan has been implemented in the following ways:

1. An organization has been formed to acquire land, and considerable yearly funds are made available for this purpose.
2. A law has been passed to stop land speculation in specific areas. In these areas, the government land acquisition agency has the right of preemption and no owner may sell his land at a price higher than that estimated by the Government Department of Public Values. 222,400 acres (mostly in the new towns) are protected by this law.
3. Between 1967 and 1969, five development missions were formed to study the projected new towns in greater detail. Expropriation of land followed, and approximately 12,500 acres have already been acquired.
4. The Paris Region has acquired several forest and recreational areas for protection purposes.
5. With regard to accessibility, an important regional express public transportation system is under construction, two lines of which are already operating.

Construction of an aerial train connection between the new town of Cergy-Pontoise and the La Défense development, has been decided upon.

To serve individual transportation, a network of freeways is projected and partly constructed. This network consists of distributory roads on the outskirts of the existing agglomerations and radial roads between these distributory roads and the new urban centers.

Within the new towns, a separation of pedestrian movement and surface traffic is visualized.

July 10th, 1970: Law passed which determines that all existing communities within the region must participate in regional undertakings. If they should refuse, the land involved can be taken from the communities and put under the jurisdiction of larger regional entities.

Administrative Organization: The seven departments of the Paris Region (Paris and the regional departments) are headed by prefects who manage local areas. Each prefect is a member of the General Council which is composed of publicly elected members. In addition, the General Delegate of the Paris Region is also the Prefect of the Paris Region, and as such oversees all important work and distributes state subsidies. This arrangement makes a cooperation between all parts of the region and city of Paris possible.

Planning Approach:
General Aims
1. High quality livability.
2. Highest possibility of choice.
3. Encouragement of good architecture.
4. Avoidance of sprawling development.
5. Concentration of development around centers of multifunctional character in order to ensure best utilization of infrastructure.
6. Establishment, for this purpose, of new towns, each projected for a population of about 500,000. At this time, the following towns are included in the master plan: Evry, Cergy-Pontoise, Marne-la-Vallée, Saint Quentin-en-Yvelines, Melun-Sénart.

The aim in general is to limit the growth of the Paris Region and to encourage growth in other provinces. Within the region, efforts are being made to limit the concentration of activities in central Paris, and encourage development of the semi-independent new towns. To further this aim, new offices are taxed highest per square meter in Central Paris, least in the new towns, and this square meter tax is completely waived for industries settling in the new towns.

Status of Project: Over 10,000 housing units are either already completed or under construction in the first three new towns. Within the next five years, the centers for Cergy-Pontoise and Evry will be partly completed, and approximately 5,000 to 10,000 additional housing units will be built. The transportation systems (public and individual) will be furthered. As far as land acquisition is concerned, important progress has already been made even though difficulties have occurred due to insufficient budget and slow procedure."

Impressions Gained During My Consultant Activities:
Since 1967, I have had the privilege of serving as consultant to the Préfecture de la Région Parisienne, l'Institute d'Amènagement de la Région Parisienne, and to a number of the individual, new town planning missions.

As far as governmental organization, quality and goals of the master plan, and availability of legal tools are concerned, this planning undertaking is, in my opinion, one of the most ambitious and promising in the world.

The enormity of the task has of course created serious problems, and part of the task in which I assisted, was to recognize and where possible, solve these problems.

To recruit the planning and technical staff necessary in the comparatively short time given, proved to be almost beyond human capability. The difficulty did not occur primarily in recruiting the necessary number of co-workers, but rather in finding the right persons for the right assignments. It was also much easier to find specialists for certain endeavours than generalists able to coordinate the diverse interests of the specialists. Yet, in the last five years, each of the five planning missions has set up physical headquarters on the site of the future city and assembled the necessary staff of urbanists, architects, transportation experts, economists, engineers etc.

The chiefs of mission, confronted with the task of planning a new city for about 500,000 inhabitants within an approximately given time span, were faced with the problem of where to begin. Should one begin with the housing units, or employment facilities, with urban centers, the creation of infrastructure, or landscaping? These decisions were complicated by the fact that financial funds were released on a year to year basis.

The second series of problems arises from the fact that though planning, land acquisition, and infrastructure are regarded as public concerns, the actual construction is to be undertaken by private enterprise. The correct line of demarcation between public and private engagement and the best method by which such transfer could be accomplished, are extremely difficult to determine. On the one hand, those responsible for the planning are desirous of carrying the planning program through to a point where the quality and integrity of the planning would be safeguarded, but on the other hand, the administrators responsible for financing, have to insist that transfer take place as soon as possible in order to recoup expended public funds.

Figure 7-54 The District of the Region of Paris.

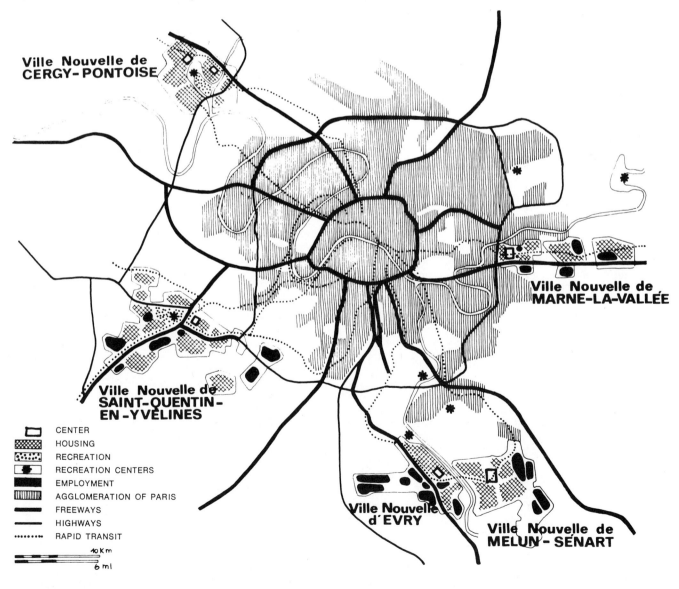

Ville Nouvelle de
CERGY-PONTOISE

Ville Nouvelle de
MARNE-LA-VALLÉE

Ville Nouvelle de
SAINT-QUENTIN-
EN-YVELINES

Ville Nouvelle
d'EVRY

Ville Nouvelle de
MELUN-SENART

CENTER
HOUSING
RECREATION
RECREATION CENTERS
EMPLOYMENT
AGGLOMERATION OF PARIS
FREEWAYS
HIGHWAYS
RAPID TRANSIT

10 Km
6 ml

Though the practices concerning timing and method of transfer vary slightly from one mission to another, it is my impression, and that of many others, that the problem has not yet been satisfactorily solved. I was therefore asked to furnish a report dealing with these problems. The following is based on this report, which I submitted in May 1971:

Authority and responsibility for the planning *and* realization of the basic structural and mechanical frame must rest with one agency, be it public or private. This agency must shoulder the responsibility of operating and maintaining the "base structure" and of enforcing those rules and regulations which are set up in order to bring about the realization of superstructures, even if this should occur in various phases. It is obvious that such authority and responsibility cannot be assumed by anybody before the responsibility for the construction of the base structure in all its parts, and the operation of it, is fully assured. Thus it is obvious that a clear division must be established between the responsibility and authority of a general development organization on the one hand, and the extent of individual responsibility for single elements on the other.

Significant new land values and the prerequisites for desirable urban development are created by public action (acquisition of land, master planning, setting up of recreational areas, construction of the entire infrastructure, including all transportation media, schools, utilities, etc.). All this is achieved by huge expenditures of funds which are derived from taxation. The presently employed practice of selling building rights on a competitive basis endangers the quality and physical arrangements of public planning and results in a government income far below the values which have been created by public action. From the point of view of the individual entrepreneurs, it is understandable that only realities are considered, without regard to future potentials which are partly visible only on paper. It is logical that each individual promoter acts in accordance to his own specific economic interests and is willing to engage only in activities related to a particular urban function in which he feels he has special experience and knowledge. Therefore separatistic tendencies develop and those planning concepts which aim at multifunctionality and small-grained patterns, are lost.

Private enterprise is not alone in this dogmatic attitude. Governmental agencies also express the wish to have large areas reserved for civic centers or university campuses etc. Thus plans established by the urbanists and architects of the governmental agencies, which try to achieve a mixing of functions in the horizontal as well as in the vertical sense, very often are, with the transfer to private enterprise, fragmentized into huge separate function areas and the original aims of avoiding ghetto formation and sprawl are negated. It is further observable that individual promoters who feel, perhaps with some justification, that they are acting as pioneers, relying on the fulfillment of settlement patterns and population quantities which are projected but appear not to be guaranteed, attempt to minimize their risks by economizing. This of course brings about the danger that the first structures which rise and which should theoretically set a standard for future development, are qualitatively poor. It therefore appears obvious that planning and execution of those features which establish the quality and type of future

urban structures, must be undertaken by large, general developers, with long-term economic view points, and the necessary financial strength, willing and able to carry the responsibility. These general developers can then, at a time when all basic criteria have been determined or even physically implemented, work with a large number of sub-developers for individual structures. Such general developers could either be the established public agencies, which would then have to extend and expand their present activity of planning, and providing of infrastructure to include the task of developing actual construction plans and constructing those parts of the multifunctional centers which have been described in Chapter 5 as the base structure. Admittedly, this would increase the public agencies' financial burden, but at the same time, it would markedly increase the possibilities of recouping much larger amounts from numerous private promoters to whom building rights could be leased on a long term basis.

If government were not willing to shoulder the added costs and responsibilities involved in acting as general developer, a second possibility would be the establishment of a development corporation which could either take the form of a Société Mixte (participants partly government and partly private organizations), or a private organization consisting of banks and insurance companies. In both cases, the timing and method of transfer would be effected. If the public authorities act as general developer, transfer would take place at a much later time, when exact plans and the implementation of the base structure were completed. In the case of a Société Mixte or a private organization becoming the general developer, the transfer of planning responsibility should take place at a much earlier time, in order to give the general developer the opportunity to influence from the beginning, the plans which he will have to execute.

Timing for the Implementation of Major Urban Centers: Another difficult decision concerns the construction of the major urban centers. When should they actually be constructed? All of them are envisaged as a concentration of all those functions which express the essence of urbanity. To the planners, it appears highly desirable that these urban centers be established at the earliest possible moment in order to create the image of urbanity and thus serve as poles of attraction, thereby encouraging settlement in the various urban sub-elements which, in the form of neighborhoods, quarters and towns, make up the entire fabric of the new city. This laudable aim however, runs head-on against the realities of free enterprise economics. No entrepreneur can rightly be expected to invest in a city center to serve a population not yet existent. On the other hand, it seems unlikely that in a democratic society, tax payers' money can be used for the creation of a city center far ahead of needs.

At the moment, there is a tendency to compromise. Certain construction is made possible by the government's willingness to construct governmental facilities such as the prefectures, almost immediately, and in the case of some of the new cities, there is an unsatisfied demand for shopping facilities in the form of not too distant already existent urban agglomerations. In these cases, it is possible to attract at least a number of stores to the new city center. These however, are planned, and even in

THE EMERGING NEW URBAN PATTERN 251

some cases constructed, in the form of typical regional suburban shopping centers with parking on the ground, and it proves almost impossible to attract major office buildings, entertainment facilities or major apartment buildings. There is a great danger that, by starting out with structures which conform both quantitatively and qualitatively to suburban standards, the chance of ever arriving at the original urban planning goals will be permanently destroyed. Thus the discrepancy between long-range public interest and short-range private interest, also affects the timing of the new city centers. It seems unlikely that the ideal solution, whereby the government would pre-invest in these ventures on the basis of expectation of returns starting to flow back in ten to twenty years, can be awaited. Therefore, as second best alternative, I recommended that the city center site be reserved and kept free of any building activity until such time as a demand for its facilities actually exist when it can be expected that private enterprise will react enthusiastically to the opportunities created by unsatisfied demand.

In order to fulfill the growing needs of the population during the waiting period, a temporary center site should be established in the proximity of the final site. The utilization of this temporary site should be permitted for strictly limited time periods only, (specified in leases) and by means of structures of a temporary nature, preferably prefabricated and movable. The public authori-

ties should also construct temporary structures for meeting rooms, health facilities, exhibition halls, etc. At that moment when the construction of the permanent city center can be undertaken, all temporary leases would expire and temporary structures could be moved to new locations in city areas not yet ripe for development.

Land Usage: Though admiring the courage and basic concepts of the Plan Directeur in general, it is my belief that the allocation of land for each "ville nouvelle" is too generous and that this over-ample supply of land might well result in densities which are insufficiently high to allow the creation of urbanity, and the introduction of public transportation. I demonstrated my apprehensions by relating them to the town of Melun-Sénart. The total land surface allocated to this town is 42,000 acres. A comparison with the city of Paris reveals that the land set aside for the new city is twice as large, and the projected population only about one-ninth of that of the city of Paris. This divergence becomes even greater if one takes into consideration the additional daytime population attracted to Paris. Paris has a residential population density of 150 persons per acre. The projected density for Melun-Sénart would be 7.2 persons per acre. This kind of low density would constitute a pattern of urban sprawl, which, in accordance to the aims of the Plan Directeur, was specifically to be avoided.

Figure 7-55 The Paris Region: Perspective sketch of the city core of Evry, illustrating the general appearance of the core and showing the loop road and its connection to the major regional road network, bridges for pedestrians and accessory public transportation (which establish a connection between the central area and the prefecture), a green belt separating the ring road and the compact core, and the terrace housing units which conceal the central garage structure.

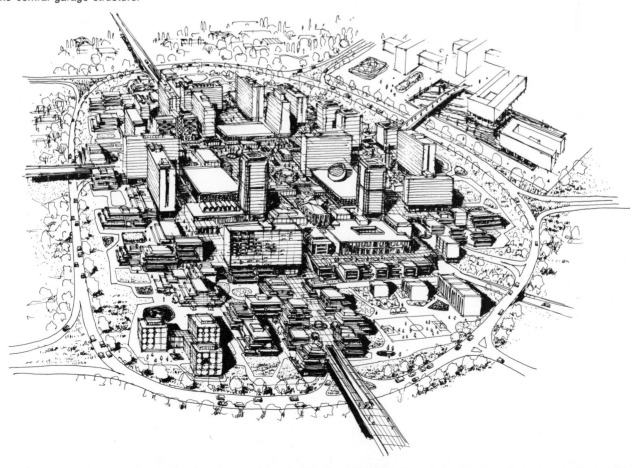

Major City Center

In order to illustrate the character of the planning for the projected city centers, I would like to mention two of them on which I had the privilege to act as consultant.

Center of the Ville Nouvelle d'Evry: Figure 7.56 indicates the location of the heart of the city and the adjoining central area which will contain housing units for a population of about 100,000. By utilizing the methods of three-dimensional planning, it was possible to achieve an average density of 4:1. Figure 7-55 depicts the general appearance of the center. In the core area, all mechanical surface traffic will be excluded.

Center of the Ville Nouvelle Marne-la Vallée: Figure 7.58 shows the location of the heart of the city which, besides all other urban functions, will provide for a population of about 15,000 and a university quarter for 15,000 students. Figure 7.59, a photograph of the working model, expresses the compact character of the core, which is surrounded by a hectagonal loop road connected to the original road network. The core itself is completely pedestrian-oriented.

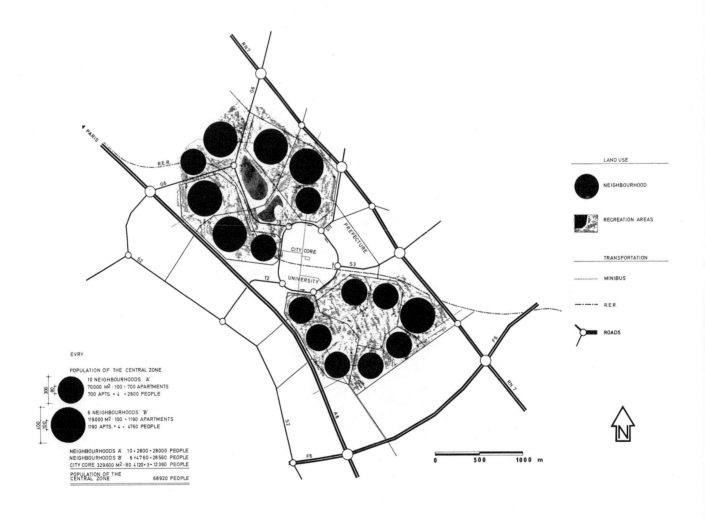

Figure 7-56   The Paris Region: The Ville Nouvelle of Evry. Schematic plan of the central area.

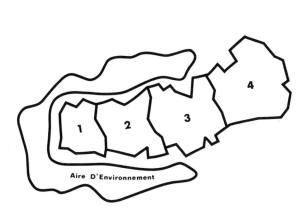

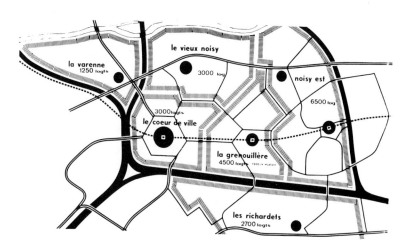

Figure 7-57 The Paris Region: Plan of the ville nouvelle Marne-la-Vallée indicating the division into four development sections.

Figure 7-58 The Paris Region: Plan of the section 1 of Marne-la-Vallée with indication of the city core (le coeur de ville), and six sub-centers.

Figure 7-59 The Paris Region: Marne-la-Vallée: Photograph of the working model. In the background, the university with student housing.

SUMMARY

By exposing my readers to four case studies of projects located in different countries and conceived to deal with radically different problems, it was my hope that we could extract some common denominators. The four case studies, as well as the thoughts developed for Civilia in England, and those reflected in the study *New Cities USA* are all aimed at finding a way out of the urban space squeeze. Each one makes its contribution to the attempt to compact the pattern of urbanization and, in doing so, to create better urban environments and conserve the natural environment.

The tabulation (Figure 7-60), examines a wide range of density patterns either as they exist in today's urban pattern or as they are projected for newly conceived ones. In this tabulation, I have stated density as a ratio between the number of urbanites on the one hand and the utilized terrain on the other. The population figures refer to gross density. That is to say that they are related not just to housing but to all urban functions, all employment facilities, public transportation, parks, recreational areas, green belts, etc.

Comparing the figures which indicate how many inhabitants there are on 100 acres, we find that the range of possibilities varies greatly. It could be even further increased if one were to consider schemes such as those proposed by the American architect Soleri, which go beyond the possibilities of presently available technological tools and therefore beyond the foreseeable future.

Any attempt to determine from this comparison which of the examples cited provides a "correct" relationship between land area and population would of course be meaningless because of the important structural differences which characteristically occur. Cities which are also national governmental centers have to devote much of their land to central governmental functions (this would apply, for example, to Paris and Vienna). Some of these cities still contain within their boundaries reserve areas for future development (for example, Vienna and Los Angeles), whereas others (for example, Paris) have utilized their municipal territory completely. Some provide space for leisure-time activities and an abundance of green areas within the city boundaries (as for example, Vienna, with 270 square feet per inhabitant), whereas others (for example, Paris) fulfill this requirement to a satisfactory degree only outside of the city boundaries. Yet on the basis of the abstract model for an urban organism for 2 million inhabitants on an urbanized area of 142.7 acres it is possible to conclude that, fully respecting those tenets which we have established for the qualities of "urbanity" and "livability," and realizing the limits of present-day technological tools, a density of 80 persons per acre is achievable.

Grave difficulties and a multitude of problems will have to be overcome before those changes can be achieved which will make the implementation of new concepts for the creating of a superior urban environment possible; yet the need to overcome these problems and difficulties evident in the global environmental crisis is so overpowering that lethargy and obstructionism on the part of government, private enterprise, and self-centered individuals will be overcome. A new urban pattern *will* emerge and the cities *will* survive.

GROSS POPULATION DENSITIES

Urban Area	Population	Area in Acres	Population Density in Persons per Acre
Los Angeles Region	6,750,000	3,100,000	2.2
New York Region	15,000,000	2,470,000	6.1
London Region	8,200,000	535,000	15.5
Vienna Inside City Boundary	1,700,000	101,300	16.8
Paris Region	7,400,000	360,000	20.5
Abstract Model Metropolitan Area	2,000,000	85,500	23.4
Louvain Second Project within City Boundary	50,000	1,760	29.5
Louvain Second Project Urbanized Area	50,000	710	70.5
Vienna Densely Developed Area	1,200,000	16,700	72.0
Abstract Model Urbanized Area	2,000,000	24,700	81.0
Louvain First Project within City Boundary	70,000	865	81.0
Paris Inside City Boundary	2,600,000	24,700	105.0
Louvain First Project Urbanized Area	70,000	280	250.0
Examples of high population densities:			
Lower East Side of Manhattan around 1900			900.0
Wah Fu Estate in HongKong	54,000	25	2,180.0

Figure 7-60 Tabulation of density patterns in existing or projected urban areas. The population and area figures used in this chart, cannot be regarded as exact, and will even be found to be in variance with some figures quoted earlier. They represent information elicited from various sources, which refer to various years. Inasmuch as no internationally accepted norm exists concerning the determination of "regional land area" an effort has been made to use comparable criteria. Thus this chart does not attempt to quote mathematically exact figures, its purpose is rather to demonstrate the wide variations of density patterns in relativity to each other.

Name Register

Place and Projects Register

Source of Information

(BOOKS, MAGAZINES, NEWSPAPERS)

Illustration Credits

The author expresses his thanks to all those who have
made illustrations available, and to all photographers.

ILLUS-TRATION NO.	SUPPLIED BY	ILLUS-TRATION NO.	SUPPLIED BY
1-1	V.G. (Author's own illustration)	2-27b	Foto Halaszi, Livonia, Michigan
1-2	James Pickerell, Camera Press, London, Photographer	2-27c	Foto Halaszi, Livonia, Michigan
		2-27d	Foto Halaszi, Livonia, Michigan
1-3	V.G.	2-28	Photograph E.N.I.T.
1-4	V.G.	2-29	V.G.
1-5	KURIER, Vienna, Austria	2-30	Mel Jacobsen, Commercial Photographer, Minneapolis
1-6	V.G.		
1-7	V.G.	2-31	V.G.
1-8	New York Times	2-32	Victor Gruen Associates
1-9	V.G.	2-33	Victor Gruen Associates
1-10	V.G.	2-34	Warren Reynolds, Infinity, Inc., Minneapolis
1-11	V.G.		
1-12	V.G.	2-35	Warren Reynolds, Infinity, Inc., Minneapolis
1-13	V.G.		
1-14	Courtesy of Rockefeller Center Pa.	2-36	Minneapolis Star & Tribune Company
1-15	V.G.	2-37	Warren Reynolds, Infinity, Inc., Minneapolis
2-1	V.G.		
2-2	Peter Mohilla, Photographer	3-1	V.G.
2-3	Chicago Architectural Photo Co.	3-2	V.G.
2-4	Maynard Parker Modern Photo, L.A., Photographer	3-3	V.G.
		3-4	V.G.
2-5	Prestel Verlag	3-5	V.G.
2-6	Prestel Verlag	3-6	V.G.
2-7	B.O.A.C. Austria	3-7	V.G.
2-8	Peter Mohilla	3-8	V.G.
2-9	V.G.	3-9	V.G.
2-10	Courtesy of the Country Club Plaza Association	3-10	V.G.
		3-11	V.G.
2-11	Peggy Gruen, Photographer	3-12	V.G.
2-12	(as in "Shopping Towns USA")	3-13	V.G.
2-13	(as in "Shopping Towns USA")	3-14	V.G.
2-14	V.G.	3-15	V.G.
2-15	V.G.	3-16	V.G.
2-16	V.G.	3-17	V.G.
2-17	V.G.	3-18	V.G.
2-18	Photograph House, Detroit, photographers	3-19	V.G.
2-19	Clark Aerial Survey Corp., Plymouth, Michigan, photographers	3-20	V.G.
		3-21	V.G.
2-20	Victor Gruen Associates	3-22	V.G.
2-21	Victor Gruen Associates	3-23	V.G.
2-22	Peter Mohilla	3-24	V.G.
2-23	Victor Gruen Associates	3-25	V.G.
2-24	V.G.	3-26	V.G.
2-25	Foto Halaszi, Livonia, Michigan	3-27	V.G.
2-26	Foto Halaszi, Livonia, Michigan	3-28	V.G.
2-27a	Foto Halaszi, Livonia, Michigan	3-29	V.G.

ILLUS-TRATION NO.	SUPPLIED BY		ILLUS-TRATION NO.	SUPPLIED BY
3-30	V.G.		5-13	Victor Gruen Associates
3-31	V.G.		5-14	Corporation of London, Dept. of Architecture and Planning
3-32	V.G.		5-15	Corporation of London, Dept. of Architecture and Planning
3-33	V.G.		5-16	David Parry Associates
3-34	V.G.		5-17	David Parry Associates
3-35	V.G.		5-18	David Parry Associates
3-36	Erich Middendorf, Berlin, photographer		5-19	V.G.
3-37	Georg Heinrichs		5-20	V.G.
3-38	Georg Heinrichs		5-21	The City Management Corp.
3-39	V.G.		5-22	Gruen Associates
3-40	V.G.		5-23	Photo Boesch, photographers
3-41	V.G.		5-24	Golden Gateway
3-42	V.G.		5-25	Planungsgruppe Zentrum Perlach
3-43	V.G.		5-26	Planungsgruppe Zentrum Perlach
3-44	V.G.		5-27	Planungsgruppe Zentrum Perlach
3-45	V.G.		5-28	V.G.
3-46	Foto Halaszi, Livonia, Michigan		5-29	Planungsgruppe Zentrum Perlach
3-47	Joshua Freiwald, San Francisco		5-30	Harris/Davis, Inc., Philadelphia
3-48	Joshua Freiwald, San Francisco		5-31	Gruen Associates
3-49	Joshua Freiwald, San Francisco		5-32	V.G.
3-50	Joshua Freiwald, San Francisco		5-33	Gordon Summers, Beverly Hills, photographer
3-51	Joshua Freiwald, San Francisco		5-34	Victor Gruen Associates
3-52	The Victor Gruen Foundation for Environmental Planning		5-35	Victor Gruen Associates
3-53	Victor Gruen Associates		5-36	Victor Gruen Associates
3-54	V.G.		5-37	Victor Gruen Associates
3-55	Peter Mohilla		5-38	V.G.
3-56	Joseph Molitor Photography, N.Y.		5-39	Victor Gruen Associates
4-1	V.G.		5-40	Victor Gruen Associates
4-2	V.G.		5-41	V.G.
4-3	V.G.		5-42	V.G.
4-4	Victor Gruen Associates		5-43	V.G.
4-5	Clark Aerial Survey Corp., Plymouth, Michigan		5-44	V.G.
4-6	Jim Sheppard, Oak Park, Michigan, photographer		5-45	V.G.
4-7	V.G.		5-46	V.G.
4-8	V.G.		5-47	V.G.
4-9	Victor Gruen Associates		5-48	V.G.
4-10	Victor Gruen Associates		5-49	V.G.
4-11	V.G.		5-50	V.G.
5-1	V.G.		5-51	V.G.
5-2	V.G.		5-52	V.G.
5-3	V.G.		5-53	V.G.
5-4	Extract from "El Amor Brujo" by Manuel de Falla		5-54	V.G.
5-5	V.G.		5-55	V.G.
5-6	V.G.		5-56	V.G.
5-7	V.G.		5-57	V.G.
5-8	Welton Beckett & Associates, Los Angeles		5-58	V.G.
5-9	Welton Beckett & Associates, Los Angeles		5-59	V.G.
5-10	Welton Beckett & Associates, Los Angeles		5-60	V.G.
5-11	Gordon Summers, Beverly Hills, California		5-61	V.G.
5-12	Julius Shulman, Los Angeles, photographer		5-62	V.G.
			5-63	V.G.
			5-64	V.G.

ILLUS-TRATION NO.	SUPPLIED BY	ILLUS-TRATION NO.	SUPPLIED BY
5-65	V.G.	6-28	Peter Mohilla
5-66	V.G.	6-29	V.G.
5-67	V.G.	6-30	Peter Mohilla
5-68	V.G.	6-31	V.G.
5.69	Michael Drummond, Montreal, Canada	6-32	Peter Mohilla
5-70	Arnott Rogers Batten Ltd., Montreal, Canada	6-33	V.G.
5-71	Arnott Rogers Batten Ltd., Montreal, Canada	6-34	Peter Mohilla
5-72	V.G.	6-35	V.G.
5-73	V.G.	6-36	V.G.
5-74	V.G.	6-37	V.G.
5-75	V.G.	6-38	Peter Mohilla
5-76	Hans Konwiarz	6-39	Wolfgang and Traude Windbrechtinger
5-77	Hans Konwiarz	6-40	V.G.
5-78	V.G.	6-41	V.G.
5-79	V.G.	6-42	Victor Gruen Associates
5-80	Hans Kampffmeyer	6-43	Victor Gruen Associates
5-81	Hans Kampffmeyer	6-44	Victor Gruen Associates
5-82	Hans Kampffmeyer	6-45	Victor Gruen Associates
5-83	Peter Mohilla	6-46	Tidyman Studios
5-84	Hans Kampffmeyer	6-47	V.G.
6-1	V.G.	6-48	Peter Mohilla
6-1	V.G.	7-1	V.G.
6-2a	Asahi Shimbun	7-2	V.G.
6-2b	Asahi Shimbun	7-3	V.G.
6-3	A. A. Wood, City Planning Officer, Norwich, England	7-4	V.G.
6-4	Robert C. Cleveland, photographer, *and* Ruhnau, Evans & Steinman, project architects	7-5	V.G.
		7-6	V.G.
		7-7	V.G.
		7-8	V.G.
6-5	Photo-Ellebé	7-9	"California Tomorrow Plan"
6-6	Stadtbildstelle, Essen, Germany	7-10	"California Tomorrow Plan"
6-7	B.O.A.C.	7-11	"California Tomorrow Plan"
6-8	V.G.	7-12	V.G.
6-9	V.G.	7-13	V.G.
6-10	V.G.	7-14	Architectural Review
6-11	V.G.	7-15	Architectural Review
6-12	V.G.	7-16	V.G.
6-13	V.G.	7-17	V.G.
6-14	V.G.	7-18	V.G.
6-15	V.G.	7-19	V.G.
6-16	V.G.	7-20	V.G.
6-17	V.G.	7-21	V.G.
6-18	V.G.	7-22	V.G.
6-19	V.G.	7-23	Gordon Summers, Photography, Los Angeles
6-20	V.G.	7-24	V.G.
6-21	V.G.	7-25	V.G.
6-22	V.G.	7-26	V.G.
6-23	V.G.	7-27	V.G.
6-24	V.G.	7-28	V.G.
6-25	Crompton Leyland Electricars Ltd., Tredegar, South Wales	7-29	V.G.
		7-30	V.G.
6-26	V.G.	7-31	V.G.
6-27	Steyr-Daimler-Puch	7-32	V.G.
		7-33	V.G.

ILLUS-TRATION NO.	SUPPLIED BY	ILLUS-TRATION NO.	SUPPLIED BY
7-34	V.G.	7-48	V.G.
7-35	V.G.	7-49	V.G.
7-36	V.G.	7-50	V.G.
7-37	Los Angeles City Planning Dept.	7-51	V.G.
7-38	Los Angeles City Planning Dept.	7-52	V.G.
7-39	Los Angeles City Planning Dept.	7-53	V.G.
7-40	Los Angeles City Planning Dept.	7-54	V.G.
7-41	Los Angeles City Planning Dept.	7-55	Paris Prefecture
7-42	Los Angeles City Planning Dept.	7-56	V.G.
7-43	Historical Map by Daniel Huber	7-57	V.G.
7-44	V.G.	7-58	Paris Prefecture
7-45	V.G.	7-59	Augustin Dumage, Paris
7-46	V.G.	7-60	Paris Prefecture
7-47	V.G.		